PENGUIN REFERENCE

THE PENGUIN DICTIONARY OF SOCIOLOGY

Nicholas Abercrombie was born in 1944 and educated at The
Queen's College, Oxford University, and the London School of
Economics. He was employed as a research officer at University
College London, before moving to the University of Lancaster first
as lecturer and then as senior lecturer. He is now Professor of
Sociology at the University of Lancaster. Professor Abercrombie
has written books and articles on the sociology of knowledge,
theory of culture, popular culture, sociological theory and class
theory. These include *Class, Structure and Knowledge* and, with J.
Urry, *Capital, Labour and the Middle Classes*. With other members
of the Department of Sociology at Lancaster, he has written
Contemporary British Society.

Stephen Hill was born in 1946 and educated at Balliol College,
Oxford, and the London School of Economics where he completed
his Ph.D. in 1973. He is Professor of Sociology at the London
School of Economics where he has also held the posts of lecturer in
sociology, lecturer in industrial relations and reader in sociology.
He has written *The Dockers* and *Competition and Control at Work*,
as well as a number of articles in his field. His main academic
interests are industrial sociology, social stratification and social history, and he is actively engaged in research on the sociology of
management and industrial relations. Professor Hill is moderator
for sociology at one of the major school examination boards.

Bryan S. Turner was born in Birmingham in 1945 and attended the
University of Leeds where he completed his BA (1966) and Ph.D.
(1970). He was a lecturer in sociology at the University of Aberdeen from 1969 to 1974 and then at the University of Lancaster
until 1978, when he returned to Aberdeen as senior lecturer and
subsequently reader. In 1982 he was appointed to the chair of sociology at the Flinders University of South Australia, where he
taught medical sociology, the sociology of religion and sociological
theory, and in 1988 he became Professor of Social Science at the

University of Utrecht. He is now Professor of Sociology at the University of Essex. His publications include *Weber and Islam*, *Marx and the End of Orientalism*, *For Weber*, *Confession* (with M. Hepworth), *Religion and Social Theory*, *The Body and Society*, *Citizenship and Capitalism*, *Equality* and *Medical Power and Social Knowledge*.

The three authors have collaborated extensively before and particularly in writing *The Dominant Ideology Thesis*, *Sovereign Individuals of Capitalism* and *Dominant Ideologies*.

THE PENGUIN DICTIONARY OF
SOCIOLOGY

NICHOLAS ABERCROMBIE, STEPHEN HILL
AND BRYAN S. TURNER

Second Edition

PENGUIN BOOKS

PENGUIN BOOKS

Published by the Penguin Group
Penguin Books Ltd, 27 Wrights Lane, London W8 5TZ, England
Penguin Books USA Inc., 375 Hudson Street, New York, New York 10014, USA
Penguin Books Australia Ltd, Ringwood, Victoria, Australia
Penguin Books Canada Ltd, 10 Alcorn Avenue, Toronto, Ontario, Canada M4V 3B2
Penguin Books (NZ) Ltd, 182–190 Wairau Road, Auckland 10, New Zealand

Penguin Books Ltd, Registered Offices: Harmondsworth, Middlesex, England

First published 1984
Published simultaneously by Allen Lane
Second edition 1988
10

Printed in England by Clays Ltd, St Ives plc
Typeset in 8/9½ pt Monophoto Times

Contents

Preface

A dictionary of sociology is not just a collection of definitions, but inevitably a statement of what the discipline is. It is also prescriptive in suggesting lines of development and consolidation. The problem of definition in a subject as diverse and dynamic as sociology is to strike a balance between an existing consensus, however fragile and temporary, and a developing potential. The unifying theme of this dictionary is our conviction that sociology is an autonomous, elaborated and vital discipline within the social science corpus. Our enthusiasm for the subject was sustained rather than diminished by the experience of seeking precision within the conflicting range of perspectives that constitute modern sociology.

Our view of sociology as a result runs counter to the usual batch of criticisms mounted against the work of sociologists. Three negative evaluations of sociology are frequently encountered; it is immature, riddled with unnecessary jargon and biased by extreme political persuasions. The notion that sociology is a young discipline – and hence inadequately developed – is a misconception which is probably based on the assumption that sociology was invented during the expansion of university education in the 1960s. In fact, sociology as a self-conscious, organized and independent discipline is well established. In order to establish the credentials of sociology, there is no need to trace the subject back to Aristotle or to the Islamic historian and legal theorist, Ibn Khaldun. The term 'sociology' was first systematically used in its modern sense in 1824 by the French writer Auguste Comte and came into wide circulation in his *Cours de philosophie positive* in 1838, replacing the older term 'physique sociale'. By the middle of the nineteenth century, small groups of intellectuals throughout Europe were busily engaged in promoting the 'new' discipline. In the late 1880s, Emile Durkheim was teaching sociology courses at the University of Bordeaux, subsequently gathering a brilliant group of sociologists around him at the Sorbonne, and founding the journal *L'Année Sociologique* in 1898.

Similar developments took place elsewhere in Europe. In Germany, early interest in sociology was stimulated by the *Verein für Sozialpolitik*, whose journal the *Archiv für Sozialwissenschaften und Sozialpolitik* dominated German sociology up to the outbreak of the First World War. The first classics of German sociology were published in the 1880s – Gumplowicz's *Grundriss der Soziologie* (1883) and Toennies' *Gemeinschaft und Gesellschaft* (1889). Georg Simmel started a lecture course in sociology in 1894 at the University of Berlin which proved one of the most popular undergraduate courses. Max Weber, professor of economics at Freiburg and Heidelberg in the 1890s, moved towards historical sociology and pioneered the comparative analysis of capitalist societies. The first major congresses in sociology were held at Frankfurt-am-Main in 1910 and in Berlin in 1912. In Italy, Roberto Ardito published his *Sociologia* in 1879, but the principal Italian contribution to classical sociology came from Vilfredo Pareto, whose *Trattato di Sociologia Generale* (1916) was an attempt to provide a systematic account of the sociological perspective. In Belgium, Guillaume de Greef published his *Introduction à la sociologie* between 1886 and 1889.

In America, particularly at the University of Chicago, sociology also enjoyed a vigorous foundation. Albion Small founded the *American Journal of Sociology* in 1895 and the American Sociological Society in 1905; the *Publications of the American Sociological Society* were first issued in 1907; and by 1910 most universities offered courses in sociology. This early development laid the foundations for the pre-eminent position which American sociology has held throughout most of the twentieth century.

In Britain, Herbert Spencer (*Study of Sociology*, 1873), Benjamin Kidd (*Social Evolution*, 1894) and Patrick Geddes (*Cities in Evolution*, 1915) had an international reputation in early sociology, but sociological courses and departments within the universities were slow to become established. A national Sociological Society was formed in 1904 and its annual publications eventually appeared as *The Sociological Review* in 1908. In 1907, T. H. Hobhouse at the London School of Economics became the first British professor of sociology, holding the newly created Martin White Chair of Sociology in the University of London. As with other subjects, sociology expanded greatly in the 1960s with the creation of a series of sociology departments in the new universities. The uneven development of sociology in Britain has often been explained by reference to the traditionalism, empiricism and individualism of British culture, but a more immediate cause may lie in the hostility of the academic establishment, especially at Cambridge and Oxford, towards the 'new' discipline. Much to the dismay of conservative academics, sociology was well established in university and secondary education by the mid 1970s, but the economic crisis of the 1980s, the attitude of the Conservative Government towards university development and the negative approach of the Economic and Social Research

Council towards sociology suggest that the future of British sociology is unpredictable. This dictionary was written in the context of this educational climate; it is intended to form part of the defence of academic sociology as an essential component of the modern curriculum.

Part of the antipathy towards modern sociology is based on the belief that the language used by sociologists is barbaric, unnecessary or, worse still, a conceptual confidence trick. Once translated back into a common idiom, this sociological jargon would impress us only by its banality. However, every academic discipline, whether in the arts or sciences, has a specialized vocabulary by which it seeks to describe the phenomena to be studied without the judgemental implications which are inevitably tied to everyday discourse. The aim of sociology is to describe, understand and explain social reality with concepts which are abstract, neutral and unambiguous. To achieve this end, it develops a terminology which is specific to its purpose. In this case, it is difficult to see how sociology differs from other human sciences, or why it should. Modern economics has its own terminology that is not accessible to the non-specialist, for example 'marginal productivity', 'perfect competition' or 'consumer price index'. The same is true of linguistics and phonetics, witness 'morphosyntactic', 'lexeme', and 'Katz-Postal hypothesis'. Of course it is also true that sociology uses a vocabulary perfectly familiar in everyday English. However, difficulty may be caused to the lay reader because sociologists rightly give these terms a more technical meaning. The words themselves may be familiar, but their use is not. Perhaps it is unfortunate, therefore, that there are so few genuine neologisms in sociology: on the whole, sociologists have been forced to adopt an existing vocabulary which is then stripped of its normative implications. This is not a perversion of the English language but a scientific necessity.

The charge that sociological theory is simply jargon has little substance. A more important objection to sociology is that it is biased, where 'biased' usually means 'Marxist'. For such critics, sociology is socialism, masquerading as a social science. There is some weight to this charge, since, for example, Saint-Simon in the nineteenth century can be regarded as the founder of both sociology and socialism. The paradox is, however, that sociology is also regarded, particularly by its left-wing critics, as a conservative discipline which sought to revive social harmony in a world being torn apart by revolution, industrialization and religious decline. It is true that in the 1970s Marxism became an influential perspective in the social sciences generally, although it never achieved anything like a monopoly in the sociology curriculum. Two points can be made about this influence. First, Marxist sociology became one of the principal vehicles for sustained criticism of orthodox Marxism. For many Marxist sociologists, the scientific claims of Marxism never survived this critical inspection. Secondly, there are strong indications in the 1980s, partly as a result of internal criticism within sociology, that the neo-Marxist paradigm has become a post-Marxist paradigm, with many sociologists showing a renewed interest in Weberian sociology, critical theory, hermeneutics and so forth. Sociology is a diverse, open and expanding subject, without any permanent commitment to any single perspective, and sociologists adhere to the conventions and procedures which in all disciplines guarantee, or at least promote, objectivity. Sociological propositions are open to public scrutiny, evaluation and refutation. Sociological evidence is collected by observation, experiment and surveys which are designed to ensure, as far as possible, reliability and replication. Unlike many public institutions, sociology as a professional discipline is open to both internal and external inquiry.

This dictionary makes no pretence that sociology is a unified approach to social phenomena. Indeed, we have made every effort to consider rival schools, controversial issues, contradictory definitions and unresolved problems. Where terms are confused and imprecise, we have said so. One reason for the existence of widespread controversy in sociology is the fact that different national schools of sociology (in France and Germany, for example) have developed in very different directions. Some forms of sociology are very close to history and philosophy, while others have sought to be quantitative and experimental, taking experimental psychology and economics as models of social science. There is an important division between American sociology, which from its inception has regarded sociology as an exact science that produces 'hard' data and contributes to the formation of public policy, and European sociology, which has adhered more closely to its roots in certain philosophical traditions, stemming for example from Hegel, Marx and, more recently, Heidegger. European sociologists are more familiar with the notion that to be useful sociology has to be critical. Encompassing this diversity within a single dictionary is difficult, but our aim has been to display the complexity of sociology rather than impose an arbitrary unity on it – a unity which in any case would be premature. Despite this lack of unity, sociology as both science and calling remains the main perspective on the central problems of living in an industrial and secular civilization.

We wish to thank the following for their help in the preparation of this dictionary: Mavis Conolly, Wendy Francis, Jenny Law, Brian Longhurst, Colm O'Muircheartaigh, John Urry, Sylvia Walby, Alan Warde. For advice in the preparation of the Second Edition, we wish to thank Lynne Ashley, Basil Bernstein, John McIntosh, John Robinson and Dennis Wrong.

July 1986   Nicholas Abercrombie
                                                            Stephen Hill
                                                            Bryan S. Turner

How to use this dictionary

In this dictionary we have tried to represent concepts, debates and schools that are both important and current. Our entries include not only technical definitions (like Standard Deviation) but also running debates (Agency and Structure, for example), types of argument (like Organic Analogy), major writers (for example, Durkheim), and whole schools (Labour Process Approach, for instance). We therefore recommend readers to use the book freely to provide guidance on any sociological topic and not only to give a simple definition of a troublesome word.

As with any dictionary, we have provided a cross-referencing system. At the end of each entry there is usually a list of other relevant entries which can usefully be followed up. For example, at the end of Anomie we suggest that you also look at Durkheim, Relative Deprivation, and Suicide. In addition, in the text of an entry, we will often use a number of technical terms which will themselves need explanation. These will be followed by the letters q.v. placed in brackets. For example, in the entry Comte the reader will find Positivism, Organic Analogy and Functionalism all followed by (q.v.), these terms also being in the dictionary. The same convention is used when names are mentioned in the text of an entry, if these are also entries in their own right. However, some terms are used so frequently that we have not given them a (q.v.). This is particularly true of Durkheim, Marx and Weber.

At the end of many entries we have suggested some further reading, the full details of which are given in the bibliography at the back of the book. In general we have given further reading for entries which cover a large subject or are technically difficult. When an author's name is followed by a date in brackets in the text of an entry, this indicates that a corresponding publication will be found in the bibliography.

A

Abstracted Empiricism. See: *Grand Theory*.

Accommodation. In the sociological analysis of race relations this describes the process whereby individuals adapt to situations of racial conflict, without resolving the basic conflict or changing the system of inequality. The term derives from experimental psychology, where it denotes how individuals modify their activity to fit the requirements of the external social world. See: *Acculturation*; *Assimilation*; *Racism*.

Accounts. The language by which people justify their behaviour when challenged by another social actor or group is an 'account'. Following the philosopher J. L. Austin (1962) who was particularly interested in 'excuses', and C. W. Mills (1940) who referred to the 'vocabulary of motives', the idea of accounts has been widely used in the sociology of deviance to study the ways in which criminals or deviants attempt to deny or to reduce their responsibility for behaviour which is regarded as untoward or socially unacceptable. The use of accounts is a method of avoiding the stigma of an accusation of criminality or deviance. For example, G. Sykes and D. Matza (1957) developed the concept of 'the techniques of neutralization' to describe the methods by which deviants justify their behaviour. Stealing from large companies may be justified by claiming that nobody really suffers or that an insurance company will cover the cost. Murder may be justified by arguing that the victim deserved it. This theory of deviant behaviour (q.v.) was further developed by D. Matza (1964) in his analysis of delinquent drift (q.v.). Because sociologists have concentrated on denials of responsibility in accounts, they have to some extent neglected the analysis of alternative responses to social accusation, such as confession. See: *Criminology*; *Delinquency*; *Differential Association*; *Labelling Theory*; *Neutralization*.

Bibl. Scott and Lyman (1968)

Acculturation. This term is used to describe both the process of contacts between different cultures and also the outcome of such contacts. As the process of contact between cultures, acculturation may involve either direct social interaction or exposure to other cultures by means of the mass media of communication. As the outcome of such contact, acculturation refers to the assimilation by one group of the culture of another which modifies the existing

1

culture and so changes group identity. There may be a tension between old and new cultures which leads to the adaptation of the new as well as the old. See: *Accommodation*; *Assimilation*.

Achievement Motivation. The need to perform well, or achievement motivation, significantly determines a person's effort and persistence in reaching some given standard of excellence or in comparison with competitors, and the level of aspiration that is involved in that standard or competition. Seen by D. C. McClelland (1961) as a major determinant of entrepreneurial activity and as a cause of rapid economic growth when widely dispersed in a society, the concept has been criticized as providing an explanation largely in terms of the characteristics of individuals and as neglecting social structural factors. See: *Asceticism*; *Capitalism*; *Protestant Ethic*.

Achievement Orientation. See: *Ascription*; *Parsons*.

Act. Sociologists distinguish between behaviour and action, where the latter involves purpose, consciousness and an objective. T. Parsons (1937) has argued that the act is the basic unit of sociological analysis, involving: (1) an agent or actor; (2) an end or future state of affairs to which action is directed; (3) a situation that comprises the conditions and means for action; (4) a set of norms by which actions are guided and means selected. G. H. Mead (1938) has conceptualized the act into its impulse, definition of the situation and consummation.

The basic distinction between action and behaviour was made originally by M. Weber (1968), when he defined sociology as a science which seeks to interpret the meaning of action. It has been argued by writers like A. Schutz

(1972) that the concept of the act is far more complex than Weber's approach would suggest. For example, it is not entirely clear what is meant by ascribing meaning to actions and situations. Another problem with the concept is that it implies an actor, but sociology has yet to provide an adequate account of what is meant by 'the actor'. For example, in some societies where the religious system involves ancestor worship, ancestral actors are in fact dead. In contemporary societies, corporations are said to have legal personalities and may be regarded as actors. See: *Action Theory*; *Agency and Structure*; *Methodological Individualism*; *Symbolic Interactionism*.

Action Research. Conventional social scientific research is concerned to describe, analyse and explain phenomena. The role of the researcher is detached, in order to minimize disturbance of the phenomena under investigation. In action research, however, the research role is involved and interventionist, because research is joined with action in order to plan, implement and monitor change. Researchers become participants in planned policy initiatives and use their knowledge and research expertise to serve a client organization. See: *Evaluation Research*.

Action Theory. Action is to be distinguished from behaviour in that it involves meaning or intention. Action theory is then analysis of action starting with the individual actor. Analysis proceeds in terms of typical actors in typical situations by identifying actors' goals, expectations and values, the means of achieving those goals, the nature of the situation and the actors' knowledge of the situation, among other elements. T. Parsons (q.v.) refers to these elements as the action frame of reference.

There are two main forms of action

theory, the 'hermeneutic' and the 'positivist', and both are also closely related to the doctrine of symbolic interactionism (q.v.). Both have their origins in the work of M. Weber. Weber distinguished four types of action: traditional, affectual, *zweckrational* and *wertrational*. Traditional actions are those performed simply because they have been performed in the past. Affectual actions are those performed simply to express an emotion. However, Weber was relatively little interested in these two forms of action, being more concerned with rational action. *Zweckrational* (instrumental action) is action in which the actor not only compares different means to a goal, but also assesses the utility of the goal itself. In *wertrational* (value-rationality), the actor takes the goal as an end in itself and may not even compare different means to that goal. Weber makes it clear that the four types of action are ideal types (q.v.) and it is empirically possible for actions to be a mixture of one or more of the types.

For Weber, it is important that action is defined in terms of 'meaningfulness' and sociological analysis must proceed by identifying the meaning that actions have for actors. Hermeneutic action theories are those which make this meaningfulness an absolute theoretical priority; acting and meaning are inextricably linked. A. Schutz (q.v.) is one writer who adopts this perspective. He argues that Weber does not provide a satisfactory account of meaningful action in that meaning is too much divorced from the actor; it becomes an objective category imposed by the sociologist.

Schutz holds that the key to the interpretation of action lies in the notion of a stream of experiences in time. Our experiences form a continuous flow. Each experience has no meaning in itself but can be given meaning by reflection on it as it recedes into the past. Actions may, however, be reflected on in what Schutz called the future perfect tense, i.e. one may reflect on future actions as if they had been in the past. For Schutz, this form of reflection is crucial, for action is the product of intention and reflection. It is that which is determined by a project or plan. Schutz further distinguishes 'in-order-to motives' from 'because motives'. The former refer to the future and are roughly equivalent to the goals for which actions are the means. The latter refer to the past and are the immediate reasons for undertaking actions. Social actions are those whose in-order-to motives contain a reference to someone else's stream of experience, and if social actions defined in this way take place on both sides, there is social interaction.

Generally, the more seriously hermeneutic action theorists take the meaningfulness of action, the less easy is it for them to include conceptions of social structure in the theory. Schutz is ambivalent on the question of the relationship of the individual actor to a determining social structure. On the other hand, positivist action theories, the most distinguished example of which is that of T. Parsons (q.v.), tend to be more interested in social structure and how it sets the goals and means available to actors. There is a tendency in the positivist theory, therefore, to make action and interaction residual concepts less important than the analysis of the social system as a whole; the notion of social structure as simply the outcome of the projects and actions of social actors is largely abandoned in favour of seeing the human actor as socialized into a common culture.

For Parsons, action is behaviour directed by the meanings attached by actors to things and people. Actors have goals and select appropriate means.

3

Courses of action are constrained by the situation and guided by symbols and values. The most important category is interaction, i.e. action oriented towards other actors. When interaction between two parties is frequent, mutual expectations will emerge. Both parties will have to adjust both their expectations and behaviour to match up with the other's behaviour and expectations. As expectations are established as reliable predictors of behaviour, they become the norms governing the interaction and following the norms not only makes action more effective, it also gives actors intrinsic satisfactions since, for Parsons, actors 'need' the approval of others. These norms are the basis of social order institutionalized in society and internalized in the individual. See: *Agency and Structure*; *Behaviourism*; *Hermeneutics*; *Methodological Individualism*; *Phenomenological Sociology*; *Rationality*; *Symbolic Interactionism*; *Verstehen*.

Bibl. Cohen, P. S. (1968); Dawe (1978)

Adaptation. See: *Evolutionary Theory*.

Addiction. This is the devotion to or enslavement by a substance, typically a drug, which is regarded as physically or socially harmful. Within the perspective of conventional criminology (q.v.) and applied sociology, research has concentrated on: (1) the analysis of addictions related to criminal behaviour (such as driving offences); (2) the social distribution of addictions according to age, class and sex; (3) the social and psychological origins of addictions (such as parental influences). Such research emphasizes learning and opportunity in addictive behaviour. By contrast, positivistic approaches which accepted behaviourism (q.v.) have been more concerned with the physiological and psychological determinants of long-term

addiction and with questions related to possible recovery.

A different approach to addiction has been based on symbolic interactionism (q.v.), and is interested in: (1) the social processes and social context by which individuals become, for example, drug-users within a deviant subculture; (2) the maintenance of a commitment to drug use; (3) social reactions to or labelling of the addict as a social deviant. Becoming an addict is conceptualized in terms of a career (q.v.) with definite stages, in which the addict comes to accept a stigmatizing label and responds to that new identity. The sociology of deviance therefore treats 'addiction' as a problematic and ambiguous label by which law enforcement agencies and public opinion exert social control over individuals regarded as harmful or anti-social. In this perspective, reactions to addiction have the unintended consequence of amplifying primary deviance. Furthermore, there is evidence of a medicalization (q.v.) of behaviour so that the notion of 'addiction' is extended to include a variety of 'harmful' activities, such as gambling. This perspective has proved valuable in sociological research, but it does not offer any practical therapeutic guidelines, being more concerned with the nature of public opinion and official responses to drug cultures. Treatment of addiction either involves some form of 'aversion therapy' in which the use of drugs comes to be associated with unpleasant experiences, or a programme of learning to reduce and remove addiction through membership of a voluntary association such as Alcoholics Anonymous. However, recovery rates under both methods are low, addiction tending to be a recurrent problem. See: *Deviancy Amplification*; *Deviant Behaviour*; *Social Pathology*; *Social Problems*.

Bibl. Duster (1970)

Adolescence. In general, the sociology of adolescence has been dominated by a 'social problems' approach, that is, basic research has centred around those phenomena which appear to characterize adolescence as a period of individual crisis. Many psychiatric and behavioural problems have their onset or greatest incidence in adolescence. Sociologists and psychologists have focused on the effect of transitions from home to school and to work on emotional stress in young people.

Sociologists have argued that the notion of a separate and specialized age group called 'adolescence' is the product of the late nineteenth century. However, historians claim that specialized youth groups can be traced back to at least the sixteenth century in France. See: *Delinquency*; *Gang*; *Generation*; *Life-Cycle*; *Peer Group*; *Social Problems*.

Adorno, Theodor (1903–1969). Associated with the Frankfurt School (q.v.), Adorno spent much of his life in his native Germany, but between 1934 and 1960 he lived mainly in the United States, where he had fled as a refugee from Nazi Germany. He had wide interests in philosophy and in social and cultural studies generally, especially music. Very much influenced by Marxism, Adorno argued that social theory had to maintain a critical edge. On this basis he attacked many of the approaches used in social studies, particularly those claiming to be scientific and quantitative, on the grounds that they did not provide a basis for the transformation of society. He is probably best known to sociologists for his critique of mass culture in the modern world. This he saw as being purveyed by a culture industry and as manipulative of the masses. Adorno's work is diffuse, but the books of most sociological interest are *Prisms* (1967), *Dialectic of Enlightenment* (1973) and *Minima Moralia* (1974). He also contributed to *The Authoritarian Personality* (1950). See: *Authoritarian Personality*; *Marcuse*; *Marxist Sociology*; *Mass Society*.

Bibl. Jay (1984)

Affectivity. See: *Parsons*.

Affinal. This refers to a relationship by marriage rather than by the real or mythical ties of descent. For example, mother-in-law is an affinal relationship in contrast to the mother–child relationship which is one of descent. See: *Descent Groups*; *Kinship*.

Affluent Worker. It was widely believed that post-war affluence in Britain had led to the embourgeoisement (q.v.) of the manual working class. J. H. Goldthorpe, D. Lockwood, F. Bechhofer and J. Platt investigated this issue among workers in Luton and published their findings as *The Affluent Worker* (1968a; 1968b; 1969). They distinguished traditional-proletarian and affluent workers. Traditional proletarians lived in closed and isolated working-class communities in single-industry areas, formed gregarious social communities of workmates, kin and neighbours, and had a conflictual, power-based class imagery (q.v.). Work formed a central life interest and was more than just a means to earn money. Traditional proletarians were found in older industries and long-established industrial areas. Affluent workers had migrated to the newer industrial centres of the Midlands, drawn by the attraction of the very high wages. They were privatized workers, in the sense of being home- and family-centred and not participating in community life. They did not see work as a central life interest or as anything more than a means of satisfying their instrumental needs for money and security, displaying none of the 'social needs' assumed by Human

Relations (q.v.). They had a non-conflictual, money image of class. These differences between traditional and affluent workers did not indicate that the Luton workers were becoming more middle-class, however, because the money class image was not similar to the middle-class prestige model, and Luton workers continued to support trade unionism and vote Labour like other workers.

Subsequent criticism and research suggest that Goldthorpe *et al.* may have exaggerated the distinctiveness of their sample, and that many of the attitudes and life-style attributes of affluent workers are widely shared in the working class: supposedly traditional workers have been shown to be similar to affluent workers. There is also a body of opinion which suggests that the money image of class structure cannot easily be distinguished from the power model. However, the main conclusion that the working class is not becoming like the classes above it is endorsed. See: *Class Consciousness*; *Life-Style*; *Orientation to Work*; *Privatization*; *Working Class*.

Bibl. Hill, S. (1981)

Agency and Structure. An important debate in sociological theory concerns the relationship between individuals and social structure. The debate revolves round the problem of how structures determine what individuals do, how structures are created, and what are the limits, if any, on individuals' capacities to act independently of structural constraints; what are the limits, in other words, on human agency. There are three main positions in this debate. (1) Some sociologists argue that structures cannot be seen as determining and the emphasis should be placed on the way that individuals create the world around them. Writers subscribing to the doctrines of Methodological Individualism (q.v.), Ethnomethodology (q.v.), or Pheno-menological Sociology (q.v.), mainly take this view; indeed, some might even argue that there is no such thing as social structure. (2) The contrary position is that sociology should only be concerned with social structures which determine the characteristics and actions of individuals, whose agency or special characteristics therefore become unimportant. E. Durkheim was an early exponent of this position. Functionalists often adopt this view, being concerned simply with the functional relationships between social structures. Many Marxists similarly argue that social relations, not individuals, are the proper objects of analysis. Individuals are only the 'bearers' of social relations. (3) The third view tries to compromise between (1) and (2), avoiding both the idea of a structure determining individuals and also that of individuals independently creating their world. One of the best-known theories of this kind is that of P. Berger and T. Luckmann (1967). They argue that there is a dialectical process in which the meanings given by individuals to their world become institutionalized or turned into social structures, and the structures then become part of the meaning-systems employed by individuals and limit their actions. For example, if a man and a woman meet for the first time on a desert island, they create their relationship and give it meaning. However, their children are born into the society made by their parents; for them it is a given which constrains their actions to a great extent. Many Marxists have also sought a similar compromise in order to give some meaning to the concept of class struggle (q.v.), conceived as actions taken by individuals or groups of individuals against the determining power of social structures. See: *Action Theory*; *Althusser*; *Hermeneutics*; *Marxist Sociology*; *Parsons*; *Social Structure*; *Structuration*; *Subject/Subjectivity*; *Verstehen*.

Agenda Setting. This is a concept employed in much recent work in the sociology of the mass media (q.v.). The suggestion is that television, radio and the press do not simply report events but rather set agendas; that is, they *select* particular issues for discussion in particular ways by particular people. From this it follows that there is a framework of presentation which excludes certain issues or points of view. For example, it is claimed that the television news coverage of industry neglects industrial accidents but reports strikes in detail.

Bibl. Glasgow University Media Group (1980)

Aging. While the political role of age groups and generations has been of considerable interest to sociologists, the general area of social aging was neglected by the mainstream of sociology until the late 1960s. Current interest in aging and gerontology (q.v.) has been stimulated by the growing proportion of the aged in the population of industrialized societies and by public concern with the aged as a social problem. In Britain, people past retiring age (women over 60 and men over 65) increased as a percentage of the population from 6·8 in 1911 to 17·7 in 1981. Social policy towards retirement has had a dramatic effect on the labour force participation rates for the elderly. At the beginning of the century, 67 per cent of men over 65 years were still employed; by the 1970s, under 19 per cent were employed. With the growth of pensions and early-retirement schemes, it has been argued that the elderly constitute an economic burden on the community. The 'burden of dependency' as a ratio is calculated as those not eligible for employment (young people below working age and those past the age of retirement) over the working population. As this dependency ratio increases, it is thought that by the end of the century

the elderly will constitute a considerable brake on economic growth for the advanced industrial societies.

While S. N. Eisenstadt (1956) provided a general perspective on age groups, sociology lacks a theoretical synthesis of existing research into demographic changes, generational politics, age stratification and aging in relation to labour markets.

While gerontology as a branch of biology treats aging as a genetically programmed process of living organisms, social gerontology is concerned with aging as (1) a contingent process relating to the social and demographic structure of human groups; (2) as an aspect of personal status in the life cycle; (3) as the dynamic component of stratification in terms of generational membership; (4) as a contemporary social problem raising questions about exploitation, victimization and stigmatization. What is of central interest to sociology is not an individual's chronological age but the criteria, in terms of social expectations and cultural values, by which an individual is labelled as 'young', 'middle-aged' or 'elderly'. For example, the problem of old age in modern societies is the product of a dramatic increase in life expectancy combined with cultural and social changes in values relating to age. In pre-literate societies, the elderly were venerated because they were social repositories of wisdom, custom and property rights. In industrial society, emphasis on achievement rather than ascription (q.v.), early retirement and the significance of youthfulness as a major criterion of personal and aesthetic values have changed the social status of the aged. These changes have given rise to a debate about old age as a disengagement from work, normative commitment and sociability.

Two important issues have come to the forefront of social research into aging. First, there is the historical debate about the changing social status of the elderly with the processes of modernization and industrialization. This issue relates to the problem of whether the decline of the extended family (q.v.) has left the aged without kinship support in industrial society. Historical evidence now suggests that households with more than two generations were uncommon in pre-industrial society and, furthermore, the social isolation of the elderly varies with residential, social class and cultural factors. Secondly, the commercialization of personal appearance in societies where youthfulness is prestigious has given rise to research into 'the mid-life crisis', sexual activity in old age, the social implications of the menopause and the general movement for health and fitness. See: *Demographic Transition*; *Demography*; *Generation*; *Life-Cycle*; *Nuclear Family*; *Social Problems*.

Bibl. Johnson and Williamson (1980); Phillipson (1982)

Alienation. This denotes the estrangement of individuals from themselves and others. It was originally a term with philosophical and religious meanings, but K. Marx transformed it into a sociological concept in the *Economic and Philosophical Manuscripts of 1844*. Marx saw human estrangement as rooted in social structures which denied people their essential human nature. He believed that this human essence was realized in labour, a creative activity carried out in cooperation with others by which people transformed the world outside themselves. The process of production is one of 'objectification', whereby men make material objects which embody human creativity yet stand as entities separate from their creators. Alienation occurs when, once objectified, man no longer recognizes himself in his product which has become alien to him, 'is no longer

his own' and 'stands opposed to him as an autonomous power'. Objectification, however, only becomes alienation in the specific historical circumstances of capitalism. In capitalist society one group of people, capitalists, appropriates the products created by others. This is the origin of alienation. Marx saw alienation both as a subjective state – as people's feelings of alienation – and as a structural category which described the social and economic arrangements of capitalism.

Marx identified four particular manifestations of alienation. (1) The worker is alienated from the product of his labour, since what he produces is appropriated by others and he has no control over its fate. (2) The worker is alienated from the act of production. Working becomes an alien activity that offers no intrinsic satisfaction, that is forced on the worker by external constraints and ceases to be an end in itself, and that involves working at someone else's bidding as forced labour. Work in fact becomes a commodity that is sold and its only value to the worker is its saleability. (3) The worker is alienated from his human nature or his 'species being', because the first two aspects of alienation deprive his productive activity of those specifically *human* qualities which distinguish it from the activity of animals and thus define human nature. (4) The worker is alienated from other men, since capitalism transforms social relations into market relations, and people are judged by their position in the market rather than by their human qualities. People come to regard each other as reifications – as worker or as capitalist – rather than as individuals.

Capital itself is the source of further alienation within a developed capitalist economy. This is because capital accumulation generates its own 'needs' which reduce people to the level of commodities. Workers become factors in the operation of capital and their activities are dominated by the requirements of profitability rather than by their own human needs. Within a market economy, the rules which govern accumulation are those of the market place. These rules constitute a set of impersonal mechanisms which dominate all economic actors, capitalists as well as workers, and the market has a coercive force. Marx noted that, although the needs of profit and capital accumulation seem to take on a life of their own, these impersonal mechanisms in fact disguise the human origins of capital and the exploitation that allows one class to appropriate what another has produced.

Since Marx, alienation has lost much of its original sociological meaning and has been used to describe a wide variety of phenomena. These include: any feeling of separation from, and discontent with, society; feelings that there is a moral breakdown in society; feelings of powerlessness in face of the solidity of social institutions; the impersonal, dehumanized nature of large-scale and bureaucratic social organizations. The first pair of usages in fact bear a considerable resemblance to the different, Durkheimian concept of anomie (q.v.) rather than to Marx's conception of alienation. The last usage echoes M. Weber's sentiments about the bureaucratic tendency of modern society.

In the 1950s and 1960s, American social scientists emphasized the subjective or psychological facet of alienation at the cost of the social structural aspect, and when they did consider structural conditions they ignored Marx's sociology of capitalism. M. Seeman (1959) separated a variety of different psychological states, which he measured by attitude scales (q.v.). The 'powerlessness' dimension of alienation refers to people's feelings that they cannot influence their social surroundings. 'Meaninglessness' is the feeling that illegitimate means are required to achieve valued goals. 'Isolation' occurs when people feel estranged from society's norms and values. 'Self-estrangement' refers to an inability to find activities that are psychologically rewarding. R. Blauner (1964) linked these dimensions of subjective alienation to the different types of work found in modern industry and claimed that production technology was the major determinant of alienation. He thought that automation (q.v.) would make jobs more satisfying and so abolish alienation. The American perspective in effect has equated alienation with people's feelings of dissatisfaction with life, which is a long way from Marx's original formulation.

The term has been used less often in recent sociology. Many modern Marxists believe that Marx abandoned alienation in his mature work in favour of exploitation and they see little point in preserving the concept. Most non-Marxist sociologists find that it has become too indeterminate to be useful. See: *Cash Nexus*; *Division of Labour*; *Reification*; *Marx*; *Weber*.

Bibl. Ollman (1971)

Alternative Medicine. These are diagnostic and therapeutic beliefs and practices which attempt to provide alternatives to scientific (allopathic) medicine which is based on the medical model (q.v.). Alternative medicine has the following characteristics: (1) it is typically homoeopathic (rather than allopathic) in treating the patient as unique with idiosyncratic problems and symptoms; (2) it follows the system laid down by S. Hahnemann (1755–1843) who argued (through his teaching on the minimum dose) that less medicine is better than more medicine; (3) it uses natural remedies and traditional (folk) cures rather than manufactured pharmaceutical products; (4) its practitioners are typically not regulated by a professional body recognized by the state; (5) the theories and treatment regimes are characteristically eclectic, drawing upon western, eastern and folk systems. Alternative medicine has developed in the twentieth century as a response to consumer, dissatisfaction with scientific medicine which is intrusive, interventionist and technologically sophisticated. The practical and philosophical roots of alternative medicine are, however, ancient. Alternative medicine includes acupuncture, chiropractic, Chinese holistic medicines, herbalism, naturopathy, iridology and psychic healing. See: *Health Care Systems*.

Bibl. Salmon (1984)

Althusser, Louis (b. 1918). A French Marxist philosopher, Althusser (1966; 1968; 1971) has had influence on contemporary sociology in four main directions.

(1) He has attempted to reformulate the base and superstructure (q.v.) model, because he objects to the economic determinism (q.v.) which he believes is implicit in most accounts of that model. Instead of seeing superstructural elements, such as ideology and politics, simply as reflections of the economic base, he proposes a scheme in which ideology and politics are conditions of existence (q.v.) of the economy. Althusser has been partly responsible for the interest shown in the concept of the mode of production (q.v.) which he considers as a complex relationship of economy, ideology and politics.

(2) Althusser has attempted to redefine the nature of ideology. He argues that ideology should be seen as a real social relation, or as a practice, not as an illusion as it is in conventional analyses.

(3) The most influential of Althusser's specific proposals is his concept of ideological state apparatuses (q.v.), itself a notion deriving from A. Gramsci. For capitalist societies to continue over time, the relations of production (q.v.) must be reproduced, a requirement that is met by the ideological state apparatuses, for example, institutions of the media and education.

(4) Althusser has advanced a number of arguments which touch on the old sociological debate about the relation of agency and structure. Essentially, Althusser objects to theories which reduce explanation to the characteristics of individuals or collections of individuals, for example, classes. Instead, individuals have to be seen as bearers or agents of the structures of social relations.

There has been a great deal of criticism of Althusserianism from within conventional sociology, concentrating on the school's theoreticism, its neglect of relevant evidence, its dogmatism and its departure from Marxist principles, particularly that of the primacy of the economy. See: *Agency and Structure*; *Marx*; *Marxist Sociology*; *Mode of Production*; *Structuralism*.

Bibl. Callinicos (1976); Thompson (1978)

Altruism. Normally contrasted with egoism and individualism, altruism is the principle of unselfish regard for the needs and interests of others. For E. Durkheim, altruistic suicide, that is suicide to serve group interests, was the result of strong collective pressure and social approval. More recently, the question of altruism over egoism has been raised by theories of exchange and reciprocity. See: *Durkheim*; *Exchange Theory*; *Reciprocity*.

Animism. As one of the basic concepts of the nineteenth-century evolutionary theory of religion, animism was held to be part of a primitive philosophy which explained such phenomena as dreams, hallucinations and death by reference to the spiritual existence of animals and plants, and the existence of the human soul. Within an evolutionary scheme of cultural development, positivist science would replace both theology and animistic philosophy. Subsequent theories saw religion more in terms of its social functions rather than as emphasizing its individual and cognitive characteristics. See: *Religion*.

Annales School. An influential group of French social historians associated with the journal *Annales: économies, sociétés, civilisations*, which was founded by L. Febvre and M. Bloch in 1929. The school has made major contributions to the empirical study of European civilization as a whole and to theoretical and methodological debates about historical analysis. Members of the school have, in particular, opposed the conventional approach to history as the chronology of political events by giving greater emphasis to social history, social structure and long-term historical trends. There is an important marriage of interests between some of the classical debates in sociology (over the transition from feudalism to capitalism, for example) and the emphasis on structure and historical process in the *Annales* school. The work of E. Le Roy Ladurie (1975) and F. Braudel (1966; 1979) has become especially important for sociologists. The influence of Braudel on contemporary social science has developed through the Braudel Center in America, under the leadership of I. Wallerstein (1974). See: *World-System Theory*.

Bibl. Burke (1980)

Année sociologique, L'. Edited by E. Durkheim between 1896 and 1913, *L'Année sociologique* has been described as a sociological laboratory rather than a journal, since it provided the principal publishing outlet of the research of the early Durkheimian school. It was certainly a major institutional factor in the dominance of Durkheimian sociology over competitive groups in France.

Bibl. Nandan (1977)

Anomie. This is a social condition characterized by the breakdown of norms governing social interaction. Anomie, like alienation (q.v.), is a concept that bridges the gap between explanations of social action at the individual level with those at the level of the social structure. The classical treatment is that of E. Durkheim in his work on suicide. In *Suicide* (1897), Durkheim argues that people can only be happy when their wants are proportionate to their means. Left to themselves, human desires are boundless and this fact of human nature, together with necessarily limited resources, creates great unhappiness or ultimately suicide. The manner in which societies cope with this problem of unattainable goals is to restrict human desires and goals by imposing a framework of norms which 'permit' only certain goals which have some chance of attainment. Anomie describes the situation when this framework breaks down, goals again outrun means and the suicide rate rises.

Durkheim's concept of anomie has been enlarged by R. K. Merton (1957) into a general theory of deviant behaviour. Merton distinguishes culturally defined goals and institutional means of achieving those goals. Societies vary in the degree to which they stress one or the other. Those societies which lay great emphasis on goals but little on means push individuals into adopting the technically most efficient means to the goal, even if these are illegitimate. An example of such an anomic society is the

United States. Crime may be normal in certain groups because, while there is a widespread emphasis on the importance of worldly success, particularly in terms of wealth, the available means to these goals are restricted by the class structure and the only means of achieving them will be deviant. See: *Durkheim*; *Relative Deprivation*; *Suicide*.

Bibl. Lukes (1967)

Anti-Psychiatry. An intellectual movement of the late 1950s and the 1960s which was critical of the theories and therapeutic treatments of conventional psychiatry. It made various criticisms. (1) The involuntary incarceration of persons regarded as insane is an infringement of basic human rights. (2) Psychiatry is a form of social control (q.v.) by which social deviance is labelled as a form of mental illness. (3) It is not insanity which creates the need for asylums, but rather asylums that create the need for mad people. (4) Diagnostic categories express, not a neutral science, but a set of dominant values, and the use of such diagnostic labels stigmatizes the mentally ill. (5) The therapeutic treatment available to psychiatry, such as electroconvulsive therapy, is degrading and of uncertain value.

The anti-psychiatry movement proposed a range of alternative forms of approach and treatment; the basic proposal was the closure of existing asylums and psychiatric units in favour of community medicine (q.v.). This movement was associated with T. Szasz (1971) in the USA, M. Foucault (1961) in France, and R. D. Laing (1959) in Britain. E. Goffman's (1961b) criticism of asylums as total institutions had an influence in sociology. Criticism of psychiatry is now less prominent, because there has been an exodus of patients from mental hospitals since the 1960s and there is a greater use of out-patient

treatment. This process of de-institutionalization or decarceration has, in part, been made possible by the improvement in antipsychotic drugs. However, critics of psychiatry would maintain that this change in policy has been produced more by the escalating costs of hospital care. See: *Alternative Medicine*; *Foucault*; *Freud*; *Goffman*; *Labelling Theory*; *Madness*; *Medicalization*; *Sociology of Health and Illness*; *Stereotypes*; *Stigma*.

Bibl. Boyers and Orrill (1972)

Appearance and Reality. K. Marx said that his method consisted in going beneath the appearance of capitalist society to the reality underlying it. Although this method seems like any scientific endeavour, Marx also made three specific proposals about the relationship between appearance and reality: (1) the appearance conceals the reality; (2) the appearance is explained by the reality; (3) the appearance is convincing and, in a sense, real. The wage-form is the classic illustration of the distinction between appearance and reality. The appearance is that labourers receive a wage as a fair price of their labour. However, the labour theory of value (q.v.) suggests that this appearance is misleading, since the capitalist exploits the labourer by paying as wages less than the value of what the labourer actually produces. The distorting appearance, the wage-form, is also explained by the real exploitative relations, since Marx believed that relations of production (q.v.) were fundamental. Lastly, the payment of wages apparently in exchange for labour is a real event even if it ultimately conceals an underlying exploitative mechanism. See: *Commodity Fetishism*; *Ideology*; *Marx*; *Marxist Sociology*.

Bibl. Abercrombie (1980)

Applied Sociology. While the methods

and substantive findings of sociology are frequently applied, the notion of applied sociology is neither a discrete and developed area of the discipline nor a term which is commonly used by sociologists. It raises problems of ethics and professional autonomy.

Aron, Raymond (1905–1983). French sociologist, philosopher and political actor, he was a professor at the Collège de France from 1970, having held a variety of other university positions from before the Second World War. He was influential in French sociology, but he was also isolated because of his criticisms and opposition to Marxism which was an important theoretical perspective in French sociology, especially before 1968. Aron (1978) divided his own contribution to sociology into four main areas. First, there was the analysis of contemporary ideologies, as in *The Opium of the Intellectuals* (1955). Secondly, he wrote extensively on the notion of industrial society (q.v.) in *Eighteen Lectures on Industrial Society* (1963b) and *The Industrial Society* (1966). Thirdly, he contributed to the analysis of international relations and warfare in *The Century of Total War* (1951), *Peace and War* (1961), *The Great Debate* (1963a), *De Gaulle, Israel and the Jews* (1968a), *The Imperial Republic* (1973b) and *Clausewitz* (1976). Fourthly, he studied modern political systems and movements in *Democracy and Totalitarianism* (1965a), *An Essay on Freedom* (1965b), *The Elusive Revolution* (1968b) and *Progress and Disillusion* (1969).

In addition, he played an important role in maintaining an awareness of the complexity and richness of the sociological tradition in *German Sociology* (1935) and *Main Currents in Sociological Thought* (1965c). He also wrote on the philosophy of history in *Introduction to the Philosophy of History* (1938) and *History and the Dialectic of Violence* (1973a).

His analysis of industrial society, in which he drew attention to pluralism (q.v.) and the complexity of values, was in many respects parallel to the concept of post-industrial society (q.v.) which has been influential in American sociology. However, he rejected the convergence thesis (q.v.), arguing that the different political systems of the USSR and the USA were distinctive; in general terms, he attempted to show that political institutions and processes were independent of social and economic relations.

Asceticism. This is a doctrine or practice in which sensuous pleasures are denied for the enhancement of the spiritual self. The notion is associated with branches of most important religions. For M. Weber, Protestant asceticism was of crucial importance for the origins of capitalism, the discipline of labour and capitalist organization. See: *Protestant Ethic*.

Ascription. Ascription means that certain qualities of individuals – status, occupation or income, for example – are given by the position into which those individuals are born or over which they have no control, rather than by their own achievements.

Asiatic Mode of Production. A Marxist concept that explains the alleged stagnation of Oriental societies, it was used by K. Marx and F. Engels in 1853 in a collection of articles published in the *New York Daily Tribune* as a description of 'Asiatic societies' from Egypt to China. Marx and Engels offered various theories to explain the origins of the Asiatic mode of production: (1) the arid conditions of these societies gave rise to the need for state-regulated irrigation systems, and (2) the self-sufficiency of village production in Asia explained the immutability of its social structure. Although there is disagreement as to the origins of the Asiatic mode of production, it has the following characteristics: absence of private property, dominance of the state over public works (such as irrigation), a self-sufficient village economy, the absence of autonomous cities, the unity of handicrafts and agriculture, and the simplicity of production methods. Marx argued that, because of the absence of private property, there was no class struggle (q.v.) based on a landowning class and peasantry. Because there was no dynamic of class conflict, there was no sociological basis for revolutionary social change (q.v.). The transformation of these societies was brought about by colonialism, because capitalist exploitation introduced private property in land and hence introduced class relationships.

This concept has given rise to considerable dispute, both within and outside Marxism. Some critics have claimed that it was neither important nor consistently used by Marx and Engels. The concept is politically sensitive for two reasons. First, it appears to justify colonialism and imperialism (q.v.), because their unintended consequences were to create the conditions for progressive social change. Secondly, it was associated with a controversy over whether pre-revolutionary Russia was a 'semi-Asiatic' society. It has been suggested, following K. Wittfogel's *Oriental Despotism* (1957), that Russian communism reproduced the social stationariness and despotism associated with the Asiatic mode of production.

On more technical grounds, the concept has been criticized by B. Hindess and P. Q. Hirst (1975) for being theoretically incoherent. It has also been rejected because it cannot account for the major social and political differences which existed between imperial China, Iran and Egypt. On empirical grounds, it has been criticized because private property did exist in, for example, Islamic societies. As an alternative framework, some Marxists have proposed a variety of modes of production to analyse the societies of Asia, such as the 'tributary mode of production' which explains the appropriation of a surplus (or tribute) from these societies. However, the concept of the Asiatic mode is no longer in general use, having been replaced by the debate on dependency (q.v.) and underdevelopment (q.v.). See: *Oriental Despotism*.

Bibl. Bailey and Llobera (1981)

Assimilation. This concept was first used in American race relations research to describe the processes by which immigrant groups were integrated into the dominant white culture. Thus, in R. Park's (1950) 'race relations cycle', the social interaction between the host society and new immigrants was conceptualized in terms of four stages – contacts, competition, accommodation and assimilation. In its original usage, assimilation was seen as a unidimensional, one-way process by which outsiders relinquished their own culture in favour of that of the dominant society. Recent research regards assimilation as reciprocal, involving mutual adjustments between host and migrant communities. Furthermore, the particular character of the ethnic group in question may enhance, retard or preclude intermarriage, participation in citizenship and social acceptance. Assimilation is often used interchangeably with acculturation (q.v.). See: *Accommodation; Racism*.

Atomism. This is the notion that societies can best be seen as entities made up of individual units ('atoms') which interact. Extreme atomistic theories argue that sociology can *only* proceed by examination of these individuals and the meanings that they place on their actions and not by analysis of whole social structures. Atomism is the opposite of holism (q.v.) in sociology. See: *Action Theory*; *Agency and Structure*; *Exchange Theory*; *Methodological Individualism*; *Utilitarianism*.

Attitude. A relatively stable system of beliefs concerning some object and resulting in an evaluation of that object, the concept of attitude is used extensively and technically in psychology but more loosely in sociology. Attitude surveys are sometimes criticized on the grounds that questionnaires do not reveal people's true attitudes, which the researcher can only know by prolonged contact as in ethnographic or participant observation (q.v.) methods, or on the grounds that knowing what people's attitudes are may not help to explain or predict their behaviour, if the researcher wishes to make inferences about this from the knowledge of attitudes. See: *Attitude Scale*; *Interview*; *Reliability*.

Bibl. Lemon (1973)

Attitude Scale. Attitude scales consist of sets of standardized statements with which people are asked to agree or disagree. Scaling assumes that an attitude will have various aspects that in their totality constitute the attitude being measured. For example, the attitude 'approval of social inequality' might embrace aspects such as class, ethnic and gender inequalities. It also assumes that people can be ranked along a continuum representing the varying degrees of 'strength' or 'intensity' with which an attitude is held. The sets of standardized statements are selected from some larger pool of items that between them cover the relevant aspects of the attitude, selection being based initially on exploratory research on which people

respond to all statements, or on the judgement of a panel of evaluators. With certain scales, factor analysis (q.v.) or cluster analysis (q.v.) may be applied to the results of the exploratory survey to test whether the selected statements in fact measure a unidimensional attitude or whether they are multidimensional. It is usual to test scales for reliability and validity before using them in the final questionnaire. The intensity or strength with which people hold the various aspects of the attitude is measured by rating scales for each item, by asking respondents how much they agree with a statement (often on a five-point scale ranging from 'strongly disagree' to 'strongly agree') or by asking them to choose between a number of different statements on each item. Attitude scales produce a single score for each individual that is constructed out of this multiplicity of items, so that each respondent can be placed somewhere along the attitude continuum. The most commonly encountered attitude scales are Guttman, Likert and Thurstone scales. See: *Attitude*; *Measurement Levels*; *Questionnaire*; *Reliability*; *Social Distance*.

Bibl. Lemon (1973)

Authoritarian Personality. This concept indicates the way in which the structure of the personality predisposes to the acceptance of anti-democratic political beliefs. Early research by E. Fromm and W. Reich argued that the family structure of capitalist societies might typically produce rigid and authoritarian personalities ready to accept fascist ideology. The classical study is by T. Adorno *et al., The Authoritarian Personality* (1950). These authors concluded that there was a prejudiced personality characterized by hierarchical and authoritarian parent–child relationships, a dichotomous view of social relationships leading to the formation of stereotypes (q.v.), conventionality, exploitative dependency, rigidity and repressive denial, all of which may culminate in a social philosophy which worships strength and disdains the weak. The authors emphasize that their study is, on the one hand, only a psychological one and, on the other, is not any necessary guide to prejudiced or discriminatory *action*. See: *Fascism*; *Frankfurt School*; *Prejudice*.

Authority. If power is the exercise of constraint and compulsion against the will of an individual or group, authority is a sub-type of power in which people willingly obey commands because they see the exercise of power as legitimate. M. Weber distinguished between legal-rational, traditional and charismatic authority. Legal-rational authority involves obedience to formal rules which have been established by regular, public procedures. The following of quasi-legal norms in formal bureaucracies is the principal example of this type of authority. By contrast, following a traditional authority involves the acceptance of a rule which embodies custom and ancient practice. In the case of charismatic authority, commands are obeyed because followers or disciples believe in the extraordinary character of their leader, whose authority transcends existing or customary practices. Any regime which has minimal public acceptance as a *de facto* government has, in Weber's terms, some basis of legitimacy even if that regime depends largely on force.

In contemporary sociology, the term is often used imprecisely to refer to the influence exercised by leadership. In social psychology, it is used in the description of group influences over individual belief and behaviour in research on the dynamics of small groups. See: *Bureaucracy*; *Charisma*; *Leadership*; *Legal-Rational Authority*; *Legitimacy*; *Power*.

Bibl. Parkin (1982)

Automation. The direction of technological change in modern industry is towards the replacement of human power and control by mechanical devices. Simple forms of mechanization provide mechanical assistance to what is primarily a manual labour process, for example when manual workers perform their tasks with the assistance of tools or machines and office workers use typewriters or calculators. More advanced forms are those in which production is primarily performed by machinery and the residual human tasks involve only the control, adjustment and regulation of machines. Automation marks the stage of technical evolution when the remaining human elements are finally removed. Truly automatic processes are 'closed-loop' systems which require no outside human intervention from the moment raw materials are inserted in a machine until the product is completed. The development of information-processing technology which provides computer control of production has had a dramatic effect: mechanization was long ago capable of replacing the manual aspect of human intervention in many production systems, but only with computerization have the intellectual and control aspects been capable of automation. Automation has also spread to office work with the computerization of many routine functions previously performed by office staff.

There has been considerable sociological interest in the consequences of automation. Sociologists have debated the effects on the content of work. R. Blauner (1964) believed that automation would benefit employees by removing the unpleasant aspects of work and leaving the more interesting and skilled parts which required employees to use their judgement and discretion. However, the subsequent development of automation has tended to remove even these aspects of work-content among lower-level manual and office workers. It has been fashionable recently to talk of the automation of human control skills as leading to de-skilling (q.v.). Against this view, others assert that a high-technology society will need a new range of skills. The evidence is inconclusive. One possible outcome is a polarization into highly skilled tasks necessary for the design and maintenance of automated processes, at one end, and de-skilled jobs at the other. The effect of automation on employment also concerns sociologists. Automation obviously reduces the number of employees needed to produce any given volume of output. This suggests an increase in unemployment. In expanding firms and economies, however, automation may not be associated with job losses if expansion counteracts the effect of labour reduction. It remains difficult to disentangle automation from economic and population factors that also determine employment levels. See: *Alienation*; *Deskilling*; *Industrialization*; *Labour Process Approach*; *Scientific Management*; *Socio-Technical Systems*; *Technology*.

Bibl. Froomkin (1968); Coombs (1985); Gill (1985)

B

Barthes, Roland (1915–1980). Often associated with French structuralism (q.v.), his idiosyncratic approach to literature and society is complex, combining sociology, semiology, literary criticism, structural anthropology and Marxism. He has made important contributions to the analysis of culture, texts and ideology. His works include *Mythologies* (1957), *Writing Degree Zero* (1953), *S/Z* (1970), *The Pleasure of the Text* (1975) and *Sade-Fourier-Loyola* (1971). See: *Myth*; *Semiotics*; *Tel Quel Group*.

Bibl. Culler (1983)

Base and Superstructure. These terms are used by Marxist sociologists in the analysis of the relationship between the economy (base) and other social forms (superstructure). The economy is defined in terms of three elements: the labourer, the means of production (which comprises both the materials worked on and the means by which this work is done) and the non-worker who appropriates the product. All economies are characterized by these three elements, but what differentiates one economy from another is the manner in which the elements are combined. There are two kinds of relation that can hold between elements, a relation of possession and a relation of property. Possession indicates the relationship between the labourer and the means of production; either he can be in possession of them, controlling and directing them, or not. In the relation of property, the non-labourer owns either the means of production or labour or both, and can therefore take the product. The superstructure is usually a residual category comprising such institutions as the state, the family structure, or the kinds of ideology prevalent in society. As to the relationship between base and superstructure, the strength of the Marxist position comes from saying that the character of the superstructure is determined by the character of the base. As the nature of the base varies, so also will the nature of the superstructure. Therefore, for example, one would expect the feudal political structure to differ from the capitalist one because the economies of these two forms are clearly different.

The model of base and superstructure has inspired a variety of studies ranging from interpretation of the eighteenth-century novel to analysis of family structure in contemporary society. The prevailing form that such studies have taken is class-theoretical (q.v.). That is, the relations of production (q.v.) in the base are taken to be relations between social classes, between workers and capitalists, for instance, and to say that base determines superstructure means that the character of the superstructure is largely determined by the economic interests of the dominant social class. Such an emphasis on class can distract attention away from the more impersonal workings of the economy.

The base and superstructure metaphor can be a fruitful analytical device but it has also excited a great deal of debate both from within and without Marxism. One point at issue is the definition of the relations of production. In that these are partly relations of ownership, they appear to involve legal definitions which the model defines as superstructural. It therefore seems difficult to separate base and superstructure analytically. In recent years attention has been concentrated on formulating a concept of relations of production which is not defined in legal terms. However, the most important bone of contention has been the notion that the base *determines* the superstructure.

A number of critics argue that the model entails an economic determinism (q.v.). In fact very few proponents of the notion of base and superstructure adopt such a determinist perspective. K. Marx and F. Engels never held that doctrine. Firstly, they suggested that superstructural elements could be relatively autonomous of the base and have their own laws of development. Secondly, they argued that the superstructure will interact with, or influence, the base. More recent Marxists have departed still further from economic determinism in claiming that superstructural elements must be seen as conditions of existence (q.v.) of the base, a notion that has been seen as robbing the economy of any primacy and giving all institutions in society equal causal efficacy. See: *Althusser*; *Engels*; *Labour Theory of Value*; *Marx*; *Marxist Sociology*; *Mode of Production*.

Bibl. Williams (1973); Abercrombie (1980)

Becker, Howard S. (b. 1928). As a contemporary representative of the tradition of the Chicago School (q.v.), his principal contributions to contemporary sociology have been in occupational socialization in *Boys in White* (1961), to the investigation of deviant subcultures and careers in *Outsiders* (1963), and to the study of youth culture and higher education in *Making the Grade* (1968) and *Campus Power Struggle* (1970a). He also wrote *Sociological Work, Method and Substance* (1970b). See: *Career*; *Deviant Behaviour*; *Labelling Theory*.

Behaviourism. This is a school of psychology that deals with observable behaviour and disregards the subjective aspects of human activity such as consciousness, intention or the meaning of behaviour to the people involved. The idea that behaviour divorced from its subjective and social meanings is a legitimate area of study is rejected by sociologists, who use the term 'action' to distinguish meaningful activity from mere behaviour. See: *Action Theory*.

Bell, Daniel (b. 1919). An American sociologist who in *The End of Ideology* (1960) claimed that apocalyptic class ideologies had declined in industrialized capitalist societies. In *The Coming of Post-Industrial Society* (1974) he suggested that 'post-industrial' society (q.v.) had superseded industrialism. His other major work is *The Cultural Contradictions of Capitalism* (1976), which postulates that the hedonistic culture typical of advanced capitalist societies is incompatible with the dominance of rationality required by the economic system. See: *End of Ideology Theory*; *Post-Industrial Society*.

Bendix, Reinhard (b. 1916). An American sociologist whose comparative study of business ideology and authority in the industrializing societies of Europe and America, *Work and Authority in Industry* (1956), remains a classic work of economic sociology. *Max Weber: An Intellectual Portrait* (1960) provides a comprehensive analysis of Weber's work. In *Nation-Building and Citizenship* (1964), he elaborated T. H. Marshall's (q.v.) view that access to political rights or 'citizenship' (q.v.) is important in incorporating the working class into modern society. He also co-authored *Social Mobility in Industrial Society* (1959) with S. M. Lipset (q.v.). See: *Incorporation*; *Social Mobility*.

Bernstein, Basil (b. 1924). Currently a professor in the sociology of education at London University's Institute of Education, Bernstein is best known for his pioneering work on the relationship between social class and children's acquisition and use of language in both family and school contexts. In recent years his work has broadened out to provide a general theory of the relationships between class relations, the distribution of power, principles of control, and communication codes. He has published widely, mostly in articles, some of which are collected into the volumes of *Class, Codes and Control* (1971; 1973; 1975). See: *Pedagogical Practices*; *Restricted Code*.

Beveridge, William Henry (1879–1963). He is best known for his role in the extension of social services and the creation of the welfare state (q.v.) in post-war Britain. In 1941, Beveridge was appointed chairman of a civil service inquiry into the management of the social services. The report of this inquiry, *Social Insurance and Allied Services* (1942), popularly known as the Beveridge Report, set out the principles which after the war guided the establishment of the welfare state. Idleness, ignorance, disease, squalor and want were identified as the major hazards facing individuals in industrial society, which should be remedied by government. The report recommended a national health service, social insurance and assistance, family allowances, and full-employment policies.

His career was varied, including a fellowship in law at Oxford University (1902–9), a subwardenship at Toynbee Hall in London's East End (1903–5), an early career in the civil service (1908–19), Director of the London School of Economics (1919–37), Liberal MP for a year (1944) and then a Liberal peer.

Bias. Systematic error or bias is the difference between the true value of a characteristic and the average value obtained by repeated investigations. Any discrepancy between the true value and research value in a *single* investigation is the sum of two factors: bias and sampling error (q.v.). The idea of bias assumes that there is a 'true' value. This assumption has been disputed on the grounds that such values do not exist independently of the measuring process used. This latter view has much to commend it in the social science field. For example, in interview situations it has been shown that the race or sex of the interviewer may substantially affect the nature of the replies given; the method of measurement here determines the data. See: *Interview*; *Non-Response*.

Birth Rate. The crude birth rate is given by the number of live births per 1,000 persons of all ages in one year. The fertility rate is the number of live births per

1,000 females of childbearing age in one year. In the UK both the crude birth rate and the fertility rate rose until the mid 1960s but have declined significantly since then. See: *Death Rate*; *Demography*; *Fertility*.

Bibl. Cox, P. R. (1970)

Blau, Peter M. (b. 1918). An American sociologist who has contributed to exchange theory (q.v.) and conducted major empirical investigations of the United States occupational structure and the structure of business organizations. His major works are: *The Dynamics of Bureaucracy* (1955); *Formal Organizations: A Comparative Approach* (1962), with W. R. Scott; *Exchange and Power in Social Life* (1964); *The American Occupational Structure* (1967), with O. D. Duncan; *The Structure of Organizations* (1971), with R. A. Schoenherr. See: *Exchange Theory*; *Social Mobility*.

Blue-collar. This is an American term used to describe manual workers.

Bogardus Scale. See: *Social Distance*.

Booth, Charles James (1840–1916). He was a British businessman, social reformer and early social statistician, concerned to improve the economic and social conditions of the mass of the population in urban England. Booth investigated empirically the conditions of the poor and other social groups and pioneered the scientific research of social problems. His mammoth surveys of poverty, industry and religion, published in 17 volumes as *Life and Labour of the People in London* (1889–1891), are unrivalled accounts of social conditions at the end of the last century. He was partly responsible for the Old Age Pensions Act of 1908.

Bibl. Simey and Simey (1960)

Bottomore, Tom (b. 1920). Until recently a professor of sociology at Sussex University and a past president of the International Sociological Association, Bottomore has written extensively on a variety of subjects. He has played a major role in presenting the ideas of Marxist sociologists, in *Karl Marx: Selected Writings in Sociology and Social Philosophy* (1961), edited with M. Reubel; *Marxist Sociology* (1975); *Austro-Marxism* (1978), edited with P. Goode. His other works on classes and politics include: *Classes in Modern Society* (1965); *Elites and Society* (1966); *Political Sociology* (1979). He was the general editor of *A Dictionary of Marxist Thought* (1983) and, with R. Nisbet, *A History of Sociological Analysis* (1978b). His recent work continues to explore the relationship between sociology, socialism and Marxism, for instance in *Sociology and Socialism* (1984). He has made a major contribution to the sociology of capitalism in *Theories of Modern Capitalism* (1985). With M. Mulkay, he is the editor of the influential series *Controversies in Sociology*.

Boundary Maintenance. This is a term typically used in functionalism, especially by T. Parsons (1951), who defines a social system as boundary-maintaining if, in relation to its environment, it preserves certain regularities of pattern. There are social processes which maintain both the boundaries *and* the equilibrium of a system relative to other systems which constitute its environment. For the continued existence of systems there must also be exchange across their boundaries with other systems. See: *Functionalism*; *Parsons*; *Social System*; *Systems Theory*.

Bounded Rationality. As used in the analysis of administrative and organizational decision-making, this concept emphasizes the constraints upon rational or optimizing decisions. Limited information is available to decision-makers regarding alternatives and consequences, and their ability to evaluate all the information that is relevant and available is also limited.

Bibl. March and Simon (1958)

Bourdieu, Pierre (b. 1930). A professor of sociology at the Collège de France, Paris, Bourdieu is best known for his work in the sociology of culture and education but deserves to be better known for his more general sociological theory. Several of his books have been translated into English, including *Outline of a Theory of Practice* (1977a), *Reproduction in Education, Society and Culture* (1977b), and *Distinction* (1984). See: *Cultural Capital.*

Bourgeoisie. This term is used loosely to describe either the middle or ruling classes in capitalist society. Both classes are assumed to have an interest in preserving capitalism in a struggle with the working class over the distribution of surplus value (q.v.). The term is perhaps more properly applied to the urban social class made up of entrepreneurs, merchants and industrialists active in the earlier stages of capitalist development. See: *Capitalism; Class; Middle Class; Periodization.*

Bureaucracy. This describes a particular system of administration. Historically it was associated with the rule of government and governmental officials, but sociologists regard it as a form of administration that is found in organizations pursuing a wide variety of goals.

As a technical term in sociology, bureaucracy is associated with M. Weber. He gave it a precise definition and suggested that it was the best administrative form for the rational or efficient pursuit of organizational goals. Weber's ideal type (q.v.) of bureaucracy comprised various elements: a high degree of specialization and a clearly defined division of labour, with tasks distributed as official duties; a hierarchical structure of authority with clearly circumscribed areas of command and responsibility; the establishment of a formal body of rules to govern the operation of the organization; administration based on written documents; impersonal relationships between organizational members and with clients; recruitment of personnel on the basis of ability and technical knowledge; long-term employment, promotion on the basis of seniority or merit, a fixed salary; the separation of private and official income. In Weber's mind these discrete elements were tied together into a coherent totality by one overarching phenomenon: rationality. Scholarly analysis of Weber's position now suggests that his idea about the rationality of bureaucracy embraced two slightly different things. In one sense the rationality of bureaucracy was that it maximized technical efficiency. The rules defined the most appropriate means to realize organizational ends, were based on up-to-date technical knowledge, and directed the behaviour of members along the most efficient lines. In the other sense, bureaucracy was a system of social control or authority that was accepted by members because they saw the rules as rational, fair and impartial – a 'legal-rational' value system. For Weber, however, bureaucracy's major quality was simply its predictability.

Weber's main preoccupation was with broad historical and comparative issues and with political administration and its impact on society, and he developed the bureaucratic ideal type for this sort of macro-analysis. His successors applied the model to the micro-sociology of business organization. Modern research has shown that many bureaucratic organizations work inefficiently and in ways that Weber's model did not anticipate. R. K. Merton (1957) demonstrates that bureaucracy becomes inflexible because of various unanticipated consequences that derive from its structure. Members may adhere to the rules in a ritualistic manner and elevate these above the goals they are designed to realize. This is inefficient if for any reason the rules do not establish the most efficient means; for example, if changing circumstances have made the rules out of date. Subordinates tend to follow orders even if these are misguided. Specialization often fosters a narrow outlook which cannot solve new problems. Colleagues within departments develop feelings of loyalty to each other and their departments, and promote these group interests when they can.

M. Crozier (1964) extends these arguments to show that bureaucracies embody vicious circles of decreasing efficiency and effectiveness. Groups of colleagues attempt to maximize their freedom of action by paying lip-service to the rules but ignoring the spirit behind these and bending them when they can. They are able to withhold or distort information so that senior managers do not know exactly what is going on. Senior managers realize that something is amiss, but they are not allowed to take arbitrary or personal action against those they suspect of failing to promote organizational goals, so they create more rules to regulate what goes on below them. These rules make the organization more and more rigid but may still fail to control subordinates. Bureaucracy becomes less efficient and provides only a limited social control. Moreover, some tasks within organizations involve unpredictable events for which standardized rules are inappropriate, and bureaucracy is particularly ineffective in such areas. See: *Bounded Rationality*; *Legal-Rational Authority*; *Management*; *Organization Theory*; *Rationalization*; *Weber*.

Bibl. Weber (1936); Albrow (1970)

C

Capital Fractions. In Marxism, capital is seen as being internally divided along several axes. One division can be drawn between large- and small-scale capital; a second occurs between industrial, financial and landed capital. These fractions are believed to have a certain commonality of interest by virtue of their all being forms of capital. This common interest, however, may be offset by sectional conflicts of interest. Such sectionalism is partly overcome by the activities of the state. See: *Capitalism*; *Relative Autonomy*.

Capital Functions. The complexity of advanced societies means that the simple division of the population into capitalists and proletarians once favoured within Marxism is no longer viable. The rise of the 'middle classes' of managers, professionals and technicians has followed the growing need to administer and co-ordinate increasingly complex production processes. At the same time, the dispersal of ownership via shareholdings, often into the hands of institutions such as pension funds, makes it more difficult to identify a capitalist class than was the case in earlier periods. A modern attempt to solve the problem of how to divide society into capital and labour is to distinguish between the legal ownership of capital and the performance of the functions of capital, which may be carried out by agents who do not legally own the means of production. These functions include the control and supervision of labour, the allocation of resources within the enterprise, and the design of products and of the labour processes to produce them. For capitalism to survive, all these functions must be performed, but the manner in which they are undertaken will vary from society to society. See: *Capitalism*; *Class*; *Management*; *Managerial Revolution*; *Middle Class*; *Profession*.

Bibl. Crompton and Gubbay (1978)

Capital Logic. This is a term applied to those analyses which attempt to explain social phenomena by reference to the needs or requirements of capital (not capitalists). For example, capital logic theories of the state argue that capital cannot, by itself, provide certain of the conditions necessary for its survival, a road network for instance, and it is therefore left to the state to ensure that they are provided. See: *Collective Consumption*; *Reproduction of Labour Power*.

Bibl. Holloway and Picciotto (1978)

Capitalism. This type of economic organization in its 'pure' form may briefly be defined by: (1) private ownership and control of the economic instruments of production, i.e. capital; (2) the gearing of economic activity to making profits; (3) a market framework that regulates this activity; (4) the appropriation of profits by the owners of capital (subject to taxation by the state); (5) the provision of labour by workers who are free agents. Historically, capitalism has mainly developed and expanded to dominate economic life along with the growth of industrialization. Some of its features, however, were to be found in the commercial sector of the pre-industrial European economy, perhaps as long ago as the medieval period, while in England, a well-developed system of capitalist agriculture predated industrialization by at least a century and a half.

Capitalism has assumed various forms in industrialized societies, which qualify the above definition. It can be misleading to talk of capitalism without some further specification of the form that is being discussed. Early industrial capitalism in Great Britain and the United States in the nineteenth century is regarded as the classical model that approximates the pure form most closely. Economic activity was carried out by a large number of small capitalist firms, owned by individuals or families, with the owners also directly managing their firms. The regulation of economic activity was provided by markets, in which competition between the suppliers of goods and services and demand from consumers were dominant. The market for labour determined wages and allocated workers between employers according to the same forces of supply and demand. The economy embodied *laissez-faire* principles, in the sense that the state did not intervene but allowed the market to determine economic activity. The role of government was

supportive rather than interventionist, providing the conditions which were necessary for the economy to flourish. This early form of industrial capitalism produced a fragmented, unstable and anarchical economic system which oscillated between booms and slumps.

Elsewhere in Europe and in Japan, however, nineteenth- and early twentieth-century governments intervened more, regulating and directing the emerging capitalist economy. The state was involved in the following activities: directly subsidizing private entrepreneurs; directing credit and investment capital; establishing state-owned firms (notably in Germany and Italy); regulating labour and product markets by political means; establishing protective tariffs; granting monopoly rights to produce certain goods or to sell in certain markets; granting government contracts. Fairly detailed control of economic life was regarded as essential, in order to enhance national power, maintain healthy state revenues and preserve social order.

Even Great Britain and the United States have moved away from the early classical model in the twentieth century. The later forms of 'monopoly' capitalism are marked by economic concentration, the domination of markets by a small number of large firms rather than there being competition among numerous small firms. Under such conditions (strictly, of oligopoly rather than monopoly), it has not been uncommon for firms to agree among themselves to limit competition and manipulate markets, so as to increase profitability and stability. The spread of joint-stock ownership early in the century led to the diffusion of ownership among a large number of shareholders and the decline of family-owned firms. Diffused ownership also weakened the old connection between ownership and the managerial function, and professional managers have come to assume control of the day-to-day administration of firms. The separation of ownership and control varies from firm to firm and when shareholders have large ownership stakes in a company or ally with others they may still exercise their ownership rights to influence company policy. The last thirty years have seen the rise of institutional ownership and the relative decline of privately owned shareholdings in commerce and industry, as financial institutions (banks, holding companies, insurance companies, pension funds) have invested in company equity on a large scale. 'Finance' capitalism marks what some Marxists see as a development of monopoly capitalism: the separation of financial from productive capital, its monopolization by a relatively small number of financial institutions, and the domination of the rest of the economy by these.

The economic role of the state has also become more influential, and *laissez-faire*, where it existed, is a thing of the past. Governments seek to create economic stability and protect the interests of indigenous capital and labour. The state has done this by using its power as a purchaser of goods and services, by means of state investment, subsidization and in Great Britain by the public ownership of parts of industry as well, by directing private investment, by regulating company formation (for example, by controlling mergers and take-overs) and by controlling wages, salaries and prices at times. There is disagreement whether the state's economic role constitutes 'state monopoly capitalism', which describes an economic system in which the state directs the economy to the benefit of a small clique of monopoly/financial capitalists, or whether it departs so far from the pure capitalist system as to constitute a post-

capitalist economy.

Early sociologists were centrally concerned with the rise and social impact of capitalism. As part of his wider interest in the 'rationalizing' tendency in modern life, M. Weber saw capitalism as a concrete manifestation of this tendency: it embodied the qualities of impersonality, calculation and the purposive-rational pursuit of interests, which together constituted efficiency. For Weber, the essential developments which gave industrial capitalism its rational character were both institutional and spiritual. The crucial institutional change was the rise of a free-market economy, particularly the free market in labour. Other important changes included the growth of a money economy and the subsequent development of banks, the rise of universal laws of contract, bureaucratic control of business enterprises, and double-entry book-keeping. The central spiritual change was the rise of ascetic Protestantism in Europe: the 'Protestant ethic' (q.v.) emphasized values of hard work and deferred gratification which favoured the creation of capital and its productive re-investment rather than consumption. The importance of such values was reaffirmed by W. Sombart (1930), who believed that the 'spirit' of capitalism was the way in which adventurous risk-taking and calculating rationality were fused, and in recent times by the continuing interest in entrepreneurial achievement motivation (q.v.) which combines hard work with a competitive attitude.

K. Marx and Weber shared a concern with the social relations involved in capitalist production. They agreed that employees were denied any part of the ownership and control of the instruments of economic production and that employees were subordinated to those who did own and control. Marx regarded such subordination as an essential feature and defining characteristic of all forms of capitalism, because this was how capital managed to extract surplus value (q.v.) from labour. Weber believed that subordination was necessary for productive efficiency in any type of industrial economy and was not confined to capitalism. For Marx, the exploitative quality of the social relations of production in capitalist economies meant that capitalism was based on coercion and a perpetual antagonism between the interests of capital and labour.

In the 1950s and 1960s, sociological interest centred on industrialism, which included both capitalist and non-capitalist economies. The Marxist revival of the 1970s led to a new concern with the distinctive features of contemporary capitalism, notably in the analysis of the labour process (q.v.) and social relations of production (q.v.) in capitalist economies, and the analysis of modes of production (q.v.).

Capitalism can also be regarded as an ideology which contains doctrines of social justice and individual rights. This ideology suggests that existing inequalities of income and wealth represent the socially just returns for the different contributions that people make to economic activity. It also contains the idea that certain freedoms and rights are necessary for the continued well-being of capitalist society, notably that individuals must be protected from the arbitrary power of the state while the state protects their economic interests by safeguarding property rights and guaranteeing the enforcement of commercial contracts. Political democracy provides safeguards against arbitrary state power and, historically, capitalism has been associated with democratic political forms. See: *Capital Fractions*; *Capital Functions*; *Convergence Thesis*; *Democracy*; *Dual Economy*; *Dual Labour Markets*; *Individualism*; *Industrial Society*; *Labour Process Approach*;

Management; *Managerial Revolution*; *Marx*; *Marxist Sociology*; *Post-Industrial Society*; *Property*; *Relative Autonomy*; *State*; *Weber*.

Bibl. Shonfield (1965); Mandel (1975); Cutler *et al.* (1977); Scott (1979)

Career. Careers may be viewed as the sequences of jobs performed by individuals in the course of their working lives. Careers may be structured into ordered sequences that relate to each other or unstructured; if structured, job sequences are frequently arranged as a hierarchy of increasing income and prestige.

The concept of career is most often applied in the study of occupations. Manual workers, particularly if unskilled, typically have unstructured careers marked by job movement of an apparently haphazard nature, though older workers have greater job stability. Skilled workers exhibit more structured patterns. In both cases, peak earnings are usually reached by the early thirties and thereafter often decline, and careers provide little advancement through an income/social prestige hierarchy. There has been a tendency among large firms over the past thirty years, notably in the United States and Japan, to develop seniority-based promotion ladders leading to jobs of greater skill or responsibility and higher pay, though these rarely lead into higher-level occupations such as management. Non-manual employees, especially men, are more likely to have structured careers. Occupationally based careers are found among professionals and semi-professionals, where individuals may shift between employers but their career progression is stable and predictable. Professions are to a large extent self-regulating and their associations protect as far as possible the earnings, status and careers of members. Organizationally based careers provide managers with structured career routes within the enterprise. Non-manual employees above the level of routine white-collar work typically enjoy rising wages throughout most of their working lives and upwards intragenerational social mobility.

H. S. Becker (1963) claimed that the concept was valuable 'in developing sequential models of various kinds of deviant behavior'. For example, he studied the stages by which a person becomes a regular marijuana user. These stages in the career included learning the technique, perceiving the effects and learning to enjoy the sensations. E. Goffman (1961b) used the notion of 'moral career' to describe the experience of mental patients in asylums. He suggested that a moral career had an objective dimension (the official institutional processing of the patient) and a subjective dimension (the personal experience of the patient). The concept is extensively used in symbolic interactionism (q.v.). See: *Deviant Behaviour*; *Dual Labour Markets*; *Middle Class*; *Profession*; *Social Mobility*; *Stratification*.

Bibl. Hall, R. (1969)

Cargo Cult. See: *Millenarianism.*

Case Study. The detailed examination of a single example of a class of phenomena, a case study cannot provide reliable information about the broader class. But it is often useful in the preliminary stages of an investigation since it provides hypotheses which may be tested systematically with a larger number of cases.

Case studies are frequently used in sociological research, sometimes as the preliminary to more extensive investigation but often as the primary research method. In the latter case, shortage of resources or difficulties in gaining access to research subjects are often reasons for this choice. Many case-study investigations in fact use more than a single case, in order to get some idea of the range of variability in the population under consideration. Cases are then selected to represent what, on the basis of theory or prior knowledge, are thought to be contrasting examples. Sociologists who use techniques of qualitative research such as ethnography (q.v.) or participant observation (q.v.), which are time-consuming and cannot easily be delegated to research assistants, almost invariably choose the case-study method. Case studies may provide data of a richness and detail that are difficult to obtain from broader surveys, but at the cost of a lack of generalizability.

Cash Nexus. This term was used by K. Marx and F. Engels in the *Communist Manifesto* of 1848 and now has a wide currency in industrial sociology. It refers to the character of employment in many modern industries, when the only tie binding employers and employees is the payment of wages for work done and when each side tries to maximize its own interests regardless of the interests of the other. The cash nexus depersonalizes employment relations by turning them into simple economic transactions subject to market forces. Some modern firms however try to create loyalty among their employees by creating ties of a non-economic nature. See: *Alienation*; *Dual Labour Markets*; *Human Relations*.

Caste. A caste system is a form of social stratification in which castes are hierarchically organized and separated from each other by rules of ritual purity. The lowest strata of the caste system are referred to as 'untouchables', because they are excluded from the performance of rituals which confer religious purity.

In this hierarchical system, each caste is ritually purer than the one below it. The caste system is an illustration of social closure (q.v.) in which access to wealth and prestige is closed to social groups whch are excluded from the performance of purifying rituals. This ritual segregation is further reinforced by rules of endogamy (q.v.). In M. Weber's study of India (1958a), caste represented an important illustration of social ranking by prestige and formed part of a wider interest in pariah groups. If castes are maintained by social closure, they originated in either the segregation of ethnic groups or in occupational specialization; in both cases, caste regulated access to the market and to social prestige in a competitive struggle between social groups.

There is considerable debate as to whether the caste system is specific to Hindu culture, or whether its principal features are more widely found in other societies where hierarchically organized, endogamous strata are present. In the first position, caste cannot be defined independently of 'caste system', which is specific to classical Hindu society. In the second argument, the term caste is extended to embrace the stratification of ethnic groups, for example in the southern states of the USA.

While the Hindu caste system is organized in terms of four major castes (Brahmin, Kshatriya, Vaisya and Sudra), there is much diversity at the local, village level, where the major castes are further divided into smaller groupings of subcastes which are called *jati*. In principle, one is born into a caste and social mobility between castes is impossible. In practice, however, it is possible for a subcaste as a whole to bring about an improvement in its standing within the hierarchy of prestige. Those special groups which can successfully acquire or imitate the ritual practices of privileged castes can experience upward mobility by a process known as 'sanskritization'.

The caste system is of interest because (1) it represents an alternative to class as a principle of social stratification, and (2) it has been regarded as a barrier to economic, specifically capitalist, development, in that caste inhibits labour mobility. Against this latter view, it has to be noted that caste does not inevitably or invariably prohibit people of different castes working together. As Weber noted, caste regulations typically end at the workplace. Given this latter possibility and the fact of mobility, the degree to which caste stands in the way of industrialization and mobility of labour is much disputed in the social sciences. See: *Ethnic Group*; *Social Closure*; *Stratification*.

Bibl. Cox, O. C. (1959); Dumont (1970)

Causal Explanation. This is a form of explanation in which one state of affairs is said to bring about another. For example, the shift to an industrial society is said to have caused the replacement of the extended by the nuclear family. Some writers argue that causal explanations in sociology are problematic for two reasons: (1) one cannot generally set up an experimental procedure with proper control groups (q.v.); (2) causal explanations cannot succeed because they assume that human beings are like natural objects when they are not, since their actions are partly determined by the meanings that they give to the world. See: *Causal Modelling*; *Correlation*; *Geisteswissenschaften*; *Hermeneutics*; *Positivism*; *Realism*; *Verstehen*.

Causal Modelling. Sociologists often wish to understand the causal connections among a number of different variables acting simultaneously, yet it is usually impossible to collect sociological data by means of the experimental method (q.v.), which would permit a precise specification of the effects of variables on each other and their interactions. Sociological data tend to provide relationships of correlation (q.v.) and not causation. Causal modelling is the generic title for a group of statistical techniques that facilitate the specification of causal linkages among correlations. These include multiple regression (q.v.), path analysis (q.v.) and log linear analysis (q.v.). The starting point is to construct a model of the assumed causal process. The model is theoretically derived by the investigator. The statistical techniques manipulate the data to see whether they fit the model. Causal models do not prove causal connections, however. Various assumptions are made when building models and these may be invalid in any particular case. One benefit of causal modelling is that, in representing causal mechanisms formally, investigators have to make their assumptions explicit. Such modelling has been used mainly on large-scale survey data, particularly in the USA, though increasingly it is applied to other data sets including historical statistical series. See: *Measurement Levels*; *Model*; *Multivariate Analysis*.

Bibl. Blalock and Blalock (1968)

Census. A census of population is the collection of demographic, economic and social data about all the people within the boundaries of a country or any other geographical unit. Censuses may be designed to provide information about topics other than population, for example, industrial production, housing and agriculture, but sociologists normally have population censuses in mind when they use the term census. National governments regularly count their people and the two oldest, continu-ous, periodic censuses are those of the United States (every ten years since 1790) and Great Britain (every ten years since 1801, except in 1941). Some commentators believe that the development of the census in the nineteenth century provided information necessary for political control of the population. See: *Socio-Economic Groups*.

Centre/Periphery. Spatial metaphors and imagery are common conceptual devices in sociological theory. There are two important uses of the centre/periphery dichotomy in sociology.

(1) E. Shils (1975) argues that the core of society is the central value system which has a sacred character and is the ultimate source of authority, legitimating the distribution of wealth, rewards and roles in the social system. While the various social elites are fundamentally involved in the centre, other social groups are located at the periphery. As the means of communication are improved with industrialization, the centre becomes more extensive within society and previously peripheral groups become increasingly involved in the central value system and subject to its authority. The emergence of the modern state was thus a condition for the extension of the centre, the creation of national identity and citizenship (q.v.) rights. However, the increasing complexity of modern society and the differentiation of roles means that consensus over central values is always partial and problematic. While Shils' theory is developed within functionalist sociology, his notion of centre/periphery has similarities with the Marxist concept of ideology.

(2) In the development theory of Marxist sociologists like A. G. Frank (1969), the centre refers, not to a core of values, but to the loci of economic power in the global organization of production

and distribution. In this perspective, the global economy is conceived in terms of a hierarchy of economic centres which, through military, political and trade arrangements, extract an economic surplus from subordinate peripheral economies and regions. The distinction between the industrialized core and the underdeveloped periphery is thus part of a more general theory of imperialism. The backwardness of peripheral economies is held to be a consequence of their dependence on various core economies and not the effect of their poor resources, illiteracy, traditionalism or political instability. The industrial development of the centre is at the cost of the underdevelopment of the periphery. The centre/periphery scheme is also used to describe regional differences within one country. The economic power of the centre, e.g. the south-east of the UK, controls peripheral regions. See: *Dependency*; *Dual Economy*; *Internal Colonialism*; *Sociology of Development*; *Underdevelopment*.

Charisma. A theological term ('gift of grace'), charismatic authority first came to prominence in M. Weber's analysis of domination. Contrasted with legal-rational authority (q.v.), charisma means the authority vested in a leader by disciples and followers in the belief that the leader's claim to power flows from extraordinary personal gifts. With the death of the leader, the disciples either disband or convert charismatic beliefs and practices into traditional ('charisma of office') or legal arrangements. Charismatic authority is, therefore, unstable and temporary. See: *Authority*; *Rationalization*.

Bibl. Weber (1946); Bendix (1960)

Chicago School. Between the two world wars, American sociology was dominated by the University of Chicago which produced an immense amount of sociological work and trained many students who subsequently became teachers in other American universities. Although covering a wide range of topics, both in theory and in empirical research, the Chicago School is best known for its urban sociology and, secondarily, for the development of the symbolic interactionist approach. Impressed by the rapid expansion of Chicago, by the intake of migrants of all nationalities, races and religions, and often influenced by humanitarian considerations, a number of sociologists, notably E. Burgess, R. Mackenzie, R. Park and L. Wirth, developed a distinctive urban theory and their students carried out detailed studies of various areas of the city. The theory was dominated by the assumption that cities manifested a particular way of life radically different from that found in the countryside. Explanation of this urban way of life was founded on the principles of urban ecology (q.v.), chiefly that the forces of competition in a bounded environment produced a set of natural areas (q.v.), each inhabited by different social groupings. These areas and groupings became the subject of detailed investigation which produced studies of the hobo, skid row, the Negro family, and the Jewish ghetto, amongst others. These studies were mostly ethnographies (q.v.), a method also used in studies of various occupations in the city: musicians, doctors and waitresses, for instance. The ethnographic tradition in Chicago became closely associated with symbolic interactionism (q.v.), in that studies of urban areas, social groups and occupations were concerned with the construction of identities by the interaction of individuals' perceptions of themselves and of others' views of them. This concern was supported by the more theoretical work, firstly by W. Thomas, and, more importantly, by G. H. Mead (q.v.). At the same time, there was an emphasis, notably in the work of W. F. Ogburn, on the collection of detailed statistical information on local communities. See: *Concentric Zone Theory*; *Rural-Urban Continuum*.

Bibl. Faris (1970); Downes and Rock (1982)

Childhood. Following the historical research of P. Aries (1960), sociologists argue that the child as a social role (q.v.) and childhood as a social category separate from adults began to develop in the eighteenth century among the nobility. The differentiation and specialization of age groups was associated with the emergence of the school as a place of moral training separate from the home. In England, this cultural development was closely connected with the emergence of the public school as a special institution for the cultivation of an elite. Before this period, children were more thoroughly integrated into the world of adults. The growth of childhood as a distinctive category was also connected with new educational theories which argued that children were innocent and required protection from adult society in order to be prepared for maturity at a later stage. By the end of the nineteenth century, this emphasis on the moral development of children required a new set of attitudes towards parental responsibilities and the importance of privacy and domesticity for the nurturing of the child. In the twentieth century, these concerns for an appropriate moral environment for children from birth were expressed by J. Bowlby (1953) in the theory of maternal deprivation (q.v.).

The growing importance of social rights for children can be seen as an extension of citizenship (q.v.), starting with the Factory Acts of the 1840s which protected children from unrestricted exploitation at work. In the twentieth century, these rights have been expanded to include rights to education and welfare. The implication of these rights for children is that the state can interfere in the household to protect the child from parental abuse. In the last decade there has, for example, been growing concern over reports of extensive sexual abuse of children in the home (primarily by fathers of their daughters). Some authors, for example J. Donzelot (1977), have suggested that developments in medicine, psychiatry and law have brought about a government of society through the family, in which the state rather than the father functions as the basis of patriarchy (q.v.).

Children have become increasingly important in social policy issues, because their position in society has become precarious as a consequence of high divorce rates, the more widespread domestic violence and sexual abuse of children, the prevalence of single-parent households, and the failure of divorced men to provide adequate financial support for children of previous marriages. Some conservative critics of society argue that this set of circumstances is a recipe for social crisis (such as mounting rates of juvenile delinquency). See: *Adolescence*; *Delinquency*; *Divorce*; *Generation*; *Marriage*.

Chi-squared Test. The test (χ^2) is a statistical technique that sociologists commonly use in the interpretation of data measured at the nominal level (data that are discontinuous and consist of mutually exclusive categories). The test allows one to assess the probability that a particular distribution might simply be the product of chance. It is also used as a simple measure of association when one variable is cross tabulated against another. See: *Cross Tabulation*; *Measurement Levels*.

Church. E. Troeltsch (1912) identified a central paradox: Christianity could either attempt to influence the whole society as a universal religion open to all people, that is as a church, or it could aim to influence society as an elite of devout followers, that is as a sect. The cost of being a church was some degree of accommodation to secular institutions, especially the state. The cost of being a sect was isolation, withdrawal and loss of general influence. Troeltsch argued that growing secularization (q.v.) spelt the end of the universal church. Contemporary sociologists, however, continue to use the term to describe large religious organizations which accept the importance of the state and other secular institutions in maintaining the social order, which have a hierarchical organization based on a priesthood and which recruit their membership through birth rather than conversion. See: *Religion*; *Sect*.

Bibl. Hill, M. (1973)

Citizenship. The concept of citizenship as a status which provides access to rights and powers is associated with T. H. Marshall (1963). Civic rights comprise freedom of speech and equality before the law. Political rights include the right to vote and to organize politically. Socio-economic rights include economic welfare and social security. In pre-industrial society these rights were confined to a narrow elite. As long as the mass was denied full civic and political rights, then revolutionary class ideologies flourished. The extension of civic and political citizenship to the bourgeoisie and working class integrated these classes into society and polity, thus leading to a decline in revolutionary class consciousness. The extension of socio-economic rights, including trade unionism, collective bargaining in the economic sphere and the growth of the welfare state, may also be viewed as significant for the integration of the modern working class. See: *Capitalism*; *Class Consciousness*; *Collective Bargaining*; *Corporatism*; *Democracy*; *Incorporation*; *Institutionalization of Conflict*; *Leninism*; *Marshall*; *Trade Unions*; *Welfare State*.

Bibl. Bendix (1964)

Civic Culture. See: *Political Culture*.

Civil Religion. A term first employed by J.-J. Rousseau in *The Social Contract* (1762) and developed by E. Durkheim in *The Elementary Forms of the Religious Life* (1912), it refers to the beliefs, symbols, rituals and institutions which legitimate the social system, create social solidarity and mobilize a community to achieve common political objectives. For example, it has been argued that, in industrial societies where there has been some secularization (q.v.) of traditional religions, national symbols and rituals serve the same function as religion in generating social solidarity.

In contemporary sociology, the term is closely associated with the analysis of American society by R. N. Bellah (1967; 1970; 1974; 1975). The American civil religion is composed of: (1) elements of the Judaeo-Christian tradition which emphasize achievement motivation (q.v.) and individualism (q.v.); (2) events from the national drama (the death of Lincoln and the Civil War); (3) secular values from the Constitution; (4) secular rituals and symbols (the flag, Memorial-Day rites and the Fourth of July). In contemporary America, where ethnic diversity and cultural pluralism create problems of social integration, Bellah argues that the civil religion generates powerful sentiments of national solidarity and purpose.

This theory of religion in American national life develops perspectives from A. de Tocqueville (q.v.) (1835),

W. Herberg (1955), and T. Parsons' (1951; 1967) analysis of religion and social integration. Bellah's version of the concept of civil religion can be criticized on a number of grounds: (1) it is highly specific to contemporary American society; (2) many societies which are ethnically and culturally diverse do not develop a civil religion; (3) it suffers from the analytical problems associated with functionalism (q.v.); (4) it represents a version of the dominant ideology thesis (q.v.). See: *Invisible Religion*; *Nationalism*; *Sacred*.

Bibl. Bellah and Hammond (1980)

Civil Society. In the social sciences, there is no consensus as to the theoretical and empirical separation of political, economic and social relations. The shifting meaning of the concept of 'civil society' indicates changing theoretical attitudes towards the relationship between economy, society and state. As sociology emerged out of political economy (q.v.), social philosophy and 'moral statistics', its province became the phenomena of social, symbolic and normative interactions which constitute 'society', while political relations (state, power, government, political parties, etc.) were left to political science, and economics became the science of the production and distribution of economic resources. Against this trend of intellectual differentiation, sociology can also be treated as, following A. Comte (q.v.), a synthetic science which attempts to integrate political, economic and social phenomena. In Marxism, also, there is a similar theoretical ambivalence. In the base and superstructure (q.v.) metaphor, the economic base is contrasted with the superstructure of law, politics and social relations. Alternatively, it is argued that, for example, the relations of production are simultaneously social, economic and legal.

In the eighteenth century, A. Ferguson (1767) treated 'civil society' as a state of civility and as the consequence of civilization. He also, however, treated 'civil society' as a political term, contrasting Western governments with Oriental despotism (q.v.). The term also had an economic connotation in that civilization was contrasted with societies (the barbaric state) in which private property did not exist. The term 'civil society' eventually came into sociology via the analyses of G. Hegel and K. Marx. In Hegel (1837), 'civil society' became an intermediate institution between the family and the political relations of the state. In K. Marx and F. Engels, we rarely, if ever, encounter the term 'society' in isolation. Rather there is a more basic dichotomy between 'civil society' (the ensemble of socio-economic relations and forces of production), and the state (the superstructural manifestation of class relations inside civil society). In *The German Ideology* (1845b), they argued that 'civil society is the true source and theatre of all history', that is, the explanation of political events, legal changes and cultural development is to be sought in the development of the structure of civil society. This Marxist conception was adapted by A. Gramsci (1971) who argued that between the coercive relations of the state and the economic sphere of production lies civil society, namely that area of social life which *appears* as the realm of the private citizen and individual consent. Gramsci's formulation of the relationship between economy, society and state in terms of two contrasts between private and public life, consent and coercion has played a fundamental role in the contemporary Marxist analysis of ideology and power. This influence is especially marked in the contrast between 'ideological state apparatus' (q.v.) and 'repressive state apparatus' in the work of L. Althusser. This modern employment of the term 'civil society' does not, however, entirely resolve the traditional problem of the relationship between base and super-structure. See: *Gramsci*; *Scottish Enlightenment*; *Society*.

Bibl. Mouffe (ed.) (1979)

Civilization. For Enlightenment thinkers, the notion of civilization was inextricably connected with the idea of social progress, namely the triumph of rationality over religion, the decline of local, particular customs and the rise of natural science. It was associated with the growth of the absolutist state and therefore with the reduction of local systems of taxation, local political autonomy and with greater cultural uniformity within states. In the nineteenth century there was growing disillusionment with progress as urban, industrial, capitalist society was seen as producing alienation (q.v.) and anomie (q.v.). See: *Progress*; *Rationalization*; *Scottish Enlightenment*; *Secularization*.

Bibl. Elias (1939a, 1939b)

Class. Sociologists identify class as one of the fundamental types of social stratification (q.v.), along with caste (q.v.) and estates (q.v.). The major theoretical tradition within class analysis derives from the work of K. Marx and M. Weber on the newly emerging class structure of industrial capitalism in the nineteenth century. In this, classes are defined in economic terms, though views differ as to what are the crucial economic determinants. An alternative tradition found in some American accounts of social stratification is that class is *not* mainly economic.

Marx analysed class in relation to the ownership of capital and the means of production. He divided the population into those who owned property and those who were propertyless, the capitalist class and the proletariat. He recognized the existence of groups which did not fit this framework such as peasants and small proprietors, but suggested that these were hangovers of the pre-capitalist economy which would vanish with the maturation of the capitalist system. Class was more than just a way of describing the economic position of different groups, because Marx saw classes as tangible collectivities and as real social forces with the capacity to change society. The incessant drive of capitalists to create profit led to the exploitation of the proletariat in work and, so Marx believed, to its increasing pauperization. In these circumstances workers would develop class consciousness and the proletariat would grow from being a class 'in itself', that is an economically defined category with no self-awareness, to become a class 'for itself' made up of workers with a class-conscious view of the world and ready to pursue class conflict against the capitalists.

Weber divided the population into classes according to economic differences of market capacity that gave rise to different life-chances (q.v.). Capital was one source of market capacity, but skill and education formed another. While property-owners were a class, as Marx had emphasized, those whose skills were scarce on the market and commanded high salaries also constituted a separate class. Thus Weber distinguished four classes: the propertied class, the intellectual, the administrative and managerial class, the traditional petty bourgeois class of small businessmen and shopkeepers, and the working class. Class conflict was common and was most likely to occur between groups with immediately opposed interests, for example between workers and managers rather than workers and capitalists. Weber also noted the significance of another principle of stratification that differed from class, namely social honour or status (q.v.).

Modern accounts of class have often rejected the Marxist definition. The separation of capital ownership from the management and control of industry makes propertylessness such a broad category that it fails to distinguish between groups with different economic positions, for example managers and shopfloor workers. Nor has the pauperization prediction been realized. British and American class theories have developed in different directions. Post-war American sociologists saw their society as classless. This was partly because they thought there were no sharp breaks in the distribution of material rewards, which they saw as being ranked simply along an unbroken continuum, and partly because they believed that individuals in modern society might just as plausibly be ranked on a whole variety of factors unrelated to economically defined class, such as occupation, religion, education, ethnicity. They took up Weber's notion of status (q.v.) and developed a multi-dimensional approach which treated social status and prestige (q.v.) as an independent factor which diluted or even replaced economically determined class. Most occupational ranking schemes used in the study of inequality assumed simply that occupations could be ranked as 'better' or 'worse' than others according to the income and prestige their incumbents received.

British sociologists in this period initially took the division of labour as the crucial determinant of class, and identified the major class divide as that running between manual and non-manual occupations. This appeared to correspond to major differences in economic and social conditions. The division formed the basis of the Registrar General's classification of socio-economic groups (q.v.) and classes. It was largely an *ad hoc* distinction but ultimately seems to have derived from the Weberian notion of life-chances. The division is no longer useful, however, because the economic and social conditions of many low-level, non-manual employees have become more like those of manual workers, and there are now significant differences between those at the bottom and top of the non-manual ladder. Class is now defined by the criteria of market and work situations. The market situation refers to material rewards and life-chances such as pay, security and opportunity for promotion. The work situation refers to work tasks and production technology, and the structure of social relations and control systems in firms. There is assumed to be a congruence between the factors, that market rewards and working conditions become progressively better as one ascends the class hierarchy. The process by which classes may be transformed from economic categories into socially meaningful groups, commonly referred to as *structuration*, has received considerable attention. Factors determining structuration include residence in single-class communities, low rates of social mobility which keep people in one class over time, and common life-styles, all of which tend to turn classes into identifiable social groups. Class variations in social values and political identification may add to the distinctiveness of classes.

The application of this conventional definition, which is now explicitly based on the Weberian approach to class, is not always easy in practice. The criteria in principle allow for a multiplicity of classes based on different levels of market rewards, different types of work situation, and different combinations of the two. This means that identifying just a few major classes is a matter of interpretation rather than being self-evident and objectively determined. The division of the population into three classes – working, intermediate and upper – is now a conventional sociological model of the British class structure. Manual workers are placed in the working class; low-level, non-manual workers, such as clerks and lower technicians, in the intermediate class; and managers, administrators and professionals in the upper. A few sociologists place clerical workers in the working class, though this is not the orthodox view.

A criticism of the conventional approach is that it concentrates on men and ignores women. Women constituted about 43 per cent of the British labour force in the early 1980s. Working women are heavily concentrated in a handful of occupations, mainly in certain professions and in clerical and sales work among the non-manual occupations, and in unskilled factory work and services (for example, cleaning) among the manual. Their jobs tend to be segregated from men's – certain jobs are largely reserved for women. They also have lower market rewards than men. If women were evenly distributed across the range of occupations, ignoring them would not affect the way class structure is conceived. But as it is, sociologists who consider only employed men may create distorted images of the shape of the class structure, because when they ignore women they also fail properly to consider whole areas of the occupational structure.

The theoretical and practical effects of treating men as central to class analysis are increasingly debated. One major problem area is the convention of making the family the unit of analysis in empirical studies of class that deal with the transmission of material and cultural inequalities through generations, for example, research into social mobility

(q.v.). In order to assign a class position to families, the class position of *all* family members has conventionally been determined on the basis of the occupation of one member, the husband/father who is regarded as the head of household and main breadwinner. With most women working, this convention becomes problematic. For example, if husband and wife can be assigned different class positions on the basis of their individual occupations, the class position of the family unit is not clear-cut. Similarly, the life-style of families with two wage-earners may differ significantly from others in the same class where there is only one wage. Moreover, some feminists suggest that women who work unpaid in the home are unjustly ignored in class theory, because their work at home supports the labour power of family members in paid employment, while they also reproduce the next generation of employees.

There has been a revival of Marxist class theory in America and Britain since the 1970s. Modern Marxists tackle the problem of where to place those occupations, such as management and the professions, which do not belong in the capitalist class or the proletariat as traditionally conceived. A distinction is made between those who perform capital functions (q.v.) and exercise the powers of ownership, in this way defining the capitalist class regardless of whether they actually own capital or not, and those who perform only the function of labour and are thus in the working class.

E. O. Wright (1976), for example, divides ownership power into three aspects: control over resource allocation and investment; control over the physical apparatus of production; and control over labour power. The capitalist class controls the overall investment process, the physical apparatus of production and labour power. The proletariat is excluded from all three aspects. The two classes stand in an antagonistic relationship. The capitalist class includes the top corporate executive – mainly the board of directors. The proletariat includes all low-level employees, both manual and non-manual. In between there are *contradictory* class locations which reflect differing strengths of control over each of the three ownership functions. Senior managers below board level have control of the physical apparatus of production and the labour power of others, but only limited influence over resource allocation and investment. Middle managers have no influence over resource allocation and only limited control of the physical apparatus and labour. Foremen have some control of labour but nothing else. Thus there are different forms of contradiction: some groups are near the boundary of the working class and others are near the capitalist class. Marxist class analysis pays more attention to the place of women in the class structure than does the orthodox Weberian one. See: *Affluent Worker*; *Class Consciousness*; *Class Imagery*; *Deferential Worker*; *Division of Labour*; *Labour Aristocracy*; *Life-Style*; *Marx*; *Marxist Sociology*; *Middle Class*; *New Working Class*; *Profession*; *Proletarianization*; *Relations of Production*; *Service Class*; *Social Closure*; *Social Mobility*; *Status Inconsistency*; *Underclass*; *Upper Class*; *Veblen*; *Voting*; *Weber*; *Working Class*.

Bibl. Parkin (1978); Heath (1981); Crompton and Mann (eds.) (1986)

Class Consciousness. Used originally by Marxists to describe a situation when the proletariat (q.v.) becomes aware of its objective class position *vis à vis* the bourgeoisie (q.v.) and its historic role in the transformation of capitalism into socialism, this term refers to the 'subjective' dimension of class. The proletariat would develop from a class 'in

itself', simply a collection of workers sharing a common class position but with no collective awareness, to become a class 'for itself'. K. Marx believed that consciousness would develop out of the working class's concrete experience of the contradiction between capitalist relations of production based on individual private property and the emerging collective forces of production which created a proletariat whose power was collectively based and experienced. *False consciousness* is a term Marxists use to describe the situation where the proletariat fails to perceive what they believe to be the 'true' nature of its interests and does not develop a revolutionary class consciousness. V. I. Lenin (1902) suggested that workers left to themselves would create only a trade-union consciousness which sought limited social and economic reforms, and that a true revolutionary awareness could only be developed by a communist party with a socialist ideology. Marxist accounts of false class consciousness raise the problem of how one is to judge class interest (q.v.).

The term has been used loosely by sociologists outside the Marxist tradition to include any feelings of self-awareness or common identity among members of a social class. M. Mann (1973) has given class consciousness greater precision and captured some of the original spirit of the Marxist usage. He identifies four elements: (1) class *identity* – the definition of oneself as working class; (2) class *opposition* – the perception that capitalists and their managers constitute an enduring opponent; (3) class *totality* – the realization that the two previous elements define one's own social situation and the whole of the society in which one lives; (4) an *alternative* society – a conception of the desired alternative which will be realized when class conflict is successfully resolved.

These elements, in practice, represent

the stages through which a developing class consciousness moves. See: *Class*; *Class Imagery*; *Commonsense Knowledge*; *Dual Consciousness*; *Gramsci*; *Hegemony*; *Leninism*; *New Working Class*; *Pragmatic Acceptance*; *Stratification*; *Working Class*.

Bibl. Ossowski (1963)

Class Dealignment. See: *Voting*.

Class Imagery. Different people perceive class structure in different ways and, whatever the objective reality of class inequality, people may have different images or models of this reality. These images, as well as the actual structure of class inequality, are often assumed to determine people's political and social attitudes and behaviour.

E. Bott (1957) has distinguished between power and prestige images. The power image divides society into the working and upper classes whose interests conflict, the upper having the power to coerce the other. These classes are seen as opposed in industry, society and politics, with little mobility between them. The prestige image portrays class structure as a finely graded ladder of positions that differ in terms of their social status, people moving up or down according to their ability. Bott suggests that one major influence on class imagery is the way people internalize the norms of their primary groups. Power models are associated with closed working-class communities where there is little geographical or social mobility and where community and work relations are superimposed. Prestige images are associated with the more open networks of social relationships typical of the middle class.

J. H. Goldthorpe *et al.* (1969) identified a third image among the manual working class, the money model. This perceives society as divided according to

differences in income and spending. Such differences create a multiplicity of different levels, with most people somewhere in the middle. This image does not emphasize social or industrial conflict and indicates low class consciousness. It is thought to be associated with manual workers who no longer live in closed working-class communities but are not part of middle-class networks.

K. Roberts *et al.* (1977) claim that there is little working-class variability, as most manual workers hold a proletarian image similar to the power model, while some have a bourgeois image that differs from the prestige and money models. Among non-manual workers there is a wider range of images than previously identified.

The analysis of imagery may be criticized in various ways. (1) It assumes that people have fairly clearly articulated and internally consistent images, when these may in fact be incoherent. (2) The classification of respondents' views depends heavily on the interpretation of the researcher, and it is possible that variations may reflect differences between researchers as well as real differences in the population. (3) The significance of class imagery has not been demonstrated – even if images are coherent, consistent and unambiguously identifiable, it remains unclear what effect, if any, they have on political or social behaviour. See: *Affluent Worker*; *Class Consciousness*; *Dual Consciousness*; *Prestige*.

Class Interest. In the debate between Marxist and non-Marxist sociologies, the notion of class interest, as the aims and aspirations of a class, is of some importance. It may be argued, for example, that the capitalist class adopts a particular ideology (q.v.) because of its class interest. Difficulties with the notion arise when the sociologist wants to ascribe an objective interest to a class when members of that class appear to be unaware of this or even to deny it. It is then not clear what evidence would confirm or deny the ascription. See: *Class Consciousness*.

Class Struggle. A diversely used term, class struggle is always assumed to belong to the Marxist canon. For K. Marx himself, the class struggle was the motive force of history. For example, the transition from feudalism to capitalism was produced by a struggle between a landed aristocracy and a rising capitalist bourgeoisie. In contemporary societies, class struggle is used to refer to conflict between social classes which occurs primarily at the economic level, manifest, for example, in wage bargaining, strikes or absenteeism and, secondarily, at the political level, manifest in such issues as the reform of trade union law, the maintenance of the welfare state and economic policy. The most important struggles in capitalist societies are those between capitalists and workers, although other classes, for example the peasantry or the middle classes, may also be involved in alliances with one or other party.

There are difficulties in deciding what is to count as evidence of class struggle, for there is a tendency for all industrial or political conflict to be interpreted as instances of struggles between classes. Within Marxism, these struggles are always seen as manifestations of, and explained by, a deeper contradiction (q.v.) between capital and labour.

In recent debates a number of Marxists, in emphasizing the manner in which structures of social relations (the economy, for instance) determine social practices, have seemed to deny class struggle any independent causal role: class struggle is not the motor of history but merely the reflection of underlying forces. The unresolved theoretical problem has been how to reconcile the notion of determining structures with the activities of people seeking to change their circumstances through struggle. See: *Agency and Structure*; *Althusser*; *Class Consciousness*; *Marxist Sociology*; *Mode of Production*.

Bibl. Friedman (1977); Hindess (1977)

Class Theoretical. Explanations which explain social phenomena by reference to the actions or existence of social classes are called class theoretical. They can be contrasted with mode-theoretical explanations which attribute causal agency to the mode of production (q.v.).

Classroom Interaction. The traditional concern of educational sociologists with pupil attainment, in which the pupil's social background or individual psychology were the main explanatory variables, gave way in the 1970s to the investigation of educational institutions themselves and the way they shape educational outcomes. Using the techniques of ethnography (q.v.) and often working within the perspective of symbolic interactionism (q.v.), investigators analysed the social interactions and values (often implicit rather than formally acknowledged) that made up the social system of the classroom or school. Since these case-study investigations are limited (often to single schools) and mainly descriptive, the generalizations that can be made about their findings are limited: (1) the hidden curriculum (q.v.), with its latent function (q.v.) of controlling pupils, is an integral part of the social system of the school; (2) there are distinct pupil subcultures of commitment to and dissent from school values; (3) these divisions within the body of pupils are influenced by the social organization of the school – for example, segregation into 'able' and 'less able' streams – and by the stereotyping and labelling of individuals by teachers and pupils alike; (4) the social interaction between teachers and pupils is highly complex, based on an asymmetrical distribution of power that sometimes promotes pupil resistance, and influenced by the way pupils accept school values, especially those of the hidden curriculum. Pupil attainment, therefore, appears to be the product not only of the intelligence or innate ability of pupils, but also of complex social processes in the school. See: *Classroom Knowledge*; *Educational Attainment*; *Labelling Theory*; *Pedagogical Practices*; *Stereotypes*.

Bibl. Hammersley and Woods (eds.) (1976); Cosin *et al.* (eds.) (1977)

Classroom Knowledge. N. Keddie (1971) links the assessment of pupils' abilities that forms the basis of streaming in schools to the criteria that teachers use to evaluate classroom knowledge. She suggests that it is knowledge defined as appropriate by the school – knowledge that is abstract and can be presented in general forms – that is relevant; teachers see this as superior to pupils' own knowledge comprising items of concrete information derived from experience. High-ability candidates are more willing to accept what is defined as appropriate knowledge and to suspend their disbelief when this fails to match their own experience. Once streamed, the more able are allowed access to more highly evaluated knowledge than those assessed as less able. See: *Classroom Interaction*; *Cultural Capital*; *Pedagogical Practices*.

Clinical Sociology. The phrase was first used by L. Wirth (1931), who observed the employment of sociologists in clinics which included psychiatrists, psychologists and social workers. These clinics were primarily concerned with behavioural problems in children, but Wirth anticipated the growth of sociological clinics which would deal with a range of social problems. The sociologist would become part of a therapeutic team providing research, teaching and practical involvement in the problems of its clients. Wirth also argued that sociology was important in providing doctors and psychiatrists with a perspective on the social dimensions of mental and physical illness. See: *Applied Sociology*; *Sociology of Medicine*; *Social Problems*.

Cluster Analysis. A group of statistical techniques used in the analysis of multivariate data to identify internal structure. Cluster analysis may be applied, for example, to identify distinct groupings (clusters) of responses to attitude surveys, or to establish what patterns of behaviour occur in activity data. It is also used to identify groups of individuals or variables. See: *Factor Analysis*.

Bibl. Everitt (1980)

Code. See: *Restricted Code*; *Semiotics*.

Coding. This is the process of translating raw research data into a form which can be used in calculation, normally by computer, by classifying data into categories and assigning each category a numerical value.

Bibl. Moser and Kalton (1979)

Coercion. There are two main senses of coercion: active and situational. (1) The actions of subordinate individuals or social groups are determined or compelled by the use or the threat of physical force. While sociologists recognize that there is an element of coercion in all societies, it is held that the use of force by the state must be supported by some form of legitimation. People accept the exercise of coercion if they believe it is administered by appropriate office-holders. (2) People are compelled to behave in certain ways by situational circumstances, that is by the structure of society and not by individuals. In K. Marx's view, the economic organization of society is coercive in that the propertyless labourer is forced to sell his labour in order to live. See: *Authority*; *Conflict Theory*; *Consensus*; *Legitimacy*; *Power*; *Social Control*; *Social Order*.

Cognitive Dissonance. L. Festinger's theory of cognitive dissonance is that people find dissonance or lack of fit between attitudes or between attitudes and behaviour unacceptable and will try to reduce it, by modifying their cognitions or adding new ones. For example, if the members of a cult expecting the arrival of aliens by flying saucers find that the saucers do not arrive on the appointed day, the inconsistency will force them either to revise their beliefs or to reinterpret the failure of the prediction.

Bibl. Festinger (1957)

Cohesion. See: *Social Order*.

Cohort. This is a demographic term describing a group of people who share a significant experience at a certain period of time. For example, all the children born in one year form the birth cohort of that year. Cohort analysis, following the history of a cohort over time, has been used to collect data relevant to the study of fertility, health care, education and employment. It can also be a particularly good method of studying social change.

Collective Bargaining. This is a method of establishing wages, working conditions and other aspects of employment by means of negotiation between employers and the representatives of employees organized collectively. As a means of accommodating competing interests in industry, it has played an important part in the regulation and

institutionalization of conflict. As an institution which provides employees with some influence over their working lives, it has extended the rights of citizenship into the economic sphere. See: *Citizenship*; *Industrial Democracy*; *Institutionalization of Conflict*; *Labour Movement*; *Trade Unions*.

Collective Behaviour. The early theory of crowd behaviour is associated with G. Le Bon (1895) who argued that, in periods of social decline and disintegration, society is threatened by the rule of crowds. In the crowd, the individual psychology is subordinated to a 'collective mentality' which radically transforms individual behaviour. In contemporary sociology, there is less interest in crowd behaviour. By 'collective behaviour', sociologists now mean the mobilization of a mass of people to change the general structure of society. Such movements to change society as a whole include both secular movements of social protest and religious attempts to change society, for example millenarianism (q.v.). The most influential general theory of collective behaviour is that of N. Smelser (1962), which draws particular attention to the importance of 'generalized beliefs' and values in directing social movements in periods of rapid social change and political disruption. See: *Social Movements*.

Collective Conscience. See: *Conscience Collective*.

Collective Consumption. This is a term introduced into urban sociology by M. Castells (1977; 1978). He argues that labour power (q.v.) must be reproduced. That is, there must be means whereby workers are able to offer their labour for sale day after day. Food, housing and transport, for example, have to be provided, as well as an educational system which trains labour power. All these items of consumption are increasingly provided in an urban setting as the population becomes more concentrated. Furthermore, their provision is more and more a matter for the state as private capital finds it unprofitable; it is a collective provision as education, transport, housing and health become state activities and hence matters for political debate and action. However, the state is persistently unable to meet the costs of collective consumption and there is therefore a tendency towards crisis in its provision which generates urban social movements (q.v.). As an explanation of the provision of urban facilities and consequent political action, the concept has been much criticized. There is some ambiguity as to whether it is a matter of collective use or collective provision. If it is the former, it is clear that many facilities, if not all, are consumed individually. If it is the latter, many items that are required for the reproduction of labour power are not provided by the state: for example, housing. Nonetheless, the concept continues to have utility, particularly as it focuses attention on the relationship of the state and private capital in the allocation of urban resources. See: *Reproduction of Labour Power*; *State*.

Bibl. Saunders (1981)

Collective Labourer. K. Marx argued that, at a certain stage in the development of capitalism, when individual workers no longer produced an entire commodity by themselves, it would be proper to speak of the collective labourer. The term refers to the cooperation of workers in a complex labour process (q.v.) characterized by a high division of labour.

Colonialism. See: *Imperialism*; *Internal Colonialism*.

Command Economy. See: *Socialist Societies*.

Commodity Fetishism. A doctrine originally formulated by K. Marx which has recently attracted attention as a result of increased interest in theories of ideology, commodity fetishism is a process by which men conceive of their social relations as if they were natural things. The doctrine depends on the prior distinction that Marx made between producing something for one's own use and producing a commodity which is an object created solely to be exchanged (for money or another commodity). Since the producers do not come into contact with each other until they exchange their products, they have no social relationships except in the act of exchange of objects. These objects come to stand for the social relationships. People's thinking about the social relations involved in their work is then characterized by a fetishism, whereby beliefs about the physical products of labour and their exchange substitute for, and mask, the social relations themselves.

The theory of commodity fetishism has been much used, together with the associated concept of reification, as a basis for theories of ideology and law, in that many forms of thought in capitalist societies are said to be fetishistic. As a theory of ideology, however, commodity fetishism has serious limitations. (1) It is based on the assumption that exchanges are between independent producers, not workers selling their labour-power to a capitalist. (2) It does not say much about the specific content of beliefs, only that they are generally fetishistic. (3) Fetishism does not exhaust the forms that ideology takes. (4) The theory better applies to economic than aesthetic or cultural beliefs. See: *Appearance and Reality*; *Ideology*; *Marx*; *Marxist Sociology*; *Reification*.

Bibl. Geras (1971); Abercrombie (1980)

Commonsense Knowledge. (1) A term used technically within phenomenological sociology to mean that knowledge which is routinely used in the conduct of everyday life: for example, knowledge of how to post a letter. The everyday world is the fundamental reality within which most people live. Consciousness of that world is characterized by the 'natural attitude' which takes the world as natural, constant and pregiven.

(2) A. Gramsci (q.v.) was interested in the way that the concept contrasted with systematic thought. Commonsense is practical, experimental and critical, but also fragmentary and incoherent. As a result, it cannot go beyond practical activity into theoretical construction. Gramsci identified commonsense thought with the mass and theoretical thought with an elite. This relates to the development of revolutionary consciousness: either a dominant class can impose a theoretical consciousness on to the masses which, although it will be at variance with commonsense, does suppress revolutionary possibilities; or an intellectual stratum (the party) can develop commonsense categories into a theoretical revolutionary consciousness. See: *Class Consciousness*; *Dominant Ideology Thesis*; *Hegemony*; *Life-World*; *Phenomenological Sociology*; *Schutz*.

Commune. In political sociology, the commune is typically a secular institution in which members, through their collective labour and common ownership of property, live together in accordance with a common ideology such as anarchism or communism. In the sociology of religion and sociology of youth cultures, the analysis of communes in industrial societies became important with the development of the commune movement, in North America particularly, in the 1960s. The maintenance of the commune as a way of life, however, proves problematic since communes have to solve basic problems of institutionalized social life, namely power, stratification and economic subsistence. See: *Cooperative*.

Bibl. Rigby (1974)

Communism. As a doctrine rather than a practice, communism refers to societies which have no private property, social classes or division of labour (q.v.). K. Marx held that these societies would be formed gradually after the revolutionary overthrow of capitalist societies. He also noted that these three features are possessed by certain tribal societies, a condition he referred to as primitive communism.

There is considerable doubt as to whether these ideals have been realized in practice in modern societies. Most communist countries have some private property, an extensive division of labour and what amounts to a class system based on bureaucratic privilege. The actual development of communist societies has produced a debate amongst theoreticians of communism, some of whom hold that some private property and division of labour may be inevitable. See: *Socialist Societies*.

Community. The term community is one of the most elusive and vague in sociology and is by now largely without specific meaning. At the minimum it refers to a collection of people in a geographical area. Three other elements may also be present in any usage. (1) Communities may be thought of as collections of people with a particular social structure; there are, therefore, collections which are not communities. Such a notion often equates community with rural or pre-industrial society and may, in addition, treat urban or industrial society as positively destructive. (2) A sense of belonging or community spirit. (3) All the daily activities of a community, work and non-work, take place within the geographical area; it is self-contained. Different accounts of community will contain any or all of these additional elements.

Many nineteenth-century sociologists used a concept of community, explicitly or implicitly, in that they operated with dichotomies between pre-industrial and industrial, or rural and urban societies. F. Toennies, for example, in his distinction between *gemeinschaft* (q.v.) and *gesellschaft*, treats communities as particular kinds of society which are predominantly rural, united by kinship and a sense of belonging, and self-contained. It became clear that societies could not be sharply divided into rural or urban, communities or non-communities, and sociologists proposed a rural–urban continuum (q.v.) instead, along which settlements could be ranged according to various features of their social structure. Unfortunately there was little agreement about what features differentiated settlements along the continuum, beyond an insistence on the significance of kinship, friendship and self-containment. This lack of agreement has made it difficult to compare the large number of studies of individual settlements carried out particularly between 1920 and 1950. In the United States there was interest in urban locations, particularly by the Chicago School (q.v.) and W. F. Whyte (1961), but in Britain rural societies commanded more attention. All these studies were based on the assumption that the communities were largely self-contained and therefore had some community spirit, but the term community no longer referred to only one kind of social structure. This community study tradition was also

important in its development of techniques of participant observation (q.v.) but has lost favour recently, partly because communities are not so self-contained as national considerations become important and partly because urban sociologists have become interested in other problems.

While, in sociology, the term community now really refers only to a set of people in a geographical area, it continues to have some normative force. For example, the rural community ideal continues to have some grip on the English imagination and town planners often aim at creating a community spirit in their designs. See: *Neighbourhood.*

Bibl. Frankenburg (1966); Bell and Newby (1971)

Community Medicine. Since the mid 1950s, in both Britain and the United States, there has been a growing emphasis on the use of community facilities (sheltered housing, community nursing, community mental-health centres and the patient's home with appropriate professional support) for treatment, rather than the general hospital. The concept is in fact general, since it embraces the care of the sick outside such institutions as hospitals and hospices; it also includes primary medical care, family medicine and general practice. The growth of interest in community care is associated with (1) the view that hospitalization is often not the most appropriate response to the patient's needs, especially in the case of mental illness; (2) disillusionment with the effectiveness of conventional, hospital-based, scientific medicine; (3) the cost of hospital services. See: *Alternative Medicine*; *Health Care Systems.*

Comparative Method. All sociological research involves the comparison of cases or variables which are similar in some respects and dissimilar in others. The term comparative method denotes a particular interest in institutional and macro-social factors analysed comparatively across different societies, or in the distribution of other specific phenomena in different societies. A major methodological issue is whether the units of comparison (whole societies, major institutions, religions, groups, and so on) and the indicators chosen to compare differences or similarities are genuinely comparable and can legitimately be used outside their specific cultural settings. Comparative method is neither a distinct methodology nor a particular theory, but rather a perspective. See: *Understanding Alien Belief Systems.*

Bibl. Vallier (ed.) (1971)

Competition. A competitive situation is one where individuals with different and opposed interests seek to maximize their own advantages or rewards. In economic theory the competition between buyers and sellers of commodities in the market is held to reduce prices, equalize profits in different enterprises and promote efficiency of production. The beneficial effects of competition were also emphasized in some early social theories. Utilitarianism (q.v.) claimed that competition had benign social consequences because it was the most reliable mechanism for producing general wealth. Social Darwinism (q.v.) made a parallel between the struggle for survival in nature and competition between people in society: in each case, the processes of natural selection ensured the survival of the fittest and improved the quality of the species. Institutional attempts to protect the weak, the unintelligent and the socially inferior – for example, state intervention to alleviate the condition of the urban poor – were regarded as interfering with natural

selection. This particular movement in sociological theory was closely associated with H. Spencer (q.v.). Popular versions of Spencer's evolutionism overlooked his argument that cooperation was the guiding principle of complex society, while competition was a central characteristic of primitive society.

In Marxism, competitiveness is not regarded as a universal, constitutive feature of human nature, but as a specific structural aspect of capitalism. In K. Marx's theory of capitalism, three types of competition can be distinguished: (1) there is competition between capitalists to control the market; (2) there is competition between workers to secure employment; (3) there is competition between capital and labour. It was in this competitive struggle with capitalists that the working class would acquire a revolutionary class consciousness. The final outcome of competitive class struggle would be the destruction of capitalist society.

For M. Weber (1922), competition was defined as peaceful conflict, consisting of attempts to gain control over scarce resources. Regulated competition was associated with social selection (for example, the competition between academics for limited posts is regulated formally by professional standards of conduct). Unregulated or violent competition was associated with natural selection (for example, the struggle for survival between species). For Weber, competitive struggles were an inevitable feature of all social relationships and not specific to capitalism.

For T. Parsons (1951; 1954), competition in capitalism is restrained by a variety of conditions: common values, codes of conduct in professional associations, reciprocity between roles and legal regulations.

Debates in sociology as to the nature of competition have thus concentrated on: (1) its extent and permanence; (2) whether it is a defining characteristic of capitalism; (3) the presence of regulation which controls competition between individuals. See: *Capitalism*; *Class Struggle*; *Conflict Theory*; *Industrial Conflict*; *Market*; *Urban Ecology*.

Bibl. Parsons (1937)

Complex Society. This is a society which has undergone structural differentiation (q.v.). The term was once popular but is now little used. See: *Comte*; *Division of Labour*; *Durkheim*; *Evolutionary Theory*; *Functionalism*; *Gemeinschaft*; *Industrialization*; *Industrial Society*; *Social Change*.

Comte, Auguste (1798–1857). Inventor of the term 'sociology', first publicly used in the fourth volume of *Cours de philosophie positive* (1838), Comte was secretary to G. Saint-Simon, and there has long been a debate over the relative importance of these two writers for socialism and sociology.

Comte thought that sociology was a science employing observation, experimentation and comparison, which was specifically relevant to the new social order of industrial Europe. Comte's scientific positivism (q.v.) was conjoined with an evolutionary view of society and thought which he saw progressing through three stages: theological, metaphysical and positive. Human societies evolve through three major stages of development (primitive, intermediary and scientific). Human thought progressed by a process of decreasing generality and increasing complexity. Employing an organic analogy (q.v.), Comte argued that society, through the division of labour, also became more complex, differentiated and specialized. The division of labour, along with language and religion, created social solidarity, but also generated new

social divisions between classes and between the private and public domains.

Sociology, standing at the pinnacle of the sciences, was to proceed in terms of an analysis of social dynamics and social statics. The first would consider the general laws of social development, while the second concentrated on the 'anatomy' of society and the mutual interaction between its constituents. Comte studied the functional contribution of social institutions (such as the family, property and the state) to the continuity of social order. While his view of the interconnectedness of elements of the social system anticipated functionalism (q.v.), Comte's view of sociology is now generally regarded as arcane. See: *Division of Labour*; *Durkheim*; *Evolutionary Theory*; *Saint-Simon*; *Sociology*.

Bibl. Coser (1971); Elias (1978a)

Concentric Zone Theory. E. Burgess, a member of the Chicago School (q.v.), argued that cities in industrialized societies take the form of five concentric rings. The innermost ring is the central business district, containing most of the better shops, offices, banks, amusement and service facilities. The second, the zone of transition (q.v.), is essentially an area in development as the central business district expands outwards. As a result, it is a run-down area of relatively cheap housing. The third zone contains the homes of manual workers, while the fourth comprises middle-class suburbs. On the fringes of the city is the commuters' zone.

Burgess proposed his theory as an ideal type (q.v.). Real cities would not conform exactly to the five zones, which would be deformed by the existence of communication routes, for example. The theory followed the principles of urban ecology (q.v.). The zones comprise natural areas (q.v.) created by impersonal forces independent of the intentions of the population. Competition for land determines the arrangement, with those activities able to afford high rents taking the best central sites. Successive waves of migration follow one another with a racial or ethnic group starting in the zone of transition and moving outwards as it prospers.

The theory has been extensively criticized. It has been argued, for instance, that cities are really in the form of sectors, not rings, and that land-values may not only be dictated by competition but by cultural values. Many of these criticisms were anticipated by Burgess and the theory remains useful, especially in its depiction of the zone of transition.

Bibl. Reissmann (1964)

Condition of Existence. A set of conditions that are required for the existence or operation of some social activity, this term is used in contemporary Marxist sociology to replace the notion of strict economic determinism. Instead of the economy being determinant, ideology and politics are conditions of existence of the economy, that is, necessary to the existence of the economy. For example, Althusser argues that the legal system in the form of the law of property and the law of contract is a condition of existence of the capitalist economy. See: *Althusser*; *Base and Superstructure*; *Determinism*.

Conflict Theory. Social conflict assumes various forms. Competition describes a conflict over the control of resources or advantages desired by others where actual physical violence is not employed. Regulated competition is the sort of peaceful conflict which is resolved within a framework of agreed rules. Markets involve competition, both regulated and unregulated. Other conflicts may be more violent and not bound by rules, in which case they are settled by the parties mobilizing their power resources.

Social theorists in the nineteenth and early twentieth centuries were concerned with conflict in society. Mid-twentieth-century functionalists, however, neglected conflict in favour of a unitary conception of society and culture which emphasized social integration and the harmonious effect of common values. When functionalists did consider the phenomenon, they saw conflict as pathological rather than the normal state of a healthy social organism.

Some sociologists in the 1950s and 1960s attempted to revive what they called 'conflict theory' against the dominant functionalism of the time, drawing on K. Marx and G. Simmel to this end. Marx had presented a dichotomous model of social conflict, in which the whole of society was divided into the two basic classes representing the interests of capital and labour. Conflict would ultimately transform society. Simmel, while emphasizing the salience of conflict, adopted neither the dichotomous model nor the assumption that conflict would in the end destroy existing social arrangements. He believed that conflict had positive functions for social stability and helped preserve groups and collectivities. L. Coser (1956; 1968) developed the Simmelian perspective to show that conflict was usually functional in pluralistic complex societies. He argued that cross-cutting conflicts, in which someone who was an ally in one dispute was an opponent in another, prevented conflicts falling along one axis and dividing society along dichotomous lines. Complex societies contained a plurality of interests and conflicts which provided a balancing mechanism that prevented instability. R. Dahrendorf (1959) similarly concluded that conflicts were cross-cutting and did not overlap, and, unlike Marx, claimed that the central conflict in all social institutions concerned the distribution of power and authority rather than capital, that it was the relationship of domination and subordination which produced antagonistic interests. He thought that the successful containment of industrial conflict within the economy, so that it no longer spilled over into other institutions, was especially important in this context.

D. Lockwood (1964) developed a distinction, implicit in Marxism, between 'system' and 'social' conflict. System conflict occurs when institutions are not in harmony: for example, when the political sub-system pursues policies which conflict with the needs of the economic sub-system. Social conflict is interpersonal and occurs only within social interactions.

Along with the decline of functionalism, the revival of Marxist and Weberian approaches to sociology in the 1970s has restored conflict to its traditional place at the centre of theory and analysis. See: *Competition*; *Consensus*; *Contradiction*; *Industrial Conflict*; *Institutionalization of Conflict*; *Social Order*; *Systems Theory*.

Bibl. Rex (1981)

Conjugal. This term refers to relationships between marriage partners, or between a man and woman living together. See: *Conjugal Role*; *Domestic Labour*; *Nuclear Family*.

Conjugal Role. The tasks typically taken up by husband and wife in the household are referred to as conjugal roles. E. Bott (1957) distinguishes *segregated* conjugal roles, in which husband and wife have quite different tasks within the home, from *joint* conjugal roles in which they have tasks which are more or less interchangeable. Segregated conjugal roles are associated with tight-knit networks of friends and kin which support husband and wife in their separate activities at home, leisure and work. Joint roles, on the other hand, are typically associated with the lack of any such network, perhaps following a period of geographical mobility. A number of studies have apparently shown that there is a trend towards more 'egalitarian' marriages, with the decline of traditional occupations and stable communities and with the increase in the number of employed wives and unemployed husbands, increasing social and geographical mobility, and separation from kin. However, a number of writers have doubted that this trend has gone at all far, pointing out, for example, that domestic chores are certainly not performed equally by men and women. See: *Domestic Labour*; *Nuclear Family*.

Bibl. Bilton *et al.* (1981)

Conjuncture. The actual balance of unevenly developed social and political forces in a society at a particular moment is referred to as the conjuncture. Analysis of specific conjunctures is distinguished from the analysis of the forces acting generally within the mode of production (q.v.), which, it is argued, may be seen only at the abstract theoretical level. For L. Althusser, the study of the conjuncture is the basis of Marxist politics because it reveals where political pressure will be most effective. See: *Althusser*; *Contradiction*.

Conscience Collective. This term played an important part in the sociology of E. Durkheim. While the notion of 'conscience' typically refers to the moral attitudes of the *individual*, for Durkheim *conscience collective* was essentially social and exterior to the individual. It referred

49

to an external normative order or social fact (q.v.) which coerced members of the group to behave and think in certain ways. As the division of labour increased, individualism also developed and the *conscience collective* declined. Societies based on organic solidarity (q.v.) are held together by restitutive law and by reciprocal relationships within the division of labour. See: *Durkheim*.

Bibl. Lukes (1972)

Consensus. The question of how social order is established and preserved in any society or social group has been a central issue of social philosophy and sociology. In sociology, following T. Parsons' (1937) treatment, this is technically referred to as 'the Hobbesian problem of order'. Broadly speaking, sociologists can be divided into those who emphasize coercion as the basis of social order and those who argue that some degree of general consensus over values and norms provides the crucial basis of any society. In practice, of course, most sociological theories of social order conceptualize the bases of order in terms of both normative consensus and physical coercion. However, in Parsonian sociology the central explanation of order is in terms of 'ultimate values' which are internalized and shared by the population as a result of common experiences of socialization within the family. The nature and extent of consensus over social values in human society has given rise to a long-standing debate in modern sociological theory. For example, there is much empirical research into the beliefs of the urban working class which suggests that dominant social values are not completely or consistently accepted by large sections of the population. Furthermore, even where common values are accepted, this acceptance may be merely pragmatic and partial. Some Marxist sociology (q.v.) has adopted notions similar to that of

value consensus, which stress dominant ideology and hegemony. Other forms of Marxism, however, have criticized the idea and have stressed the importance not of unity but of class and class conflict. See: *Coercion*; *Conflict Theory*; *Dominant Ideology Thesis*; *Gramsci*; *Hegemony*; *Parsons*; *Pragmatic Acceptance*; *Social Order*; *Value*; *Working Class*.

Bibl. Cohen, P. S. (1968)

Content Analysis. This is the analysis of the content of communication, which involves classifying contents in such a way as to bring out their basic structure. The term is normally applied to the analysis of documentary or visual material rather than interview data, but the same technique may in fact apply to the analysis of answers to open-ended questions in survey research. Researchers create a set of categories which illuminate the issues under study and then classify content according to these predetermined categories. It is essential that the categories are precisely defined to minimize bias resulting from the judgements of different investigators. This technique produces quantitative data which can be processed by computer and analysed statistically. However, content analysis is sometimes criticized as involving subjective judgements which may create data that are quantifiable but not valid. See: *Coding*.

Bibl. Holsti (1969)

Contest Mobility. See: *Sponsored Mobility*.

Contradiction. Two social activities are said to be in contradiction when, because of their very nature, they are incompatible. The term is used most frequently in Marxist sociology. For example, there is a contradiction between labour and capital because of the way that capital exploits labour by the extraction of surplus value (q.v.).

Contradictions, although they are systematic in the structure of society, do not necessarily issue in actual conflict. In the case of capital and labour the presence of actual conflict will depend on the organization of class forces and the activities of the state. The more fundamental are the contradictions involved and the more different contradictions are fused together, the more serious will be any resultant conflict. See: *Conflict Theory*; *Marx*; *Marxist Sociology*; *Systems Theory*.

Bibl. Althusser (1966)

Control Group. In social science experiments a control group is a group of people matched as closely as possible on relevant variables with an experimental group. The experimental group is exposed to the independent variable whose effects are being investigated while the control group is not exposed. Any differences which are found between the two groups after the experiment are attributed to the independent variable. For example, in studying the effect of television on children, besides exposing the experimental group to television one has to create a similar group matched by important characteristics (for example, age, sex, education, class) which is not exposed to television. Without such a control, the investigator cannot tell whether any observed effect is due to television or to some other feature of the environment.

Control groups may also be used when experiments are impracticable. A comparison of two groups is made, matching the members as closely as possible, but where only one group has in the past been exposed to the independent variable. The hypothesis that this variable has an influence is tested by comparing the two groups. This method works from the past to the present and is known

as a *cause-to-effect* design. Alternatively, two groups selected because they are known to differ in some significant aspect are matched as closely as possible and their past is investigated to find an explanation of the difference. This is an *effect-to-cause* method. See: *Experimental Method*.

Bibl. Moser and Kalton (1979)

Convergence Thesis. This argument claims that the process of industrialization produces common and uniform political, social and cultural characteristics on societies which, prior to industrialization, may have had very different historical backgrounds and social structures. All societies converge to a common point because industrialization requires certain characteristics in order to function effectively. These are: (1) an extended social and technical division of labour; (2) the separation of the family from the enterprise and the work place; (3) a mobile, urbanized and disciplined work-force; (4) some form of rational organization of economic calculation, planning and investment. Theories of industrial convergence suggest in addition that, given the 'logic of industrialism', all industrial societies will tend to be secular, urban, mobile and democratic. The convergence thesis is thus linked, on the one hand, with the 'end of ideology theory' in suggesting that industrial society will be based on a new form of consensus and, on the other, with development theory which regards Western society as the only appropriate model for rapid economic progress.

There are a number of theoretical problems associated with the convergence thesis. (1) It is not clear whether all societies must assume a common form with industrialization or whether considerable institutional variation is compatible with a common industrial base. (2) There is an ambiguity in whether it is the presence of the large industrial enterprise, industrialization as a process, or certain technological conditions of production which is held to be the cause of social convergence. In the latter case, the argument assumes a crude form of technological determinism which treats the social context of industrialization as directly dependent on changes in industrial technique. (3) Not all industrial societies are empirically converging towards a common pattern. (4) Some people argue that the characteristics of industrial society are those of capitalism. Insofar as social convergence takes place, this may be explained by the dominance of capitalism rather than by the process of industrialized production itself. (5) The convergence thesis was typical of the optimistic analysis of industrial society which was common in the early 1960s. The subsequent experience of industrial decline, inflation and unemployment in certain industrialized economies has shown that regional imbalance, de-industrialization and economic decline may create important variations between and within industrial societies. See: *Capitalism*; *End of Ideology Theory*; *Industrial Society*; *Industrialization*; *Post-Industrial Society*.

Bibl. Kerr *et al.* (1962); Scott (1979)

Conversational Analysis. A relatively recent field of study in sociology, conversational analysis has grown out of ethnomethodology (q,v.), especially the work of H. Sacks. The use of natural language in conversations provides order and management of the social settings in which the conversations take place. Conversational analysis provides *descriptions* of the way in which conversations achieve this order. Empirical studies include the way in which the first five seconds of telephone conversation are structured and the manner in which courtroom conversational interaction is

ordered. Conversational analysis represents a move away from the earlier ethnographic studies conducted by ethnomethodologists, towards more rigorous scientific and quantitative methods of data collection.

Bibl. Sociology (1978)

Cooperative. Voluntary organizations characterized by the absence of a distinct ownership and capital-providing class, cooperatives are jointly owned and wholly or in part financed by their members, who also determine policy. The origins of the cooperative movement are associated with the ideas of C. Fourier in France and R. Owen in Great Britain in the early nineteenth century. Owen's aim was to create a self-supporting cooperative community where producers and consumers were the same people. In practice, cooperatives have usually divided into separate consumer and producer forms. Owen's community ideal has rarely been realized, though Owenism was the inspiration for the modern Mondragon cooperative community in Spain.

Consumer cooperatives are widespread and have a long and successful history, notably in Great Britain and Sweden. Producer organizations include farming cooperatives which purchase, process and market. These are widespread in Europe and America. Producer cooperatives in manufacturing industry have in the past usually proved unsuccessful. The difficulty of raising sufficient capital and the inadequate management of member-controlled organizations reduced the commercial viability of cooperatives. However, the number of producer cooperatives in Western Europe and the USA is now growing. The Mondragon group of cooperatives shows that the financial and managerial problems can be overcome, in which case producer cooperation is highly efficient.

The commitment and application of cooperative members to organizational goals exceeds that of employees in conventional firms, and industrial relations are transformed when all employees are co-owners. Cooperatives incorporate socialized ownership as an alternative to conventional capitalism yet retain the market economy, which is why K. Marx and modern Marxists disparage them as 'worker capitalism'. See: *Commune*.

Bibl. Thornley (1981); Bradley and Gelb (1983)

Corporatism. A form of social organization in which the key economic, political and social decisions are made by corporate groups, or these groups and the state jointly. Individuals have influence only through their membership of corporate bodies. These include trade unions, professions, business corporations, political pressure groups and lobbies, and voluntary associations. Corporatism may be contrasted with decision-making via the market, in which individuals who make their own private market choices collectively and cumulatively shape society. At the political level, corporatism may also be contrasted with the traditional form of liberal democracy in which political decisions were taken only by governments representing the electorate directly.

The theory of the corporate state, that the political community includes a number of corporate groups and individuals are to be represented politically via their membership of these groups rather than as individual electors, was adopted in Italian fascism.

Some commentators have suggested recently that many Western European democracies were moving towards a tripartite form of corporatism in the 1970s, that governments made social and economic policy in consultation and negotiation with the powerful vested interests of trade union movements and employers' associations. It is claimed that politicians allowed corporate bodies to influence state decisions in return for these bodies controlling their members: corporations delivered the support of their members in return for an influence over political decision-making. Trade unions restrained their members' strike activity and pay demands, employers aligned the pursuit of their private interests with those of the state, while governments in return protected labour and pursued economic expansion. Corporatism was particularly strong in the Scandinavian nations, the Low Countries, West Germany and Austria, with weaker versions in Italy and the UK. In the 1980s, the effect of economic downturn has been to weaken the trade union movement and, outside Scandinavia, business and government have eroded tripartite corporatism as they find less need to cooperate with unions to curb worker militancy. Sociologists disagree whether corporatism represents an attempt by the state to incorporate and pacify militant trade unionism at the cost of employees' interests, or whether it marks the successful use of workers' power to constrain business and the state. Where corporatism survives in the 1980s, employees' interests seem to be better protected than where market forces are allowed to dominate economic life, with lower rates of both unemployment and inflation. See: *Democracy; Fascism; State; Trade Unions*.

Bibl. Panitch (1980); Goldthorpe (ed.) (1985)

Correlation. It is normal to record a variety of data simultaneously in sociological research: for example, to measure respondents' educational attainments and occupational levels in surveys. If one datum provides information about another they are associated or correlated. In the example of educational attainments and occupational levels, it is generally found that the higher the occupational level the higher the educational attainment – i.e. the correlation is normally *positive*, which means that the values of the two variables tend to increase or decrease together. A *negative* correlation describes the case when the value of one variable increases while the other decreases. There are various types of correlation coefficient that are used with different sorts of data, but all measure the strength of the association between two or more variables. The fact that two variables are correlated does not establish which one is antecedent or causes the other, or indeed that they are causally related at all, since they may both be caused by a third factor.

Counter Culture. A term made popular in the 1960s, when student radicals and others formulated new and unconventional theories and policies about politics, work and family life that ran counter to conventionally accepted values and patterns of behaviour. Common themes of the counter culture included the repressive qualities of conventional family life, the desirability of letting people 'do their own thing', experimentation with drugs of various kinds, and the virtues of sexual freedom.

Counterfactual. A proposition which states what would have happened had something not been the case. It is often claimed that to make any sociological proposition meaningful and testable, there must be a corresponding counterfactual proposition. For example, to argue that the industrial revolution caused the decline of the extended family means that one must have some idea of what would have happened to the family

had there not been an industrial revolution. Again, to claim, as in some studies of power, that a particular action is against the interests of an individual or group, one must know what actions *would* be in the interests of that group. See: *Falsificationism*.

Bibl. Lukes (1974)

Credentialism. This term refers to a modern tendency in society to allocate positions, particularly occupational positions, on the basis of educational qualifications or credentials. The pursuit of such credentials then becomes an end in itself, a process sometimes known as the 'Diploma Disease'. As a result, not only is the educational process distorted but the qualifications demanded and gained may have very little to do with the skills actually used in a job. Qualifications in the much expanded higher education system, for example, may merely serve as a method of restricting entry to certain occupations and not as a training for them.

Bibl. Dore (1976)

Crimes Without Victims. In most crimes there is a clearly defined victim. However, there is a limited number of crimes which have no victims, sometimes referred to as 'service' crimes. These include drug abuse, gambling and prostitution. Typically these are not reported to the police, because both parties to the crime derive a 'benefit' from it.

Criminal Statistics. In England and Wales, the official statistics used to estimate the crime rate are based on the recording by the police of notifiable offences. Notifiable offences are in effect those crimes for which a suspect has the right to trial by jury, which marks the difference between more and less serious crimes. The majority of convictions in

British courts are in fact for motoring offences, which do not enter the estimation of the crime rate because, with the exception of reckless driving and the theft or unauthorized taking of a vehicle, they are not notifiable. Notifiable offences that are unknown to the police or that the police choose not to record do not appear in the criminal statistics. The annual rate of increase in recorded crime averaged about 10 per cent between 1963 and 1983. Crime is (1) concentrated in the urban population; (2) committed mainly by males between the ages of 14 and 28, with a peak between 14 and 18; (3) concentrated in certain social groups, especially the working class; (4) committed by a growing proportion of females, notably by those aged between 13 and 15, with the consequence that the male–female ratio of offenders had closed to 5 : 1 in 1983 from about 7 : 1 in 1963.

It is generally agreed that all criminal statistics, including notifiable and unnotifiable crimes, prosecutions and convictions, are unreliable as guides to the actual extent of crime, for several reasons. (1) Crimes known to the police are a small fraction, possibly as low as one quarter, of crimes unknown to the police – this is the so-called 'dark figure'; many trivial offences are not fully reported, while certain types of serious crime such as fraud, blackmail, incest and rape are also under-reported. (2) Criminal statistics may also reflect police bias (notably leniency towards women, white people and middle-class offenders) and changes in public opinion about specific crimes such as mugging. (3) The size and composition of criminal statistics are also shaped by the efficiency, deployment and size of the police force. (4) Changes in law clearly determine the incidence of crime; for example, attempted suicide and homosexuality between consenting adults ceased to be

crimes in the post-war period. (5) There is also judicial bias in the variability of treatment of alleged offenders by the courts. As a result, sociologists tend to treat criminal statistics as evidence, not of actual criminality, but of changes in police practice, public opinion and judicial process; that is, they attempt to go behind the statistics to understand the social processes that determine how these statistics are collected and categorized.

In order to get a better idea of actual rather than recorded crime, many nations initiated crime surveys in the 1960s and 1970s. These large-scale surveys of national populations ask people whether they have been victims of crime. The first British crime survey was conducted in 1982, the second in 1984. The British surveys show that only about 1 in 5 incidents of vandalism, thefts in dwellings, and other household thefts was reported to the police. 1 in 3 assaults, thefts involving personal contact and other thefts from the person was reported. 2 in 3 burglaries were reported. In all, about two thirds of all crimes mentioned by victims have not been reported to the police. Many offences that are reported by victims do not get recorded by the police, or are not recorded in the proper category. Surveys do not necessarily provide the 'true' record of crime, because they do not cover corporate victims, respondents are likely to understate offences involving drugs, alcohol abuse and sex between consenting partners, and there are obvious problems of fabrication and recall among victims. Interestingly, the British evidence suggests that surveys may be less accurate than police statistics of serious sexual offences, because victims tend not to report these to interviewers. See: *Crimes Without Victims*; *Official Statistics*.

Bibl. Box (1971); Hough and Mayhew (1985); Bottomley and Pease (1986)

Criminology. This is the scientific study of criminal behaviour, that is of infractions of the law, especially criminal law. Criminology is (1) the study of the causes, nature and distribution of crime in society; (2) the study of the physical, psychological and social characteristics of criminals; (3) the study of the victims of crime and their interaction with criminals. Criminology also includes the more specific discipline of penology (q.v.). Three major and damaging criticisms have been made of the subject: (1) the legal definition of criminal behaviour is inappropriate from a sociological perspective; (2) if the notion of 'crime' is replaced by that of 'deviance', it becomes clear that no single theory of deviant behaviour can explain the complexity of such heterogeneous phenomena; (3) the overlap between the theoretical objectives of criminology and the policy objectives of law enforcement agencies calls into question the objectivity and autonomy of criminological research.

While the sociology of deviance was an important development in the 1960s, various Marxist perspectives contributed in the 1970s to the emergence of a 'critical' or 'new' criminology which emphasized power, conflict and class in the explanation of crime. In more recent years, sociology, increasingly influenced by feminism (q.v.), has given more attention to women as victims and perpetrators of crime. Women commit fewer serious crimes than men and are overrepresented in shoplifting and minor sex offences. Various criminological explanations have been suggested: (1) sexrole socialization; (2) sex differences in opportunities to commit crimes; (3) differences in police response; (4) variations in societal reaction. See: *Addiction*; *Crimes Without Victims*; *Criminal Statistics*; *Delinquency*; *Delinquent Drift*; *Deviancy Amplification*; *Deviant Behaviour*; *Differential Association*; *Gang*; *Social Pathology*; *White-Collar Crime*.
Bibl. Box (1983)

Critical Theory. This form of social analysis is often equated with the Frankfurt School (q.v.) of critical sociology in the twentieth century, but the notion of criticism is clearly older and more comprehensive than this simple equation would suggest. Criticism means the exercise of negative judgement, especially concerning manners, literature or cultural products in general. Textual criticism developed as a weapon of religious conflict during the Reformation, when biblical criticism was held to be a negative but objective judgement on conventional ecclesiastical practice and dogma. Criticism then came to mean uncovering hidden assumptions and debunking their claims to authority, as well as simple fault-finding. G. Hegel (q.v.) saw human history as a progression of human self-awareness which constantly transformed and went beyond existing social constraints. In Hegelian philosophy, therefore, criticism was more than a negative judgement and was given the positive role of detecting and unmasking existing forms of belief in order to enhance the emancipation of men in society.

This Hegelian critique of ideological forms of consciousness was enthusiastically espoused by the so-called Left Hegelians who proposed to apply 'critical criticism' to all spheres of human activity, especially in relation to religion and politics. It was in this context that K. Marx and F. Engels framed their project (1845b) of criticizing society so as to unmask religion and all other forms of bourgeois thought.

For Marx, the idea of critique was not simply a negative *intellectual* judgement on ideological systems of thought, but a practical and revolutionary activity. Under the slogan 'The philosophers have only interpreted the world in various ways; the point is, to change it', Marx (1845) began to develop the idea that in order to be effective philosophical criticism had to become an instrument of the working class in its revolutionary struggle against the bourgeoisie (q.v.). For Marx, critique was now conjoined with *praxis*. While this idea of praxis (q.v.) or practice is particularly complicated in Marxism, in one respect it signifies that intellectual criticism can only be actualized fully in the activity of men in society. This conception of the relationship between valid knowledge of the world and revolutionary practice was taken one step further by G. Lukacs (1923), for whom true consciousness was the exclusive property of the proletariat as a class acting in its real interests, even when these interests were clouded by 'false' consciousness.

The development of critical theory by the Frankfurt School arose out of their dissatisfaction with the use of 'criticism' by institutionalized Marxism to legitimate political decisions of the Communist Party. Critical theorists also had a deeper perception of the value and importance of 'critique' in its Hegelian form. By its very nature, criticism has to be *self*-critical. Consequently, the Frankfurt School developed an open and often syncretic attitude to any philosophical tradition which held out the promise of human emancipation through social critique. Critical theorists recognized that, since capitalism had changed fundamentally, it was impossible to remain entirely within the framework of Marx's criticism of nineteenth-century capitalism. The principal target of critical theory, therefore, became the claims of 'instrumental rationality' (in particular, natural science) to be the only valid form of any genuine knowledge. The critique of the rational foundations of science and capitalism led critical

theory not only to reappraise classical German philosophy, but to debate M. Weber's analysis of capitalism as a rationally organized 'iron cage'. The recent work of the critical theorists in Germany has revitalized the traditional discussion of the similarities and differences between Marx and Weber in their analyses of capitalism. See: *Capitalism*; *Frankfurt School*; *Habermas*; *Hermeneutics*; *Marx*; *Marxist Sociology*; *Neo-Kantianism*; *Positivism*; *Verstehen*.

Bibl. Connerton (ed.) (1976)

Cross Tabulation. A common way of presenting data is in two-way tables which relate the values of one variable to those of another. The following example is of a cross tabulation of voting intention by social class among 200 people:

	Conservative	Labour	Total
Middle Class	80	20	100
Working Class	30	70	100
Total	110	90	200

The purpose of cross tabulating variables is to see what association they have with each other. It is possible to elaborate the analysis by bringing in further variables, for example by introducing sex into the illustration above to see if the relationship between class and voting is the same for both men and women.

Cult. In its anthropological usage, a cult is the beliefs and practices of a particular group in relation to a god or gods. In sociology, it is often associated with the discussion of church-sect typologies. The cult is regarded as a small, flexible group whose religion is characterized by its individualism, syncretism and frequently esoteric belief. While it has been suggested that religious sects emphasize fellowship and cults enhance private, individual experience, in practice it is often theoretically difficult to distinguish religious groups in these terms. The modern proliferation of cults, often with specifically Oriental religious ideas, has brought into question the nature and extent of secularization in Western industrial societies. See: *Church*; *Sect*; *Secularization*.

Bibl. Jackson and Jobling (1968)

Cultural Capital. For P. Bourdieu (1973) (q.v.), success in the educational system is largely dictated by the extent to which individuals have absorbed the dominant culture, or how much cultural capital they have got. He argues that those in power control the form that culture takes and are thus able to sustain their position. See: *Cultural Reproduction*.

Cultural Deprivation. The failure of children from the working class and some ethnic minorities to reach the same average levels of educational achievement as middle-class children has often been explained in terms of cultural deprivation, the failure of the home and neighbourhood to provide these children with the motivational and linguistic attributes necessary for success within the educational system. It is less often used now, because it implies personal inadequacy when the issue may simply be one of cultural *difference*: the school embodies social values and conceptions of appropriate knowledge which may differ from those of large sections of the population. See: *Bernstein*; *Classroom Knowledge*; *Cultural Capital*; *Educational Attainment*; *Restricted Code*.

Bibl. Keddie (1971)

Cultural Lag. The idea of a cultural lag was developed by W. F. Ogburn (1950) in response to crude economic determinism (q.v.) in which cultural, political and social phenomena change in direct and immediate response to changes in the economic basis of society. Ogburn noted that changes in culture were not always or necessarily congruent with economic changes. For example, he argued that economic changes influencing the division of labour in the family had not been accompanied by a change in the ideology that 'a woman's place is in the home'. A cultural lag exists when two or more social variables, which were once in some form of agreement or mutual adjustment, become dissociated and maladjusted by their differential rates of change. Although Ogburn's formulation of the problem of social change is no longer central to contemporary sociology, his hypothesis of cultural lag did anticipate debates in sociology about the relationship between the economic base and cultural superstructure of society. See: *Base and Superstructure*; *Social Change*.

Cultural Relativism. (1) This is a method whereby different societies or cultures are analysed objectively without using the values of one culture to judge the worth of another. A favoured way of achieving this aim is to describe the practices of a society from the point of view of its members. The method is one of the hallmarks of 'modern' anthropology in contrast to the ethnocentrism (q.v.) of nineteenth-century anthropology. (2) A more commonsense meaning is that beliefs are relative to a particular society and are not comparable between societies. See: *Comparative Method*; *Rationality*; *Understanding Alien Belief Systems*.

Cultural Reproduction. This term was introduced into British sociology by P. Bourdieu (1973), who sees the function of the education system as being to reproduce the culture of the dominant classes, thus helping to ensure their continued dominance. See: *Cultural Capital*; *Dominant Ideology Thesis*; *Hegemony*; *Social Reproduction*.

Culture. Sociologists and anthropologists use 'culture' as a collective noun for the symbolic and learned, non-biological aspects of human society, including language, custom and convention, by which human behaviour can be distinguished from that of other primates. Cultural anthropology (as distinct from physical anthropology) takes as its special province the analysis of the culture of human societies. Anthropology recognizes that human behaviour is largely culturally and not genetically determined. This has given rise to debates about cultural diffusion and the uniqueness of cultures and cultural relativity.

In the Anglo-French tradition, the concept of culture is often used synonymously with 'civilization'. There has been no special problem in equating 'to cultivate' and 'to civilize'; both culture and civilization are traditionally opposed to barbarism. In Germany, however, under the romantic tradition, culture was held to be the repository of human excellence, artistic achievement and individual perfection, while civilization was regarded as a process of material development which threatened individual culture by creating an urban mass society (q.v.). The contrast in Germany between *Kultur* and *Zivilisation* became part of the critique of modern industrial society which was perceived as an impersonal force which standardized human culture and consciousness. This romantic criticism of modern society came to influence the approach of the Frankfurt School (q.v.) to mass society and aesthetics, and also the sociology of N. Elias.

In American and British sociology, the concept of culture does not have this critical ambience. While Anglo-American can sociologists do refer to the culture of social groups as the total set of beliefs, customs or way of life of particular groups, they more commonly employ more differentiated concepts such as 'belief system', 'system of values' or even 'ideology' (q.v.). The notion of the culture of social groups thus occurs most frequently in the areas of the sociology of knowledge or deviance. Indeed, since sociologists typically regard the culture of industrial society as fragmented and diversified, they are more likely to conceptualize contemporary society as a plurality of life-worlds rather than as possessing unified cultural systems. It is for this reason that the sociology of deviance approaches modern society in terms of conflicting subcultures (q.v.), thereby rendering the idea of a coherent normative culture problematic. The assumption that modern societies do not have a common culture, however, raises the problem of how consensus is maintained in industrial society and, in Marxism, how a dominant ideology functions to incorporate social classes. In contemporary sociology there is, as yet, no theoretical agreement as to whether contemporary societies possess either a dominant culture or a dominant ideology which creates some social consensus despite the fragmentation which is produced by social differentiation, ethnic diversity, class structure or regional variation. See: *Civilization*; *Consensus*; *Custom*; *Dominant Ideology Thesis*; *Gramsci*; *Hegemony*; *Nature/Nurture Debate*; *Norm*; *Sociobiology*; *Value*.

Bibl. Elias (1970)

Custom. This term is used mainly in anthropology, to denote established patterns of behaviour and belief. It refers both to the routines of daily life and to the distinctive features which mark off one culture from another. See: *Culture*.

D

Dahrendorf, Ralph (b.1929). A German sociologist who has contributed to class theory and role theory, Dahrendorf was formerly a professor of sociology in Germany, then a European Economic Community Commissioner, and recently Director of the London School of Economics. His major works are: *Class and Class Conflict in an Industrial Society* (1959); 'Conflict after Class' (1967a); *Society and Democracy in Germany* (1967b); *The New Liberty* (1975); *Life Chances* (1979). See: *Conflict Theory*; *Imperatively Coordinated Association*; *Institutionalization of Conflict*; *Service Class*.

Dark Figure. See: *Criminal Statistics*.

Darwinism. See: *Social Darwinism*.

Davis–Moore Debate. See: *Stratification*.

Death Rate. The crude death rate is the number of deaths per 1,000 living members of a population per year. The standardized death rate is the number of deaths for any given cohort (q.v.) or age group per year. The standardized rate is a common measure in demography since, in this particular instance, the death rate among people of 65 years of age is obviously much higher than that among teenagers. Comparisons of crude death rates and crude birth rates (q.v.) provide the sociologist with basic measures of fertility (q.v.) and population increase. For example, the 'net rate of natural increase' is the excess of the crude birth rate over the death rate. See: *Birth Rate*; *Demography*.

Bibl. Cox, P. R. (1970)

Deductive. See: *Hypothetico-Deductive Method*; *Induction*.

Deferential Worker. This is a type of working-class conservative who defers to the old-established ruling class as the natural leaders of society. D. Lockwood (1966) suggests that deferential workers are to be found in farming and small firms, where regular contact with and dependence upon superiors create deference and lead to the assimilation of these superiors' attitudes and values. This has been disputed by H. Newby (1977). See: *Working-Class Conservatism*.

Deferred Gratification. A concept used to refer to behaviour in which sacrifices are made in the present in the hope of greater future reward. It is often said that this is a feature of middle-class upbringing, accounting for the relatively greater educational success of middle-class children. It is also claimed that deferred gratification is a precondition of both the accumulation of capital and the striving for success that were important in the earlier stages of capitalism. See: *Achievement Motivation*; *Capitalism*.

Definition of the Situation. The importance of the subjective perspectives of social actors for the objective consequences of social interaction is often summarized in sociology by the notion of 'defining the situation'. It was first specified by W. I. Thomas (1928) in a well-known aphorism – 'if men define situations as real, they are real in their consequences'. One implication of this sociological viewpoint is that, for sociology, the truth or falsity of beliefs ('definitions of the situation') are not important issues; what matters is the outcome of social interaction. Thus, if a particular minority group is regarded as 'a threat to society', then there will be major objective consequences – exclusion, intimidation, expulsion – even where the minority group is not a real threat to social order. This approach to what Thomas (1927) called 'situational analysis' has had an important influence on subsequent studies of the conditions for stable interaction and role-taking in symbolic interactionism (q.v.) and ethnomethodology (q.v.).

Bibl. McHugh (1968)

De-industrialization. The importance of manufacturing industry has declined in a number of industrial societies, when measured by the share of manufacturing in total output or the proportion of the population employed in manufacturing. In part, this relative decline simply reflects the growth of output and employment in the service sector of the economy which changes the relative shares of manufacturing and services. Employment changes further reflect the implementation of labour-saving technologies which reduce the volume of employment in manufacturing for any given level of output. De-industrialization, defined as a decline in manufacturing, is a feature of such structural shifts within capitalist economies. In the UK and USA, however, de-industrialization has also followed the declining international competitiveness of manufacturing industries in these countries. Britain, for example, became a net importer of manufactured goods in the mid 1980s for the first time since the Industrial Revolution. See: *Industrialization*.

Delinquency. This term covers a wide variety of infringements of legal and social norms, and in criminology it is typically specified as juvenile delinquency to indicate the high level of indictable offences committed by young males between the ages of 12 and 20 years. The typical crimes of younger males are larceny and breaking and entering, while violent crimes are more common in the age groups over 17 years. Most sociological theories of juvenile delinquency attempt to explain these crimes in terms of the organization of urban gangs, delinquent subcultures (q.v.), and the limitations on opportunity for working-class males and deprived social groups. For example, the Chicago School (q.v.) analysed juvenile delinquency in terms of the social structure of local neighbourhoods and the role of the peer group (q.v.) in the socialization (q.v.) of adolescent generations. Alternatively, delinquency has been explained as the product of anomie (q.v.) or as the result of delinquent drift (q.v.). Critical criminologists have occasionally regarded delinquency as an expression of opposition to dominant values and social inequality. See: *Adolescence*; *Criminal*

Statistics; *Criminology*; *Deviancy Amplification*; *Deviant Behaviour*; *Differential Association*; *Gang*; *Labelling Theory*; *Merton*; *Social Problems*; *Subculture*.

Delinquent Drift. An explanation of delinquent conduct developed by D. Matza (1964; 1969), it claims that delinquents often 'neutralize' legal and moral norms by subjectively defining such norms as inapplicable, irrelevant or unimportant. Once a person feels indifferent towards the law, he may commit unlawful acts without a strong sense of guilt or shame. A delinquent who thus neutralizes legal norms may be said to drift into a subculture (q.v.) of delinquency, which makes him available for delinquent acts. See: *Criminology*; *Delinquency*; *Deviant Behaviour*; *Neutralization*.

Democracy. Sociological discussion of democracy has gone through several phases. Many nineteenth-century accounts, like that of A. de Tocqueville, concentrated on the social consequences of allowing greater political participation to traditionally subordinate groups, and this theme has been developed in the work of the mass-society (q.v.) theorists. More recent work has explored the connections between social development and parliamentary democracy, which is conceived of as the election of leaders by ballot with a universal franchise by means of a competitive party system. Various attempts have been made to correlate democracy with degree of industrialization, level of educational attainment, and national wealth. It has been argued that democracy is naturally encouraged by higher levels of industrial development which create pressures for wider participation in politics. Other approaches have investigated the way in which democracy may lead to bureaucracy in trade unions (q.v.) and the relationship between democracy and citizenship (q.v.).

Marxists have been interested in exploring the relationship of capitalism and democracy, often within the general context of theories of the state. Earlier arguments that parliamentary democracy was effectively a sham, and that the state was really an instrument of the dominant capitalist class, have given way to more complex accounts. See: *Capitalism*; *Citizenship*; *Elite*; *Industrial Democracy*; *Michels*; *Political Participation*; *Political Parties*; *State*; *Voluntary Associations*; *Voting*.

Bibl. Bottomore (1979)

Demographic Transition. The theory of demographic transition attempts to specify general laws by which human populations change in size and structure during industrialization (q.v.). The theory holds that pre-industrial societies were characterized by stable populations which had both a high death rate (q.v.) and birth rate (q.v.). In the first stage of the transition, death rates begin to fall with improvements in nutrition, food supply, food distribution and improved sanitation and health standards. Since the birth rate continues to remain high relative to the declining death rate, there is a rapid increase in the size of the population. In the second stage, changes in social attitudes, the introduction of cheap forms of contraception and increases in life-expectancy create social pressures for smaller families and for a reduction of fertility (q.v.). The populations of advanced, urban industrial societies are now stable with low birth and death rates. The growth pattern of human populations is thus held to be S-shaped, involving a transition from one type of demographic stability with high death and birth rates to another type of plateau with low death and birth rates. This demographic transition can be illustrated by a diagram:

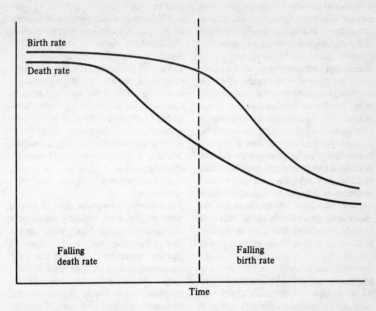

Birth rate

Death rate

Falling
death rate

Falling
birth rate

Time

Demographic transition theory can be criticized under three broad headings. (1) It may provide a *description* of the general features of demographic change in certain Western societies, but it does not provide a sophisticated causal explanation because the theoretical connections between the key variables, and their nature, are often not precisely stated. (2) As a *general* theory, the notion of a common process of population change is difficult to reconcile with specific population changes in modern Africa, Asia and Latin America. (3) Recent research in historical demography also presents a far more complex picture of European population history. The stability of pre-industrial populations in north-eastern Europe was caused by low fertility as a consequence of late marriage and celibacy, while the population stability of societies which lay east of a line connecting Trieste and St Petersburg was

the result of early marriage with strictly enforced low fertility. These revisions of traditional transition theory now place greater importance on marriage practices and family structure than on simple technological change in the explanation of population growth. See: *Aging*; *Demography*; *Social Change*; *Urbanization*.

Bibl. Wrong (1966); Andorka (1978)

Demography. This can be defined as the analysis of the size, structure and development of human populations, although it is occasionally employed to cover the study of animal populations. The crude statistics of population size and change are provided by the relationship between the birth and death rates and by migration and emigration. Two central features of population structure are the sex and age composition of human groups. Demographic analysis also includes the geographical distribution of populations, population and natural resources, genetic composition, population projections, family planning, and demographic features of the labour supply. Because the demography of human populations is crucial for economic and social planning, the development of demographic analysis has become important for national and international government forecasting. Partly in response to government requirements and partly because of the nature of demographic data, demographers have developed sophisticated mathematical models of population change and structure which permit statistical forecasting, population projections and the creation of actuarial life-tables. It is now commonplace, therefore, to distinguish between formal or mathematical demography, which is concerned with the mathematical structure and functions of human populations, and social or historical demography, which studies the historical conditions of population change such as the nature of demographic transition.

The demographic characteristics of human populations are clearly of major importance for any sociological understanding of human society. Population change in both size and structure has a direct bearing on, for example, the availability of housing, education, health and employment. Despite these obvious connections between demography and sociology, it is perhaps surprising that the two disciplines have tended to develop as separate and distinct approaches to human society. Although the question of population density played an important part in early sociological theories of social contract and division of labour, subsequent sociological theory and research did not take the demographic features of society to be of central *analytical* significance in sociological explanation. One explanation of the neglect of demography by sociolo-

gists may lie in the fact that sociologists like T. Parsons came to equate an interest in the demography of society with a 'biologizing' tendency in sociological theory. Biological determinism attempts to employ the study of animal populations as the basis for the study of human groups, perceiving the latter in terms of basic laws of population growth in relation to fixed resources. While demographers were inclined to ignore the cultural and social factors which mediate between population and environment, sociologists have neglected population variables between society and environment.

This mirror-image ignorance between demography and sociology has now changed fundamentally with recent developments in the social history of human populations which is centrally concerned with such questions as marriage practices, bastardy, family structure and generally with the impact of social conditions on fertility, mortality and migration. Historical demography employs the method of 'family reconstitution' in which parish records are used to study the major demographic events – births, deaths and marriages – of each family. The use of this method by, for example, the Annales School (q.v.) transformed sociologists' understanding of the family. In particular, it helped to destroy the myth of the extended family (q.v.) in pre-industrial Europe. Historical demography, especially under the impact of the Cambridge Centre for the Study of Population and History, has made a major contribution to the re-evaluation of conventional sociological perspectives on the family, fertility and social class, and the social aspects of population change. This expansion in historical demography has consequently made important contributions to the sociological analysis of social change (q.v.) by improving our understanding of the relationship between population change, social structure and technological improvement. See: *Aging*; *Birth Rate*; *Cohort*; *Death Rate*; *Demographic Transition*; *Fertility*; *Malthus*; *Mortality*; *Nuclear Family*.

Bibl. Wrigley (ed.) (1966); Laslett (ed.) (1972); Wrigley and Schofield (1982)

Dependency. The theory of dependency can be understood as a critical response to the *laissez-faire* model of international trade and economic development which can be traced back to A. Smith's (1776) explanation of the economic benefits of the division of labour (q.v.). Smithian theories of international trade suggest that economic growth is maximized by regional specialization and the reduction of trade tariffs. Since natural resources, climate and labour supplies are unequally distributed between societies, each society should specialize its production around these 'natural gifts' so that international trade exchanges will maximize productivity in certain raw materials, commodities and services.

Dependency theory was advanced by P. Baran (1957), who argued that the economic development of industrial societies in the West rested on the expropriation of an economic surplus from overseas societies. Third World countries were underdeveloped as a consequence of their precarious reliance on export-oriented primary production. This theory was further elaborated by A. G. Frank (1969), who analysed underdevelopment in terms of a global network of exploitation between metropolis and satellite societies. Dependency theory argues that the global economy cannot be conceived in the Smithian manner as a system of *equal* trading partners precisely because the superior military, economic and political power of the centre (the industrial societies) imposes conditions of unequal exchange

on the periphery (underdeveloped societies depending on the export of raw materials and labour). Historically speaking, colonialism undermined nascent industrial production in the Third World by ensuring favourable conditions for the export of commodities from capitalist societies. By forcing dependent societies to specialize in the production of raw materials (cotton, rubber, tea and so forth), the industrial societies maintained this system of unequal exchange and forced these exporters into dependence on an unstable world market for such commodities. It is argued that the system of dependency between centre and periphery, while no longer organized under direct colonialism, is still maintained through the power of multinational corporations which dominate international trade by controlling the price of basic materials. Criticism of dependency theory cannot be separated from recent objections to the sociology of underdevelopment. See: *Centre/ Periphery*; *Imperialism*; *Internal Colonialism*; *Underdevelopment*; *World-System Theory*.

Bibl. Amin (1976)

Dependent/Independent Variables. In sociological accounts of the relationships between variables, a phenomenon that is explained or caused by something else is called a 'dependent' variable, while the causal or explanatory variable is referred to as 'independent'. For example, in social mobility studies the dependent variable is usually the level of occupational attainment of individuals while the independent variables include other phenomena that may explain this level, such as the occupations of parents and the educational achievements of the individuals concerned.

Deprivation. Sociological analysis defines deprivation broadly as inequality of access to social goods. It includes poverty (q.v.) and wider forms of disadvantage. M. Brown and N. Madge (1982), surveying the huge volume of research sponsored jointly by the Social Science Research Council and the Department of Health and Social Services in Britain in the 1970s, conclude that the concept is in fact slippery and fraught with problems. Researchers have adopted a wide range of operational definitions, measurement has proved extremely difficult, while the fact that deprivation may occur in several areas of social life diffuses the concept further. *Multiple deprivation* refers to the tendency noted in some studies for inequalities of access in different areas to overlap. Thus low income or unemployment may go together with poor housing, poor health and access to inferior education. The multiplication of deprivation seems particularly prevalent in inner-city areas in Britain. *Transmitted deprivation* refers to a view that deprivation is transmitted across generations. A popular stereotype is that inadequate parenting produces inadequate children, who in turn become inadequate parents. Sociologists suggest that individual attributes are less important than structured inequalities that persist over time. In fact, research shows that transmitted deprivation is less than was once thought. See: *Distribution of Income and Wealth*; *Poverty Trap*; *Relative Deprivation*; *Unemployment*; *Welfare State*.

Derivations. See: *Pareto.*

Descent Groups. A descent group is any social group in which membership depends on common descent from a real or mythical ancestor. Thus a lineage is a unilineal descent group in which membership may rest either on patrilineal descent (patrilineage) or on matrilineal descent (matrilineage). In cognatic descent, all descendants of an ancestor/ancestress enjoy membership of a common descent group by virtue of any combination of male or female linkages. However, cognatic descent is sometimes used synonymously with either 'bilateral' or 'consanguineal' descent. A clan is a unilineal descent group, the members of which may claim either patrilineal descent (patriclan) or matrilineal descent (matriclan) from a founder, but do not know the genealogical ties with the ancestor/ancestress. A phratry is a grouping of clans which are related by traditions of common descent. Mythical ancestors are thus common in clans and phratries. Totemic clans, in which membership is periodically reinforced by common rituals such as sacred meals, have been of special interest to social anthropologists and sociologists of religion. Where the descent groups of a society are organized into two main divisions, these are known as moieties (halves).

The analysis of descent groups is crucial for any anthropological study of pre-industrial society, but in most Western industrial societies the principle of descent is not prominent and descent groups are uncommon. In modern Britain, for example, we recognize our cognates as kin and surnames are patrilineally acquired, but there are no descent groups as such. See: *Endogamy*; *Exogamy*.

Bibl. Keesing (1975)

De-skilling. Several writers concerned with the social impact of technological change in the 1960s and 1970s, for example D. Bell (1974), believed that the average skill requirements of industrial work were being upgraded, with a consequential transformation of the occupational structure and an expansion of the middle class. H. Braverman (1974) rejected this view, suggesting that manual and lower-level non-manual jobs were being de-skilled. He believed that the strategy of employers was to reduce the skills required in their production processes, often by means of new technologies which simplified tasks. He saw the possession of skills as providing workers with power to resist managerial domination at work, because skilled workers were in short supply on the labour market and because production systems could not function without their expertise. Braverman saw employees becoming proletarianized rather than middle class.

Evaluation of these competing accounts involves several difficulties. (1) Skill is a social construct as well as a reference to real attributes of knowledge and/or manual dexterity, and is thus an ambiguous concept. Official occupational classifications often show the skill levels of jobs to be increasing, yet among lower-level occupations at least this apparent increase is mainly the result of a simple upwards reclassification of jobs whose 'real' skill level has not increased. (2) Some occupations resist de-skilling, notably the professions. Organized resistance may also affect definitions of skill; for example, some craft unions in Britain have successfully retained the skilled label for their members, who are paid accordingly by managers and keep their traditional craft control over certain aspects of the production process, even though the work has less 'real' skill than before. (3) There is a distinction between *jobs* and *workers*. Jobs may be de-skilled but for various reasons workers may not. When de-skilling takes place during periods of economic growth, the actual number of jobs available to skilled workers may increase even though they decline as a proportion of all jobs. De-skilling in the past often resulted from new industries with lower skill requirements growing alongside older ones: the loss of skills which might how through in statistics would not reflect any de-skilling of existing workers and jobs in existing industries and firms, but the changes in the industrial structure. See: *Automation*; *Labour Process Approach*; *Proletarianization*.

Bibl. Wood (ed.) (1982)

Determinism. Usually a term of abuse in sociology, determinism is used in several senses. (1) Theories are said to be deterministic to the extent that they emphasize the causal primacy of social structure to the exclusion of the autonomy or 'free-will' of the human subject. Explanations have to be sought in the nature of social structure, not in the characteristics of individuals. (2) Marxist sociology is often accused of using an economic determinism in which all social phenomena are explained in terms of the economic structure or relations of production (q.v.). (3) Technological determinist theories are those that suggest that social change is dependent on technological change. (4) Occasionally social scientists argue that social phenomena are to be explained by reference to biological or genetic characteristics. These would manifest a biological determinism. See: *Agency and Structure*; *Base and Superstructure*; *Methodological Individualism*; *Reductionism*; *Sociobiology*; *Technological Determinism*.

Deviancy Amplification. This term was originally coined by L. T. Wilkins (1964) who used the expression 'deviation amplification'. The concept is an important element within the sociological critique of conventional criminology (q.v.). It suggests that much of the alleged deviance in society is the unintended consequence of police control, mass-media coverage and popular reaction to deviant stereotypes. The theory suggests that distorted information and ignorance about minorities in a mass society (q.v.) produce inappropriate responses to perceived deviance. In turn, this distorting knowledge results in a further amplification of deviance. Thus, societal reaction and deviant response create a 'spiral of deviancy' by which relatively minor patterns of deviance may be amplified. The concept of deviancy amplification has been particularly useful in studies of police reaction to drug abuse and sexual offences. The theory of the spiral of deviancy has been criticized by J. Ditton (1979) for failing to show how these spirals are eventually terminated, diminished or abandoned. The theory of amplification was associated with labelling theory (q.v.) and the concept of stigma (q.v.) as an explanation of crime and deviance. In addition, it provided one basis for a critical sociology of the mass media (q.v.). While the theory may be particularly relevant to certain crimes (e.g. sexual offences), it may be inapplicable in others (e.g. murder). Public reaction to crime is in fact far more variable and ambiguous than deviancy theory would suggest. See: *Deviant Behaviour*; *Stereotypes*.

Bibl. Young, J. (1971)

Deviant Behaviour. The study of deviant behaviour or the sociology of deviance is most adequately understood as a reaction against criminology (q.v.). There are three important areas where criminology and the sociology of deviance sharply diverge.

Criminology has historically been largely concerned with the infraction of legal norms, whereas deviancy research has taken a much broader definition of deviance as any socially proscribed departure from 'normality'. Thus, many different forms of behaviour may be socially condemned or challenged even though the behaviour is not specifically illegal – foul language, keeping 'bad

company', habitual failure to keep appointments, and heavy drinking would be obvious examples. The sociology of deviance thus takes a far broader, more heterogeneous category of behaviour as its object of study than is the case for traditional criminology. It also tends to include any behaviour which is socially defined as 'deviant' as an operational definition. Deviancy studies have embraced a great diversity of behaviour from drug abuse to football hooliganism to witchcraft as behaviour which is labelled as deviant.

The second area of difference is that traditional criminology concentrated on the causes of crime which were seen to reside, as it were, within the individual criminal, whereas the sociology of deviance maintains that at least some categories of criminal behaviour are the result of the imposition of social control on subordinate or marginal social groups. Paradoxically the enforcement of law may have the unintended consequence of amplifying deviance in society. Deviancy theory has been particularly concerned with the role of criminal stereotypes and stigma (q.v.) in the creation of deviant careers.

Thirdly, there was little analytical distinction in criminology between the existence of crime in society, the criminal personality or character and the criminal act. It seemed that to explain why criminals existed was also to explain the presence of crime in society. The sociology of deviance suggests that the question of deviance in society and the making of a deviant should be kept analytically separate.

The criminological definition of crime as simple infractions of legal norms raises a variety of problems. Legal definitions are subject to change (with judges' decisions and with changes in legislation) so that 'crime' is an unstable, shifting phenomenon. On the other hand, the notion that deviance is simply any deviation from accepted, common normative standards implies that societies are, or must be, characterized by some normative consensus. An alternative view is that modern industrial society does not have any cultural uniformity or value consensus, but on the contrary is typified by a wide pluralism in values and norms. In this case, the distinction between 'normality' and 'deviance' becomes blurred and imprecise. The claim that 'deviance' is simply behaviour so labelled runs into similar difficulties. It presupposes that the social reaction to deviance is unambiguous and normally sufficient to confer a deviant stigma on the offender – in other words, it assumes some form of value consensus.

The assumption of a deviant identity is normally assumed to involve a successful process of stigmatization, social isolation, membership of a deviant subculture and acceptance of a deviant role. In this perspective, the deviant is the product of definite social processes which ostracize individuals from 'normal' roles and groups, forcing them to adopt deviant self-conceptions and restricting the availability of conventional roles and activities. Primary deviance, the initial infraction of social norms, leads through social isolation to secondary deviance. For example, if a person is sentenced for some sexual offence, such as homosexual abuse of children, this may severely limit the range of 'normal' sexual contacts such an individual might subsequently make. The isolation from normal sexual interaction may further increase the likelihood of additional deviance. In order to cope with social isolation and stigmatization, the deviant may find support in membership of a deviant subculture (q.v.) and thereby adopt the role of permanent deviancy. E. Lemert (1951; 1967) made the distinction between primary and secondary deviation in order to draw attention to the importance of social reactions to deviance. Individuals who commit deviant acts find that they need to cope with negative social reactions. The process of coping may involve individuals in redefining themselves in ways that promote further deviance.

Underlying this model is the idea of a career (q.v.). The deviant career may be seen as a process of development over time, leading through identifiable stages towards the end state of permanent deviancy. The end may be in doubt to participants until it is reached, but each stage of the unfolding career progression is recognized by the deviant and other people. As just described, career has a strong meaning: there is a conventional and structured pattern of rule-breaking which over time socializes an individual into deviance. A weaker use is simply that any deviance can be described after the event as having a pattern. While the strong version may help us to understand deviant careers in sexual and drug offenders, it is less relevant to other forms of crime such as murder. It also assumes that deviants uniformly accept and adopt external social labels as personal self-conceptions. There has been very little exploration of the possible conflicts and contradictions between such social labels and personal identities in the social formation of the deviant. The limitations of the symbolic interactionist paradigm, however, have brought into prominence the need for a theory of deviance which incorporates the notion of 'social control' as a central feature. See: *Addiction*; *Becker*; *Career*; *Deviancy Amplification*; *Delinquency*; *Delinquent Drift*; *Differential Association*; *Gang*; *Goffman*; *Labelling Theory*; *Moral Panic*; *Norm*; *Social Problems*; *Stereotypes*; *Subculture*; *Symbolic Interactionism*.

Bibl. Taylor, Walton and Young (1973); Downes and Rock (1982)

Deviant Subculture. See: *Subculture*.

Diachronic. Although originally used specifically in linguistics, diachronic is now more widely used to refer to the analysis of change, while *synchronic* refers to the analysis of static states.

Dialectical Materialism. Materialism (q.v.) rejects idealist explanations of social and other phenomena and suggests that *all* phenomena are material. The notion of *dialectic* expresses the view that development depends on the clash of contradictions and the creation of a new, more advanced synthesis out of these clashes. The dialectical process involves the three moments: thesis, antithesis and synthesis. K. Marx used the notion to account for social and historical events, but Engels extended the scope of dialectical analysis so far as to establish it as a general law of development that applied equally in social, natural and intellectual spheres. He believed both that the real world, whether of society or nature, developed according to dialectical sequences of contradiction and synthesis, and that dialectical logic was the means by which one could comprehend this development. See: *Engels*; *Historical Materialism*.
Bibl. Kolakowski (1978a)

Differential Association. A general theory of criminal behaviour developed by E. H. Sutherland (1934) on the basis of an earlier theory by G. Tarde. It attempts to explain crime in terms of cultural transmission; crime is learned within primary groups whose members are criminally inclined. People become criminal as a consequence of an excess of social definitions favourable to crime over unfavourable definitions. The theory is in fact more concerned with differential definitions than differential association. It was subsequently developed and expanded by D. R. Cressey (1955) and D. Glaser (1956). The theory was further revised by Sutherland and Cressey (1955). The theory was important as a critique of explanations which treated criminals as abnormal persons, because it located the cause of crime in general social processes. While the theory is valuable in the study of professional criminals who have a deviant career, it is less relevant in the case of crimes like homicide which are typically single, isolated acts. See: *Criminology*; *Deviant Behaviour*.
Bibl. Lemert (1967)

Differentiation. A notion with a long history in sociology, differentiation is mainly used in theories of social change. It refers to a process whereby sets of social activities performed by one social institution become split up between different institutions. Differentiation represents an increasing specialization of the parts of a society, giving greater heterogeneity within the society. For example, whereas the family once had reproductive, economic and educational functions, in modern societies specialized institutions of work and education have developed outside the family.

For classical nineteenth-century sociology, differentiation was an important concept in the analysis of social change and in the comparison of industrial and pre-industrial societies. There was often an explicit analogy between the social and the biological. For H. Spencer (q.v.), for example, differentiation was a necessary accompaniment of the growth in size of both biological and social aggregates. As units grow, there must be differentiation of structures if the unit is to survive. With increased specialization of parts, there is a corresponding requirement for a greater interdependence and integration of parts.

Contemporary analyses continue classical themes by tying differentiation to functionalist or evolutionary theories of social change. T. Parsons (q.v.), for example, argues that social evolution has proceeded by variation and differentiation from simple to progressively more complex forms. He shows that social systems (q.v.) differentiate into sub-systems, each of which has distinct functions with respect to various environments which include other sub-systems. This process continues over time, producing a greater range of sub-systems, each with its own peculiar structure and function, all tending to the general enhancement of adaptive capacity.

A good example of the empirical use of the concept of differentiation is that provided by N. Smelser (1959). He tries to analyse nineteenth-century industrialization in terms of the differentiation of family structure in relation to the changing economy. There is a sequence of change where an existing structure generates discontent which eventually leads to a more differentiated structure.

There are some similarities between the concepts of differentiation and division of labour (q.v.), except that the latter mainly concentrates on the specialization of tasks within the economic sphere. Occasionally differentiation is used, not as a concept in theories of social change, but to indicate the way in which various groups in a society are separated from one another and ranked along a hierarchy of status or wealth. In this sense it is equivalent to social stratification (q.v.). See: *Comte*; *Division of Labour*; *Durkheim*; *Evolutionary Theory*; *International Division of Labour*; *Organic Analogy*.

Bibl. Parsons (1966)

Diploma Disease. See: *Credentialism*.

Discourse. This is a domain of language-use that is unified by common assumptions. For example, M. Foucault (q.v.) describes the existence of discourses of madness – ways of talking and thinking about madness – which have changed over the centuries. In the early medieval period, the mad were not seen as threatening but almost as possessing an inner wisdom. In the twentieth century the discourse of madness emphasizes the condition as an illness in need of treatment. In the intervening centuries there have been other discourses of madness, treating madness and the mad in quite different ways. For Foucault there may also be similarities (or articulations) between discourses of different topics at any one time. He suggests that the discourse of political economy in the eighteenth and nineteenth centuries, for instance, takes the same *form* as the discourse of natural history. However, it is also important to stress that, although discourses may overlap or reinforce each other, they may also conflict. For example, at certain moments in the history of Western societies, different and often contradictory discourses of the individual have coexisted, some of which stress a freedom to act, others of which emphasize the individual's duty to society.

Sociological attention also concentrates on the social function of discourses, most importantly on their ability to close off possibilities. Within a discourse, there are literally some things that cannot be said or thought. This means that discourses may have an effect similar to that of ideology. That is, a discourse, as a ready-made way of thinking, can rule out alternative ways of thinking and hence preserve a particular distribution of power. See: *Ideology*; *Madness*.

Discrimination. See: *Prejudice*.

Three Types of Distribution

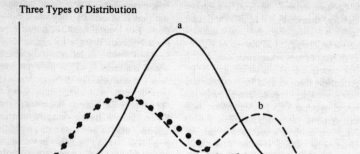

(a) Unimodal Symmetrical
(b) Bimodal
(c) Skewed

Distribution. In statistics this refers to the set of values, together with their relative frequencies, of any variable, often expressed graphically. Sociologists need to ascertain and then explain the particular shape of any distribution. The diagram above shows three common types of distribution.

A commonly encountered unimodal symmetrical distribution is the *normal* distribution with mean 0 and variance 1. This forms the basis of probability theory and many important statistical measures derive from its mathematical characteristics, including the measure of variability known as the standard deviation (q.v.). Empirically, distributions in many different situations often do closely approximate this normal distribution.

Distribution of Income and Wealth. The spread of material resources among the population is an important indicator of social inequality, while changes in this distribution over time indicate whether society is becoming more or less equal. The investigation of the spread of per-

sonal income and wealth, however, is fraught with difficulty because of inaccuracies in the data, the problem of deciding the relevant unit of analysis (whether to use individuals, families or households), how to assess the non-monetary benefits derived from government expenditure, and the way individuals' positions may change over the life-cycle.

Between 1974 and 1979, the Royal Commission on the Distribution of Income and Wealth conducted a comprehensive investigation of the position in Britain. On *income* distribution, the Commission used data from income tax returns, which do not provide a completely reliable coverage of either income or the population in receipt of income, and supplemented these with information from other sources such as the Family Expenditure Survey and the New Earnings Survey. It reached these conclusions: (1) In 1976–7, the spread of pre-tax income from all sources (earnings from employment and self-employment, pensions, cash benefits, investment income and rent) was such that the upper half of the population received 75·9 per cent of all income while the lower half received 24·1 per cent, and the top decile (ten per cent) of the population received 26·2 per cent while the bottom decile received 2·5 per cent. Taxation reduced inequality somewhat, the share of the upper half declining to 73·1 per cent after tax and that of the top decile to 23·2 per cent, the lower half's share rising to 26·9 per cent and that of the bottom decile to 3·0 per cent. More recent data show a slight widening of the gap between top and bottom in the period 1976–83, for both pre- and post-tax incomes. (2) To establish trends over time, income tax data alone provide a long enough series, so the figures are less accurate and differ slightly from those cited above, but they do indicate trends: between 1949 and 1976–7, the distribution of earnings after tax became slightly less unequal, with the top decile's share declining from 27·1 per cent to 22·4 per cent while the bottom half increased its share from 26·5 per cent to 27·6 per cent. (3) Taking households as the units of analysis instead of individuals and adjusting for the different needs of differing households, disparities in the after-tax distribution of income are further reduced: the top decile had only 21·4 per cent of the total and the bottom decile had 4·3 per cent in 1976–7.

Wealth distribution is more difficult to investigate because of the greater unreliability of the data, which depend largely on estate tax returns that are inaccurate and so require extensive adjustment, the difficulty of establishing a consistent set of data over time, and the problem of whether to define wealth simply as marketable assets or to include non-marketable assets (for example, the capital value of state and occupational pension schemes). Taking marketable assets as the measure, the Commission's evidence suggested a number of con-

clusions. (1) Personal wealth has been even less equally distributed than income: in 1976, the top 1 per cent of the population alone owned 25 per cent of all personal wealth, the top decile owned 60 per cent, and the bottom 80 per cent of the population had but 23 per cent. (2) The trend until the late 1970s was towards less inequality: the share of the top 1 per cent has declined since 1923 when it was about 60 per cent of personal wealth; as recently as 1966 the top decile owned a 68 per cent share. However, the evidence may not be a reliable measure of the trend, partly because of data errors and partly because of fluctuations in asset prices (notably the value of company shares and to a lesser extent land values) which may be expected to have a significant impact on the share of the top 1 per cent at any particular moment. With the rise in these asset values since 1976, inequality has stabilized and shown no further decline. (3) The reduction in inequality has stemmed in part from the wider distribution of home ownership. (4) The ingredients of wealth differ for different groups: the top 1 per cent relies far more on company shares and land than the remainder of the top decile, for whom homes and life assurance policies are more significant. (5) Inheritance is the major source of wealth among the top 1 per cent, and appears to account for about a quarter of the total personal wealth in the population as a whole. (6) High income earners spend part of their incomes in savings and other forms of capital accumulation and over their working lifetimes can accumulate wealth in sizeable amounts by the standards of the bottom 80 per cent of the population, though not by those of the top 1 per cent. (7) Bringing in pensions, by assigning them a capital value even though they are not marketable assets when provided by the state or an occupational pension scheme, virtually doubled the share of the bottom 80 per cent of the population, to 45 per cent of all personal wealth in 1976. See: *Class*; *Poverty*; *Stratification*; *Welfare State*.

Bibl. Atkinson, A. B. (ed.) (1980); Royal Commission on the Distribution of Income and Wealth (1980); *Social Trends 16* (1986)

Division of Labour. This concept has been used in three ways: (1) in the sense of the *technical* division of labour it describes the production process; (2) as the *social* division of labour, it refers to differentiation in society as a whole; (3) as the *sexual* division of labour, it describes social divisions between men and women.

(1) The eighteenth-century economist A. Smith (1776) used this term to refer to the extreme specialization in the process of production that results from minutely subdividing work into limited operations performed by separate workers. He recommended this technique to raise the productivity of labour, by increasing people's dexterity as they endlessly repeated one simple task, reducing time lost in shifting between tasks, and simplifying operations in a way that facilitated the introduction of machinery. C. Babbage (1832) noted another advantage: the separation of work into components, some of which were simpler than others and all of which were simpler than the whole. This enabled the employer to purchase cheaper (less skilled) labour to do the simpler jobs instead of using expensive, skilled workers to do the whole process as before. The division of labour thus forms the basis of modern industrial production.

For K. Marx, in his early writings, the division of labour produced social conflict and was a primary cause of social class inequality, private property and alienation (q.v.). In capitalist society, it destroyed all the interesting and creative aspects of work, leaving only boring and repetitive operations. In his later works, he suggested that the technical division of labour was required in any industrial society, and would continue even under socialism and the abolition of private property and inequality, indicating that class and the division of labour were separate phenomena. Some Marxist sociologists assert that the extreme division of labour found in many firms is not technically required for efficiency and that managers use it to increase their power in the workplace by weakening the control over production of skilled operatives. Unlike specialization which allows those with the greatest aptitude to do various expert activities, the division of labour tries to reduce all specialisms to simple components which anyone can do.

(2) While A. Comte (q.v.) recognized that the division of labour tended to increase social solidarity by creating mutual relations of dependence between individuals, he also emphasized negative aspects of the process which were divisive of society. Following this view, E. Durkheim thought that the division of labour in modern societies created a new basis for social integration which he called 'organic solidarity'. The growing complexity and differentiation of society created a new basis of reciprocity arising from socio-economic specialization rather than from commonly held beliefs.

(3) While in classical political economy the concept referred to the specialization of technical and economic processes, some modern sociologists have extended and elaborated the concept to include, for example, the sexual division of labour, the division of activities and roles between men and women. While this sexual division is often explained biologically by reference to the reproductive functions of women, feminists see these

divisions as an effect of patriarchy (q.v.) and as a feature of the separation of the domestic domain and the public sphere in capitalist society. See: *De-skilling*; *Differentiation*; *Domestic Labour*; *Dual Labour Markets*; *Durkheim*; *Evolutionary Theory*; *International Division of Labour*; *Labour Process Approach*; *Marx*; *Mental/Manual Division*; *Scientific Management*.

Divorce. This term denotes the dissolution of a valid marriage while both partners are still alive, who are then free to remarry. Divorce rates have increased markedly in most industrial societies in recent times, from less than 3 people per thousand of the married population in Britain in 1961 to nearly 12 people per thousand in 1981. For approximately every three marriages per year there is one divorce in Britain. Rates vary: people who marry in their teens or early twenties are more likely to divorce than those who marry later; people whose parents have divorced are more likely to divorce; marriages across class or ethnic divisions have a higher divorce rate. The increased propensity to divorce does not necessarily reflect any growth in family disorganization, because it appears that many marriages used effectively to break down though they did not end in divorce. Legal changes have made divorce easier, in particular the 1971 Divorce Reform Act which added irretrievable marriage breakdown as a reason for divorce to the older notion of matrimonial offence, when one or both parties had to be 'guilty' of cruelty or adultery. Social values have also changed and now sanction divorce as an appropriate response to marital disorganization. Legal and attitudinal changes explain much of the higher incidence of divorce. Marriage, however, remains a popular institution and remarriage among divorcees is common: one or both parties

to every third marriage in 1979 had previously been married and divorced.

Sociological interest in divorce comes from those who treat it as a form of anomie (q.v.) that involves a loss of normative regulation for the individual or society, and those who are concerned with the practical consequences that divorce creates for individuals in terms of financial and social difficulties. Sociologists have mainly concentrated on women and divorce, and little is known about men's reactions to this event. See: *Marriage*.

Bibl. Hart (1976); Haralambos (1980)

Domestic Division of Labour. See: *Domestic Labour*.

Domestic Labour. This term refers to those tasks in the household, performed by men and women, that are needed to keep it going from day to day, including cooking, cleaning, child care and looking after the sick and elderly. The domestic division of labour, that is the allocation of domestic tasks between men and women, is notably unequal with women taking on the very much greater burden. There is not a great deal of evidence that it is becoming any more equal or that women are spending less time at domestic labour. The introduction of machines of various kinds, for example, has not helped greatly, for this has often meant the transfer of a task from men to women as it has become mechanized, and women have set higher standards which their family come to expect. Nor has the growth of women's paid employment outside the home altered the division and women continue to perform the same domestic chores as well as working outside.

The division of labour between men and women in the home is reproduced in employment, for women also tend to have routine and badly paid jobs. Furthermore, women's domestic work is largely unpaid, although it is absolutely necessary for society for people to be fed, cared for and reproduced. Two interpretations have been offered of this apparent paradox. Firstly, it has been argued that women are exploited by men who have services performed for them free of charge. Secondly, a number of writers have suggested that women's work, and the institutions of the family generally, serve a function for capitalism in feeding, clothing and caring for workers (and future workers) without any cost: it is capital that exploits women. See: *Conjugal Roles*; *Nuclear Family*; *Patriarchy*; *Sexual Divisions*; *Symmetrical Family*.

Bibl. Oakley (1974); Barrett (1980)

Dominant Ideology Thesis. Modern Marxists frequently explain the political passivity of subordinate classes as the consequence of ideological incorporation. They interpret K. Marx as claiming that the ruling class everywhere establishes its own ideology as dominant in society, and that this indoctrinates subordinates who uncritically accept it as true. The thesis has been criticized both on theoretical grounds, that it is not a correct interpretation of what Marx actually believed, and empirically, that throughout history subordinate groups have developed their own beliefs and frequently rejected those of dominant classes. See: *Gramsci*; *Hegemony*; *Ideology*; *Incorporation*; *Social Order*.

Bibl. Abercrombie *et al.* (1980)

Dore, Ronald P. (b. 1925). Presently director of the Centre for Japanese and Comparative Industrial Research, and Visiting Professor at Imperial College, London, he has made a major contribution to the understanding of modern Japan in *City Life in Japan* (1958), *Land Reform in Japan* (1959), *Education in Tokugawa Japan* (1965),

British Factory, Japanese Factory (1973), *Shinohata* (1978) and *Flexible Rigidities* (1986). He has also written on economic development and, in *The Diploma Disease* (1976), on the role of education in developing societies. See: *Credentialism*.

Dramaturgical. This approach within symbolic interactionism (q.v.) is particularly associated with E. Goffman (q.v.). The basic idea is that in interaction people put on a 'show' for each other, stage-managing the impressions that others receive. Social roles are thus analogous to those in a theatre. Thus people project images of themselves, usually in ways that best serve their own ends, because such information helps to define the situation and create appropriate expectations. See: *Sociodrama*.

Dual Career Families. Families in which both husband and wife have careers (q.v.).

Dual Consciousness. People are said to manifest a dual consciousness when they hold two apparently inconsistent sets of beliefs at the same time. The term is most commonly applied to members of the working class in contemporary European societies, who have sets of beliefs formed by the dominant culture through the educational system as well as different sets of beliefs generated by the experience of work and working-class life. The former type of belief is typically revealed in questionnaire research which tends to ask abstract questions, while the latter shows most clearly in practical activities. For example, it has been shown that many people will say, in response to social survey interviewers, that they disapprove of unofficial strikes, while participating in such strikes at their own workplace. See: *Class Consciousness*; *Dominant Ideology Thesis*; *Gramsci*;

Pragmatic Acceptance; *Working Class.*

Dual Economy. This term was originally associated with J. H. Boeke's analysis in the early twentieth century of economic growth in underdeveloped nations. European-owned plantations in Java, run along rational and efficient capitalist lines, coexisted with an indigenous agrarian economy where peasants made no effort to emulate the European model. This was a dual economy of advanced and backward sectors which remained distinct. Europeans were dominated by economic needs whereas the Javanese peasants had social needs. The economic laws valid for capitalist societies were not valid for dual economies where capitalism coexisted with a peasant economy embodying precapitalist social values and relationships. His theory is not entirely accepted, but his description of economies segmented into advanced and backward sectors continues to inform the study of developing societies.

More recently the idea of dualism has been applied *within* advanced capitalist economies, notably Japan and the United States. The structure of both economies is thought to embrace a 'core' sector of corporations that are large, prosperous and stable, and have sufficient economic power to manipulate their environments in order to reduce the disruptive effects of competition. There are also 'peripheries' of smaller, less prosperous and less stable firms. Where the two sectors relate, the relationship is asymmetrical because some firms on the periphery may depend on large corporations for business, whereas the latter do not depend on the former. See: *Centre/Periphery*; *Dependency*; *Dual Labour Markets*; *Internal Colonialism*.

Bibl. Averitt (1968)

Dual Labour Markets. Economists now believe that national labour markets comprise interrelated yet non-competing submarkets. Dual labour market models suggest that there are primary and secondary markets. *Primary* markets are composed of jobs which offer high wages, career structures (albeit with low ceilings for manual employees), the chance to acquire skills on the job, and stable and secure employment. Internal labour markets are often held to be characteristic of primary employment. In these, firms recruit from outside for certain fairly low positions and then fill higher-level vacancies by the promotion of existing employees. *Secondary* labour market jobs provide low wages, few possibilities for advancement or the acquisition of skills, and unstable, insecure employment. To some extent the primary/secondary labour market division corresponds to the divisions within the dual economy (q.v.): 'core' firms tend to offer primary jobs and peripheral firms to offer secondary ones. The overlap is not complete because 'core' firms may also offer secondary jobs. In the United States, where the dual labour market is highly developed and well documented, certain groups of workers tend to get jobs in one market rather than another: ethnic minorities and women are more likely to be selected for secondary jobs; white males for primary ones.

Institutional economists such as P. B. Doeringer and M. J. Piore (1971) attribute duality mainly to technological factors: advanced technology is believed to require firm-specific skills and stable labour forces, which in turn lead firms to offer training and to commit workers to their jobs by means of high pay, a career structure and good benefits. Because technological demands are not constant for all jobs within a firm, companies frequently work with a mix of primary and secondary markets. Women and minorities are stereotyped as making

77

insufficiently reliable and stable employees, which is why they are discriminated against and excluded from the better jobs. Job changing and absenteeism have tended on average to be higher among these groups, hence employers' stereotypes. But it may be the case that an apparent lack of job commitment follows from the inferior jobs on offer in the secondary market rather than the characteristics of employees. Equally, the labour-force attachment of women now seems to be changing, since women work for more of their lifetime than in the past and, when they are working, do not appear to change jobs any more often than men. Oligopolistic product markets are needed if firms are to pass on the extra costs of creating a privileged stratum. Radicals such as M. Reich *et al.* (1973), who prefer *segmented* to 'dual' because there are more than just two submarkets, suggest that segmentation is a managerial strategy of divide-and-rule. Because 'monopoly' capitalism in the twentieth century created larger enterprises, standardized production methods and de-skilled craftwork, the working class began to grow more homogeneous and potentially more able to organize collectively against capital. Management has therefore created artificial divisions and bought off a large segment of labour in order to prevent organized class struggle. Neither account of segmentation gives much weight to trade unionism, yet experience in America and elsewhere is that unions and professional associations also help to develop and maintain segmentation, insisting that companies adopt employment practices that are beneficial to their members and protecting their members against competition from new arrivals on the labour market. Institutional and radical economists distinguish between upper and lower parts of the primary market. The lower comprises manual and lower white-collar employees who lack transferable skills and are therefore dependent on their employers. The upper section comprises managers, professionals and certain craftsmen with transferable skills, who are not tied to a single employer and move among firms seeking the best deal.

Sociologists now take account of segmentation in the analysis of internal stratification within the working class, the study of the position of women and ethnic minorities in employment, and accounts of work and industrial relations. There is evidence that market segmentation is fairly universal, so that men and women, for example, tend to be employed in different sectors. Outside the USA and Japan, however, there is less evidence of the prevalence of some of the features of primary markets that are postulated by economists, namely internal labour markets, career ladders, and skill acquisition. Segmentation models differ from the labour process approach (q.v.) which claims that labour *has* been homogenized. See: *Career*; *De-skilling*; *Human Capital*; *Labour Aristocracy*; *Sexual Divisions*; *Stereotypes*; *Underclass*; *Women and Work*; *Working Class*.

Bibl. Edwards (1979); Amsden (ed.) (1980); Berg (ed.) (1981); Gordon *et al.* (1982)

Durkheim, Emile (1858–1917). He is widely acknowledged as a 'founding father' of modern sociology who helped to define the subject matter and establish the autonomy of sociology as a discipline. He taught first at the University of Bordeaux and then at the Sorbonne in Paris.

He was greatly influenced by the French intellectual tradition of J.-J. Rousseau, C. H. Saint-Simon (q.v.) and A. Comte (q.v.). His work is marked by an opposition to the utilitarian tradition in British social thought, which explained social phenomena by reference to the actions and motives of individuals. He adopted a collectivist perspective throughout his sociological analysis. He denied that the utilitarian version of individualism could provide the basis on which to build a stable society. He also asserted that the sociological method was to deal with social facts (q.v.).

In his first major work, *The Division of Labour in Society* (1893), he argued against the British writer H. Spencer that social order in industrial societies could not adequately be explained as an outcome of contractual agreements between individuals motivated by self-interest, because the pursuit of self-interest would lead to social instability, as manifest in various forms of social deviance such as suicide. He distinguished the forms of social order found in primitive and modern societies. Mechanical solidarity in primitive societies was based on the common beliefs and consensus found in the *conscience collective* (q.v.). As societies industrialized and urbanized and became more complex, the increasing division of labour destroyed mechanical solidarity and moral integration, thus rendering social order problematic. He was well aware at the time he was writing that industrial societies exhibited many conflicts and that force was an important factor in preventing social disruption. He believed, however, that a new form of order would arise in advanced societies on the basis of organic solidarity. This would comprise the interdependence of economic ties arising out of differentiation and specialization within the modern economy, a new network of occupational associations such as guilds that would link individuals to the state, and the emergence within these associations of collectively created moral restraints on egoism. T. Parsons (1937; 1968a) interpreted organic solidarity as the continuation of the *con-*

science collective in a modified form, suggesting that Durkheim's analysis of social order in modern society demanded a prior consensus and moral order, and this view has proved influential. Evidence for this interpretation can be drawn from a variety of Durkheim's publications. For example, in two pamphlets written during the First World War Durkheim noted that the communal experience of warfare had created a moral consensus in France and involvement in public ceremonies which resembled religious festivals. In his sociology of religion, Durkheim also argued that modern society would require some form of *conscience collective* relevant to contemporary circumstances – an argument clearly dependent on Saint-Simon's conception of the New Christianity. However, it is difficult to reconcile this view of the continuing importance of religious values in modern societies, which Durkheim appears to have accepted towards the end of his life, with the argument of *The Division of Labour in Society* which recognized the importance of economic reciprocity (q.v.) in creating social consensus. There has been considerable controversy over the continuity of the theme of moral consensus in Durkheim's sociology. Parsons (1937) argued that the early emphasis on social facts in a positivistic framework collapsed as Durkheim adopted a voluntaristic action framework. An alternative view suggests that the central theme of Durkheim's sociology was the idea of moral compulsion and normative constraint. The changes in Durkheim's epistemology did not produce significant discontinuities in his sociology of moral life.

He saw the domain of sociology as the study of social facts and not individuals. He believed both that societies had their own realities which could not simply be reduced to the actions and motives of individuals, and that individuals were moulded and constrained by their social environments. In 1895 he wrote *The Rules of Sociological Method*, in which he demonstrated that law was a social fact, embodied in formal, codified rules and not dependent on individuals or on any particular act of law enforcement for its existence.

In *Suicide* (1897), he explained how even apparently individual decisions to commit suicide could be understood as being affected by the different forms of social solidarity in different social settings. He identified four types of suicide (q.v.) on the basis of his analysis of the suicide statistics of different societies and different groups within them. 'Egotistic' and 'anomic' forms of suicide were most commonly found in modern societies where, as *The Division of Labour in Society* had previously shown, traditional forms of social regulation and integration like the *conscience collective* of mechanical solidarity had declined. The higher incidence of 'egotistic' suicides among modern Protestants than Catholics reflected an individualistic ethos in which individuals were responsible for their own salvation. 'Anomic' suicides occurred when the individual experienced a state of normlessness or when norms conflicted. Both forms were to be found when the social checks on individual behaviour typical of traditional societies had lost their force. In primitive societies and in armies in modern societies, where mechanical solidarity was stronger, 'altruistic' suicides for the good of the group were more common. Fatalistic suicides, for example among slaves, were the result of excessive social regulation. Although there have been major criticisms of his approach (Atkinson, 1978), Durkheim's *Suicide* represents the most influential sociological contribution to this issue.

He came to see social norms as regulating people's behaviour by means of institutionalized values which the individual internalized, rather than society simply acting as an external constraint. In 1912, in *The Elementary Forms of the Religious Life*, he suggested that primitive religions embodied the idea of society and that sacred objects were so because they symbolized the community. Religious culture consisted of the collective values which comprised a society's unity and personality. Religious ceremonies served to reinforce collective values and reaffirm community among individuals. This process was clearly identifiable in primitive societies, though Durkheim recognized how difficult it was to find similar sacred objects and collective rituals in modern organic societies. His approach to the sacred/profane dichotomy represents a major alternative to arguments about secularization (q.v.). Durkheim was concerned to understand the universal functions of religious systems for the continuity of society as such. In *Primitive Classification* (1903), written with M. Mauss, he argued that the fundamental categories of human thought, such as number, time and space, were modelled upon features of social organization.

In his political writings he expressed concern at the dangers to society of individuals who do not feel that social norms are meaningful to them, who are in a state of anomie (q.v.). He saw the attraction of socialism to the working class as a protest against the disintegration of traditional social bonds and values, rather than as a desire for the abolition of private property *per se*. He advocated guild socialism as a means of rebuilding cohesive and solidary social communities. See: *Differentiation*; *Division of Labour*; *Guild*; *Norm*; *Official Statistics*; *Religion*; *Sacred*; *Social Order*; *Social Pathology*; *Suicide*.

Bibl. Lukes (1972); Giddens (1978)

Dysfunction. A social activity or institution has dysfunctions when some of its consequences impede the workings of another social activity or institution. Any particular activity may have dysfunctions for one other activity and *eufunctions* (helpful functions) for another or, indeed, a mixture of dysfunctions and eufunctions for the same activity. See: *Functionalism.*

E

Ecological Fallacy. This is the fallacy of drawing conclusions about individual people from data that refer only to aggregates. For example, sociologists often conduct their studies by comparing the social characteristics of collectivities. The relationship between voting and social class might be studied by comparing a geographical area with a high proportion of, say, manual workers with one containing a high proportion of professional managerial workers, and seeing how many votes each political party receives in each area. This is a permissible technique, because some evidence of a connection between the social class composition of an area and voting behaviour can be established. However, such a study would commit the ecological fallacy if it led to imputations about *individual* voting behaviour on the basis of data that derived from collections of individuals.

Ecology. See: *Suicide*; *Urban Ecology*.

Economic Determinism or **Economic Reductionism.** See: *Determinism*; *Economism*; *Reductionism*.

Economic Sociology. The study of the relations between the economic and non-economic aspects of social life was central to the interests of most sociologists in the nineteenth and early twentieth centuries. The intellectual dominance of functionalism (q.v.) and cultural sociology in the mid twentieth century led to a declining interest in economic activities, which continued until the 1970s when sociologists rediscovered in M. Weber and K. Marx the central place of the economy in the understanding of society. Economic sociology is a generic title covering various theoretical traditions and areas of substantive interest, neither a distinct 'school' nor a narrowly limited area.

Economism. This term has two distinct meanings in Marxist sociology, both pejorative. (1) Economism in the sense of economic reductionism explains all social, political and cultural activity in terms of the economic base, which denies the 'superstructure' any independent significance. A related meaning is that the key to the subordination of one class by another is found in the organization of production. (2) A variant meaning widely used in industrial sociology describes the class consciousness (q.v.) and aspirations of the working class as economistic, when workers' activities are geared to improving their material conditions within capitalism rather than to its overthrow. This variant is similar to the use of 'trade-union consciousness' by V. I. Lenin (1902). See: *Base and Superstructure*; *Determinism*; *Leninism*; *Marxist Sociology*; *Reductionism*; *Trade Unions*.

Education, Sociology of. See: *Sociology of Education*.

Educational Attainment. Despite formal equality of opportunity and access to education, levels of educational attainment vary systematically within Western societies. Children from lower social class families do less well than those from higher, and girls do less well than boys. Because of the linkage between educational qualifications and occupations, sociologists concerned with social mobility (q.v.) and class (q.v.) have been especially interested to explain class variations in attainment.

British educational sociologists in the 1950s and 1960s identified a number of factors affecting social class differences in attainment. (1) The organization of schooling, with selection on the basis of a competitive examination (the 11 +) for different types of public secondary school and the streaming of children within schools, was one factor. The spread of comprehensive schools since the late 1960s has largely ended selection in public education, while the point at which streaming takes place has been raised in many schools. Comprehensive education has not existed for long enough to ascertain its effect on attainment. But the continuation of private selective schools (accounting for 8·2 per cent of British schoolchildren in 1980) and streaming may perpetuate class differences. The experience of countries with longer comprehensive traditions, with less emphasis on streaming and with relatively smaller private sectors, such as the USA, suggests that systematic differ-

ences in attainment may survive changes in the overall organization of the school system. Research in Britain by M. Rutter *et al.* (1979) indicates that even within one type of school (comprehensive), differences in the internal organization of individual schools will lead to different levels of achievement in public examinations. (2) Teachers' expectations were thought to be influential, since teachers appeared to expect higher levels of achievement from middle-class pupils than working-class ones, and pupils responded to these different expectations. Moreover, middle-class children shared the same culture as middle-class teachers. (3) Working-class culture was thought to be one of cultural deprivation (q.v.), marked by low aspirations for educational attainment in family and community, and embodying a restricted code (q.v.). The second and third factors emphasized cultural phenomena as important sources of difference, and this emphasis has been continued in more recent treatments of classroom interaction (q.v.), classroom knowledge (q.v.) and cultural reproduction (q.v.).

Gender differences have recently attracted the attention of sociologists, though they are less well researched than class differentials. In Britain, girls do better than boys until adolescence and gain more passes at Ordinary level and CSE. But they do less well at Advanced level and are less likely to attend university. They are also less likely than boys to study mathematics, sciences or engineering. These inequalities, however, are declining. Attainment differences have often been explained by the sexual division of labour outside school. In a society where a woman's primary role is domestic, as housewife and mother, and where women's work is inferior to men's and takes second place to domestic commitments, girls are socialized with different expectations from boys'. Schools may reinforce these expectations via the hidden curriculum (q.v.). S. Sharpe (1979) has suggested that teachers will treat boys and girls differently, acting on the stereotype that girls should be submissive and passive, and that their primary adult roles will be domestic. In addition, girls are expected to study 'feminine' subjects, which do not include mathematics, physics or engineering. In coeducational schools, boys reinforce these stereotypes so that girls experience pressure to conform from teachers and peers alike. The slow reduction in attainment differentials suggests, however, that sociologists have not yet fully explained gender differences. See: *Bernstein*; *Equality*; *Intelligence*; *Nature*/*Nurture Debate*; *Peer Group*; *Sponsored Mobility*; *Stereotypes*; *Women and Work*.

Bibl. Banks (1976); Stanworth (1983).

Egoism. See: *Suicide*.

Elaborated Code. See: *Restricted Code*.

Elias, Norbert (b. 1897). After fleeing from Germany in 1933, Elias held academic posts in sociology at the universities of Leicester (1954–62) and Ghana (1962–64). He was also professor emeritus at the University of Frankfurt and visiting professor at the Institute of Interdisciplinary Research at the University of Bielefeld. His major work (*Über den Prozess der Zivilisation*) was neglected at the time of publication in 1939, but has subsequently come to be regarded as a classic of historical sociology since its recent publication as *The Civilizing Process* (1939a and 1939b). His major interest has been the pacification of medieval society through the development of individual, moral forms of restraint in codes such as table-manners and etiquette. The development of the state as a system of social regulation has been accompanied by the emergence of civilized systems of self-control. In *The Court Society* (1969), he studied the evolution of ceremony in the French court before the Revolution, the economic decline of aristocratic society as a result of its internal competition for influence, and the emergence of bourgeois society. The impact of individual norms of restraint on the process of dying in a secular society has been outlined in *The Loneliness of the Dying* (1982). He has also made important contributions to theoretical problems in sociology. For example, in *What is Sociology?* (1970) he developed the idea of figurational analysis; the reciprocity between people creates the figurations of social interaction which develop in ways which are unplanned. Concepts like group or community refer to figurations of interdependent individuals. His contribution to the sociology of knowledge has been published in *Involvement and Detachment* (1986).

Elite. This refers to a minority group which has power or influence over others and is recognized as being in some way superior. The sociology of elites has traditionally dealt with the ruling elites within societies, as in the work of V. Pareto (q.v.) and G. Mosca (q.v.), or within organizations as in the study of political parties conducted by R. Michels (q.v.). The assumption has been that there will always be a divide between the rulers and the ruled or those with power and those without, even in nominally democratic societies and institutions. Ruling elites vary in the extent to which they are open to outside influences: in some societies elites recruit new members from the non-elite and/or are open to pressures from below, whereas elsewhere elites may be less open to outside recruits and influence. Elites also vary in the extent to which they are integrated into socially cohesive or solidary groups. The traditional sociological model of the United States was of a plurality of elites in different spheres which remained unintegrated and acted as checks and balances on each other. C. W. Mills (q.v.), however, has claimed to have found a well-integrated and partly self-perpetuating power elite. He has noted that the top groups in political, economic and military organizations are linked by ties of family and friendship and share common social backgrounds.

Ruling elites are sometimes distinguished from ruling classes in terms of the fluidity of their membership and the way outside pressures influence them. This is a poor criterion, since some elites are not fluid or open and the concept of class (q.v.) does not entail that dominant classes do not recruit from lower classes or remain uninfluenced by outside pressures. The difference between class and elite rests largely on the fact that classes are defined in terms of economic position and power, whereas elites may have a non-economic basis. Indeed, a ruling elite is sometimes simply that section of the dominant class with political power. See: *Miliband–Poulantzas Debate*: *Oligarchy*; *Political Parties*.

Bibl. Giddens (1973)

Embourgeoisement. An explanation of declining working-class support for radical political movements, as the result of increased affluence causing workers to adopt middle-class (bourgeois) values and life-styles, embourgeoisement was a popular argument in Britain in the 1950s and 1960s. It was criticized in the Affluent Worker (q.v.) research. The notion of proletarianization (q.v.) holds, conversely, that some of the middle class are becoming like the working class. See: *Class Imagery*; *End of Ideology Theory*; *Life-Style*.

Bibl. Goldthorpe and Lockwood *et al.* (1969)

Emergent Properties. This concept was formulated by T. Parsons (1937) in his analysis of social systems. There are three related notions. First, social systems have a structure which emerges from the process of social interaction. Secondly, these emergent properties cannot be reduced to the biological or psychological characteristics of social actors; for example, culture cannot be explained by reference to biology. Thirdly, the meaning of a social act cannot be understood in isolation from the total context of the social system within which it occurs. The concept is thus an element of Parsons' argument against reductionism (q.v.). See: *Agency and Structure*; *Parsons*; *Social System*; *Systems Theory*.

Empathy. In sociology the concept of empathy – the ability to assume or take on the social roles and attitudes of other social actors – appears in a variety of different contexts. (1) In the social psychology of G. H. Mead (q.v.) the ability to empathize with social roles and positions is a basic social skill, acquired in the process of socialization. In order to anticipate the response of others to our social gestures it is important for us to be able to put ourselves in the social position of other actors. (2) In the sociology of development, empathy has been treated by D. Lerner (1958) as a basic psychological concomitant of modernization which requires social actors to identify with new political leaders and programmes, new economic commodities and modern social institutions. In an open, democratic society, each citizen has to be able to imagine alternative social arrangements and different political policies. (3) In methodological terms, the ability of the sociologist to empathize with the individuals who are being studied is often mistakenly confused with M. Weber's concept of 'interpretative sociology'. Weber's methodology is less concerned with sympathetic interpretation and more with the attribution of meaning to actions and motives by the use of theoretical constructs. See: *Hermeneutics*; *Verstehen*.

Bibl. Outhwaite (1975)

Empirical An empirical statement or theory is one which can be tested by some kind of evidence drawn from experience.

Empiricism. This is an epistemological doctrine based on the supposition that the only source of knowledge is experience. In sociology, it is used positively to describe that style of sociology that tries to avoid untested theoretical speculation and to aim always at the provision of quantitative, empirical evidence. Negatively, as is often the case in British sociology, it is suggested that empiricism tends to reduce the importance of theory on the one hand and, on the other, underestimates the technical and theoretical difficulties of gathering reliable data. See: *Attitude*; *Interview*; *Official Statistics*; *Positivism*; *Theory-Laden*.

End of Ideology Theory. In the 1950s, American sociologists, especially D. Bell (q.v.) and S. M. Lipset (q.v.), put forward the theory that, because of important changes in the nature of capitalism, democratic participation of the working class in politics and the growth of welfare, the old ideologies of the right and the left had lost their relevance and force. Western societies, having solved their earlier social problems, were thus characterized by a consensus and by a pragmatic approach to the remaining problems of the distribution of resources.

Although the theory, to some extent, adequately reflected the existence of consensus and welfare politics in the 1950s and early 1960s, it was subsequently thought that the prevalence of racial conflict in America, the student riots in Europe, the polarization of attitudes during the Vietnam war and the upsurge of industrial conflict in the 1970s were sufficient empirical disconfirmation of the notion of the 'end of ideology'. Other writers suggested that the 'end of ideology' was itself an ideology of welfare consensus. See: *Citizenship*; *Consensus*; *Ideology*; *Institutionalization of Conflict*; *Social Order*.

Bibl. Waxman (ed.) (1968)

Endogamy. All human societies possess social rules which specify certain categories of persons who are regarded as eligible marriage partners. The rules for marrying within and without certain defined kinship groups are fundamental to any study of kinship. The rule of endogamy permits or prescribes marriage within a specified group, based on kinship, tribal, class or religious affiliation. See: *Descent Groups*; *Exogamy*.

Engels, Friedrich (1820–1895). A German-born industrialist whose family partly owned a textile business in Manchester, Engels spent most of his adult life working in England. He was the close collaborator and friend of K. Marx, introducing him to economics in the 1840s, later supporting him financially, then spending years preparing the manuscripts of *Capital*, vols. 2 and 3, for publication after Marx's death.

In 1844 Engels published a newspaper article, *Outlines of a Critique of Political Economy*, which analysed capitalism as an economic system based on private property and class conflict and criticized the contradictions of liberal economics. This led to the association with Marx, and jointly they wrote *The Holy Family* (1845a), *The German Ideology* (1845b) and the *Communist Manifesto* (1848). Engels' own contributions to the development of Marxism were varied. (1) After Marx's death, he suggested that superstructural elements such as law and ideology had some independence of the economic base and might on occasion determine it, separating the economic from other factors in a way that Marx rarely did. (2) He laid the foundations of what came to be known as dialectical materialism (q.v.) in *Anti-Dühring* (1877–8) and the posthumously published *Dialectics of Nature* (1952). (3) Influenced by C. Darwin, he believed that social development followed evolutionary principles and he emphasized the notion of unilinear development more strongly than Marx. (4) He attempted to develop Marxism on a natural scientific basis, natural science being conceived as both materialistic and following dialectical laws.

His work also covered history, anthropology and military commentary. *The Condition of the Working Class in England* (1845), based mainly on direct observation of Manchester and Salford, remains the classic description of working-class life in industrializing England, though modern historians debate whether the wretched living standards Engels describes were in fact an improvement on what went before or, as Engels claims, a deterioration. *The Origin of the Family, Private Property and the State* (1884) is notable for its condemnation of women's subjugation and its association of patriarchy (q.v.) with private property, though its anthropological base is discredited. See: *Base and Superstructure*; *Ideology*; *Marx*; *Matriarchy*.

Bibl. McLellan (1977)

Entrepreneurship. The economist J. Schumpeter (1934) saw innovation as the criterion of entrepreneurship. Entre-

preneurial activity formed the engine of economic development because profits were created by doing new things or finding new ways of doing existing things. Managers in business organizations were entrepreneurs when they made creative and innovative decisions. This view of the determinants of economic growth has been influential in sociological analyses of developing societies, and it has been suggested at times that the extent to which social values favour the emergence of the entrepreneurial personality influences the likelihood of economic development. This interest in entrepreneurship links with M. Weber's famous discussion of the Protestant Ethic (q.v.) and the socio-religious values and personality type conducive to the emergence of modern capitalism. See: *Achievement Motivation*; *Capitalism*.

Epidemiology. This is the study of the incidence and distribution of diseases and illness in human populations. In medical sociology, it involves the study of how such factors as social class, age, sex and culture influence the presence of illness. While orthodox epidemiology examines social factors in the distribution of disease, it has been criticized by some sociologists because it treats disease as a problem for the individual in relation to the social environment and ascribes responsibility for illness to the individual, rather than treating illness as an effect of social structure. Because epidemiology has been developed in the framework of the medical model (q.v.), it does not give sociological variables a central place in the causal explanation of disease and its social distribution. However, some medical sociologists describe themselves as social epidemiologists. See: *Sociology of Health and Illness*.

Epistemology. In philosophy this concept

is used technically to mean the theory of knowledge, or the theory of how it is that men come to have knowledge of the external world. The term is more loosely used in sociology to refer to the methods of scientific procedure which lead to the acquisition of sociological knowledge. For example, a sociology founded on realism (q.v.) would have a different epistemology from one founded on positivism (q.v.).

Bibl. Keat and Urry (1975).

Equality. It is conventional to identify four types of equality: (1) the doctrine of equality of persons, or ontological equality; (2) equality of opportunity to achieve desirable goals; (3) equality of condition, in which the conditions of life are made equal by legislation; (4) equality of outcome or result.

Ontological equality is normally associated with a religious belief. For example, in Christianity there is the doctrine that all people are equal, because God is the Father of humanity. The spread of secularization (q.v.) has made such beliefs problematic.

The idea of equality of opportunity is the legacy of the French Revolution, the idea being that all positions in society should be open to a competitive system of entry by means of educational attainment, on the basis of personal talent. This form of equality requires universalistic criteria in the selection of people to positions in society and also places a value on achievement motivation (q.v.). By employing the analogy of society as a competitive contest, equality of opportunity suggests that all persons, regardless of race, gender or age, have the right to compete. Critics of this standard of equality argue that, as a result of cultural capital (q.v.), many people entering the competition already enjoy many advantages. This argument was frequently used in Britain in the

1960s against the 11 + examination as a means of selection for grammar-school education, on the grounds that it reinforced existing inequalities; children from middle-class homes already possessed many cultural advantages over working-class children. This argument was put forward by J. W. B. Douglas (1964), who claimed that there was a 'wastage of ability' in Britain as a consequence of inequalities of condition. To insure a more fundamental equality, it is argued that, by means of legislation on welfare and education, there should be an equality of condition to compensate for social disadvantage. Positive discrimination in favour of minority groups to promote social mobility (q.v.) would be a further illustration of changes designed to bring about equality of condition.

Radical critics of society argue that equality of opportunity is a position supported by liberalism and equality of condition is a form of change which aims to reform rather than abolish the prevailing system of inequality. Radical objections against these two forms of equality also argue that the analogy between society and a competition itself reflects the dominant ideology of capitalism. For example, in the nineteenth century, Social Darwinism (q.v.) conceptualized society in terms of a struggle for survival. Against these metaphors, socialists argue for equality of outcome through a programme of political and economic revolution which would remove the social causes of inequality. The aim of socialism is to destroy inequalities (the ultimate cause of which is private ownership of the means of production) and to satisfy human needs equally regardless of the accidents of birth (such as sex).

These types of equality have been criticized as either not feasible or not desirable. For example, it is argued that the achievement of radical equality is unrealistic, because it would require the socialization (q.v.) of children away from the family in order to minimize the inheritance of cultural benefits, the abolition of all forms of inheritance of property, the prohibition of competition and achievement, and a universal training programme in cooperative values and altruism (q.v.). Critics argue that empirical research shows that radical attempts to secure equality over a long period (the Israeli kibbutz, religious communities, secular communes, peasant revolutions and communist revolutions) have not been successful, because inequalities of class, status, power and authority can never be wholly eradicated. It is further argued that equality of condition and outcome are not necessarily desirable, because they conflict with other values such as personal freedom and individualism (q.v.). For example, in Britain it is often claimed that parents have a right to choose private education for their children and that governments should not, in the name of equality of opportunity or condition, prevent freedom of choice with respect to the type of education parents desire for their children. Against this, it has been suggested that privileged social groups use an ideology (q.v.) such as 'freedom of choice', not to defend freedom, but to maintain the privileges they enjoy as a consequence of continuing inequality.

While sociologists have devoted considerable energy to the study of inequality, the conditions for equality and the development of egalitarian social movements have been neglected in mainstream sociology. The contemporary value placed on equality is the product of egalitarian ideologies (such as socialism), the expansion of social rights as a consequence of citizenship (q.v.), the erosion of status hierarchies as

a result of urbanization (q.v.) and the development of mass consumption as an aspect of the rise of a mass society (q.v.). In Britain, the welfare state (q.v.) played an important part in bringing about greater equality of opportunity and condition. These social changes were largely based on the implementation by governments of the economic ideas and policies of J. M. Keynes (1883–1946). In the economic recession which has dominated the world economy since 1973, government has moved away from Keynesianism towards a monetaristic policy which cuts state expenditure on welfare in order to encourage investment and profitability. The result has been an increase in inequality and a greater tolerance, at least on the part of governments, of inequality. See: *Capitalism*; *Caste*; *Class*; *Class Imagery*; *Classroom Knowledge*; *Commune*; *Competition*; *Cultural Deprivation*; *Democracy*; *Dual Consciousness*; *Educational Attainment*; *Estates*; *Industrial Democracy*; *Industrial Society*; *Justice*; *Life-Chances*; *Marshall*; *Progress*; *Stratification*.

Bibl. Tawney (1931); Turner, B. S. (1986b).

Equilibrium. Societies or social systems are said to be in equilibrium when the forces acting within them are balanced and the society is consequently stable. T. Parsons (q.v.) holds that societies are systems which always tend to equilibrium, even if they do not reach it. He conceives of social change as the movement from one equilibrium position to another (or one tendency to another) as the internal forces are changed and rebalance themselves. This is referred to as dynamic equilibrium. See: *Pareto*; *Systems Theory*.

Error. See: *Bias*; *Sampling Error*.

Estates. A system of stratification (q.v.)

found historically in Europe and Russia which, like caste (q.v.), contained sharp differences and rigid barriers between a small number of strata. Unlike castes, estates were created politically by man-made laws rather than religious rules. These laws served both to define the system and control mobility between strata, and also to create an orderly framework of rights and duties which applied to all. Each estate had its own code of appropriate behaviour (for example, etiquette). Estates were commonly found in feudalism (q.v.) and the post-feudal, early modern period. The normal divisions were threefold: clergy, nobility and the commons, though sometimes fourfold when the commons were separated into city dwellers and peasants.

Estimation. This refers to the method of estimating characteristics of a population from sample data. Sampling (q.v.) on a random basis allows statistical distribution theory to be used to make estimates of a known degree of accuracy.

Ethnic Group. There has been much conceptual confusion in sociology with respect to the distinctiveness of such terms as 'ethnic group', 'racial group', 'caste' and 'social stratum'. In general, sociologists have rejected the notion that human groups can be unambiguously defined in terms of their genetic constitution. Social groups in sociological theory are more commonly defined by reference to shared culture such as language, customs and institutions. There is a difference between a group which claims ethnic distinctiveness and one which has distinctiveness imposed upon it by some politically superior group in a context of political struggle. Ethnicity may, therefore, become the basis either for national separatism or for political subordination. The ambiguity of the definition of 'ethinic group'

thus reflects the political struggles in society around exclusive and inclusive group membership. See: *Caste*; *Group*; *Internal Colonialism*; *Nationalism*; *Racism*; *Social Closure*; *Stratification*.

Ethnocentrism. This term, first coined by W. G. Sumner (1906), is used to describe prejudicial attitudes between in-groups and out-groups by which *our* attitudes, customs and behaviour are unquestionably and uncritically treated as superior to *their* social arrangements. The term is also used to criticize sociologists and anthropologists who, often unwittingly, import narrow, parochial assumptions drawn from their own society into their research. See: *Cultural Relativism*; *Prejudice*; *Understanding Alien Belief Systems*.

Ethnography. The direct observation of the activity of members of a particular social group, and the description and evaluation of such activity, constitute ethnography. The term has mainly been used to describe the research technique of anthropologists, but the method is commonly used by sociologists as well. See: *Participant Observation*.

Ethnomethodology. This is a term, literally meaning 'people's methods', invented by H. Garfinkel (q.v.) to describe a branch of sociology which he initiated. In its origins the subject was based on a critique of mainstream sociology, which Garfinkel saw as imposing a set of sociological categories on the ordinary person. Conventional sociology re-describes what ordinary people do, treating their own accounts as somehow deficient. For example, the concept of social structure is an invention to the extent that it departs from people's own sense of structure. At the same time, sociology is really a commonsense practice, not a technical one, for the sociologist uses his or her commonsense categories for organizing data. The subject as conventionally practised, therefore, claims to be something it is not, and treats people as 'cultural dopes'.

Instead, ethnomethodology proposes to investigate how people ('members') construct their world. The assumption is that everyday life is fairly orderly and that is a quality requiring investigation. Members have to work continuously at making their own activities make sense to others, yet despite this, the way in which the social world is constructed is entirely taken for granted. One important feature of everyday life is the indexical character of 'conversation'. The understanding of conversation depends on the participants being able to fill in a set of background assumptions unique to every interaction. Members, therefore, have to 'repair' indexicality (q.v.), perhaps by glossing (q.v.).

Ethnomethodology aims to study members' methods as they are persistently used in the construction of the social world. There are two main varieties of investigation. The first is illustrated by Garfinkel's experiments in the disruption of everyday life. Garfinkel asked his students to go home and behave as if they were lodgers. The reactions of parents and relatives were dramatic, at first puzzled and then hostile. For Garfinkel this illustrates how carefully constructed, yet delicate, is the social order of everyday life and, in other studies (of jurors, for example), he investigated how people constructed this order in different settings while taking it entirely for granted. The second type of ethnomethodological investigation is conversational analysis (q.v.), the study of the social organization of talk.

Ethnomethodology was a topic of considerable debate in sociology in the early 1970s but is less prominent now. It

has been criticized on a number of grounds: (1) it deals with trivial subjects; (2) it presents an over-ordered notion of everyday life which is, in fact, riven by conflict and misunderstanding; (3) it has no notion of social structure and consequently neglects the way in which the activities of people are constrained by social factors; (4) it uses the methods of inquiry which it criticizes in others. See: *Phenomenological Sociology*; *Schutz*; *Symbolic Interactionism*.

Bibl. Cicourel (1964); Turner, R. (1974).

Ethology. This is the comparative study of animal behaviour, particularly its non-learned aspects. There have been unsuccessful attempts to apply the lessons learned with animals, particularly primates, to human behaviour. However, as a method of study that emphasizes the limitations imposed on behaviour by genetic structure, it complements social scientists' concern for what is learned and socially created. See: *Sociobiology*.

Bibl. Hinde (1982)

Eufunction. See: *Dysfunction*; *Functionalism*.

Eugenics. A term coined by F. Galton in 1883 to refer to the improvement of the human race by the use of a 'genetic policy' based on the principles of heredity (q.v.). As a social movement, it was influential in the United States between 1890 and 1920, where it was associated with Social Darwinism (q.v.). The American Genetic Association was founded in 1913. The aim of eugenics was to maintain and improve human populations by positive means (the encouragement by financial support of parents who were thought to be intelligent or in some sense superior) and negative means (the prohibition on reproduction by parents who were allegedly inferior). These ideas began to have a practical application in the United States when the state of Indiana adopted a sterilization law in 1907. During a period of massive migration to the United States, eugenics was used to give expression to anxieties about the consequences for American culture of a sustained policy of immigration. Sociologists have been critical of the use of biological models in the explanation of social action and interaction; they have also criticized the organic analogy (q.v.). Although eugenics as such is no longer fashionable, the basic issues are still important in the nature/nurture debate (q.v.). See: *Intelligence*; *Sociobiology*.

Evaluation Research. Social scientists are increasingly called upon to use their research expertise to evaluate the success of policies in reaching goals. Evaluation research is often linked to action research (q.v.). It has been employed most widely in the United States.

Evolutionary Theory. This doctrine embraces a variety of principles in different usages and there is no real agreement as to its essence. There are two types of evolutionary theory: (1) that which postulates the unilinear, ordered or progressive nature of social change; (2) that which is based on an analogy with evolution in plant and animal populations, following Darwinian theory.

(1) Evolutionary perspectives were central to the nineteenth-century approach to the study of society. Some commentators saw *any* change as evolutionary, but the major sociological contributions emphasized the ordered and directional nature of change. C. H. Saint-Simon (q.v.) started from the idea, conventional in late eighteenth- and early nineteenth-century conservatism, of society as an organic equilibrium, stabilized by the fact that individuals and social classes depended on the success of the whole for their survival. To this he added an evolutionary idea of social development, a sequential progression of organic societies representing increasing levels of advancement. Each society was appropriate in its own time but was later superseded by higher forms. He saw the growth of knowledge as defining and determining evolution, and his three stages were later elaborated in A. Comte's (q.v.) evolutionary scheme. Comte linked developments in human knowledge, culture and society. Societies passed through three stages, the primitive, intermediary and scientific, which corresponded to the forms of human knowledge arranged along a similar continuum of theological, metaphysical and positive reasoning. All mankind inevitably passed through these stages as it developed, suggesting both unilinear direction and progress. Moreover, Comte saw society in organismic terms, as an entity made up of interdependent parts which are in balance with each other and create an integrated whole. He saw evolution as the growth of functional specialization of structures and the better adaptation of parts.

H. Spencer (q.v.) also displayed a linear conception of evolutionary stages. The degree of complexity in society was the scale on which he measured progress. The trend of human societies was from simple, undifferentiated wholes to complex and heterogeneous ones, where the parts of the whole became more specialized but remained integrated. He worked with an organic analogy but did not describe society *as* an organism. The concern with change and stages of development can also be found in nonorganismic thought in the second half of the century, among anthropologists interested in the comparative study of cultures, in the succession of modes of production (q.v.) outlined by K. Marx and F. Engels, and in E. Durkheim's view of the progressive division of labour (q.v.) in society.

(2) Twentieth-century anthropologists and sociologists have mainly been less interested in evolution, except for a revival of interest among American functionalists in the 1950s and 1960s. This revival is sometimes referred to as *neo-evolutionism*, which tends to utilize the principles of natural selection and adaptation drawn from evolutionary theory in the biological sciences. Functionalism (q.v.) used an organismic model of society and found in Darwinian evolutionary theory an explanation of how organisms changed and survived that appeared compatible with its own assumptions. The starting point was the adaptation of societies to their environments. Environments included both the natural world and other social systems. Changes in society, deriving from whatever source, provided the basic material of evolution. Those changes which increased a society's adaptive capacity, measured by its long-run survival, were selected and became institutionalized, following the principle of the survival of the fittest. Sociological functionalism located the main source of adaptation and selection in differentiation, the process whereby the main social functions were dissociated and came to be performed by specialized collectivities in autonomous institutional spheres. Functional differentiation and the parallel structural differentiation would enable each function to be performed more effectively. Anthropological accounts have often referred to specific evolution (the adaptation of an individual society to its particular environment), whereas sociologists have concentrated on general evolution which is the evolution of superior forms within the total development of human society.

This general perspective suggested a unilinear direction of change and that some societies were higher than others on a scale of progress, assumptions that specific evolution did not make. See: *Differentiation*; *Division of Labour*; *Durkheim*; *Marx*; *Organic Analogy*; *Parsons*; *Progress*; *Social Darwinism*; *Urban Ecology*.

Bibl. Parsons (1966); Eisenstadt (1968a); Peel (1969a)

Exchange Theory. The conceptualization of social interaction, social structure and social order in terms of exchange relations has a long history in anthropology and more recently has been adopted by some sociologists. Two approaches can be identified; individualistic and collectivist exchange theories.

The American individualistic approach, as found in the work of G. C. Homans (1961) and P. M. Blau (1964), follows the hedonistic, utilitarian perspective that individuals seek to maximize their own private gratifications. It assumes that these rewards can only be found in social interaction and that people seek rewards in their interactions with each other. Exchange theorists see a similarity between social interactions and economic or market transactions, namely the expectation that benefits rendered will produce a return. The basic paradigm is a two-person interaction model. There is an emphasis on mutual reciprocity, though the basis of exchange remains calculative and involves little trust or shared morality. This approach faces several criticisms. (1) Its psychological assumptions are naive and exaggerate the self-seeking, calculative elements of personality. (2) The theory is stunted because it cannot go beyond the two-person reciprocity level to social behaviour on a larger scale. (3) It does not explain social processes such as domination or generalized values that cannot be derived from the paradigm of two-person exchange. (4) It is an elegant conceptualization of the sociologically trivial.

The traditional emphasis on collective exchange in French anthropology, associated with M. Mauss and C. Lévi-Strauss (q.v.), is not subject to these criticisms. The emphasis is on generalized exchange involving at least three actors, in which any individual participant may not receive from the person to whom he gave, rather than on mutually reciprocal exchange. Exchange involves shared values and trust, the expectation that others will fulfil their obligations to the group or society rather than pursue self-interests. In Lévi-Strauss's work, exchange theory explains the development of these integrative cultural ties through the social networks which generalized exchanges create. Although directed at non-industrial societies, Lévi-Strauss deals with issues of social structure and culture that are more relevant sociologically than the concerns of individual exchange theories. See: *Utilitarianism*.

Bibl. Ekeh (1974)

Exchange Value. See: *Labour Theory of Value*.

Exogamy. The concept of exogamy refers to those formal rules or social preferences compelling marriage outside the immediate group. See: *Endogamy*.

Experimental Method. In the physical sciences experimentation is a method of research whereby changes are deliberately made in a process and their effects are observed and measured. The experiment allows the investigator to control all the factors that might affect the phenomenon under study. In sociology it is seldom, if ever, possible to achieve complete control and many investigations are better described as uncontrolled observational studies. In order to provide some estimation of cause and effect within such studies, various techniques may be used. One method is that of the control group (q.v.), which reduces, but does not eliminate, the uncontrolled factors. When the investigation is of social processes where control groups cannot be used – the majority of research situations – causal modelling (q.v.) of the data may be attempted.

Bibl. Moser and Kalton (1979)

Explanans/Explanandum. In any explanation, the thing that is to be explained is called the explanandum. The explanans refers to the set of statements which together constitute the explanation of the explanandum.

Explanation. See: *Agency and Structure*; *Causal Explanation*; *Causal Modelling*; *Dependent/Independent Variables*; *Explanans/Explanandum*; *Falsificationism*; *Functionalism*; *Hermeneutics*; *Hypothetico-Deductive Method*; *Naturalism*; *Phenomenological Sociology*; *Positivism*; *Realism*; *Rule*; *Sociology as Science*; *Structuralism*; *Verstehen*.

Extended Family. This is conventionally defined as a social unit comprising parents and children and other more distant relatives, perhaps including grandparents or uncles and aunts, living under one roof. It is now more widely used to describe a looser set of relationships in which the nuclear family keeps in contact with wider kin, and receives practical assistance with a variety of tasks, from child rearing to buying a house. The typical family form in modern industrial societies is not, therefore, the isolated nuclear family but is a modified extended family. See: *Conjugal Role*; *Group*; *Kinship*; *Nuclear Family*.

Bibl. Anderson, M. (1975); Morgan (1975)

F

Facticity. This term, drawn from phenomenological sociology (q.v.), and sometimes confused with alienation (q.v.), refers to the way in which the external social and natural world appears to individuals as solid, taken-for-granted, and 'thing-like'. See: *Schutz*.

Bibl. Berger and Luckmann (1967)

Factor Analysis. This statistical technique is often used in the analysis of survey data to identify any common components or factors underlying a set of items. Frequently, attitude scales that deal with a variety of different items – for example, politics, industrial relations, inequality, capital and corporal punishment, the family, sexual morality – may be shown to contain a single general factor (perhaps authoritarianism in this hypothetical case) that contributes to all items.

Bibl. Harman (1967)

False Consciousness. See: *Class Consciousness*.

Falsificationism. This doctrine, originally associated with K. Popper (q.v.), claims that scientific advance can only come about through the testing and falsifying of hypotheses, which are then replaced by new hypotheses, also subject to test and falsification. One cannot ultimately verify, only falsify. It is further argued that hypotheses are only meaningful to the extent that a test can be conceived that would falsify them.

It has been argued against this position, originally by T. Kuhn (1970), that scientific change does not come about through the systematic testing and falsification of hypotheses, but through the replacement of one paradigm (q.v.) by another. It is also argued that science depends critically on propositions that cannot be falsified, like 'every event has a cause'. See: *Counterfactual*; *Positivism*.

Family. See: *Sociology of the Family*.

Fascism. Mussolini's corporatist political system, fascism, existed in Italy between 1922 and 1945. The term fascism is often applied, however, to cover somewhat similar political movements elsewhere, for example German nazism and the Spanish Falange. Fascism was an authoritarian, nationalistic and illiberal political movement arising out of the social and economic crises following the First World War, which were perceived as proving the inadequacy of liberalism and the democratic process. It had no developed or coherent political philosophy but embraced nationalism, a hatred of communism, a distrust of democratic politics, commitment to the single-party state and faith in charismatic leaders. It glorified violence and supported totalitarianism. In Germany, nazism was also racialist and anti-semitic. The social support of fascist movements came from the military, middle-class groups who felt threatened by the social disorder and economic depressions of the inter-war period and by the rise of socialist movements, and some parts of the working class.

The Fascist state was corporatist in the sense that many of the autonomous institutions of democratic pluralism (q.v.) were suppressed, in order that the state should be the sole representation of the social collectivity. Independent trade unions and political parties were the notable casualties. Italian fascists at one time suggested that professions and industries should act as representative groups which would link the people to the state, but in practice this idea was ignored.

There are a number of theories which seek to explain fascism. (1) W. Reich (1933) argued that fascism resulted from sexual repression in an authoritarian and inhibited society; he concentrated on the sexual symbolism of fascist collective rituals. (2) B. Moore (1968) argued that whether capitalism developed along the lines of democracy or dictatorship depended on the forms of alliance between the landed classes, the peasantry and the urban bourgeoisie; where capitalist agriculture is slow to develop (as in Prussian Germany) and repressive forms of agricultural production predominate, a repressive, fascist state apparatus is necessary for the continued subordination of agricultural labourers. (3) N. Poulantzas (1974) argues that fascism is the result of a deep economic and ideological crisis of the dominant class. When no fraction of the dominant class can impose its leadership on the 'power bloc', the fascist state replaces demo-cratic, parliamentary politics as a solution to the crisis of capitalist society which is threatened by the organized working class. The petty bourgeoisie, which is squeezed by the concentration of large capitalist enterprises, comes to play an important part in government because it is being forced into the working class by capitalist development. The collapse of traditional parliamentary politics results in a reorganization of the political system through the formation of the fascist party and the use of 'extra-parliamentary means' with the support of monopoly capitalism. The conclusion to these class struggles is the dominance of finance capitalism over other capital fractions (q.v.) within the political system. See: *Authoritarian Personality*; *Class Struggle*; *Corporatism*; *Nationalism*.

Bibl. Woolf (ed.) (1968); Kitchen (1976)

Fecundity. It is conventional in demography to distinguish between the biological capacity for reproduction (fecundity) and actual reproduction (fertility). Fertility (q.v.) is less than fecundity in all societies, and varies considerably among societies without any apparent relation to differences in fecundity.

Feminism. This is a doctrine suggesting that women are systematically disadvantaged in modern society and advocating equal opportunities for men and women. This idea has had a great and deserved influence in sociology in recent years. Feminist sociologists have argued that sociologists, who are mostly men, have neglected the sociological significance of women in all areas of the subject. For example, many studies of social stratification have concentrated on the paid work of men as a determinant of the class position of women family members. Again many investigations of clerical work have tended, until recently, to consider only male clerks, neglecting the fact that three-quarters of this section of the workforce are female. See: *Class*; *Domestic Labour*; *Patriarchy*; *Sexual Divisions*.

Feminization. Occupations are said to be feminized when women enter them in significant numbers. For example, the proportion of clerks who are women has increased from 20 per cent in 1911 to 71 per cent in 1971. The degree of feminization of an occupation is often said to be related to its proletarianization (q.v.), in that as the work becomes less skilled it is cheaper for employers to employ women. See: *Sexual Divisions*.

Fertility. This is defined as the actual number of live births in a population unit in one year, while 'cohort fertility' is the number of live births for a group or cohort of women during their span of reproduction. 'Fertility' – actual live births – is thus contrasted in demography with 'fecundity' which is the *potential* capacity for biological reproduction. The principal factors influencing fertility in a population are the age of marriage, the availability of contraception and attitudes towards family size. A decline in fertility is characteristic of urban, industrial societies and has significant social and economic consequences for the size of the workforce. See: *Birth Rate*; *Demographic Transition*; *Demography; Fecundity*.

Feudalism. The social, economic and political structure known as feudalism was found in its most developed form in northern France in the twelfth and thirteenth centuries. Feudalism is conventionally a label applied also to Japan and to other parts of Europe where feudal characteristics have been found, and the system is thought to have lasted in Europe for the five hundred years known

as the Middle Ages. Feudalism cannot be defined exactly because of the diversity of cases and the fact that no individual case remained unchanged over the half millennium of the feudal period in Europe.

J. Prawer and S. N. Eisenstadt (1968) list five characteristics common to most developed feudal societies: (1) lord–vassal relationships; (2) personalized government that is mainly effective at local rather than national level and where there is relatively little separation of functions; (3) a pattern of landholding based on granting fiefs in return for services, primarily military; (4) the existence of private armies; (5) rights of lords over the peasants who are serfs. These characterize a political system that was decentralized and depended on a hierarchical network of personal ties within the ranks of the nobility, despite the formal principle of a single line of authority stretching upwards to a king. This provided for collective defence and the maintenance of order. The economic base was the manorial organization of production and a dependent peasantry who provided the surplus that lords needed to perform their political functions.

Sociological interest in feudalism has taken the following directions. M. Weber (1922) was concerned with its political and military arrangements, especially with the socio-economic structure which was required to maintain a feudal cavalry. Weber contrasted the feu (a heritable, traditional title to land) and the benefice (a title which could not be inherited) as the basis of a contrast between feudalism and prebendalism. K. Marx and F. Engels dealt only briefly with pre-capitalist modes of production, but in the 1970s some Marxist sociologists became interested in the feudal mode of production (q.v.). Unlike capitalism, where workers were dispossessed of all control over the means of production, feudalism did permit peasants effective possession of some of these means (though not legal title). Class struggle between lords and peasants centred on the size of the productive units allocated to tenants, the conditions of tenancy, and control of essential means of production like pasture, drainage and mills. In contemporary Marxist approaches, therefore, it is argued that, because the peasant-tenant has some degree of control over production through, for example, possession of customary rights, 'extra-economic conditions' are required to secure control over the peasantry by landlords. These conditions are basically forms of political and ideological control. The feudal mode of production is thus one which secures the appropriation of surplus labour in the form of rent. Feudal rent may assume a number of forms – rent in kind, money or labour. Variant forms of the mode can be defined in terms of these variations in rent. For example, rent-in-labour requires a particular type of labour process which is the combination of independent production by tenants with demesne production under the supervision of the lord or an agent. The transition of feudalism to capitalism is, in this perspective, the outcome of continuous struggle over the nature and extent of appropriation by rent. However, there are competing theories of transition; causal primacy may be given to exchange relations, markets, relations and forces of production, and to cultural factors. See: *Patrimonialism*; *Relations of Production*.

Bibl. Coulborn (ed.) (1956); Bloch (1961); Hindess and Hirst (1975); Holton (1985)

Field Work. Sometimes this is used as a synonym for ethnography (q.v.), and more loosely to describe the activity of collecting data in empirical sociological research. See: *Participant Observation*.

Folk Society. A concept used by R. Redfield to designate one pole of a continuum between folk and secular or urban societies, his version of F. Toennies' distinction between *gemeinschaft* (q.v.) and *gesellschaft*. Folk societies are relatively more isolated, homogeneous, and traditionally organized, and less secular and individualistic. See: *Rural-Urban Continuum*.

Folkways. This concept, introduced by W. G. Sumner (1906), describes the everyday activities within a small-scale society which have become established and are socially sanctioned. Folkways differ from mores (q.v.) in that they are less severely sanctioned and are not abstract principles.

Forces of Production. A concept used within Marxist sociology, the forces of production refer to both the materials worked on and the tools and techniques employed in production of economic goods. They have to be distinguished from relations of production (q.v.). See: *Marx*; *Mode of Production*.

Fordism. See: *Scientific Management*.

Formal Organization. All social collectivities involve some form of organization, but the term formal organization is reserved for collectivities that have developed formal procedures for regulating relations between members and their activities. The sociological investigation of such collectivities is the domain of organization theory (q.v.), which focuses primarily though not exclusively on economic and political or governmental formal organizations. *Informal Organization* describes social relationships and actions that do not coincide with formal procedures and roles. See: *Bureaucracy*; *Role*.

Formal Sociology. This approach, associated particularly with G. Simmel (q.v.) and early twentieth-century

German sociology, took the *form* of social relationships as the object of analysis and studied relationships which differed in substance but displayed the same formal properties. For example, competition may be viewed as a relationship with distinct formal characteristics, no matter what the setting – whether it occurs in the market place, on the sports field, or in the political arena. M. Weber (1922) outlines the basic forms of human interaction which occur in any society, such as power, competition and organization.

Foucault, Michel (1926–1984). Representative of a pervasive French influence in contemporary sociology, Foucault has provided a major critique of conventional methodology and assumptions in historiography and sociology. His approach has been particularly influential in historical studies of the asylum, prison and clinic. The main topics of his published works are knowledge, power and the human body. In *Discipline and Punish* (1975), he studied the development of new systems of knowledge (penology and criminology), new forms of architecture (panopticism) and new disciplines of social regulation. In *Madness and Civilization* (1961), he traces social reaction to madness from the medieval 'ship of fools' through the asylum to the nineteenth-century 'moral treatment'. Similarly, *The Birth of the Clinic* (1963) and *The History of Sexuality* (1976) are focused on the control of the body through the medium of rational, systematic knowledge. The more abstract problems of discourse are dealt with in *The Order of Things* (1966) and *The Archaeology of Knowledge* (1969). See: *Discourse*; *Madness*.

Bibl. Cousins and Hussain (1984); Smart (1985)

Frankfurt School. An influential movement in contemporary Marxism, the Frankfurt School was a group of social scientists who worked in the Institute of Social Research (1923–1950) which was connected to the University of Frankfurt. Members of the Frankfurt School were predominantly Jewish and as a group went into exile during the Nazi ascendancy. The Institute moved to Columbia University, New York, at this time, returning to Frankfurt in 1949. Although principally important for their theoretical writing on epistemology, Marxism and culture, the School undertook important empirical research in America on racism and prejudice resulting in the publication of *The Authoritarian Personality* (1950). Leading figures in the School included T. W. Adorno, W. Benjamin, E. Fromm, M. Horkheimer and H. Marcuse.

Their principal interests were: (1) the development of a criticism of economism (q.v.) in orthodox Marxism; (2) the elaboration of an appropriate epistemology and critique of advanced capitalism; (3) the incorporation of Freudian psychoanalysis into K. Marx's theory of society; (4) an attack on instrumental rationality as the basic principle of capitalist society. The Frankfurt School is typically regarded as 'neo-Marxist' and 'revisionist' because: (1) it attempted to revise conventional Marxism by criticizing economic determinism; (2) it was eclectic in borrowing from psychoanalysis and sociology to fill gaps it perceived in Marxist theory; (3) it was pessimistic with regard to the possibility of revolutionary change of capitalism by working-class struggle; (4) it emphasized the importance of culture rather than economics and produced influential studies of music, literature and aesthetics. See: *Adorno*; *Authoritarian Personality*; *Critical Theory*; *Habermas*; *Marcuse*; *Positivism*.

Bibl. Jay (1973); Held (1980)

99

Freud, Sigmund (1856–1939). Born in Moravia of Jewish parents, he was brought up in Vienna where he studied medicine. His early work was in the histology of the nervous system, but, influenced by J. Breuer's use of hypnosis, he made an important contribution to the study of hysteria by the use of free association (or 'talking therapy'). Their research on hysterical phenomena and psychotherapy was published as *Studies on Hysteria* (1895). As a consequence of this clinical work, Freud developed the basic concepts of psychoanalysis (the unconscious, repression, abreaction and transference), which were described in, for example, *Five Lectures on Psycho-Analysis* (1910). Freud became interested in how jokes and dreams might reveal the nature and problems of human sexuality in *The Interpretation of Dreams* (1900) and *Jokes and their Relation to the Unconscious* (1905a). He applied the same approach to the study of lapses of memory and verbal slips in *The Psychopathology of Everyday Life* (1901). Freud also developed a psychoanalysis of art in *Leonardo da Vinci* (1910), where he argued that paintings like 'Madonna and Child with St Anne' were products of Leonardo's homosexuality, rejection of parental authority and narcissism. The theory of childhood sexuality was outlined in *Three Essays on the Theory of Sexuality* (1905b); his conception of the dynamics of personality was published in *The Ego and the Id* (1923). Freud and his colleagues founded the International Psycho-Analytical Association in 1910 in Nuremberg; they also created journals to disseminate their ideas. These were *Central Journal for Psycho-Analysis* and *Internal Journal for Medical Psycho-Analysis*. Freud wrote an account of these institutional and theoretical developments in *On the History of the Psycho-Analytical Movement* (1914) and *An Autobiographical Study* (1925).

Although Freud's psychoanalytical research covered a wide variety of issues, it was his perspective on the conflict between the instinctual gratification of the individual and the requirements of social order which was particularly influential in sociology. In his later work – *The Future of an Illusion* (1927), *Civilization and its Discontents* (1930), and *Moses and Monotheism* (1934–8) – Freud emphasized the contradiction between the satisfaction of sexuality and aggression for the individual and the importance of social control for civilization. The social order is a fragile compromise between sexual fulfilment, social discipline and work.

Freud's theories have been influential in both sociology and Marxism. T. Parsons (q.v.) adopted Freud's account of personality development to provide the psychological underpinnings of the socialization process, but, in stressing the complementarity between personality and social systems, Parsons neglected the contradictory relationship between sexuality and social order. In Marxism, L. Althusser referred to Freud's discovery of the unconscious as parallel to K. Marx's discovery of the laws of modes of production. In the Frankfurt School (q.v.), psychoanalytical theories were adopted to develop a materialist conception of personality as a companion to Marx's materialist analysis of society. See: *Althusser*; *Feminism*; *Foucault*; *Gellner*; *Gender*; *Myth*; *Patriarchy*; *Taboo*.

Bibl. Bocock (1983)

Functional Imperative or **Functional Prerequisite.** These concepts refer to the basic needs of a society which have to be met if it is to continue to survive as a functioning system. For example, a system of social stratification is said to be necessary to ensure that the most able people are recruited to the most important positions, a requirement for an efficient society. The concept has been much criticized on the grounds that it is difficult to establish what are the functional imperatives in any society. See: *Evolutionary Theory*; *Functionalism*; *Need*; *Parsons*; *Stratification*; *Teleology*.

Functional Theory of Stratification. See: *Stratification*.

Functionalism. Now a controversial perspective within sociology, functionalism has a long history. Nineteenth-century sociologists were greatly impressed by the way in which the various elements of a society were interdependent, and they often explained this interdependence in terms of evolutionary theory (q.v.) or the organic analogy (q.v.). Just as the heart has the function of circulating the blood, so also do social institutions have functions for society as a whole. Functionalist ideas were also introduced into sociology via social anthropology.

As a minimal definition, functionalism accounts for a social activity by referring to its consequences for the operation of some other social activity, institution, or society as a whole. There are a large number of types of functionalist argument, but three have been especially important. (1) A social activity or institution may have latent functions (q.v.) for some other activity. For example, some functionalists contend that whatever the intentions of individual members of families, the change from an extended family form to a nuclear one benefited (had latent functions for) the process of industrialization; namely, that people were freed of family ties and were able to be geographically mobile. This claim of latent functionality for industrialization is part of an explanation of the change in family structure. (2) A social activity may contribute to the maintenance of the stability of a social system (q.v.). For example, E.

Durkheim argued that religious practices were best understood as contributing to the integration and stability of a society. Some theorists would go so far as to say that one should look at all social institutions as performing this function. (3) A social activity may contribute to the satisfying of basic social needs or functional prerequisites (q.v.). T. Parsons (q.v.) argued that societies have certain needs that must be met if they are to survive, and institutions have to be seen as meeting those needs.

There has been a great deal of debate about functionalist argument, much of it very repetitive, although the debate has lessened in the last fifteen years. Four important arguments have been adduced against one or all of the variations of functionalism outlined above. (1) Functionalism cannot account for social conflict or other forms of instability, because it sees all social activities as smoothly interacting to stabilize societies. Functionalists have responded to this claim by suggesting that social conflict may, in fact, have positive functions for social order, or, in the concept of dysfunction (q.v.), admitting that not all social activities will have positive functions for all other activities. (2) Functionalism cannot account for change, in that there appears to be no *mechanism* which will disturb existing functional relationships. The functionalist response to this has been to employ concepts such as differentiation (q.v.). (3) Functionalism is a form of teleology (q.v.) in that it explains the existence of a social activity by its consequences or effects. (4) Functionalism neglects the meanings that individuals give to their actions by concentrating simply on the consequences of actions. See: *Holism*; *Latent Function*; *Malinowski*; *Radcliffe-Brown*; *Reciprocity*; *Social Structure*; *Stratification*; *Systems Theory*.

Bibl. Cohen, P.S. (1968); Ryan (1970)

G

Gang. This term is typically used to refer to small groups which are bound together by a common sense of loyalty and territory, and which are hierarchically structured around a gang leader. Although the term occurs in a variety of contexts – such as 'work gang' – it is most commonly employed in the sociology of deviance to refer to groups of male adolescents engaged in various deviant activities. In F. Thrasher (1927) and W. F. Whyte (1955), the existence of delinquent gangs was seen to be the product of the urban disorganization of working-class communities providing young men with a sense of identity and excitement. Thrasher demonstrated that gangs were not loosely organized collections of individuals, but integrated groups, bound together by conflict with the wider community, with a strong sense of loyalty and commitment. A. Cohen (1955) treated working-class gangs as subcultures (q.v.) which rejected middle-class values. He argued that the gang values were non-utilitarian, negative and delinquent. R. Cloward and L. Ohlin (1961) argued that delinquent gangs were caught between the opportunity structures of the working and middle classes; this gave rise to three different subcultures, namely criminal (concerned with illegal methods of making money),

conflict (concerned with violence) and retreatist (concerned with drugs). Subcultures were seen as defensive reactions to limited social opportunities by young (predominantly male) adolescents. This theory was an application of anomie (q.v.) to juvenile delinquency (q.v.). Recent debates have questioned whether gangs are tightly organized, primary groups or merely diffuse, impermanent groups. More recently, sociologists have turned to the study of women and crime. Cloward and Piven (1979) consider the function of gangs in the socialization (q.v.) of girls. See: *Adolescence*; *Chicago School*; *Deviancy Amplification*; *Deviant Behaviour*; *Differential Association*; *Group*; *Peer Group*; *Primary Relationship*.

Bibl. Yablonsky (1967); Brake (1980)

Garfinkel, Harold (b. 1917). Responsible for initiating a school of sociology known as ethnomethodology (q.v.), Garfinkel is interested in analysing the methods used by people in everyday life to describe and make sense of their own activities. His main publication is a collection of essays, *Studies in Ethnomethodology* (1967).

Geisteswissenschaften. A generic term used to cover the human sciences, it is usually associated with a particular view of human sciences as disciplines employing methods radically distinct from those of the natural sciences, particularly as they involve an *understanding* of human beings. See: *Empathy*; *Hermeneutics*; *Simmel*; *Verstehen*; *Weber*.

Bibl. Outhwaite (1975)

Gellner, Ernest (b. 1925). Born in Paris and currently professor of social anthropology at the University of Cambridge, he is highly critical of linguistic philosophy in *Words and Things* (1959) and of the reluctance in modern anthropology to engage in rational criticism of other societies in *Saints of the Atlas* (1969). In *Thought and Change* (1964), he argues that the promotion of wealth through industrialization and government by co-nationals are the principal bases of legitimacy of modern societies. In *Legitimation of Belief* (1974), he criticizes modern pluralism and relativism. In *Muslim Society* (1982), he considers the impact of social change on Islamic cultures. His work is noted for its use of social anthropology to explore traditional philosophical issues and vice versa. In *The Psychoanalytic Movement* (1985) he has provided an explanation of the social success of Freudian therapy, which calls into question the basic assumptions of psychoanalysis as a coherent theory or effective practice.

Gemeinschaft. Usually translated as 'community', this term is contrasted with *gesellschaft* or 'association'. Societies characterized by *gemeinschaft* relations are homogeneous, largely based on kinship and organic ties, and have a moral cohesion often founded on common religious sentiment. These relationships are dissolved by the division of labour (q.v.), individualism (q.v.) and competitiveness, that is, by the growth

of *gesellschaft*-relationships. Whereas F. Toennies (1887) regarded *gemeinschaft* as the expression of real, organized life, *gesellschaft* is an artificial social arrangement based on the conflict of egoistic wills. See: *Civilization*; *Community*; *Rural-Urban Continuum*; *Toennies*; *Urban Way of Life*.

Gender. If the sex of a person is biologically determined, the gender of a person is culturally and socially constructed. There are thus two sexes (male and female) and two genders (masculine and feminine). The principal theoretical and political issue is whether gender as a socially constructed phenomenon is related to or determined by biology. For example, in the nineteenth century various medical theories suggested that the female personality was determined by anatomy and women's reproductive functions. These views have been challenged by feminism (q.v.). Anthropological research has also shown the cultural specificity of notions about gender, sexuality and sex-roles. For example, M. Mead (q.v.) showed in a number of cross-cultural studies that, while gender differentiation is widespread, the social tasks undertaken by men and women are highly variable. There is no general relationship across societies between social roles and biological sex. Social psychologists have treated gender-identity as the product of child training rather than as biologically given. Ethnomethodology (q.v.) studies 'gender' as the problem of how individual sexuality is assigned.

More recently, critics have challenged these interpretations, because (1) while sociologists distinguish between sex and gender, they often treat the latter as an expression of the former, thereby giving biology a determining significance, and (2) they fail to provide the connection between the economic subordination of women and its expression through the family and personal life. In the radical critique, it is the place of women in relation to economic production which ultimately determines male/female differences. In this sense, it can be argued that 'gender' is analogous to class relationships. The task of establishing systematic, causal connections between capitalism (q.v.), class (q.v.) and patriarchy (q.v.) has, however, proved to be highly problematic. Theoretical attempts to develop a sociological perspective on biological sex, gender, sex-roles and personality have nevertheless transformed many taken-for-granted assumptions in a number of sociological topics. For example, feminists within the psychoanalytic tradition have challenged the basic ideas of Freud (q.v.) by showing that the Oedipus complex, penis envy and castration complex should be interpreted as features of the symbolic world of patriarchal power. See: *Domestic Labour*; *Nature/Nurture Debate*; *Patriarchy*; *Sexual Divisions*; *Sociology of Gender*.

Bibl. Oakley (1972); Weitz (1977)

Gender Stereotyping. See: *Dual Labour Markets*; *Educational Attainment*; *Stereotypes*.

Generalized Other. See: *Mead*.

Generation. While in biological and genealogical terms the concept of 'generation' has a precise meaning as the regular descent of a cohort (q.v.) from a common ancestor, it has proved difficult to give the term a clear meaning in sociology. Since there is always a continuity of births in a society, there is no definite cut-off point between one generation and the next. It is important, therefore, to distinguish between 'contemporaries' (those alive at the same time) and 'coevals' (those of the same

age). In sociology, genealogy is less important than the consciousness of a group, born at the same time, of common experiences, interests and outlook. Despite the conceptual confusion, the concept has played an important part in sociology, especially in political sociology where political behaviour is thought to correlate with generation. 'Generation' is sometimes claimed to be as important as 'social class' or 'gender' in the explanation of individual and group differences in culture, interests and behaviour (Mannheim, 1952). 'Generational conflicts' and the stratification of society by 'age groups' is thus held to be parallel or analogous to 'class conflict'. See: *Aging*.

Bibl. Eisenstadt (1956)

Gerontology. The study of aging (q.v.), old age and the problems of the elderly, it was in the 1960s dominated by the welfare needs of the elderly within a social-policy framework. Recent social gerontology, however, has been influenced by the cultural movements of the 1970s and by the political organization of the elderly (by such associations as the Gray Panthers in the United States). There is now considerable interest in the social construction of the concept of age, the politics of aging, the experience of aging and in the idea of aging as a normal (as opposed to pathological) process. Despite these changes, gerontologists are still concerned with social rather than sociological questions. See: *Demographic Transition*; *Demography*; *Health Care Systems*; *Sociology of Medicine*.

Bibl. Jerrome (ed.) (1983)

Gesellschaft. See: *Gemeinschaft*.

Ghetto. Although this term is commonly applied to the Jewish quarter of pre-war European cities, in sociology it refers to any urban area, often deprived, which is occupied by a group segregated on the basis of religion, colour or ethnicity. In contemporary debates, it has been suggested that the notion of an 'internal colony' is a more accurate description of the racial segregation of the black community in North America. However, while the colonial analogy implies the possibility of social change (that is, 'decolonization'), in historical terms ghetto-status was permanent.

Bibl. Neuwirth (1969)

Giddens, Anthony (b. 1938). Currently professor of sociology and fellow of King's College, Cambridge, he has contributed extensively to the interpretation of classical sociological theory in *Capitalism and Modern Social Theory* (1971), *Politics and Sociology in the Thought of Max Weber* (1972), *Emile Durkheim* (1978) and *Sociology* (1982). He attempted a resolution of the traditional problems of class analysis in *The Class Structure of the Advanced Societies* (1973). The central theme of his perspective has been to develop the theory of action, agency and structure (q.v.), and the knowledgeability of the social actor, through a theory of structuration (q.v.), in *New Rules of Sociological Method* (1976), *Studies in Social and Political Theory* (1977), *Central Problems in Social Theory* (1979), *Profiles and Critiques in Social Theory* (1983) and *The Constitution of Society* (1984). More recently, he has begun an extensive critique of the theoretical limitations of historical materialism (q.v.) in *A Contemporary Critique of Historical Materialism* (1981). He has also presented an innovative framework for an integration of sociology and geography in the analysis of time and space (1984). He has criticized sociology for its failure to provide an analysis of the development of the state and the impact of international conflicts on social relations in *The Nation-State and Violence* (1985).

Gift. The analysis of gifts has played an important part in the anthropology of kinship systems where, especially in the case of cross-cousin marriages, the exchange of women between families is an instance of a gift relationship. The exchange of gifts is either regarded as a method of creating and reinforcing binding social relationships or as an exhibition of superior wealth. While the study of gifts has not been particularly important in sociology, M. Mauss (1925) sees them as illustrations of social exchange. See: *Exchange Theory*.

Glass, David V. (1911–1978). A British demographer and sociologist, his contributions to the development of historical demography and the empirical study of social mobility were of major significance. He held the senior chair in sociology at London University and was on the faculty of the London School of Economics. His major contributions to historical demography were *Population and History* (1965), edited with D. Eversley, and *Population and Social Change* (1972), edited with P. Revelle. He supervised the pioneering investigation into British social mobility, published with other contributors as *Social Mobility in Britain* (1954). He was a founder of *The British Journal of Sociology* and of *Population Studies*, and was elected a Fellow of the Royal Society – a unique distinction for a sociologist. See: *Social Mobility*.

Glossing. For ethnomethodologists, all utterances and actions are indexical, that is, their meaning is uniquely given by their context. Actors have to make sense of such utterances and actions by referring to their context; they have to 'repair' indexicality. Since specification of the context can be an unending task, actors produce a shorthand description, or gloss, of what is going on, of what makes sense to them. See: *Ethnomethodology*; *Indexicality*.

Bibl. Cuff and Payne (eds.) (1979)

Goffman, Erving (1922–1982). In contemporary sociology, he has made a major contribution to the study of social interaction, encounters, gatherings and small groups in *Behaviour in Public Places* (1963), *Interaction Ritual* (1967), and *Relations in Public* (1971). He has also made important contributions to role analysis in *Encounters* (1961a). His principal concern has been with the constituents of fleeting, chance or momentary encounters, that is with the sociology of everyday life. To grasp the orderliness of such meetings, Goffman employed drama as an analogy for the staging of social meetings in *The Presentation of Self in Everyday Life* (1959). For Goffman, the social order is always precarious because it is disrupted by embarrassment, withdrawal and the breakdown of communication; these issues are explored in *Stigma* (1964). He has also contributed to the analysis of inmates in mental institutions in *Asylums* (1961b). His recent publications include *Frame Analysis* (1974) and *Gender Advertisements* (1979). See: *Dramaturgical*; *Ethnomethodology*; *Role*; *Stigma*; *Symbolic Interactionism*; *Total Institution*.

Bibl. Ditton (ed.) (1980)

Goldthorpe, John H. (b. 1935). Presently a fellow of Nuffield College, Oxford, he was co-director with D. Lockwood (q.v.) of the Affluent Worker (q.v.) investigation and co-authored the three volumes (1968; 1968b; 1969) resulting from this research. He subsequently directed a part of the Social Mobility Group's investigation at Nuffield College, leading to the publication of *The Social Grading of Occupations* (1974), with K. Hope, and *Social Mobility and Class Structure in Modern Britain* (1980). He has published papers on class, industrial relations and inflation, and edited *The Political Economy of Inflation* (1978) with F. Hirsch, and *Order and Conflict in Contemporary Capitalism* (1985). See: *Class Imagery*; *Privatization*; *Social Mobility*.

Gouldner, Alvin Ward (1920–1980). Born in New York, he was professor of sociology at Washington University (1959–67), President of the Society for the Study of Social Problems (1962), professor of sociology at Amsterdam (1972–76) and Max Weber Professor of Sociology at Washington University (from 1967). His early works such as *Patterns of Industrial Bureaucracy* (1954) and *Wildcat Strike* (1955b) explored aspects of M. Weber's theory of bureaucracy in relation to strikes, management and control. He emphasized the capacity for working-class action and industrial disruption despite the constraints of bureaucracy. Features of Weber's sociology of religion were explored in *Notes on Technology and the Moral Order* (1962): he argued that certain moral orders (the Apollonian) which emphasized order, reason and activism were causally important in the development of technology.

An important change of direction occurred in the 1960s when he turned to theoretical debates with Marxism and scientific sociology. He worked on a project which would provide a historical and critical study of social theory from Plato (in *Enter Plato*, 1965) to Marxism (in *The Two Marxisms*, 1980) to contemporary sociology (in *Against Fragmentation*, 1985). In these publications Gouldner rejected the fashionable distinction between neutral science, moral discourse and political commitment. These criticisms were first formulated in *The Coming Crisis of Western Sociology* (1970), a major and controversial study of functionalism (q.v.) and Marxism as it had developed as a scientific theory within the Soviet bloc. In 1974, he founded the influential journal *Theory and Society*, which has done much to develop and elaborate his views on critical theory.

Gouldner was always concerned with the possibilities for progressive social change, and specifically with the role of intellectuals in directing and contributing to change in *The Future of Intellectuals and the Rise of the New Class* (1979). He called upon sociologists to be more reflexive about their theories and role in society in *The Dialectic of Ideology and Technology* (1976).

Following his death, there has been much debate as to the dominant intellectual forces which shaped his vision of critical theory. His views on rationality and criticism were influenced by the Frankfurt School (q.v.), but his radical style and outlook were also shaped by C. Wright Mills (q.v.). However, his concern for bureaucracy, power and knowledge reflected his debt to the Weberian tradition.

Gramsci, Antonio (1891–1937). Initially a journalist, then a militant in the Italian Communist Party and imprisoned for ten years by Mussolini, Gramsci was one of the most important Marxist thinkers of the twentieth century. His work, a deliberate attempt to unify social theory and political practice, was dominated by a rejection of economic determinism (q.v.) and the attempt to find an alternative way of interpreting K. Marx. This rejection was achieved in two ways: (1) by insisting on the independence of politics and ideology from economic determination; (2) by emphasizing the way

that men and women can change their circumstances by struggle.

Gramsci argued that the domination of the capitalist class could not be secured by economic factors alone but required political force and, much more importantly, an ideological apparatus which secured the consent of the dominated classes. In capitalist societies, these apparatuses were effectively the institutions of civil society (q.v.), the churches, the family and even trade unions. Political coercion was essentially the province of the state. The stability of capitalist societies was mostly dependent on the ideological domination of the working class. Gramsci suggested that this domination could not be complete, however, for the working class has a dual consciousness (q.v.), one part of which is imposed by the capitalist class while the other part is a commonsense knowledge (q.v.) derived from the workers' everyday experience of the world.

This commonsense knowledge is potentially revolutionary but requires development by party intellectuals to make it an effective force. For Gramsci, radical social change can only come about when a revolutionary consciousness is fully developed, and hence the role of the party is crucial in articulating and promoting this consciousness. The class struggle (q.v.) is very largely a struggle between intellectual groups, one beholden to the capitalist class and the other to the workers. See: *Class Consciousness*; *Dominant Ideology Thesis*; *Hegemony*; *Leninism*; *Marxist Sociology*.

Bibl. Mouffe (ed.) (1979)

Grand Theory. A term coined by C. W. Mills (q.v.) to refer, pejoratively, to sociological theories couched at a very abstract conceptual level, like those of T. Parsons (q.v.). He similarly criticized abstracted empiricism, the practice of accumulating quantitative data for its own sake. Instead he advocated sociology as the study of the relationship of the individual's experience to society and history.

Grounded Theory. In contrast to formal, abstract theory obtained by logico-deductive methods, grounded theory is grounded in data which have been systematically obtained by social research. The development of grounded theory was an attempt to avoid highly abstract sociology. Grounded theory was part of an important growth in qualitative analysis (q.v.) in the 1970s which sought to bridge the gap between theoretically-uninformed empirical research and empirically-uninformed theory by grounding theory in data. It was a reaction against grand theory (q.v.) and extreme empiricism. The concept is a truism, because one cannot collect data without theory or develop theory without an empirical reference.

Bibl. Glaser and Strauss (1968)

Group. Social groups are collectivities of individuals who interact and form social relationships. C. H. Cooley (1909) classified groups as *primary* and *secondary*. The former are small, being defined by face-to-face interaction. They have their own norms of conduct and are solidaristic. Within this category may be included the family, groups of friends and many work groups. The latter are larger and each member does not directly interact with every other. Some secondary groups, for example trade unions, can be described as associations when at least some members interact, when there is an identifiable normative system and some shared sense of corporate existence.

There was a remarkable growth of interest in small groups in the 1930s based on three distinct approaches that have subsequently fused. E. Mayo and colleagues in the business school at Harvard University investigated industrial work groups as part of their sociological approach to the study of human relations in industry; experimental psychologists associated with K. Lewin became interested in groups as the result of investigations of leadership; and J. L. Moreno pioneered sociometry (q.v.), the empirical investigation of the structure of social interaction and communication within small groups. The resulting social psychology of groups has been concerned with issues of group structure and cohesion, morale, group leadership, and the effects on the individual. The relevance of this small-group sociology to an understanding of larger social collectives has still to be shown, although the work of R. F. Bales greatly influenced T. Parsons' (q.v.) analysis of social systems. See: *Homans*; *Human Relations*; *Leadership*; *Primary Relationship*; *Self*.

Bibl. Homans (1950; 1961)

Guild. Guilds were occupational associations of pre- and early industrial society which communicated the lore and skills of a trade by means of formal apprenticeships, control of members' occupational activities, and the exclusion of outsiders from practising the trade. They were normally fraternal and corporate bodies.

H

Habermas, Jürgen (b. 1929). Habermas is one of the principal exponents of critical theory (q.v.) and is also closely associated with the Frankfurt School (q.v.). The main theme of Habermas' theory (1970a; 1970b) is that valid knowledge can only emerge from a situation of open, free and uninterrupted dialogue. In *Towards a Rational Society* (1970c) and *Theory and Practice* (1963) he argued that the idea of a neutral apolitical science, based on a rigid separation of facts and values, is untenable since questions of truth are inextricably bound up with political problems of freedom to communicate and exchange ideas. He has been a prominent critic of positivism (q.v.) and economic determinism (q.v.) in *Knowledge and Human Interests* (1968). Habermas has also been highly critical of systems theory (q.v.), engaging in a prolonged debate with N. Luhmann in *Theorie der Gesellschaft oder Sozialtechnologie?* (1971). He has also been influential in recent studies of the state and the decline of normative legitimacy in *Legitimation Crisis* (1973). His most recent study is *Communication and the Evolution of Society* (1979). See: *Hermeneutics.*

Bibl. McCarthy (1978)

Halévy Thesis. E. Halévy (1961) explained the social and political stability of England in the nineteenth century in terms of the importance of Protestantism. He said that Wesleyan Methodism acted as a social ladder between artisan, nonconformist dissent and the Anglican establishment, thereby contributing to the process of social embourgeoisement (q.v.) and reducing social conflicts.

Bibl. Hill, M. (1973)

Halsey, A. H. (b. 1923). Currently professor of social and administrative studies and a fellow of Nuffield College at the University of Oxford, he has written extensively on education and social mobility. As director of the Oxford Social Mobility Project, he published *Origins and Destinations* (1980), with A. F. Heath and J. M. Ridge, which analysed the interrelationships of family, education and class in twentieth-century Britain. He gave the Reith Lectures for 1977, published as *Change in British Society* (1978). His other major publications include: *Social Class and Educational Opportunity* (1957), *Education, Economy and Society* (1961), *Power in Co-operatives* (1965), *Social Survey of the Civil Service* (1968), *The British Academics* (1971), *Trends in British Society since 1900* (1972), *Power and Ideology in*

Education (1977) with J. Karabel, and *Heredity and Environment* (1977).

Hawthorne Studies. See: *Human Relations.*

Health Care Systems. This term encompasses the various institutions by which the health needs of a society are satisfied. In medieval Europe, the Church provided some charitable relief through the hospice (for sick pilgrims) and the lazar-houses (for the victims of venereal disease and leprosy). The period of religious foundations (335–1550) was followed by the age of the charity hospital (1719–1913). Health care delivery in industrial societies is highly complex. The modern hospital, offering both general and specialized service, has dominated modern health care systems following improvements in care (associated with the professionalization of medicine and nursing) and in hygiene for the management of infections. In the majority of industrial societies, there was a significant programme of construction and modernization of hospitals in the mid-1960s. With the escalation of the cost of hospitalization, there has been, since the mid-1970s, a new emphasis on containment. In the period of hospital expansion, there was, in America, the growth of an alliance between private industry, the state and the medical profession, which sociologists called 'the medical-industrial complex' (B. and J. Ehrenreich, 1970). However, in the period of economic recession, there has been a greater emphasis on preventive medicine (for example, anti-smoking campaigns), community medicine (q.v.) and other local services (such as health centres).

Health care systems can be considered in terms of the levels of health delivery and the means of funding. In terms of levels, it is conventional to distinguish between primary, secondary, and tertiary care. Primary care refers to all forms of out-patient care, typically provided by a general practitioner. Secondary care refers to more specialized forms of service, such as the services of a cardiologist. Tertiary care incorporates complex procedures provided within a specialized hospital or hospital unit such as open-heart surgery. Furthermore, health care systems can be considered along a continuum of private and public health care. At one extreme, health care in the United States is decentralized and depends extensively on private health insurance and private sources of funding; at the other extreme, the USSR has a highly centralized, unitary system funded by the state. Societies like Britain and Sweden fall in the middle of the continuum, combining both public provision and private insurance schemes. There has been much controversy as to the desirability of different types of health care delivery. The basic issue is that a public system of health (such as the National Health Service in Britain) provides a minimum standard of health which is more or less egalitarian, but the economic cost of such a service is very high. By contrast, private health schemes are not an economic burden on the state, but they are highly inegalitarian, since privileged social groups enjoy far higher standards of health. The dispute is, therefore, about equality (q.v.) versus efficiency.

It is difficult to resolve this debate by the use of comparative health statistics. Societies have different procedures for measuring morbidity rates and for evaluating effectiveness. The statistics are also complicated by the fact that populations may have different age structures. There are also important cultural variations in attitudes towards sickness and hospital care. For example, in Japan a period of treatment in a hospital is regarded as an important form of rest. In Japan, the average length of hospitalization was 42·9 days, whereas in Britain it was 13·1 days, according to a World Health Organization survey of 1977. However, the principal difficulty in evaluating different systems is the disagreement over objectives, whether these are to achieve a more egalitarian distribution of health or an efficient system which is economically sensitive to consumer demand. The health care systems of industrial societies are, as a result, a topic of intense political debate. See: *Sociology of Medicine*; *Sociology of Health and Illness*.

Bibl. Rodwin (1984)

Hegemony. This is a term used by A. Gramsci (q.v.) to describe how the domination of one class over others is achieved by a combination of political and ideological means. Although political force – coercion – is always important, the role of ideology in winning the consent of dominated classes may be even more significant. The balance between coercion and consent will vary from society to society, the latter being more important in capitalist societies. For Gramsci, the state was the chief instrument of coercive force, the winning of consent by ideological domination being achieved by the institutions of civil society (q.v.), the family, the Church and trade unions, for instance. Hence the more prominent is civil society, the more likely it is that hegemony will be achieved by ideological means.

Hegemony is unlikely ever to be complete. In contemporary capitalist societies, for example, the working class has a dual consciousness (q.v.), partly determined by the ideology of the capitalist class and partly revolutionary, determined by their experiences of capitalist society. For capitalist society to be overthrown, workers must first establish their own ideological supremacy derived from their revolutionary consciousness. See: *Class Consciousness*; *Dominant Ideology Thesis*; *Ideological State Apparatus*; *Marxist Sociology*.

Bibl. Anderson, P. (1976a)

Heredity. The basic principles of the science of heredity – the study of the transmission by breeding of discrete units of inheritance (genes) from parents to children – were discovered by G. J. Mendel (1822–1884) through a study of peas in 1865. These experiments laid the foundations for genetics (the science of heredity), a term coined by W. Bateson in 1905. These laws of genetic inheritance in the natural world were adopted by F. Galton (1822–1911), who developed the idea of eugenics (q.v.) as a science for the improvement of humanity through the adoption of 'genetic politics'.

Mendelian principles of heredity or genetic transmission may be expressed crudely in the idea that 'like begets like'. Although this theory proved to be useful and important in biology, its application to anthropology and sociology has been much contested. In nineteenth-century sociology, assumptions about genetic inheritance were used to suggest that 'criminals beget criminals'. As a consequence of Social Darwinism (q.v.), it was argued that people with poor genetic attributes should be discouraged or prevented from breeding, because it would have disastrous consequences for society. Sociologists have challenged these assertions on the grounds that: (1) it is very difficult to prove the truth of Mendelian laws in the case of human populations; (2) culture (q.v.) is more important than biological inheritance in social groups, and the symbol (q.v.) not the gene is the basic unit of transmission; (3) eugenics is morally objectionable. See: *Intelligence*; *Nature/Nurture Debate*; *Racism*; *Sociobiology*.

Bibl. Sahlins (1977).

Hermeneutics. This is the theory and method of interpreting meaningful human action. It has a long history, being rooted in the problems of biblical interpretation. Before printing, when bibles were produced by hand-copying, numerous errors were introduced. Hermeneutics referred to the problem of recovering the 'authentic' version. In the early part of the nineteenth century, hermeneuticians became interested in how to interpret any text, not just by concentrating on the text itself, as in the case of biblical interpretation, but also by reference to the experiences of the author.

The subject became more developed in the work of W. Dilthey, who argued that there is a marked difference between the study of nature and the study of human action, which, being an expression of 'lived experience', requires a special method of analysis. Dilthey effectively provided two such methods. In the first, the focus was on the relationship of the creator of an act, a book or a picture to the interpreter. The latter understands by putting himself in the position of the former. Understanding is possible because both share a common humanity or, in another formulation, because they are both expressions of the Spirit. In the second, the characteristics of individuals are disregarded. Instead, hermeneutics understands human action in relation to some wider whole which gives it meaning. For example, a painting is understood by reference to the outlook or world-view (q.v.) of the society in which it is produced. Similarly, the analyst can construct such a world-view out of its individual manifestations. This circular relationship between a whole and its parts is known as a hermeneutic circle.

K. Mannhiem (q.v.) advances similar arguments. He suggests that individual cultural manifestations can be understood by seeing them as part of a larger world-view. The analyst attaches 'documentary meaning' to human action. This has nothing to do with intentions, but makes sense in the context of a world-view. For example, the documentary meaning of a painting can be understood by locating it within the world-view of the society or group which produced it.

Hermeneutics has formed part of a general critique of positivism in sociology, in which human action is seen as caused by social structures of various kinds. However, the difficulty of hermeneutic analysis has always been how to validate interpretations. On the face of it, one interpretation of the meaning of an action or a text is as good as another. The solution offered to this problem is the 'hermeneutic circle' mentioned above. The most distinguished recent writer to advocate this solution is H. G. Gadamer, who insists that hermeneutics has to understand the part in terms of the whole, and the whole in terms of the part. The interpreter, in judging a book, for example, has to recapture the perspective within which the author formulated his or her views. For Gadamer, the spatial and temporal gap between author and interpreter is bridged by tradition and by what he calls a 'fusion of horizons'. However, the gap can never be completely bridged; there can never be a completely correct interpretation. Interpretations are therefore always tentative and subject to revision in the hermeneutic circle. See: *Geisteswissenschaften*; *Phenomenology*; *Positivism*; *Verstehen*.

Bibl. Connerton (1976); Bauman (1978)

Hidden Curriculum. Most educational institutions have a formal curriculum comprising those areas of academic knowledge which pupils are expected to acquire, e.g. mathematics. Besides this academic and explicitly taught curriculum, however, there is also a set of values, attitudes or principles, a hidden curriculum, that is implicitly conveyed to pupils by teachers. The hidden curriculum is believed to promote social control at school and in society at large by training people to conform and to obey authority, teaching them to regard social inequalities as natural, and ensuring cultural reproduction (q.v.).

S. Bowles and H. Gintis (1976) argue that schools have an important role in teaching punctuality, discipline, obedience and diligence, which are the qualities they believe are needed by the workforce in a capitalist society. Pupils who are creative or independent do relatively poorly at school, while those with the first set of qualities do well. In this account, the success of the school in teaching technical skills and knowledge is less important than its success in imparting a hidden curriculum that corresponds to the real needs of the economy. This principle of correspondence has been criticized, on the grounds that many pupils are not socialized to become disciplined workers by schools, as is shown by the prevalence of industrial conflict and employee resistance to managerial control. Resistance may be found even within the school itself, since pupil subcultures that reject authority and school values have been identified, mainly among the academically less successful. See: *Classroom Interaction*; *Classroom Knowledge*; *Educational Attainment*.

Histogram. Any distribution of variables measured on an interval scale may be presented pictorially as a histogram, where blocks of differing areas represent the number of observations falling within each interval on the scale used to measure the variable. For example, the

following table, which gives the age distribution of a sample of respondents in a survey, can also be presented as a histogram.

Age	Number
Under 10 years	5
10 and under 20	10
20 and under 30	20
30 and under 40	30
40 and under 50	20
50 and under 60	25
60 and under 70	10
Total	120

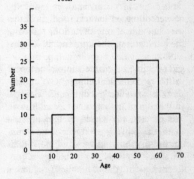

Historical Materialism. K. Marx propounded the materialist interpretation of history that social, cultural and political phenomena were determined by the mode of production of material things. This gave causal priority to the economy rather than to ideas in the explanation of historical processes, summarized in the base–superstructure (q.v.) distinction. See: *Dialectical Materialism*; *Materialism*.

Historical Sociology. In the past twenty years, the two disciplines of history and sociology have converged in terms of empirical interests and methodological approaches. For example, the Annales School (q.v.) employs quantitative methods for the analysis of historical data, while historians of European witchcraft often depend on anthropological theories of magic for historical analysis. Similarly, sociologists frequently utilize detailed historical studies of the working class in one locality in order to build a picture of the development of a national working class during industrialization. This convergence has occurred despite acrimonious debates which proclaim the necessary divisions between the two disciplines.

The term 'historical sociology' can have two trivial meanings. These are either that historical analysis should be more concerned with the social context or that sociology should be given a deeper historical background. P. Abrams (1982) provides a more compelling definition of historical sociology in terms of three theoretical concerns. (1) Sociology is specifically concerned with the transition to industrialism as an historical process. (2) Sociology is concerned with the pattern of freedom and constraint in the life-histories of individuals in social contexts. (3) Sociology is concerned with the dynamic interaction between human agency and social structure, not as an abstract problem, but as an empirical issue in world history. In this sense, all sociology is historical sociology because it is inevitably concerned with change, process and development. See: *Comte*; *Evolutionary Theory*; *Historicism*; *Periodization*; *Progress*; *Social Change*.

Bibl. Braudel (1969)

Historicism. (1) As used by K. R. Popper (q.v.) (1957), this refers to interpretations of history that purport to show the existence of fixed laws of historical development.

(2) In a different sense, historicism refers to the doctrine that every age can only be understood in its own terms and that meaningful comparison cannot be made across historical periods. This view is usually associated with a conception of the human sciences contrary to natural-ism (q.v.) and utilizing such concepts as *Verstehen* (q.v.). It has been argued that historicism falls into a relativism (q.v.) in providing no independent means of validating claims about any society or historical period. See: *Geisteswissenschaften*; *Hermeneutics*.

Holism. This is the doctrine that societies should be seen as wholes, or as systems of interacting parts. Analysis should, therefore, start from large-scale institutions and their relationships, not from the behaviour of individual actors. Societies, in this view, have properties as wholes which cannot be deduced from the characteristics of individuals. See: *Action Theory*; *Atomism*; *Functionalism*; *Methodological Individualism*; *Social System*; *Systems Theory*.

Homans, George C. (b. 1910). An American sociologist concerned with the functioning of small groups and face-to-face social interaction, he has made notable contributions to exchange theory (q.v.). His major works are: *The Human Group* (1950), *Social Behaviour: Its Elementary Forms* (1961), *Sentiments and Activities* (1962) and *The Nature of Social Science* (1967). In a famous paper (1964) he argued that all social phenomena are to be explained in terms of the characteristics of individuals rather than social structures. See: *Group*; *Methodological Individualism*.

Homoeostasis. See: *Social System*.

Housework. See: *Domestic Labour*.

Housing Class. The theory of housing classes was introduced by J. Rex and R. Moore (1967). Their argument is that the population can be grouped into distinct housing classes, the owners of houses or council-house tenants for example, that are usually geographically segregated. The constitution or numbers of classes will vary from place to place. Housing classes are independent of social classes, although they are also a feature of social inequality since not all housing is equally desirable. Rex and Moore assume that everybody wants suburban housing but not everybody has access to it, and hence there is competition and struggle between housing classes which is responsible for much apparently racial conflict. The regulation of access to housing classes is of great importance, since it tends to confine ethnic minorities to city centres. The theory has been criticized because it is difficult to draw the boundaries of housing classes, a very large number of classes are often introduced, conflicts are as often within housing classes as between them, suburban housing is not universally desired and, most important, housing classes are really a function of the social class structure. See: *Zone of Transition*.

Human Capital. Individuals who invest time and money (including foregone earnings) in education, training and other qualities that increase their productivity and thus their worth to an employer, are said to have a greater endowment of human capital. The idea of differing human capitals is used by many labour economists to explain inequalities in the labour market: variations in pay are assumed to reflect the different values of the human capital that different employees bring to work. Groups who are apparently disadvantaged in the labour market, including women and ethnic minorities, are held to owe at least part of their inferior rewards to their lower investments in human capital, whether these be education and training or, particularly in the case of women, lack of continuous work experience. A problem with the concept is

that productivity is not in fact measured directly but is only inferred from the higher pay received by, for example, the better educated men. The inference depends on an assumption that employers are rational people who maximize profits by paying only what the productivity of each individual employee justifies. See: *Dual Labour Markets*; *Women and Work*.

Bibl. Amsden (ed.) (1980); Granovetter (1981)

Human Ecology. See: *Urban Ecology*

Human Relations. This interdisciplinary movement in the study of social relations in industry, embracing sociology, social anthropology and social psychology, was influential between the late 1930s and early 1960s in academic and managerial circles. It focused on the behaviour of employees in groups, and marked a shift away from the scientific management (q.v.) view of employees as isolated individuals maximizing income, to regard employees as oriented towards groups and needing socially supportive relationships at work, placing group interests above their own individual financial rewards. Pioneering research carried out in the Western Electric Co. by E. Mayo and colleagues between 1927 and 1932, sometimes known as the Hawthorne Studies after the name of the main plant, suggested that employee productivity was influenced by group factors. In one experiment, output increased when the creation of small work groups raised morale. However, in another, work-group norms restricted output. Subsequent investigation has concentrated on the factors influencing work-group formation, such as the technology and layout of production systems, and the ways of channelling group dynamics to the benefit of the company – for example, by training supervisors to act as group leaders. Criticisms of

Human Relations include: (1) that it has ignored the wider social system of the organization, including conflict between workers and management; (2) that it has ignored the influence on output of trade unions and the wider economic environment; (3) that it exaggerates the 'social' needs of employees. See: *Affluent Worker*; *Cash Nexus*; *Group*; *Industrial Conflict*; *Pareto*; *Scientific Management*; *Socio-Technical Systems*.

Bibl. Rose, M. (1975)

Humanism. A concern with man rather than with God or nature is the central tenet of humanism. Humanist Marxist sociology is that which takes mankind, rather than social structure, as its central focus.

Hypothesis. A proposition or set of propositions put forward for empirical testing. The word is often used more loosely to mean suggestion, explanation or theory. See: *Hypothetico-Deductive Method*.

Hypothetico-Deductive Method. This is a method of inquiry in which a theory is verified or refuted by empirically testing hypotheses deduced from it. It is, in practice, not often adhered to in sociology, nor, according to some critics, in the natural sciences. See: *Falsificationism*; *Hypothesis*; *Positivism*.

I

Iatrogenesis. See: *Sociology of Health and Illness*.

Idealism. In philosophy, this is the position that the external material world is either constructed by or dependent upon the mind. In sociology, subjectivist idealism is occasionally employed to describe such positions as symbolic interactionism (q.v.) in which the external social reality cannot exist independently of the everyday interactions and subjectivity of social actors. Marxists argue that sociology as a whole is idealist because it neglects or minimizes the causal role of objective economic conditions. For some Marxists, the economic base determines the superstructure of beliefs. However, it should be noted that Marxists in recent years have often appeared to stress the causal importance of the superstructure, while the emphasis on subjectivity in sociology has the merit of drawing attention to the active role of social actors in the construction of social reality. See: *Base and Superstructure*; *Determinism*; *Materialism*.

Bibl. Benton (1977)

Ideal Type. There has been considerable confusion surrounding the exposition of ideal-type constructions in sociology. M. Weber first drew attention to ideal types in order to make explicit the procedures by which he believed social scientists formulate general, abstract concepts such as 'the pure competitive market', the 'church-set typology' or 'bureaucracy'. He suggested that social scientists selected as the defining characteristics of an ideal type certain aspects of behaviour or institutions which were observable in the real world, and exaggerated these to form a coherent intellectual construction. Not all the characteristics will always be present in the real world, but any particular situation may be understood by comparing it with the ideal type. For example, individual bureaucratic organizations may not exactly match the elements in the ideal type of bureaucracy (q.v), but the type can illuminate these variations. Ideal types are therefore hypothetical constructions, formed from real phenomena, which have an explanatory value. 'Ideal' signifies 'pure' or 'abstract' rather than normatively desirable. However, the precise relationship between ideal types and the reality to which they refer remains obscure. Weber did suggest that major discrepancies between reality and an ideal type would lead to the type being redefined, but he also argued that ideal types were not models to be tested. However, other sociologists treat them as testable models of the real world.

Further confusion may arise since Weber himself often implicitly used ideal types as testable models. See: *Model*; *Weber*.

Bibl. Rogers (1969)

Ideological State Apparatus (ISA). A term popularized by L. Althusser (q.v.). This refers to one of the means by which the domination of the capitalist class is secured. ISAs, examples of which are religious and educational institutions, the media of communication, the family, even trade unions and political parties, function by incorporating all classes in societies within a dominant ideology. The hegemony (q.v.) of dominant classes can also be secured by Repressive State Apparatuses (RSA) which operate by force rather than ideology. The balance between ISAs and RSAs will vary from society to society. The concept of ISA has been criticized for exaggerating the impact of ideology in making societies coherent. See: *Dominant Ideology Thesis*; *Gramsci*; *Ideology*; *Incorporation*.

Bibl. Abercrombie (1980)

Ideology. One of the most debated concepts in sociology, ideology may be provisionally defined as beliefs, attitudes and opinions which form a set, whether tightly or loosely related. The term has been used in three important senses: (1) to refer to very specific kinds of belief; (2) to refer to beliefs that are in some sense distorted or false; (3) to refer to any set of beliefs, covering everything from scientific knowledge, to religion, to everyday beliefs about proper conduct, irrespective of whether it is true or false.

(1) Ideology in this sense has figured mainly in the American political science literature and is defined as a tightly knit body of beliefs organized around a few central values. Examples are communism, fascism and some varieties of nationalism. Ideologies in this sense are frequently oppositional to dominant institutions and play a role in the organization of devotees into sects or parties. Investigation of these sorts of belief typically takes the form of studies of the ideological personality or of the social functions that ideology performs, as in, for example, the industrialization of a society.

(2) This conception of ideology is associated with the Marxist literature. There are many different usages but the fundamental arguments are that, firstly, the character of ideologies is largely determined by the economic arrangements of a society and, secondly, in class societies such as capitalism, ideologies are distorted by class interest (q.v.). The first argument is represented in the notions of base and superstructure (q.v.) and in the idea that membership of a social class determines ideology. The second is often expressed in the concepts of a dominant class ideology and false consciousness.

Areas of debate revolve around the degree of economic determination and the consequences of holding that ideologies are necessarily distorted in capitalist society. It has been argued that some sorts of ideology – concerning art, for example – are relatively unaffected by the economy or class membership. Again, social groups other than class have been shown to have an influence on the character of ideology. Various arguments have been advanced concerning the mechanism by which distorted beliefs are produced. For instance, class interest is said to narrow and constrain perceptions of the world, and Marx's ideas on commodity fetishism (q.v.) have also been invoked. These arguments do, however, raise the difficulty of how one obtains objective knowledge. Thus, if the economic base or class interests distort knowledge in capitalist societies, how is one to obtain a perspective outside capitalism in order to claim that there is distortion?

(3) The notion of ideology as constituting any set of beliefs, true or false, is found in the sociology of knowledge (q.v.). The idea here is simply that all beliefs are socially determined in some way or another, although there is no assumption that any one factor, the economy for instance, is most important. For example, it has been argued that bureaucracies generate particular styles of thought. There is, therefore, room for argument about the degree of social determination and about which social groups generate ideologies. Some writers have argued that the principle that beliefs are socially caused creates a difficulty in that this seems to imply that these beliefs are false. Against this, it has been suggested that social causation does not imply falsity, and showing that a proposition is false and that it is socially caused are quite separate activities. Other writers, working within the tradition of hermeneutics (q.v.), have argued that it is incorrect to speak of social factors *causing* beliefs.

Contemporary European debates about ideology have fused (2) and (3). There are three major points of argument. (a) There has been a general movement against economic determinism and towards the recognition that ideology may be relatively independent of class or the economic structure. (b) Many recent writers have argued against the notion that ideology consists of 'ideas in people's heads'. First, it is suggested that ideology should be seen not only as an intellectual product but also as comprising the ideas of ordinary men and women. Second, some writers have argued that ideologies are not ideas at all, but rather should be viewed as practices engaged in every day by everybody in an entirely unreflecting way. Third, it may be that discourse (q.v.), a unified and structured domain of language-use that constrains what can be

said or thought, is equivalent to ideology. (c) More abstractly, the role of the subject, the individual human agent, in ideological creation and function has been the subject of extensive debate, particularly where sociology overlaps with other disciplines like linguistics. See: *Althusser*; *Appearance and Reality*; *Class Consciousness*; *Culture*; *Determinism*; *Dominant Ideology Thesis*; *End of Ideology Theory*; *Gramsci*; *Hegemony*; *Interpellation*; *Myth*; *Semiotics*; *Subject/Subjectivity*; *World-View*.

Bibl. Larrain (1979); Abercrombie (1980); Belsey (1980)

Idiographic. A term used to describe methods of study of individual, unique persons, events or things. It contrasts with nomothetic methods in which the object is to find general laws which subsume individual cases. See: *Empathy*; *Hermeneutics*; *Historicism*; *Verstehen*.

Imperatively Coordinated Association. This is a term used by R. Dahrendorf (1959), derived from M. Weber, to describe groups which possess an authority structure, such as the state and firms. See: *Dahrendorf*.

Imperialism. In its broad and conventional meaning, imperialism is the imposition of the power of one state over the territories of another, normally by military means, in order to exploit subjugated populations to extract economic and political advantages. As a form of conquest and domination, empires are an ancient form of political rivalry between human societies. In the social sciences, attitudes towards imperialism are sharply divided. Liberal economists, like J. A. Schumpeter (1951), have argued that the imperialist expansion of European societies in the nineteenth century was not a necessary feature of capitalist growth and competition, but in fact contrary to the political and economic characteristics of capitalism. Imperialism was simply the survival into capitalism of the militaristic nationalism of absolute monarchies. By contrast, radical writers have treated imperialism as an essential feature of capitalist development at a particular stage. V. I. Lenin (1915) associated capitalist imperialism with the dominance of finance capital, the export of capital in response to domestic stagnation of the economy, the growth of international trusts and the capitalist division of the globe. Economic theories of imperialism either claim that capitalism is pushed into imperialism because of a crisis of profitability in home markets or pulled into imperialism by the need for cheap raw materials. Critics of these Marxist theories point out that (1) imperialism pre-dates capitalism and (2) political rather than economic causes explain imperialist rivalry.

The terms 'imperialism' and 'colonialism' are often used interchangeably, but colonialism – the settlement of foreign territories, the separation of foreign and indigenous peoples by legal means, and the growth of racialism – can be regarded as a special or direct form of imperialism. 'Neo-colonialism' refers to a situation where, despite formal political independence, previous colonies are still dependent upon and subordinated to a metropolis. See: *Capitalism*; *Dependency*; *International Division of Labour*; *Underdevelopment*; *World-System Theory*.

Bibl. Barratt Brown (1974); Mommsen (1980)

Income. See: *Distribution of Income and Wealth*

Incorporation. The process of incorporation refers to the channelling of working-class political and economic activity into existing institutions, rather than allowing it to remain on the outside where it poses a threat to the established order. This process is thought to involve both the growth of citizenship (q.v.) and a change in working-class culture from radical, oppositional values based on class consciousness to an acceptance of the socially dominant values in society. Whereas T. H. Marshall (q.v.) and R. Bendix (q.v.) believed that the growth of citizenship established effective democratic participation that destroyed privilege, Marxist sociologists have argued that inequality remained and incorporation was mainly the result of growing bourgeois ideological hegemony (q.v.) over the working class and the 'betrayal' of the working class by their political and trade-union leaders. See: *Class Consciousness*; *Dominant Ideology Thesis*; *Ideological State Apparatus*; *Institutionalization of Conflict*; *Oligarchy*; *Trade Unions*.

Index. (1) In survey analysis a number of variables may be combined into a composite measure or index which is expressed as a single score. For example, an investigator may ask several questions about various aspects of social inequality, such as housing, education, income and health, and then combine the answers into a single measure of reported inequality. Each respondent can then be assigned a single score on this composite scale.

(2) Index can also refer to an indicator of something that is not measured directly. For example, voting for socialist political parties is sometimes used as an index of politically militant attitudes among manual workers.

Indexicality. Ethnomethodologists argue that all actions and utterances are indexical, that is, they depend for their meaning on the context in which they occur. This feature means that actors will normally make sense of actions and utterances of others by referring to their context, an activity which requires work, even if unconscious, particularly as each context is unique. See: *Ethnomethodology*; *Glossing*.

Bibl. Cuff and Payne (eds.) (1979)

Individualism. This term refers to a collection of doctrines which stress the importance of the individual in relation to other entities. For example, Protestantism is a form of religious individualism in that it argues for a direct relationship between individuals and God, rather than one mediated by the Church. See: *Methodological Individualism*.

Induction. This is a process by which the truth of a proposition is made more *probable* by the accumulation of confirming evidence, a common pattern in scientific and sociological research. It cannot ever be ultimately valid because there is always the possibility of a disconfirming instance. Induction is contrasted with deduction, in which valid conclusions can be logically deduced from valid premises. Sociological arguments are rarely strictly deductive in form, even if they may claim to be. See: *Falsificationism*; *Hypothetico-Deductive Method*.

Industrial Conflict. The relationship between the owners and managers of industry on the one hand and working people on the other is frequently one of conflict. The term refers both to the forms which conflict may take and to the sources of conflict. There is general agreement among industrial sociologists that the forms of conflict are various and include absenteeism, sabotage, restriction of output and non-cooperation, all of which may occur on an individual or collective basis, and collective bargaining and strikes which are collective manifestations.

There are competing accounts of the sources of conflict. The Human Relations (q.v.) movement suggested that conflict occurred when industry failed to integrate workers into a socially supportive community at work and that conflict between managers and workers was not inevitable. Other approaches believe that conflict is inevitable. R. Dahrendorf (1959) claimed that there would always be conflict between those with authority and those without. Many Weberian sociologists attribute conflict to the clash of economic interests in employment, because workers and managers have different interests with regard to wages and effort. Marxists also adhere to an economic explanation, namely that employment in capitalism is by nature exploitative and places management and labour in opposed camps. Economic accounts have had primacy in recent years.

Accounts of conflict reflect three alternative models of the firm and the employment system. Human Relations had a *unitary* model of the firm as a homogeneous community with shared interests and values, with the potential of great harmony. The Marxist perspective is *dichotomous* and oppositional, emphasizing the fundamental and all-embracing nature of conflict. Exploitation means that firms are split into two camps which have no identity of interests and workers are compelled to work against their will. Modern Weberian economic accounts are usually *pluralist*, since they see firms as containing a plurality of divisions and competing interests, that is within the ranks of management and labour as well as between them. Moreover, pluralism suggests that the various parties within the firm have an interest in cooperating, since by working together they do better than they would on their own, and so conflict occurs within this broader cooperative framework. An assumption of some accounts is that, because people

121

can choose whether or not to work, employment should not be seen as coercive. See: *Collective Bargaining*; *Imperatively Coordinated Association*; *Industrial Democracy*; *Inflation*; *Institutionalization of Conflict*; *Labour Process Approach*; *Pluralism*; *Scientific Management*; *Strikes*; *Trade Unions*.

Bibl. Fox (1974); Hyman (1977); Hill, S. (1981)

Industrial Democracy. This concept refers to the participation of workers in industrial decisions which affect their working lives. The mechanisms by which democracy may be promoted are various. They include: (1) trade unionism and collective bargaining; (2) works councils and consultation between management and employees; (3) co-determination, which provides employee representatives with seats on company boards and a share in company decision-making; (4) workers' control of industry. Workers are primarily interested in having influence in the areas that most directly affect their working lives, such as wages, working conditions and the power of managers over employees. Trade unionism and collective bargaining have proved effective at this level in Britain, while in continental Europe works councils have formed the main vehicle of participation on issues other than wages. However, certain crucial issues, such as new investments or plant closures, are beyond the scope of trade unions working through collective bargaining or works councils dealing with day-to-day problems, and other mechanisms of industrial democracy are required in addition. In a number of European countries, employees have representation on company boards and participate in high-level decision making, but, being in the minority, these employees do not determine the outcome of decisions. In Yugoslavia, the law has established self-management, and companies are managed by employees who also share the profits, which is a form of workers' control. The other form is found in enterprises structured as cooperatives. See: *Citizenship*; *Collective Bargaining*; *Cooperative*; *Trade Unions*.

Bibl. Poole (1975)

Industrial Relations. This phrase covers the employment relationship and the institutions associated with it. It embraces the relations between workers, work groups, worker organizations and managers, companies and employer organizations. The study of industrial relations is an interdisciplinary enterprise, drawing heavily on industrial sociology, labour economics and trade-union history, and to a lesser extent on psychology and political science.

Industrial Society. The defining characteristics of an industrial society are (1) the creation of cohesive nation-states organized around a common language and culture; (2) the commercialization of production and the disappearance of a subsistence economy; (3) the dominance of machine-production and the organization of production in the factory; (4) the decline of the proportion of the working population engaged in agriculture; (5) the urbanization of society; (6) the growth of mass literacy; (7) the enfranchisement of the population and the institutionalization of politics around mass parties; (8) the application of science to all spheres of life, especially industrial production, and the gradual rationalization (q.v.) of social life. Industrial society is frequently associated with mass society (q.v.). Western Europe and North America went through the process of industrialization in the period 1815–1914, although there was considerable variation in the rate of change for individual societies.

The principal area of controversy in the analysis of industrial society has centred on whether such societies are cooperative or conflictual, adaptive or self-destructive. In the nineteenth century, sociologists like H. Spencer and E. Durkheim emphasized the cooperative, integrative nature of the division of labour (q.v.) in industrial society. Similarly, contemporary structural functionalism (q.v.) has treated industrial society as a highly differentiated and coherent social system. In contrast, Marxist sociologists regard industrial society as inherently conflictual by pointing to, for example, the contradictory interests of wage labour and capitalist owners and managers. While sociologists treat both capitalism and socialism as industrial societies, Marxists typically regard industrial society as specific to capitalism, emphasizing the essentially exploitative nature of capitalist relations. For Marxists, however, the technological basis of machine-production in industrial society is incidental to the defining characteristics of capitalism, namely the separation of the worker from the means of production, production of commodities by wage labour and the realization of an economic surplus in the form of profits. The crises of capitalist production result in class struggle and imperialism. Not all conceptions of industrial society have been formulated in such sharp contrasts between cooperation or conflict. Both M. Weber and the economist J. M. Keynes recognized the instability of the capitalist market without accepting a Marxist analysis. Weber recognized the instability of competitive capitalism and the discipline of factory production, while denying that socialism could avoid completely the sociological characteristics of industrialism. Keynes (1936) thought that the basic problem of the business cycle was inadequate aggregate consumer demand, which could be solved by state provision of programmes of public works rather than through war and class conflict. The debate about the role of the state in relation to the crises of industrial capitalism has remained central to much recent sociological analysis. See: *Automation*; *Capitalism*; *Convergence Thesis*; *Division of Labour*; *Industrial Conflict*; *Industrialization*; *Post-Industrial Society*; *Socialist Societies*; *Technology*.

Bibl. Aron (1962); Scott (1979)

Industrialization. This term refers to sustained economic growth following the application of inanimate sources of power to mechanize production. Industrialization initially took the form of factory production, later spreading to agriculture and services. Compared with pre-industrial organization, it has involved division of labour (q.v.), new social relations of production (q.v.) between the owners of capital, managers and workers, urbanization and the geographical concentration of industry and population, and changes in occupational structure. Initially a development within capitalist economies, industrialization now transcends any single economic system. The understanding of the nature and consequences of industrialization and industrial society has always been central to sociology from the nineteenth-century 'founding fathers' through to the present. See: *De-industrialization*; *Industrial Society*; *Post-Industrial Society*; *Urbanization*.

Bibl. Aron (1962)

Inequality. See: *Deprivation*; *Distribution of Income and Wealth*; *Equality*; *Justice*; *Stratification*.

Inflation. This is a rise in the general level of prices which has the effect of reducing the purchasing power of a given amount of money. The investigation of inflation has mainly been confined to economics, but sociologists are now interested in the social processes that lie behind this phenomenon.

Within market economies the interests of capital and labour conflict with regard to the distribution of the product between profits and wages, with both sides trying to maximize their own interests. Historically, when labour was weak – as the result of high unemployment levels, a political and legal system that favoured business interests, and a poorly organized labour movement – pressure to raise wages was resisted. In the post-war era through to the recession of the late 1970s, all these conditions changed and business was less able to resist pay demands. These demands became inflationary to the extent that higher wages did not reflect more output; by increasing prices, business resisted the reduced profits implied by increased wage costs. Governments played a part by increasing the money supply to permit higher money wages to be accommodated without widespread business bankruptcies.

This analysis suggests a number of important social conditions. (1) There is little natural harmony of interests between employers and workers. (2) There is no effective set of shared social values which restrain workers' aspirations and demands – a state of anomie (q.v.). (3) The balance of power within industry and in politics between labour and capital is now more evenly balanced. (4) Government plays a significant role in reconciling economic conflicts. See: *Corporatism*; *Industrial Conflict*.

Bibl. Hirsch and Goldthorpe (eds.) (1978)

Infrastructure. See: *Base and Superstructure*.

Inner City. See: *Zone of Transition*.

Insanity. See: *Anti-Psychiatry*; *Madness*; *Medical Model*; *Medicalization*.

Instinct. A term used in sociology to indicate unlearned, pre-social, or genetically coded characteristics of human beings. See: *Ethology*; *Nature/Nurture Debate*; *Need*; *Sociobiology*.

Institution. The term is widely used to describe social practices that are regularly and continuously repeated, are sanctioned and maintained by social norms, and have a major significance in the social structure. Like role (q.v.), the term refers to established patterns of behaviour, but institution is regarded as a higher-order, more general unit that incorporates a plurality of roles. Thus a school as a social institution embraces pupil roles, teacher roles (which usually include different roles for junior, senior and head teachers) and, depending on the degree of autonomy a school has from outside agencies, parent roles and the managerial/inspectorial roles associated with the relevant educational authority. *The* school as an institution embraces these roles across all the schools that jointly constitute the school system in a given society.

Five major complexes of institutions are conventionally identified. (1) Economic institutions serve to produce and distribute goods and services. (2) Political institutions regulate the use of, and access to, power. (3) Stratification institutions determine the distribution of positions and resources. (4) Kinship institutions deal with marriage, the family and the socialization (q.v.) of the young. (5) Cultural institutions are concerned with religious, scientific and artistic activities.

Institutionalization is the process whereby social practices become sufficiently regular and continuous to be described as institutions. The notion is a useful corrective to the view that institutions are given and unchanging entities, indicating that changes in social practice both modify existing institutions and create novel forms. This is the correlate of the idea in role theory that people have some freedom to 'role make' in their interactions with others and do not simply act out prescribed patterns of behaviour.

The concept of institution is widely used in sociology, though often without precise specification. Different schools of sociology treat it in different ways. For example, functionalists can see institutions as fulfilling the 'needs' of individuals or societies, while phenomenologists may concentrate on the way in which people create or adapt institutions rather than merely respond to them. See: *Comparative Method*; *Need*; *Norm*; *Social Structure*.

Bibl. Eisenstadt (1968b; 1968c)

Institutionalization of Conflict. Early capitalist industrialization was marked by violent social conflict in industry and society which at times threatened to culminate in revolution. As capitalism has matured, so conflicts have declined and become less threatening. A major sociological explanation is the institutionalization of conflict.

It is assumed that one reason why conflict was severe during early capitalism was the destruction of traditional, pre-industrial social bonds and normative regulation. With the completion of the transition to mature industrialism, new regulatory and integrative institutions and values developed. Institutionalization results from the separation and autonomy of political and industrial conflict, so that one is no longer superimposed upon the other. The growth of citizenship rights such as universal suffrage and political representation means that the interests which dominate industry no longer control politics. Citizenship directly integrates workers into society as well. Another process is subsumed under institutionalization: the development of specialized institutions for regulating conflict in industry once industrial conflict has been separated from political. Trade unions, together with collective bargaining between employers and trade unions, are institutions which negotiate and reconcile the differences between employers and workers. See: *Citizenship*; *Collective Bargaining*; *End of Ideology Theory*; *Industrial Conflict*; *Strikes*; *Trade Unions*.

Bibl. Hill, S. (1981)

Instrumentalism. This term describes the orientation of workers who seek instrumental satisfactions from work, such as high pay or secure employment. It is sometimes contrasted with the orientation of those who value satisfactions relating to the intrinsic nature of work tasks or the social community aspects of work. In practice people usually appreciate a combination of all three. T. Parsons (q.v.) also uses the term to describe an orientation to action. See: *Affluent Worker*; *Cash Nexus*; *Orientation to Work*.

Bibl. Hill, S. (1981)

Integration. (1) One of the abiding problems of classical sociological theory was how the various elements of society hold together, how they integrate with each other. Various accounts of social integration are proposed, the two most important being integration by commonly held values and integration by interdependence in the division of labour (q.v.). The concept has been criticized as implying an over-integrated view of societies, ignoring the possibilities of conflict. (2) Integration also refers to the process by which different races come to have closer social, economic and political relationships. See: *Dominant Ideology Thesis*; *Durkheim*; *Parsons*; *Social Order*.

Intelligence. Defined as an innate ability, it is measured in terms of an individual's performance in mental tests which provide an intelligence quotient (the IQ) giving the ratio of a person's intelligence to the average of 100. A. Binet (1857–1911), a French psychologist, was commissioned in 1904 by the French minister of public instruction to inquire into the education of retarded children. He constructed an intelligence test which graded children in terms of their mental age (determined by a variety of cognitive tests) and their chronological age. This technique was developed by W. Stern, who invented the IQ by dividing the mental age by chronological age and multiplying by 100. This arithmetical device produced a single number which was regarded as an index (q.v.) of a child's ability.

Considerable controversy surrounds the concept. (1) Is intelligence a fixed, innate ability or is it a skill which can be developed? (2) Do intelligence tests measure ability or performance which is determined by other factors such as class, race or gender? (3) Do the tests measure a child's conformity to classroom expectations which are set by the teacher? (4) Some critics suggest that IQ tests are produced by representatives of the middle class in terms of the prevailing culture of such privileged groups, and that IQ tests are biased towards certain dominant norms. There is general agreement in sociology that intelligence tests are not neutral or reliable, and that intelligence is not static or wholly innate. See: *Classroom Interaction*; *Classroom Knowledge*; *Nature/Nurture Debate*.

Interaction. See: *Action Theory*; *Ex-*

change Theory; *Parsons*; *Simmel*; *Symbolic Interactionism*.

Interaction of Variables. This term describes the situation when there are two or more independent variables which interact together to influence a dependent variable. For example, an investigation of the effect of teaching methods (an independent variable) on educational achievement (the dependent variable) might show that formal methods produce higher levels of achievement among school pupils than informal methods. Introducing the IQ score of pupils as a second independent variable, however, could produce an interaction effect between the independent variables, with the result that formal teaching methods would not produce improvements in educational achievement for all IQ scores: pupils at the extremes, with very high and very low IQ scores, might achieve higher levels with informal methods whereas the great bulk of pupils might do better with formal. The main effect of formal methods in this hypothetical example is to raise achievement levels, but interaction means that the effect of one independent variable is not the same for every category of another independent variable. See: *Dependent/Independent Variables*; *Multivariate Analysis*.

Bibl. Moser and Kalton (1979)

Intergenerational Mobility. See: *Social Mobility*.

Internal Colonialism. This concept was used by Marxists like V. I. Lenin and A. Gramsci to describe political and economic inequalities between regions within a given society, by political sociology to characterize the uneven effects of state development on a regional basis, and by race relations theory to describe the underprivileged status and exploitation of minority groups within the wider society. These variations in application have a number of common elements: (1) they reject the assumption that industrial development will, in the long run, produce an integrated society, bound together by common culture and by equality of citizenship rights; (2) regional inequalities are not temporary but necessary features of industrial society. In colonialism the relationship between metropolis and colony is unequal and exploitative; in internal colonialism the relationship between the core and its geographical periphery is also exploitative. An internal colony produces wealth for the benefit of those areas most closely associated with the state. The members of these colonies may be differentiated by ethnicity, religion, language or some other cultural variable; they are then overtly or covertly excluded from prestigious social and political positions which are dominated by members of the metropolis. This model has been used recently to explore the role of Celtic regions within British national development. See: *Centre/Periphery*; *Underdevelopment*.

Bibl. Hechter (1975)

Internalization. This concept refers to the process by which an individual learns and accepts as binding the social values and norms (q.v.) of conduct relevant to his or her social group or wider society. See: *Socialization*.

International Division of Labour. The concept of the division of labour (q.v.) calls attention to the way in which the production process is progressively broken up into different tasks. The result is a greater degree of specialization which can operate at a number of different levels. Individual workers will specialize, but so also will whole companies or parts of a country which come to play one particular role in a production process that spreads over a wide geographical area. The division of labour now has an international dimension, in that different countries tend to specialize in one phase of the production process of particular commodities. This tendency reproduces internationally the class system that is produced nationally by the division of labour, with Third-World countries being forced into specialization and advanced industrial countries benefiting by acting as the coordinators of the process. See: *Centre/Periphery*; *Dependency*; *Imperialism*; *Uneven Development*; *World-System Theory*.

Interpellation. This idea was introduced by L. Althusser (q.v.) to explain the way in which ideology (q.v) works. It expresses the view that ideologies are not ideas or beliefs in people's heads but should be more broadly conceived as *social processes*. Ideology works in a manner analogous to naming a person or hailing him or her in the street; that is, ideologies 'address' people and give them a particular subjectivity (q.v.) Ideologies, therefore, play a crucial role first in constructing individuals' identities and then in giving them a particular position in society. For example, religious ideology gives believers a certain identity in relation to God and other human beings. The concept has been criticized for being too rigid. It does not allow people to resist ideology.

Bibl. Therborn (1980)

Interpretation. See: *Empathy*; *Geisteswissenschaften*; *Hermeneutics*; *Phenomenological Sociology*; *Rule*; *Verstehen*.

Intersubjectivity. Many forms of sociological theory have, as their starting point, the experiences of the individual subject. Such theories have to explain how it is that individuals relate to one another, that is, how intersubjectivity is created. See: *Action Theory*; *Phenomenological Sociology*; *Schutz*; *Symbolic Interactionism*.

Bibl. Berger and Luckmann (1967)

Intervening Variable. This is a variable that mediates the effect of one variable on another. For example, the positive correlation between the occupational levels of fathers and sons is mediated by several intervening variables, one of the most important being educational attainment. See: *Correlation*.

Interview. The interview is an important research technique in empirical sociology. Interviews may either be formal, using a structured interview schedule, or informal, the interviewer being able to follow up points made by the interviewee. Interviews may also provide either quantitative or qualitative data. Doubts have been expressed concerning the reliability of the interview. Thus its very formality may mean that the respondent does not act 'typically'. The interview is not a neutral social relationship and the respondents' perceptions of the interviewer may well affect replies. See: *Bias*; *Ethnography*; *Participant Observation*; *Qualitative Analysis*; *Questionnaire*; *Unobtrusive Measures*.

Interviewer Bias. See: *Bias*; *Interview*; *Replication*.

Intragenerational Mobility. See: *Social Mobility*.

Invisible Religion. P. L. Berger and T. Luckmann (1963) criticized the conventional sociology of religion for its narrow focus on Christian institutions; they argued that the sociology of religion and the sociology of knowledge (q.v.) were both alike in explicating the processes by which the everyday world is rendered meaningful. They argued in *The Social Construction of Reality* (1967) that religion was fundamental to the creation and preservation of social reality. These perspectives on religion were further developed in Berger (1969) and Luckmann (1967). Luckmann claimed that individualism (q.v.) in contemporary, urban, consumer society contained elements of transcendence and sacredness which were components of an invisible religion. These themes of contemporary individualism were the pursuit of individual autonomy through self-expression and self-actualization. He associated this emphasis on individual experience and expression with social mobility (q.v.), achievement motivation (q.v.), sexuality, and the privatized world of the modern family. His theory of religion is consequently a significant challenge to the conventional view of secularization (q.v.). See: *Civil Religion*; *Privatization*; *Profane*; *Sacred*; *Religion*.

J

Joint Conjugal Role. See: *Conjugal Role*.

Justice. As a concept fundamental to ethical theory and political philosophy, justice is associated with the notion of equity (or impartiality) and equality (q.v.), especially with the injunction to treat equals equally. From Aristotle (*c*.384–322 BC), it is conventional to distinguish between (1) distributive justice, which is concerned with questions of who should get what, and (2) corrective (or commutative) justice, which is concerned with the treatment of individuals in social transactions (especially punishing an individual for an offence). The notion of distributive justice is important in contemporary social philosophy and policy as social justice. A modern theory of distributive justice has been put forward by the American philosopher J. Rawls in *A Theory of Justice* (1971), in which he defends individualism (q.v.) while also arguing a case for equality. His general definition is that 'All social values – liberty and opportunity, income and wealth, and the bases of self-respect – are to be distributed equally unless an unequal distribution of any, or all, of these values is to everyone's advantage' (1971, p. 62). We can take two examples. It may be 'to everyone's advantage' to have legislation prohibiting the possession of firearms; instead, society has an unequal distribution of firearms to the police force in order to maintain an equal security of life. Secondly, it may be 'to everyone's advantage' to prohibit young people under a certain age from riding a motorbicycle. In both illustrations there is a tension between personal liberties and social justice. An alternative view of justice, that emphasizes liberties, has been propounded by R. Nozick in *Anarchy, State and Utopia* (1974) in an argument supporting private property, individual rights and self-determination. For Nozick, the state can be justified provided it is minimal, that is, it does not interfere with the enjoyment of personal freedoms.

The concept has been the topic of perennial dispute in philosophy. In practice, the principles of justice are often ambiguous and therefore difficult to apply. In the case of distributive justice, when we say 'treat equals equally' it is often difficult to determine in what sense people are equal. In the case of corrective justice, there are always problems associated with criminal responsibility, retribution and the justification of punishment. The ancient principle of *lex talionis* ('an eye for an eye') expressed a basic notion of justice,

129

but most contemporary legal systems prefer to support some notion of correction and rehabilitation. While justice may be difficult to define and achieve, few governments have ever entirely abandoned the appeal of justice (especially as fairness), since justice is an essential feature of legitimacy. (q.v.). See: *Citizenship*; *Relative Deprivation*.

Bibl. Runciman (1966)

K

Kinship. The social relationships deriving from blood ties (real and supposed) and marriage are collectively referred to as kinship. Anthropologists often distinguish between ties based on descent and ties based on affinity, i.e. ties resulting from marriage.

Kinship is universal and in most societies plays a significant role in the socialization of individuals and the maintenance of group solidarity. In simple societies kinship relations may be so extensive and significant that in effect they constitute the social system. For this reason, the concept is vitally important to anthropologists. In more complex societies kinship normally forms a fairly small part of the totality of social relations which make up the social system. Sociologists are less concerned with kin relations, therefore, and treat these as important mainly in the sociology of the family. See: *Conjugal Role*; *Descent Groups*; *Extended Family*; *Marriage*; *Network*; *Nuclear Family*; *Sociology of the Family*.

Knowledge, Sociology of. See: *Sociology of Knowledge*.

L

Labelling Theory. In the sociology of deviance, the 'labelling theory of deviant behaviour' is often used interchangeably with the 'societal reaction theory' of deviancy; both phrases point equally well to the fact that sociological explanations of deviance treat it as a product, not of individual psychology or of genetic inheritance, but of social control. Labelling theory was significantly influenced by the Chicago School (q.v.) and symbolic interactionism (q.v.). The foundations for this view of deviance were first established by E. Lemert (1951) and were subsequently developed by H. S. Becker (1963). The perspective of 'the definition of the situation' (q.v.) is employed to assert that, if individuals or groups are defined as deviant, there will be important and often unanticipated consequences at the level of behaviour. Labelling theory has subsequently become a dominant paradigm in the explanation of deviance. The theory is constituted essentially by two propositions. The first is that deviant behaviour is to be seen not simply as the violation of a norm, but as any behaviour which is successfully defined or labelled as deviant. The deviance does not inhere in the act itself but in the response of others to that act. The second proposition claims that labelling produces or amplifies deviance. The deviant's response to societal reaction leads to secondary deviation by which the deviant comes to accept a self-image or self-definition as someone who is permanently locked within a deviant role. The distinctiveness of the approach is that it draws attention to deviance as the outcome of social imputations and the exercise of social control.

Labelling theory has now spread outside the confines of the sociology of deviance; for example, the imputation of the label 'insane' to a person may represent an important stage in the process of becoming mentally ill. Labelling theory has also been used to explain witchcraft. The theory has thus proved a fruitful development of sociological understanding of the relationships between deviance, self-conceptions, social reaction and control. It is important to remember, however, that labelling theory is not a causal explanation of primary deviance, but only of secondary deviance as a response to imputed deviance from norms.

Labelling theory has been criticized from various perspectives. Radical criminologists such as I. Taylor, P. Walton and J. Young (1973) suggest that it neglects the significant effect of power and economic influence on the detection of crime. It is also argued that the theory neglects the victim by concentrating on the deviant and the criminal. Labelling theory has, however, been significant in generating an important body of empirical research evidence on crime and deviance. See: *Criminology*; *Delinquency*; *Delinquent Drift*; *Deviancy Amplification*; *Deviant Behaviour*; *Differential Association*; *Madness*; *Stigma*; *Symbolic Interactionism*; *Witchcraft*.

Bibl. Gove (1975)

Labour Aristocracy. This refers to an upper and privileged stratum of the manual working class which, by means of scarce skills, strategic position, or organizational and trade-union strength, establishes better conditions for itself. It has been influential among Marxist accounts of the nineteenth-century British working class, where the existence of a labour aristocracy has been used to explain the lack of revolutionary class action in the second half of that century. Their claim is that the labour aristocracy was divided from the rest of the working class by its favourable conditions and was more likely to collaborate with the bourgeoisie than to oppose it. Although correctly highlighting the internal divisions within the nineteenth-century working class – social historians point to many other sources of division as well – the concept remains vaguely defined and its use ambiguous. It appears to have little relevance for understanding modern class structure in Britain, although it can be applied to Japan and the USA, where workers in the primary labour market do have a highly privileged position. See: *Dual Labour Markets*; *Labour Process Approach*; *Working Class*.

Bibl. Moorhouse (1978); Gray (1981)

Labour Markets. See: *Dual Labour Markets*; *Human Capital*; *Women and Work*.

Labour Movement. Worker dissatisfaction and protest are ubiquitous in industrial society. The organizations which develop to give effective voice to these sentiments constitute the labour movement.

American social scientists for long regarded the term 'labour movement' as being interchangeable with trade unionism, and unionism as being concerned with collective bargaining. However, the European experience and that of presently industrializing societies show that there is a wide range of organizational forms. Individual labour movements often comprise both trade unions and political parties. The British labour movement, for example, embraces the Trades Union Congress and the Labour Party; indeed, trade unions finance the political party. Nor do trade unions always value collective bargaining as the means of promoting workers' interests: French trade unions, for example, acted largely to mobilize worker support for political parties until recently. See: *Collective Bargaining*; *Institutionalization of Conflict*; *Trade Unions*.

Bibl. Sturmthal and Scoville (eds.) (1973)

Labour Power. K. Marx distinguished between the labourer's work (labour) and his capacity to work (labour power). In capitalism, the employer buys labour power and not labour. See: *Labour Theory of Value*; *Marx*; *Marxist Sociology*; *Surplus Value*.

Labour Process. This term refers to the process of production, in which labour power is applied to raw materials and machinery to produce commodities. The substitution of 'labour' for the term 'production' reflects the Marxist view that it is labour which creates all value and that the more conventional term disguises this fact. See: *Labour Process Approach*; *Labour Theory of Value*.

Labour Process Approach. H. Braverman in *Labor and Monopoly Capital* (1974) claimed that the labour process (q.v.) in advanced capitalist economies should be seen as determined by capitalist social relations, and not as a product of technological or organizational factors which have their own requirements irrespective of the form of economic ownership. He contended that the way labour processes are organized and carried out reflects the antagonism that is inherent in capitalism, which is based on the exploitation of labour by capital. This antagonism means that the managers who represent capital in modern corporations cannot rely on labour voluntarily to work diligently and effectively to produce surplus value (q.v.). Managers therefore look for ways of maximizing their own control over the labour process and minimizing that of workers. According to this account, the evolution of production technology and the organization of work are determined by capital's need to dominate the labour process and weaken any power labour has to resist. Historically management has attempted to do this by introducing Scientific Management (q.v.) principles of work organization and new technologies that are less dependent on workers' skills, which together de-skill labour, and in the future may reduce their dependence on workers altogether by replacing people with automated machinery where possible. Equally, since the profitability of capital may be increased by reducing labour costs, economic pressures reinforce the trend towards de-skilling and technological replacement, in order to cheapen labour.

Braverman was responsible for a major intellectual shift within industrial sociology leading to a new concern with the nature of the labour process, including the evolution of managerial practices and production technology and the character of the social relations involved in production.

Research has qualified Braverman's arguments. (1) The resistance of employees to de-skilling and tight control has often retarded and modified managerial policy, particularly where trade unions have been strongly established. (2) The long-term trend towards the automation (q.v.) of production and routine office tasks may reduce overall skill requirements and employment opportunities; nevertheless, the new technologies will themselves create a demand for new skills, for example in design and maintenance. (3) Managers want a compliant labour force that will produce profits, and control of the labour process is only one possible way of ensuring compliance. Another way is to create conditions that foster the voluntary commitment of employees to managerial goals. R. Edwards (1979) suggests that in bureaucratized employment systems in the USA, employees are treated fairly and according to impartial rules, are offered long-term employment and the prospect of career advancement via internal labour markets and, in firms in the primary sector of the dual economy (q.v.) and dual labour market (q.v.), are paid above the rates elsewhere. These employment characteristics minimize the awareness of exploitation and develop employee loyalty to the company. The Japanese form of corporate paternalism has a similar effect. Bureaucracy and dual labour markets segment employees and create a privileged stratum or labour aristocracy (q.v.) that is amenable. (4) A number of profit-conscious managers now see unacceptable costs in tight control of the labour process. Where automation is not sufficiently advanced to dispense altogether with labour, the cost of close supervision can be high. If companies can reduce their supervisory personnel and still achieve adequate output from employees, there is a strong financial incentive to do so. Thus some firms experiment with job redesign which is intended to make work more satisfying and give more autonomy to workers. See: *Bureaucracy*; *Capitalism*; *Deskilling*; *Division of Labour*; *Industrial Conflict*; *Mental/Manual Division*; *Paternalism*; *Relations of Production*.

Bibl. Gordon *et al.* (1982); Littler (1982); P. Thompson (1983)

Labour Relations. See: *Industrial Relations*.

Labour Theory of Value. For K. Marx, the aim of any economy is the creation of use values, that is, useful objects. However, in many economies, especially capitalist ones, people do not produce things for their own use directly, but for exchange with other commodities. All commodities are produced by labour and, ultimately, it is the labour time expended in their production that determines exchange value. Commodities may not, however, actually exchange at their values, because their prices will be determined by a whole range of factors, including supply and demand. See: *Surplus Value*.

Labour Unions. See: *Trade Unions*.

Latent Function. This term refers to the unintended and unrecognized consequences of social action upon other social actors or institutions. In an example used by R. Merton (q.v.), the Hopi Indians engage in ceremonial dances designed to encourage rain. Whatever the effects on the weather, these dances have the unintended consequence or latent function of uniting the tribe. See: *Functionalism*; *Manifest Function*.

Bibl. Merton (1957)

Latifundia. A large estate, characteristic of the agrarian structure of Latin America, in which the labourer is subject to the authoritative control of the normally absentee *patron*. The *latifundismo* is a system of such estates. See: *Paternalism*.

Law, Sociology of. See: *Sociology of Law*.

Lazarsfeld, Paul F. (1901–1976). An Austrian sociologist who emigrated to the USA in 1933, he has been the major influence on the growth of modern quantitative sociology. In the early 1940s he founded the Bureau of Applied Social Research at Columbia University as the first university-based social survey centre. His main contributions to research methodology included the systematic development of cross tabulation (q.v.) as a technique for the analysis of survey data, the construction of indicators, and the training of a generation of quantitative sociologists. His substantive work was in the area of mass communications and political, applied and mathematical sociology.

Lazarsfeld taught in the Sociology Department of Columbia University from 1940 to 1969, where he collaborated with R. K. Merton (q.v.). He published widely in scholarly journals and monographs. Among his best-known works are: *Mathematical Thinking in the Social Sciences* (1954); *Personal Influence* (1955), with E. Katz; *Latent Structure Analysis* (1968), with N. W. Henny; *The People's Choice* (1969, 3rd ed.), with others; *Qualitative Analysis: Historical and critical essays* (1972).

Leadership. In social psychology, leadership is frequently treated in the analysis of small groups. In sociology, it is defined as the exercise of influence or power in social collectivities. Weberian sociology has identified three types of leadership corresponding to the different forms of authority. Charismatic leaders lead by virtue of the extraordinary powers attributed to them by their followers. Traditional leaders lead by virtue of custom and practice, because a certain family or class has always led. Legal leadership based on expertise and implemented according to formal rules is typically found in public administration and modern business enterprises. From this perspective, modern management represents the exercise of leadership on the basis of technical or professional competence.

Recent sociologists have emphasized power rather than leadership, being particularly concerned with the structural conditions that allow some to exercise power over others. They have questioned the Weberian assumption that leadership roles must be legitimated by subordinates. See: *Authority*; *Charisma*; *Group*; *Human Relations*; *Legitimacy*; *Power*.

Legal-Rational Authority. For M. Weber (1922), legal-rational authority is the characteristic form of authority in modern society. Within bureaucracy, a command is held to be legitimate and authoritative if it has been issued from the correct office, under the appropriate regulations and according to appropriate procedures. The authority of officials depends, not on tradition or charisma (q.v.), but on a consensus as to the validity of rules of procedure which are perceived as rational, fair and impartial. See: *Authority*; *Bureaucracy*; *Legitimacy*.

Legitimacy. The modern problem of legitimacy is a problem of political representation and consent. The issue of political legitimacy emerges with the disappearance of direct political relationships in small-scale societies; the modern problem thus centres on which individuals are legitimately entitled to act as representatives of political power. Legitimacy is consequently bound up with the nature of political leadership.

In classical civilization there was no essential difference between 'lawfulness' and 'legitimacy'. Legitimate power was simply lawful power. In modern discussions of political legitimacy, law and morality have been partially separated. The positivist definition of law treats law as a command supported by appropriate sanctions, and the moral content of law is secondary. Governments can have legal authority without being morally just governments.

Modern theories of legitimacy are often subjectivist in defining legitimate power as power which is believed to be legitimate. M. Weber's theory of legitimacy is one which stressed the importance of followers' beliefs. There are three ideological bases of legitimacy (traditional, charismatic and legal-rational) which may confer authority on rulers. Since Weber thought that the state could not be legitimated by any absolute standards based on natural law, the modern state has a 'legitimation deficit'; its operations are extended beyond the scope of public consent. Notions of legitimation deficits and crises have become common in political sociology. See: *Charisma*; *Leadership*; *Legal-Rational Authority*; *Natural Law*; *Power*.

Bibl. Merquior (1980)

Legitimation. See: *Habermas*; *Leadership*; *Legal-Rational Authority*; *Legitimacy*; *Legitimation Crisis*.

Legitimation Crisis. A term introduced in the work of J. Habermas (q.v.), who argues that all social systems have to have some mechanism that gives them legitimacy (q.v.). Modern capitalist societies require extensive state planning of the economic system. This state intervention is given legitimacy by parliamentary democracy which, for Habermas, boils down to periodic and occasional voting by citizens who are otherwise politically inert. This inertia, or civil privatism, is necessary for the survival of the system. However, civil privatism is undermined by the very process of state intervention and planning, which systematically interferes in citizens' private lives, thus generating a potential crisis of legitimacy.

Bibl. Habermas (1973)

Leisure Class. Coined by T. Veblen (1899), a leisure class is defined by its sense of the indignity of manual labour, and this disdain for work is expressed through conspicuous consumption, waste and leisure. The weakness of Veblen's approach was its conflation of aristocracy, bourgeoisie (q.v.) and *nouveau riche*, although he was, however, more concerned with social criticism than with sociological precision.

Leninism. The Russian revolutionary leader, V. I. Lenin, produced little systematic theory but certain of his political doctrines have had some influence in sociology. His analysis of labour movements (1902) suggested that workers spontaneously produced only a reformist outlook which sought piecemeal improvements of the working class's lot within capitalism rather than seeking to overthrow the system. Trade unionism, according to this perspective, is reformism *par excellence*, since its objectives of improving pay and conditions at work and persuading governments to act in the realms of social welfare and labour law can be met and, once achieved, serve to incorporate

workers within capitalism. Moreover, trade unionism encourages sectionalism between different trades and occupations within the working class. He believed that the revolutionary socialist party, led by Marxist intellectuals, was necessary to furnish the working class with a true revolutionary class consciousness rather than trade-union consciousness. These ideas, that there are inherent limitations to working-class ideology, that unions are sectional bodies, and that class consciousness has to be taught by a political party, have informed some recent analyses of class consciousness and the labour movement. Lenin himself also produced analyses of imperialism (q.v.) and uneven development (q.v.). See: *Class Consciousness*; *Economism*; *Gramsci*; *Incorporation*; *Trade Unions*.

Bibl. Kolakowski (1978b)

Lévi-Strauss, Claude (b.1908). While Lévi-Strauss has made an enormous contribution to modern anthropology in *Structural Anthropology* (1958), to the study of mentality in *The Savage Mind* (1962b) and, more generally, to structuralism in *Mythologiques* (1964), he has had only a slight influence on contemporary sociology. The point of his anthropology is primarily to provide an understanding of human conceptual activity, and thus to contribute to the study of the human mind. While his structuralist analyses of myth, totemism (1962a) and primitive classifications often appear to bear a close affinity with the social anthropology of E. Durkheim and M. Mauss, Lévi-Strauss himself claims to have been influenced by the Anglo-Saxon tradition of empirical anthropology, but his analysis of myth depends on structural linguistics and cybernetics.

Lévi-Strauss's anthropology is essentially cognitive anthropology aimed at an analysis of the relationship between nature and culture in terms of language. His work has been organized around three areas: kinship theory (1949), the analysis of mythology and the nature of primitive classifications. These three areas are connected by social exchange, especially the exchange of women, words and commodities. Structuralist analysis is applied to these social phenomena to isolate the underlying patterns, regularities and types which, for Lévi-Strauss, point to the universal features of the neuro-physiological constitution of the human brain. His autobiographical work, *Tristes Tropiques* (1955), is a major guide to the nature of the anthropological imagination. See: *Exchange Theory*; *Foucault*; *Lacan*; *Myth*; *Semiotics*; *Structuralism*; *Taboo*.

Bibl. Leach (1970)

Life-Chances. The chances an individual has of sharing in the economic and cultural goods of a society are referred to in Weberian sociology as 'life-chances'. The distribution of such goods is usually asymmetrical. Material rewards are clearly distributed unequally in most societies, and so are cultural goods, as is shown, for example, by differential access to education. Asymmetrical distribution may reflect different class access to goods. See: *Class*; *Stratification*.

Bibl. Dahrendorf (1979)

Life-Cycle. This term is used primarily to describe the development of a person through childhood, adolescence, midlife, old age and death. The sociological concept of 'life-cycle' does not refer to the purely biological process of maturation, but to the transitions of an individual through socially constructed categories of age and to the variations in social experience of aging. For example, men and women have very different social experiences of biological aging, while the length and importance of 'childhood' varies between cultures.

There is a secondary meaning of the concept which may refer to the history of individual families rather than to persons. In this alternative sense, the life-cycle of a family is a process which includes courtship, marriage, child-rearing, children leaving home and dissolution of the family unit. See: *Aging*; *Generation*.

Bibl. Berger and Berger (1976)

Life-Style. In the British sociology of stratification of the 1960s and 1970s there was an interest in the differences between social groups, in patterns of social relationships, the consumption of material goods, and culture, which together constitute life-styles. Such differences are visible indicators of class position, and life-styles form one of the ways in which economic classes have a social presence. The debate about embourgeoisement (q.v.) revolved around the assertion that workers were adopting middle-class life-styles. The Affluent Worker (q.v.) research disproved this claim. In American sociology, the notion of style of life has been used to distinguish between rural and urban, urban and suburban forms of social life. See: *Class*; *Rural-Urban Continuum*.

Life-World. This refers to the everyday world as it is experienced by ordinary men and women. For phenomenological sociology (q.v.), the life-world is the 'paramount reality' and the main object of sociological inquiry. Its chief characteristic is that it is unproblematic and is taken for granted, and is therefore to be contrasted with the world of scientists and sociologists in which natural objects and social interactions are not taken for granted. See: *Commonsense Knowledge*; *Schutz*.

Lineage. See: *Descent Groups*.

Lipset, Seymour M. (b.1922). A professor of government at Stanford University, his intellectual contributions are diverse and cover social movements (q.v.) and political radicalism, modernization, democracy in trade-union government and social mobility (q.v.). He is regarded as one of the leading figures of post-war American sociology. His major works are: *Agrarian Socialism* (1950); *Union Democracy* (1956) with others; *Social Mobility in Industrial Society* (1959) with R. Bendix (q.v.); *Political Man* (1960); *The First New Nation* (1963); *Revolution and Counter Revolution* (1969); and *The Politics of Unreason* (1971) with E. Raab. See: *End of Ideology Theory*.

Lockwood, David (b. 1929). A British sociologist who has contributed to the theory of social conflict and social class, and to the empirical investigation of stratification in Britain, presently professor of sociology at Essex University. His study of clerks, *The Blackcoated Worker* (1958), was significant for its conclusion that the historically privileged position of clerks was threatened (though he disputed that clerks were becoming more proletarian), and as a contribution to modern Weberian class theory. Two papers in 1956 and 1964 contributed to the conflict–consensus debate from the conflict perspective. He was one of the senior members of the research team which conducted the Affluent Worker (q.v.) investigation; this used his conceptual typology of the British working class (1966). See: *Class Imagery*; *Conflict Theory*; *Deferential Worker*; *Orientation to Work*.

Log Linear Analysis. The techniques of multivariate data analysis used by sociologists have largely been borrowed from other disciplines and depend on assumptions that may be inappropriate for sociological research findings. In particular, sociologists may wrongly believe that their data fit the assumptions of the general linear model and erroneously use regression (q.v.) and path analysis (q.v.) techniques deriving from the model. For example, it is not uncommon for sociologists to treat ordinal variables as if they had the properties of interval scales or to use nominal categories in the 'dummy variable' regression procedure, but they run a risk of spurious results.

Log linear analysis transforms nonlinear into essentially linear models by the use of logarithms, and has been developed to meet the specific needs of sociologists. Its main application is in the elaboration of contingency tables comprising many variables, some or all of which are nominal or ordinal measurements, and in the causal modelling (q.v.) of data. Like other modelling devices, it requires that the user specify a theoretical model that is then tested against the data. Analysis usually proceeds by testing successive models against the data until the best 'fit' is found. The use of logarithms in regression models is another application. See: *Measurement Levels*; *Model*; *Multivariate Analysis*.

Bibl. Gilbert (1981)

Longitudinal Study. See: *Panel Study*.

Lukács, Georg (1885–1971). Partly a political organizer but more of a Marxist theoretician, Lukács has contributed a good deal to Marxist theory, especially the critique of epistemology and ontology (q.v.) in *The Ontology of Social Being* (1978). As far as sociologists are concerned, his major works are *History and Class Consciousness* (1923) and *The Historical Novel* (1955). In the analysis of consciousness he developed the notion that the working class had a unique in-

139

sight into historical truth. However, because there were occasionally divergences within the working class and it was prey to false consciousness, he argued that the analyst might have to impute a consciousness to it. He also argued for the importance of the concept of reification (q.v.) for the analysis of capitalist society. He made a major contribution to the sociology of literature in *Essays on Thomas Mann* (1964), *Goethe and his Age* (1968) and *Studies in European Realism* (1972). He suggests that the novel was realistic in the nineteenth century and reflected man's experience as a whole because the bourgeoisie (q.v.) was triumphant. The novel becomes modernist, reflecting only a fragmented experience, in the twentieth century, because of the rise of a potentially revolutionary working class. His work on the novel argues for a connection between social class and literary form. Lukács suggested in *The Destruction of Reason* (1954) that there was a strong current of irrationalism in German intellectual history which had contributed to the rise of fascism (q.v.). See: *Marxist Sociology*.

M

Macro-Sociology. In sociology there are different levels of analysis. Macro-sociology is the analysis of either large collectivities (the city, the Church) or, more abstractly, of social systems and social structures. See: *Micro-Sociology.*

Madness. In psychiatry and abnormal psychology, mental illnesses are divided into neuroses and psychoses; the term 'madness' rarely appears in standard works on mental abnormalities. The causes of mental illness are either organic malfunctioning or in personality conflicts which have their origin in childhood.

Psychoses (for example, schizophrenia) involve a loss of contact with reality; neuroses (for example, anxiety neurosis or reactive depression) are less severe, involving an over-reaction to reality. Phobias (such as agoraphobia) are regarded as a sub-category of anxiety neurosis. Critics of these categories argue that (1) they are not logically coherent and (2) they reflect, behind the neutral language of science, commonsense views on social deviance (q.v.).

The sociology of madness, by contrast, treats psychological abnormalities from a critical perspective. 'Madness' is a social label for classifying and controlling deviancy. 'Madness' belongs to a collection of labels – 'witchcraft', 'vagrancy' and 'hysteria' – by which deviants may be incarcerated. While there may be organic causes of insanity, insane behaviour contravenes social norms and treatment is a form of social control. T. Szasz (1971) has drawn attention to the loss of individual rights which follows from the attribution of mental illness to deviants. Similarly, M. Foucault (1961) has examined historical changes in the criteria used to incarcerate people, from leprosy to venereal disease to madness. Scientific psychiatry does not represent an advance in knowledge, but merely a more subtle and sophisticated form of social control. For Foucault, psychiatry is the triumph of 'reason' over 'madness' in the form of social exclusion and confinement.

There is also a feminist critique which makes several claims. (1) Women are more likely than men to be labelled as insane. (2) Psychiatry, by accepting the values of a patriarchal society, treats women as hysterical or neurotic. (3) Psychoanalysis also treats women as deficient. (4) These negative stereotypes (q.v.) of women are reflected in different forms of treatment and rates of admission; for example, in Britain while one man in twelve will be a psychiatric in-patient at some point in his life, one

141

woman in eight will be admitted as a psychiatric in-patient. (5) Marriage seems to protect, but also exposes women to mental illness. See: *Anti-Psychiatry*; *Foucault*; *Freud*; *Labelling Theory*; *Medical Model*; *Medicalization*; *Sociology of Health and Illness*; *Witchcraft*.

Bibl. Scheff (1966); Mangen (1982)

Malinowski, Bronislaw (1884–1942). He did anthropological field-work among the Trobriand Islands, New Guinea, shortly after the First World War, publishing *Argonauts of the Western Pacific* in 1922. His academic life was subsequently spent at the London School of Economics where he became reader in anthropology (1924) and professor of anthropology (1927). Malinowski made major contributions to the study of magic in *Coral Gardens and Their Magic* (1935), functionalist theory in *A Scientific Theory of Culture* (1944), and the study of sexual behaviour in *Sex and Repression in Savage Society* (1927).

The principal features of the empiricist tradition in British anthropology following Malinowski's perspective were: (1) a concentration on intensive, detailed empirical study of small-scale societies; (2) an emphasis on direct participation with native informants; (3) an adherence to functionalist theory in which cultural institutions were treated as direct expressions of human needs. See: *Functionalism*.

Malthus, Thomas (1766–1834). His *Essay on Population* (1789) argued that human capacity for reproduction exceeded the rate at which subsistence from the land can be increased. Living conditions of the working class could not be improved without the population increasing, thereby reducing living standards by decreasing the food supply. Human populations were checked by positive means (famine, disease or war) or negative means (late marriage and chastity). Social Darwinism (q.v.) adopted Malthusian demography, arguing that working-class poverty resulted from moral licence. See: *Demographic Transition*; *Demography*.

Bibl. Petersen (1979)

Management. Sociological interest in management is focused on three issues: (1) a concern with managers as an elite social grouping; (2) the character of the social relationships internal to management hierarchies in enterprises; (3) management as a process with both technical and social control functions.

(1) The occupational category of managers and administrators has grown considerably in this century, from 3.6 per cent of the employed population in the British census of 1911 to 10.0 per cent in 1981. Managers are placed at or near the top of the class structure in all accounts of stratification. In modern Weberian accounts, managers have an elite position by virtue of their market and work situations. The market position and life-chances (q.v.) of managers are highly favourable, with regard to income, terms and conditions of employment, prospects of career advancement, and pensions. The managerial work situation normally provides more interesting work and autonomy than many other occupations. These market and work advantages increase the higher the level of a manager in the managerial hierarchy. Entry to managerial careers has become more selective over time, especially in terms of required educational qualifications. Modern Marxist class analysis places management in the upper of two classes because managers in capitalist economies are held to perform the various capital functions (q.v.).

(2) Along with the growth in numbers there has gone an increasing elongation of the organizational hierarchy and

greater division of labour and specialization within the ranks of management. It is now usual to distinguish top management including the board of directors, concerned with corporate strategy and with the distribution of resources in the enterprise; middle management, with functional responsibilities such as production, research and development, marketing, personnel, accountancy and finance; and first-level operational management, including foremen and supervisors. An increase in the number of vertical levels and greater horizontal division as the result of specialization of functions creates a complex structure of relationships within the management hierarchy. The sociological investigation of these has become a specialized area in its own right that is conventionally known as organization theory (q.v.).

(3) The process of management has two important attributes. Management is in one sense an economic resource that comprises the technical functions connected with administering other resources. These include planning, organizing and integrating a complex division of labour and directing the activities that occur within an enterprise. Management is secondly a structure of control which ensures the compliance of subordinates and the direction of their activities along the lines laid down from above.

The social control aspect has become prominent in recent sociology. Starting from the premise that subordinates do not share the same interests as management, which may variously be explained as a consequence of exploitation as in Marxist accounts, of an inevitable conflict between those with and without authority as in R. Dahrendorf's account (1959), or of the competing claims between wages and profits, attention is focused on how managers persuade or compel others to comply with their commands. From this perspective, a

large part of the history and development of management in the twentieth century may be seen as the attempt to impose control over recalcitrant employees. See: *Bureaucracy*; *Class*; *Industrial Conflict*; *Labour Process Approach*; *Managerial Revolution*; *Middle Class*; *Scientific Management*; *Service Class*.

Bibl. Hill, S. (1981)

Managerial Revolution. J. Burnham, in *The Managerial Revolution* (1941), suggested that the rise of professional managers would create a new class to replace the old ruling class of capitalists. Along with A. Berle and G. Means (1932) he was responsible for highlighting changes in the way modern firms were run, with the managerial employee replacing the owner as the controller of the corporation. This separation of the ownership of firms from their administration and control resulted from the way share ownership was becoming fragmented and dispersed among numerous small shareholders instead of being concentrated in a few hands.

Some commentators believed that the new influence of salaried employees at the top of corporations would lead to changes in the running of firms. Managers were thought no longer to maximize profits like old-style capitalist owners and to be more socially responsible. In particular, as R. Dahrendorf (1959) suggested, it was thought that the nature of managerial authority would change, creating a new state of shared interests in place of the old conflicts between labour and capital. Managerial legitimacy was thought to depend on managers' claims to technical and professional competence.

Research conducted in the 1970s and after has shown that the managerial revolution thesis was overstated. There are still a few giant corporations where individuals and families retain control by virtue of their large private shareholdings. The recent trend towards the institutional ownership of shares by pension funds, insurance companies and other corporations means that the older tendency of shareholdings to fragment has been reversed (though this new trend does not re-establish individual private ownership, of course). There is no evidence, moreover, that salaried managers are any less interested in company profitability than capitalist owner-controllers, nor that they run their firms differently.

The phenomenon of what are known as corporate networks has also attracted attention. It is normal both in Britain and the USA for the boards of directors of large companies to include non-executive, outside directors who also sit on the boards of other companies. Many of these directors have links with the financial institutions that own the bulk of company shares. The precise significance of such networks is not clear, but one implication is that, at the highest level, the business world is more integrated than was thought previously. See: *Capital Functions*; *Capitalism*; *Class*; *Industrial Conflict*; *Management*.

Bibl. Scott (1979); Hill, S. (1981); Stokman *et al.* (1985)

Manifest Function. The intended and recognized consequences of social action upon other social actors or institutions. See: *Functionalism*; *Latent Function*.

Bibl. Merton (1957)

Mannheim, Karl (1893–1947). He was born in Hungary, fled to Germany in 1919 where he became a university teacher, left Germany in 1933 after the emergence of nazism and moved to England, where he continued his academic career at the London School of Economics. His major works, many of which were collected and published in English after his death, are *Ideology and Utopia*

(1936), *Essays on Sociology and Social Psychology* (1953), *Essays on the Sociology of Culture* (1956), *Essays on the Sociology of Knowledge* (1952), *Man and Society in an Age of Social Reconstruction* (1940), *Diagnosis of Our Time* (1943), and *Freedom, Power and Democratic Planning* (1951).

His work can be divided into two phases. The first saw the development of his sociology of knowledge. (1) He insisted that a sociology of knowledge was possible, that there was an association between forms of knowledge and social structure, and that membership of particular social groups conditioned belief. (2) He attempted to deal with what he saw as the relativistic implications of the sociology of knowledge. He assumed that, if all beliefs could be socially located, then there was no place for true beliefs and no socially independent criteria of truth. He experimented with various solutions to this problem, initially by postulating a class of socially independent propositions, and latterly by recognizing that his initial assumption that social origins determined truth was incorrect. (3) He rejected Marxist explanations of knowledge or ideology (q.v.), which he regarded as reducing all knowledge to class membership. In Mannheim's view, a number of social groups or processes (e.g. generation, sect, class and competition) could be correlated with forms of knowledge.

In the second, less appreciated phase of his work, Mannheim argued for the necessity of social reconstruction. Contemporary societies had become mass societies, disordered groups of atomized individuals with no social ties. Such societies were the outcome of liberal capitalism, and their repair was to be effected by social planning. See: *Ideology*; *Mass Society*; *Relativism*; *Sociology of Knowledge*.

Bibl. Abercrombie (1980)

Marcuse, Herbert (1898–1979). Trained at the universities of Berlin and Freiburg, Marcuse was influenced by the phenomenology of E. Husserl and M. Heidegger. In 1934 he joined the Frankfurt School (q.v.) in exile at Columbia. Approaching Marxism via phenomenology and critical theory (q.v), his central question has been with the possibility of authentic existence in industrial capitalism in, for example, *One-Dimensional Man* (1964), which argued that modern societies generate artificial needs, giving the working class a false consciousness. Believing that Marxism had failed to conceptualize the individual, he turned to S. Freud (q.v.) to provide an analysis of sexuality in *Eros and Civilization* (1955). Marcuse's critical views on American liberal democracy were reflected in *An Essay on Liberation* (1969), but he was equally critical of Soviet society in *Soviet Marxism* (1961). Marcuse is also known for his controversial studies of philosophy in *Reason and Revolution* (1954) and of sociology in *Negations* (1968). See: *Marxist Sociology*.

Market. The market has always occupied a central place in economic theory but has been less significant in sociological analysis. In its broadest sense, a market is an arena of exchange in which individuals attempt to maximize their own advantages. In the process, the market also serves to coordinate activities. The market in this sense has been used mainly in a branch of social theory, namely exchange theory (q.v.), and has not spread widely among other sociologists.

In a more restricted application, that of the market economy, the concept has been more widely used. A market economy is one where the greater part of the economic activities of production, distribution and exchange are carried out by private individuals or corporate bodies following the dictates of demand and supply, in which state intervention is minimized. Weberian sociology has placed emphasis on this economic aspect. M. Weber himself regarded the rise of a market economy as a major contribution to the growth of capitalist industrialism, and in his analysis of class assumed that stratification reflected the distribution of different life-chances (q.v.) in the market place.

Modern Weberian class analysis has followed this track, and there is a growing interest in the workings of labour markets. Marxist and Weberian schools often join in characterizing labour markets as agencies by which one group or class dominates another, since the parties to the exchange are not of equivalent strength. See: *Capitalism*; *Class*; *Competition*; *Dual Labour Markets*; *Industrial Society*; *Marriage*.

Bibl. Weber (1922)

Market Situation: See *Class*

Marriage. Mate selection operates rather like a market, and the rules of selection determine the forms of exchange between partners and their households. These rules in human societies are extremely complex but they may be regarded as a continuum from arranged to formally free marriages. In a closed market, selection is made by parents to consolidate property and form family alliances. Parental choice is more important than affection, because marriages are based on prudence and calculation. In open markets, romantic attachment becomes the basis of marriage, parental wishes are minimized and, in principle, partners select from an infinite range of eligibles. Marriage is a cultural phenomenon which sanctions a more or less permanent union between partners, conferring legitimacy on their offspring. As an institution, marriage is either monogamous (being married to one person at a time), or polygamous (having more than one marriage partner at a time). Polygamy includes: (1) polygyny (one man and two or more wives); (2) polyandry (one woman and two or more husbands); (3) group marriage (several husbands and wives in a common marital arrangement). The eligibility of partners in any form of marriage is determined either by exogamy (q.v.) or endogamy (q.v.). The permanence of the marriage union is also variable. Common law marriages have a stability without legal recognition; they are based on custom and may result in a legal union. Legislation in Britain (under various matrimonial causes acts) has extended the grounds for divorce and made litigation less costly. The increase in divorce results in 'serial monogamy' where most divorcees subsequently remarry. Feminists argue that marriage may reinforce the subordination of women by men. For example, it is clear that in many marriages men can be physically violent towards their wives without much fear of intervention by the police. See: *Divorce*; *Domestic Labour*.

Bibl. Goode (1964)

Marshall, Thomas H. (1873–1982). A professor of sociology at the London School of Economics, he is best known for his influential analysis of citizenship (q.v.) and social class in the course of industrialization, contained in the essay 'Citizenship and Social Class' (1949), republished in *Sociology at the Crossroads* (1963). In *Social Policy* (1965) he analysed the development of welfare policies between 1890 and 1945 as an illustration of the expansion of social rights. Marshall (1981) saw modern capitalism as a 'hyphenated society' where there are inevitable contradictions between democracy, welfare and class.

Martin, David (b. 1929). Currently professor of sociology at the London School of Economics and professor of human values at the Southern Methodist University, Dallas, Texas (1986–88), he has made a major contribution to the sociology of religion, in which he has been a leading critic of the contention that industrial societies are characterized by an inevitable process of secularization (q.v.). In *A Sociology of English Religion* (1967), he showed that the evidence on belief and practice did not support the secularization thesis and, in *The Religious and the Secular* (1969a), he challenged the implicit historical and sociological assumptions behind the theory. He has shown, in *A General Theory of Secularization* (1978a), that it is important to combine political sociology and the sociology of religion in order to understand the divergent patterns of state–church relations. He has also contributed to the sociological analysis of pacifism (1965) and to our understanding of the Christian challenge to violence in *The Breaking of the Image* (1980). Professor Martin has written extensively on the problem of the loss of authority and continuity in modern cultures in *The Dilemmas of Contemporary Religion* (1978b), *Anarchy and Culture* (1969b) and *Tracts against the Times* (1973). He has played a major role in defending the traditional 'Book of Common Prayer', about which he has written extensively since 1979. His current writing is on the theoretical relation of religion to politics and of religion to sociology.

Marx, Karl (1818–1883). A political revolutionary and social theorist, Marx was born and educated in Germany. After finishing his education, he married and became a journalist but, being unable to find permanent employment, he migrated to Paris in 1843. There he mixed with émigré radicals, became a socialist and met F. Engels (q.v.) with whom he formed a life-long friendship and collaboration. Expelled in 1845, he moved to Brussels and, after travelling around Europe, finally settled in London in 1849. There he stayed for the rest of his life in considerable poverty, occupied in writing and political activity, and supported financially largely by Engels and occasional journalism.

Marx's major works of sociological importance are: *The German Ideology* (1845b), with F. Engels; *The Poverty of Philosophy* (1847); *Manifesto of the Communist Party* (1848), with F. Engels; *The Eighteenth Brumaire of Louis Bonaparte* (1852); *Capital* (1867, 1885, 1894); and two manuscripts published after his death, *The Economic and Philosophic Manuscripts of 1844* (1964) and *Grundrisse* (1973).

Marx has been a major influence on the development of sociology, as often a subject of criticism as of inspiration. There are five important sociological areas covered by his writings.

(1) In his early work Marx was interested in the concept of alienation (q.v.). One of the senses that he gave to the term was that of alienated labour, in which condition man had work imposed on him by others, a theme that was to run through all his subsequent contributions.

(2) Marx is best known for his views on the relationship between economic life and other social institutions. It is often suggested that he was an economic determinist, believing that the nature of a society was determined by the manner in which its economy was owned and organized. This is certainly not the case. Although he thought that human labour was the basis of social activity, he also held that social institutions, like the state or the family, were relatively independent of the economy in their development and even had an influence on the operation of the economy. Marx's views on this question are best summed up in the theory of base and superstructure (q.v.).

(3) Although Marx was influenced by his anthropological reading and speculated on primitive states of human society, he was primarily interested in the analysis of societies organized into social classes. The basis of social classes lay in the relations of production (q.v.) in the economy. Those who own and control the means of production, and are able to take the product, form one class and those depending on their own labour alone the other. The form of the relations of production will vary from society to society, producing different class relations. For example, in capitalist societies the relationship between capitalists and workers is based in the control the capitalist has over both the forces of production (q.v.) and the product. He can direct the use to which equipment is put, control the labour process, and take the product whatever it is. In feudal societies, however, the lord does not have direct control over the means of production, which remains in the hands of the peasant, but he can appropriate the product. For Marx, the basic model of such societies is of a two-class structure. He argued, however, that in all real societies the picture will be more complicated, with several classes, particularly those left over from earlier stages of society. Marx's analysis of social class as applied to contemporary capitalist societies has attracted a great deal of criticism, because of the difficulties in fitting the middle class into his scheme and of identifying a class of *persons* who own and control the means of production when ownership of capital passes increasingly to institutions such as pension funds. For Marx, the relations of production necessarily involve conflict because the owners of the means of production, for example capitalists within a capitalist society, effectively exploit workers by appropriating the product of their labour.

(4) This conflict, or contradiction

(q.v.), at the heart of class societies also suggests a theory of social change. Marx argues that class struggle (q.v.) is the 'motor of history'; the rising capitalist class overthrew the feudal aristocracy and will be similarly displaced by the working class. In capitalist societies Marx suggests that, other things being equal, the society will become polarized with the working class becoming poorer and poorer. It should be clear that change does not follow automatically from changes in the economic structure; class struggle as the *active* intervention of human beings is necessary. Historical change takes the form of a succession of societies dominated by different modes of production (q.v.), feudalism or capitalism for example, each of which represents greater technological control over nature. Marx's analysis of class struggle and social change has proved controversial. It has been argued that class struggle has little to do with change from one society to another and, specifically for capitalist society, there is no sign of impending disintegration, polarization, or progressive impoverishment of the working class.

(5) Marx was pre-eminently a theorist of capitalist society. *Capital*, his most detailed work, spells out the economic mechanisms of capitalist society, developing the labour theory of value (q.v.), the theory of capital accumulation, and the possibilities of capitalism's internal collapse. Also in *Capital* is a discussion of other issues which have become important recently, for example, commodity fetishism (q.v.) and appearance and reality (q.v.). See: *Althusser; Bourgeoisie; Capital Fractions; Capital Functions; Capitalism; Class; Determinism; Division of Labour; Feudalism; Historical Materialism; Ideology; Labour Power; Labour Process; Labour Process Approach; Marxist Sociology; Mental/ Manual Division; Periodization; Political Economy; Praxis; Ruling Class; Socialist Societies; Surplus Value.*

Bibl. McLellan (1973); Bottomore (1978)

Marxist Sociology. Since Marx's death in 1883, an enormous literature has grown up around his work. A good deal of this has been critical and much early sociology, that of M. Weber (q.v.), for example, was partly formed by a critique of Marx. There has also been a stream of work that is broadly Marxist, often involving reinterpretations of Marx, although that term is now employed so widely that it has begun to lose all meaning. There are several areas of sociology where Marx's work has been extended, while remaining faithful to at least some of his principles.

(1) In the analysis of class structure, several early Marxists argued that Marx's scheme had to be revised because there was no real sign of the collapse of capitalism or of heightened class struggle. A good deal of effort has been expended in trying to adapt the basic idea of a necessary conflict between capital and labour to the conditions of contemporary capitalism. This has taken the form of new theories of social class (q.v.) to take account of changes in the patterns of property ownership, the growth of the middle class (q.v.), and changes in relationships at work. In addition some Marxists have given attention to the notion of class consciousness (q.v.) as a prerequisite for class struggle (q.v.), especially A. Gramsci (q.v.), V. I. Lenin and G. Lukács (q.v.).

(2) In the analysis of politics, arguments that the state is the instrument of the ruling class have given way to a more complex analysis of the state as relatively autonomous of the ruling class, responsive to pressures from the working class via the institution of parliamentary democracy, but ultimately favouring the

interests of capital.

(3) Revisions of Marx's economics have taken the form of distinguishing different capital fractions (q.v.), and of providing an account of the monopoly phase of capitalism which is distinctively different from the earlier, competitive phase dominant in Marx's day.

(4) A feature of twentieth-century capitalism noted by Lenin was its capacity to seek markets in under-developed countries and often to colonize and control those countries. Following Lenin's account of im-perialism (q.v.) many studies have connected the persistence of under-development in the world with capital-ism's need for expansion.

(5) A great deal of twentieth-century Marxist sociology has been dominated by an interest in the analysis of ideology (q.v.). In particular, it has been argued that the continued persistence of capital-ism has been due in large part to the ideological control exercised by the dominant class. This sort of analysis has often been inspired by the notion of hegemony (q.v.) as propounded by Gramsci or by the writings of the Frankfurt School (q.v.).

(6) There has been a continuing inter-est in the study of the philosophy and method of Marxism, particularly in the Frankfurt School and Critical Theory (q.v.), and more recently in the work of J. Habermas (q.v.) and followers of L. Althusser (q.v.). Very often the study of methodology has been informed by an attempt to rescue Marxism from posi-tivism (q.v.).

(7) Many sociologists have utilized the work of Marxist historians interested in the analysis of social change through class struggle and, more recently, in the utility of the concept of mode of pro-duction (q.v.) for historical analysis. See: *Capital Functions*; *Capitalism*; *Class Theoretical*; *Conditions of Existence*; *Conjuncture*; *Dominant Ideology Thesis*; *Economism*; *Engels*; *Feudalism*; *Histori-cal Materialism*; *Ideological State Ap-paratus*; *Labour Process*; *Labour Process Approach*; *Leninism*; *Marx*; *Mental/ Manual Division*; *Miliband–Poulantzas Debate*; *Overdetermine*; *Patriarchy*; *Poli-tical Economy*; *Power*; *Relative Auton-omy*; *Reproduction of Labour Power*; *Socialist Societies*.

Bibl. Anderson, P. (1976b); Bottomore (1978)

Mass Observation. This was an organ-ization founded in 1936 with the aim of conducting social surveys of the popu-lation and reporting the results as widely as possible. The founders believed that social science should not be purely aca-demic. To this end they carried out a large number of studies based on diaries and reports from regular participants as well as questionnaires. Their methods may not always have been technically perfect but they furnished a very full picture of British social change before and during the Second World War.

Mass Society. The concept of mass society is central to an influential social theory which holds that contemporary society has the following characteristics: most individuals are similar, undiffer-entiated and equal, showing no indivi-duality; work is routine and alienating; religion has lost its influence and there are no deeply held and important moral values, although the masses are prone to ideological fanaticism; the relationships between individuals are weak and secon-dary and ties of kinship are not import-ant; the masses are politically apathetic and open to manipulation by dictator-ships and bureaucracies; culture – art, literature, philosophy and science – has become a mass culture, that is, reduced to the lowest level of taste.

Writers who describe society in these

terms use the concept of mass society pejoratively and usually attribute the ills of society to capitalism or industrialization. Some of these themes are present in the work of nineteenth-century social theorists, A. de Tocqueville (1835) and F. Toennies (q.v.) for example, and in the very general dichotomy between pre-industrial and industrial society current at that time. However, the specific theory of mass society was developed between 1920 and 1960 in three main directions. (1) In England, a number of writers, especially literary critics like T. S. Eliot and F. R. Leavis, concentrated on the loss of excellence in literature and culture generally and the disappearance of a cultivated public. Theirs was essentially a conservative reaction to capitalist society and was taken up by a number of sociologists, especially K. Mannheim (q.v.). (2) Members of the Frankfurt School (q.v.), especially after their flight from Hitler's Germany to the USA, analysed the political rather than cultural aspects of mass society. Their argument was that capitalism had, by producing a mass society, created the conditions for the political manipulation of the masses by ruling elites. This showed a rather more socialist response to the social and international problems of the inter-war period. (3) In making use of the concept of mass society, some American writers saw it more positively. For E. Shils (1962), for example, the masses were being drawn into political participation, thus making elitist politics more difficult.

Some early research into the mass media was influenced by mass society theory, particularly that of the Frankfurt School, in that the audience was seen as relatively undifferentiated and easily influenced (or manipulated) by programmes. However, the concept of mass society is not now influential in sociology. (1) Contemporary societies are not seen as undifferentiated masses but as made up of numbers of competing groups. (2) Subordinate classes are not manipulated by an elite but are quite capable of active dissent. (3) There has not been a breakdown of family and community ties. See: *Dominant Ideology Thesis*.

Bibl. Giner (1976); Swingewood (1977)

Materialism. In sociology, this term has a specific sense in referring to theories in which economic relations are the basic cause of social phenomena. More generally, materialist explanations in which concrete social relations are determinant are contrasted with idealist explanations in which ideas are seen as the ultimate cause of social relations. See: *Dialectical Materialism*; *Engels*; *Historical Materialism*; *Idealism*; *Marx*; *Marxist Sociology*.

Maternal Deprivation. It has been argued, most notably by J. Bowlby (1953), that young children need a stable, continuous and affectionate relationship with their mothers, and that maternal deprivation, the absence of such a relationship, may result in mental illness or delinquency. The theory has important implications for women in society, suggesting that they ought to stay at home with their children. Feminists have attacked it as an ideology which keeps women out of the labour force. Recent research suggests that stable relationships with a range of adults may be more important for mental health than an intense maternal relationship. See: *Socialization*.

Bibl. Rutter (1972)

Matriarchy. A term used in nineteenth-century anthropology to designate a society ruled by women. In contemporary use, it refers more narrowly to a form of the family in which the mother is the head and descent is reckoned through her. The notion of matriarchal systems of domination is controversial. F. Engels (q.v.), in *The Origin of the Family, Private Property and the State* (1884), argued that pre-modern societies, before the emergence of private property, had been matriarchal. These societies were eventually replaced by patriarchal systems with the transition from nomadic (hunter-gatherer) to agricultural communities. An alternative argument is that patriarchy (q.v.) results from conquest. The archaeological evidence to support or to refute these theories is clearly difficult to obtain. The concept is important, however, because it is now used to add weight to the feminist perspective on the differences between gender (q.v.) and biologically determined sex roles. Matriarchy suggests that male domination has not been universal. The term is also used more loosely to designate family forms dominated by the mother. See: *Feminism*; *Nature/Nurture Debate*.

Mead, George H. (1863–1931). Although publishing little in his lifetime, Mead, through his lectures, came to have a profound effect on the development of symbolic interactionism (q.v.) in American sociology. His lecture notes were posthumously published in a number of major volumes – *Mind, Self and Society* (1934), *The Philosophy of the Act* (1938) and *The Philosophy of the Present* (1959). In Mead's philosophy, the self emerges through the process of social interaction with others. In his social behaviourism, the conditioned responses of human beings include gesture and role-taking, which are the bases of social life. Gestures and conversation are crucial features of the symbolic interaction, the distinctive feature of which is that the individual can imagine the effect of symbolic communication on other social actors. Human actors carry on an 'internal conversation' with the self and

anticipate the response of other actors. We imaginatively assume other social roles and internalize the attitudes of 'the generalized other' – the attitudes of the social group. See: *Action Theory*; *Chicago School*; *Role*; *Symbolic Interactionism*.

Bibl. Strauss (1964)

Mead, Margaret (1901–1978). An American cultural anthropologist whose early field work was on child-rearing in the Pacific, she has made a major contribution to the nature/nurture debate (q.v.) and the study of culture (q.v.) and socialization (q.v.). While not denying the importance of biology and the natural environment, Mead demonstrated the central role of culture in shaping human behaviour and attitudes through a series of empirical studies of different societies. There is a social division around social activities which are assumed to be relevant to gender (q.v.), but these divisions have no general or systematic relationship to biological sex. In short, her studies of culture in *Coming of Age in Samoa* (1928), *Growing Up in New Guinea* (1930) and *Sex and Temperament in Three Primitive Societies* (1935) emphasized the importance of nurture over nature. Her anthropological ideas provided significant support for feminism (q.v.) and her contribution to the development of sexual politics was further reinforced by *Male and Female* (1949). Her field work also showed how primitive societies were relatively tolerant towards the sexual behaviour of adolescents, contrasting sharply with the anxiety shown in Western (especially Protestant) cultures towards sexual development. Her interpretations of her own empirical research in *Culture and Commitment* (1970a) contributed to a more sympathetic understanding of the conflict of generations. Her anthropological studies generated controversial debate, but she retained an enduring commitment to the development of aboriginal societies within the modern world in *New Lives for Old* (1956). She contributed to the debate on race in *Science and the Concept of Race* (1970b) and remained optimistic about the future developments of religion, sexuality and culture in *Twentieth Century Faith* (1972).

Her work has been challenged by D. Freeman (1983) on the grounds that her basic field work was unreliable: she did not learn the Samoan language, her period of research in Samoa was too short, and her informants were not reliable. Freeman has argued that her results do not support her theories and that cultural anthropology is not an adequate paradigm (q.v.). Against Freeman, it has been argued that Mead did not deny or neglect heredity (q.v.) and that her subsequent research more than adequately replicated her earlier findings.

Mean. The arithmetic mean or average of a set of values is obtained by adding the values together and dividing by the number (n) of items in the set.

Meaning. See: *Action Theory*; *Empathy*; *Hermeneutics*; *Phenomenological Sociology*; *Rule*; *Verstehen*; *Weber*.

Meaningful Action. Action which actors invest with meanings deriving from definite motives and intentions, rather than that which follows from mere habit or instinct (q.v.), is meaningful action. See: *Action Theory*; *Phenomenological Sociology*; *Rule*; *Verstehen*.

Measurement Levels. Data can be measured at different levels, on scales of measurement of different strengths. The lowest level is the *nominal* scale. In this, a score indicates simply to which group an individual datum belongs. For ex-

ample, a population replying to an attitude survey might be divided into those replying 'yes' and 'no' to various questions, 'yes' being given the scale point 1 and 'no' point 2. The numbers denote categories and nothing else: those saying 'yes' could just as easily be numbered 2, while 2 carries no sense of being of a greater order of magnitude than 1. Indeed, the two categories could be given any other numbers.

The next level of measurement is the *ordinal* scale. In this, categories are arranged in a hierarchy. For example, attitude surveys often use a technique of measuring attitudes know as the Likert scale, which asks respondents to indicate the strength of their agreement with certain statements according to the following ordinal categories: Strongly Disagree; Disagree; Uncertain; Agree; Strongly Agree. Each point is given a number, in this case 1 to 5. Replies are ordered and movement along the scale indicates an increasing or decreasing magnitude of agreement. Ordinal scales, however, do not allow measurement of the differences between categories: it is not possible to say that Strongly Agree indicates a feeling that differs from Agree by a precise amount.

Interval-level scales are also ordered, but have the additional property that the distances between points on the scale are uniform. Thus scores on an interval scale can be compared in terms of the distances between them as well as their order, since they represent equal units of measurement. *Ratio* measurement shares the properties of interval scales and in addition has an absolute zero point. The Centigrade scale for measuring temperature is an interval scale, because 0° in fact refers to the amount of heat available at the freezing point of water and not to the absence of heat. The Kelvin scale, however, is based on ratio measurement because 0° here represents an absolute zero at which no heat is present. Measurement at the interval and ratio levels is metric, while nominal and ordinal levels are non-metric.

Measurement levels are important because they influence the sorts of statistical techniques that can be used in the analysis of research data. At the nominal level, there is a restricted range of techniques based on frequencies or counting, such as the mode, chi-squared test (q.v.), contingency tables and cross tabulation (q.v.). Ordinal-level measurement is appropriate for the full range of non-parametric (q.v.) statistics. Interval and ratio levels allow all statistical techniques to be employed. See: *Attitude*; *Log Linear Analysis*; *Regression*.

Mechanical Solidarity. See: *Durkheim*.

Media Sociology. See: *Sociology of the Mass Media*.

Median. In a distribution of values, the median is the point with half the distribution on either side.

Medical Model. As the basic paradigm (q.v.) of medicine since the development of the germ theory of disease in the nineteenth century, it is the principal form of explanation in scientific medicine. Its fundamental assumptions are: (1) all disease is caused by a specific aetiological agent (the 'disease entity') such as a virus, parasite or bacterium; (2) the patient is to be regarded as the passive target of medical intervention, since scientific medicine is concerned with the body as a sort of machine rather than the person in a complex social environment; (3) restoring health (a state of equilibrium (q.v.) in the body conceptualized as a machine with functional parts) requires the use of medical technology and advanced scientific procedures.

This model has been criticized on the following grounds: (1) it is an ideology (q.v.) which justifies the use of medical technology, thereby precluding alternative therapies and procedures; (2) the model was developed as a response to infectious diseases in the nineteenth century, but, partly because of the aging (q.v.) of populations, modern societies require health care systems (q.v.) which can respond to chronic illness; (3) the model is inappropriate in the treatment of mental illness and deviance (q.v.); (4) it is not appropriate to regard the patient as simply an organism, and therapy is more likely to be effective where the patient is regarded as a person with social and psychological needs. See: *Alternative Medicine*; *Anti-Psychiatry*; *Clinical Sociology*; *Madness*; *Medicalization*; *Sick Role*; *Sociology of Health and Illness*; *Sociology of Medicine*.

Bibl. Veatch (1981)

Medical Sociology. See: *Sociology of Medicine*.

Medicalization. This refers to the increasing attachment of medical labels to behaviour regarded as socially or morally undesirable. The implication is that modern medicine can cure all problems (including vandalism, alcoholism, homosexuality, dangerous driving or political deviance) once these are recognized as 'diseases'. The term is used by critics of modern medicine who argue that doctors have too much political influence in issues where they are not in fact professionally competent to make judgements. See: *Addiction*.

Bibl. Zola (1972)

Members' Methods. See: *Ethnomethodology*.

Mental/Manual Division. In K. Marx, the division between mental and manual labour was a marked feature of the division of labour (q.v.) in capitalist society and related to human alienation. In Marxist literature, the dichotomy between hand and head in the labour process (q.v.) has a variety of meanings: (1) the emergence of supervisory roles within the factory which manage the labourer, whose activities become devoid of imagination, choice or intellect; (2) the development of machinery and computers in which human intelligence is stored with the consequent de-skilling (q.v.) of labour; (3) the specialization of labour into separate mental and manual functions resulting in internal divisions within the working class; (4) the social denial of the unity of hand and head as the natural condition of the human species. While this distinction has been an important feature of Marxist analyses, some sociologists argue that it is difficult to see how in practice it can be distinguished from more conventional notions such as manual/non-manual occupations.

Bibl. Sohn-Rethel (1978)

Meritocracy. In a meritocracy, social positions in the occupational structure would be filled on the basis of merit in terms of universal criteria of achievement, not on ascribed criteria of age, sex or inherited wealth. The meritocratic ideal is faced with the problem of securing objective measurement of talent independently of inherited advantages. See: *Credentialism*; *Stratification*.

Merton, Robert K. (b.1910). An American sociologist and the author of very wide-ranging work, chiefly in essay form, much of which is collected in Merton (1957). Most influential have been his theory of anomie (q.v.), his views on bureaucracy (q.v.), his account of functionalism (q.v.), and his sociological account of the growth and direction of science in the seventeenth century. See:

Latent Function; *Middle-Range Theory*.

Metaphysical Pathos. This phrase describes the underlying mood of pessimism informing analyses of bureaucracy. R. Michels and M. Weber, for example, assumed that all large-scale social activity necessarily results in bureaucracy and the loss of democratic freedom. See: *Bureaucracy*; *Michels*; *Oligarchy*; *Weber*.

Bibl. Gouldner (1955a)

Meta-Theory. This term refers to the general background of philosophical assumptions that provide rules for the construction of particular sociological theories and justify particular sociological methods. There are several such meta-theories in sociology, an example of which is hermeneutics (q.v.).

Methodenstreit. This term refers to the dispute over methodological principles and procedures which was central to debates within the social sciences in Germany in the 1890s. The key issue was whether the new discipline of sociology could be based on the epistemology (q.v.) and methodology of the natural sciences or whether it required special methods peculiar to the study of social action and social institutions. See: *Hermeneutics*; *Naturalism*; *Neo-Kantianism*; *Positivism*; *Verstehen*.

Methodological Individualism. This is the doctrine that all sociological explanations are reducible to the characteristics of individuals. It was originally formed in opposition to the work of such sociologists as E. Durkheim who argued that the characteristics of individuals could safely be ignored in sociological explanations; 'social facts' have an existence of their own and can be studied independently of individuals whose actions they determine. Less radically, many functionalists argue that social groups have emergent properties (q.v.), that is, characteristics that are produced when individuals interact but are not reducible to individuals. Against this, methodological individualists claim that all such functionalist arguments rest ultimately on assumptions about individual behaviour.

Debates about methodological individualism are not as popular as they were some twenty years ago. In discussion of the relationship of individual to society, or of psychology to sociology, attention has shifted to other issues such as agency and structure (q.v.). While it may be trivially said that societies are collections of individuals, this does not show that sociological explanations are *reducible* to psychological or biological ones. Furthermore, it is quite possible that individual characteristics are socially derived in the interaction between individuals. See: *Social Fact*; *Subject/Subjectivity*.

Bibl. Lessnoff (1974)

Metropolitan Fringe. On the outskirts of many industrial cities lies a belt of commuter housing, often located in scattered villages. It has been argued that a distinctive style of life prevails in these areas, characterized chiefly by a radical separation between middle-class commuters and old-established working-class residents. See: *Concentric Zone Theory*; *Suburban Way of Life*.

Bibl. Pahl (1975)

Michels, Robert (1876–1936). A German sociologist and economist, he wrote on nationalism, socialism, fascism, the role of intellectuals, social mobility and elites. He is best known for *Political Parties* (1911), in which he stated the 'iron law of oligarchy' in democratic organizations. See: *Elite*; *Oligarchy*; *Political Parties*; *Trade Unions*.

Micro-Sociology. This level of sociological analysis is concerned with face-to-face social encounters in everyday life and with interpersonal behaviour in small groups.

Middle Class. Sociologists have long debated the limits, homogeneity, and even existence of the middle class, which is usually defined as comprising those in non-manual occupations. The motive for the debate comes from two directions. (1) There is a continuing argument around the allegedly Marxist notion that there are two main classes in society and hence little room for a genuine middle class. (2) The growth in occupations usually referred to as middle class has also inspired debate. In the period 1911–81, for example, the size of the manual worker group fell from some 80 per cent to just over 48 per cent of the employed population of Britain, while higher professionals increased from 1 per cent to over 3 per cent, lower professionals from 3 per cent to almost 9 per cent, and clerks from almost 5 per cent to 15 per cent. There are two main lines of argument, the first stressing the middle class as fairly large, enjoying pay and conditions of work more favourable than those of the working class, but less so than the upper class. This relatively favourable market capacity of the middle class is often said to be based on the possession of educational and technical qualifications. The second and more popular view is that the middle class is composed of a number of discrete segments with one segment effectively part of the working class, another smaller one part of the upper class, leaving a relatively small grouping truly in the middle. This second view therefore undermines the significance of the distinction between manual and non-manual occupations.

There is widespread agreement that there is a considerable gap between manual and non-manual earnings. However, this comparison is misleading since a number of non-manual categories, clerks and shop assistants for example, have earnings very little different from manual workers. In respect of hours of work, fringe benefits, pension schemes, sick pay schemes and job security, these routine white-collar workers may be a little better placed than manual workers, though the differences are being eroded. It has recently been argued that clerks have good promotion prospects and that this occupation is, for very many, a route to managerial positions. However, this seems to apply almost entirely to male clerks and, since some three-quarters of those employed in this occupation are women, overall promotion prospects are not particularly good. White-collar conditions of work may be little better, as an increasing division of labour (q.v.) and the introduction of computers and other equipment have affected office work, making it much more routine, less demanding, less skilful, more controlled by management and offering reduced scope for independent action. A similar process of proletarianization (q.v.) may also, in some degree, be affecting some lower professional occupations. What is not so clear is whether these changes in the market and work situation of some white-collar occupations result in changes in beliefs, political action and trade-union membership and militancy among white-collar workers, but there are still differences between them and manual workers.

In contrast with the position of routine white-collar workers, the upper sections of the middle class, especially higher professionals and higher managers, have high levels of pay with well-defined career expectations, shorter hours of work, and better pension and sick pay arrangements. Their work situation is also more favourable, allowing much greater independence, a measure of

control over others, and opportunities to use their skills. The situation of these occupations is in many respects like that of the traditional upper class of employers, and it has been argued that only middle management, smaller businessmen and lower professionals truly constitute a middle class. See: *Career*; *Class*; *Class Imagery*; *Credentialism*; *Management*; *Professions*; *Service Class*; *Social Mobility*; *Trade Unionism*; *Unionateness*; *Upper Class*; *Working Class*.

Bibl. Abercrombie and Urry (1983)

Middle-Range Theory. This term was coined by R. K. Merton who believes in the necessity for sociological theory constructed between 'minor working hypotheses' and 'master conceptual schemes'.

Bibl. Merton (1957)

Migration. Migration is either external (between societies) or internal (between regions). There is, for example, an important internal pattern of labour migration in Italy between the poor south and the industrialized north. Large-scale external labour migration has played a crucial part in the economic development of post-war Europe. In the north-western industrial regions of Europe, there were in the early 1970s over eleven million foreign migrant workers; in Germany and Britain, one in seven manual workers was a migrant. The causes of external labour migration can be classified in terms of 'push' and 'pull' factors. In the latter are the size and structure of the indigenous labour force. Increases in full-time education postponed the entry of young people into the labour market, creating a gap for unskilled migrants, while indigenous workers also moved into better-paid, white-collar, skilled occupations. The 'push' factors are the unemployment, poverty and underdevelopment of labour-exporting countries, which have high rates of population increase, high unemployment and low *per capita* incomes. Migration does not provide economic development for poor regions which remain underdeveloped and dependent on the centres of industrial capitalism.

Bibl. Castles and Kosack (1973)

Miliband–Poulantzas Debate. In *The State in Capitalist Society* (1969), R. Miliband criticized the view that power in industrial societies is held by a plurality of competing elites rather than by a dominant class, by showing that the members of these elites were held together by a multiplicity of familial, religious, educational and cultural ties. These elites constituted a single homogeneous ruling class. N. Poulantzas (1969) in turn criticized Miliband, arguing that the interpersonal ties between individual members of the dominant class were largely irrelevant to the argument, because the state and social class are objective structures and cannot be reduced to the personal characteristics of their members. In his reply, Miliband (1970) defended the importance of empirical analysis, charging Poulantzas with 'structural super-determinism', that is, with eliminating the possibility of organized political action to change the objective conditions of political life. See: *Pluralism*; *State*.

Bibl. Urry and Wakeford (eds.) (1973)

Millenarianism. In Christianity, the belief that the Messiah would return for a thousand years (millennium) has given rise to numerous social movements among the poor. In sociology, a millenarian movement is a collective, this-worldly movement promising total social change by miraculous means. Millenarianism in Europe flourished between the eleventh and sixteenth centuries among the disprivileged, for example, the Anabaptist movement. Anthropologists sometimes include Melanesian 'cargo cults' and 'nativistic movements' in this category. Millenarian movements in this wider context (e.g. North American Indian Ghost Dance or Islamic Mahdi movements) are pre-political responses to social tensions following European colonialism. See: *Social Movements*.

Bibl. Lanternari (1963)

Mills, C. Wright (1916–1962). An American professor of sociology, he was highly critical of conventional social science for perpetuating prevailing prejudices regarding political power and social inequality. In *White Collar* (1951) he looked at the social characteristics of the American middle class. In *The Power Elite* (1956) he explained the power structure of the United States as an integrated array of elites in different spheres. These elites were to some extent self-perpetuating. In *The Sociological Imagination* (1959) he provided a historical interpretation of the evolution of the social sciences in America and a vigorous polemic against the dominance of functionalism (q.v.) and empiricism (q.v.) in sociology. See: *Elite*; *Grand Theory*.

Mobility, Social. See: *Social Mobility*.

Mobilization. In modernization (q.v.) theory, the term refers to the process by which peasants or workers are brought together to achieve collective goals. Political mobilization is the process by which a population is brought into the political arena by the formation of new parties and other political institutions. The 'mobilization system' is the ensemble of values, institutions and groups which are organized to achieve societal goals (such as the creation of a nation-state). See: *Nationalism*.

Mode of Production. This concept, of

great importance in Marxist theory, has also had considerable influence in various areas of sociology, especially in the sociologies of development, ideology and politics. A mode of production is the relationship between the relations of production (q.v.) and the forces of production (q.v.). Modes of production can be distinguished from one another by the different relationships between the forces and relations of production. For example, in the feudal mode of production, the lord does not have direct control over the peasant's forces of production, tools and land, but does have control over the disposition of the peasant's produce. In the capitalist mode of production, on the other hand, the capitalist controls both the forces of production and the disposition of the product. Many theorists argue that different modes of production have, associated with them, different forms of ideology and politics. For example in the feudal mode of production, ideology in the form of religion is prominent. Although attention has largely focused on the feudal and capitalist modes of production, other types have been distinguished, particularly the Asiatic and slave modes of production.

The concept of mode of production is intended as an abstract analytical model. No society is likely to contain only one mode of production. This will be so particularly in periods of social change when more than one mode will co-exist in the same society. Recent work has concentrated on three main areas: (1) the concept has been given more precision by defining relations of production more tightly; (2) the relationship of the economy or relations of production to politics and ideology has been redefined, so that these are now treated as conditions of existence (q.v.) of the economy; (3) forms or stages of modes of production have been differentiated. An example of this

last point is the separation of the monopoly form of the capitalist mode of production from the competitive form. See: *Althusser*; *Asiatic Mode of Production*; *Base and Superstructure*; *Capitalism*; *Feudalism*; *Ideology*; *Marx*; *Marxist Sociology*; *Oriental Despotism*; *Patriarchy*; *Slavery*; *Underdevelopment*.

Bibl. Abercrombie, Hill and Turner (1980)

Model. This is an abstract way of presenting the relations between social phenomena. Models of social processes will not necessarily perfectly represent the actual social world but will provide devices which simplify and aid understanding of the essential mechanisms involved. For example, social networks or family structures may be modelled. More formal models may also be employed in which relations between elements are expressed mathematically. See: *Causal Modelling*; *Ideal Type*.

Modernization. Modernization theory was a dominant analytical paradigm in American sociology for the explanation of the global process by which traditional societies achieved modernity. (1) Political modernization involves the development of key institutions – political parties, parliaments, franchise and secret ballots – which support participatory decision-making. (2) Cultural modernization typically produces secularization (q.v.) and adherence to nationalist ideologies. (3) Economic modernization, while distinct from industrialization, is associated with profound economic changes – an increasing division of labour, use of management techniques, improved technology and the growth of commercial facilities. (4) Social modernization involves increasing literacy, urbanization and the decline of traditional authority. These changes are seen in terms of increasing social and structural differentiation (q.v.). Modernization theory has been criticized on two grounds: (1) modernization is based on development in the West and is thus an ethnocentric model of development; (2) modernization does not necessarily lead to industrial growth and equal distribution of social benefits, since it is an essentially uneven process resulting in underdevelopment and dependency (q.v.). Marxist alternatives to modernization theory stress the negative aspects of modernity on traditional societies. See: *International Division of Labour*; *Mobilization*; *Sociology of Development*; *Urbanization*; *World-System Theory*.

Bibl. Lerner (1958)

Monogamy. The practice whereby people marry only one spouse at a time. This is the form of marriage generally practised in Europe, the Americas and Australasia, but there are societies in which it is the custom for a man to have several wives at the same time (*polygyny*) or a woman several husbands (*polyandry*).

Montesquieu, Charles-Louis de Secondat, Baron de (1689–1755). A French aristocrat who travelled widely in Europe and developed a comparative perspective on the political systems of his time, he was elected to the French Academy in 1727 and became an important figure in the Enlightenment. His social theory was dominated by the problem of political despotism. His *Persian Letters* (1721) was a fictional correspondence between two Persian travellers in Europe which allowed him to reflect upon French society. In his sociological analysis of the harem, Montesquieu argued that any society based on total force or despotism was not viable in the long term. This theme was further pursued in *Considerations on the Causes of Roman Greatness* (1734), a comparative analysis of the social causes of the rise and fall of

empires. His most significant contribution came in *The Spirit of the Laws* (1748), where he argued that, following the English experience of parliamentary government, despotism could be avoided by the institutional separation of the executive, legislative and juridical functions of the state. This involved an important 'separation of powers' which would prevent the absolute power of despotism. In this work, Montesquieu wrote a comparative sociology of institutions that showed the interconnections between religion, education, government and geography. He established a sociological tradition which continued to be influential in the nineteenth-century work of N. Fustel de Coulanges, E. Durkheim and A. de Tocqueville. See: *Comparative Method*; *Durkheim*; *Oriental Despotism*; *Tocqueville*.

Moore, Barrington, Jr. (b.1913). A lecturer in sociology and senior research fellow in the Russian Research Centre at Harvard University since 1951, he has made a major contribution to comparative and historical sociology (q.v.). His most influential work is *Social Origins of Dictatorship and Democracy* (1968). In this, he examined the relationship between social classes (especially the peasantry and landlords) in England, France, the United States, Imperial China, Japan and India to see how historical class formations have determined the forms of politics in the modern world, giving rise to bourgeois democracy (England and America), fascism (pre-war Japan and Germany), and communism (China). In *Soviet Politics* (1950) and *Terror and Progress USSR* (1954), he adopted a functionalist framework in political sociology (q.v.) to analyse the contradictions between totalitarian politics, industrialization (q.v.) and ideology in post-revolutionary Russia.

He has also contributed to political and sociological theory in *Political Power and Social Theory* (1958). His historical and political studies can be seen as social inquiries into the relationships among freedom, truth and happiness. These issues were reflected in a collection of essays in honour of H. Marcuse (q.v.) that he edited with K. H. Wolff (1967). In his later works, he turned to certain major ethical and social issues. In *Reflections on the Causes of Human Misery* (1972), he addressed himself to 'war, cruelty and general human nastiness'; in *Injustice* (1978), he studied the bases of political authority, obedience and revolt by means of an historical inquiry into the German working class. Finally, he has contributed to the sociological analysis of privacy (1984). See: *Comparative Method*; *Peasants*.

Bibl. Smith, D. (1983)

Moral Panic. This expression refers to the alleged over-reaction of the mass media, police and local community leaders to delinquent offences which are in fact relatively trivial, both in terms of the nature of the offence and the number of people involved. For example, in Britain minor acts of vandalism by youth groups have often been regarded both as characteristic of all young people and as threats to the moral order of society. The analysis of moral panic suggests that newspapers indulge in sensationalism by exaggerating trivial social events, but the effects may be more serious, resulting in calls for more severe penalties and even the creation of new criminal offences. See: *Deviancy Amplification*.

Bibl. Cohen, S. (1972)

Moral Statistics. An aspect of the nineteenth-century French antecedents of sociology, moral statistics involved the collection of aggregate social data, which were regarded as a feature of social pathology (q.v.) – suicide, divorce, homicide and illegitimacy. See: *Durkheim*; *Official Statistics*; *Suicide*.

Mores. W. Q. Sumner (1906) defined mores as the patterns of cultural and moral action which contributed to the continuity of the human group. Mores are traditional, prescriptive standards which maintain the social group by regulating individual behaviour. See: *Culture*; *Custom*; *Folkways*.

Mortality. Mortality data are normally expressed in terms of the number of deaths per thousand individuals as specified by age, sex and social class. Mortality rates provide indicators of important social arrangements. The infant mortality rate, especially the neo-natal rate (covering the first four weeks of life), provides a sensitive indicator of general social welfare in different societies and different regions within any one society. Differential mortality rates between social classes indicate inequalities in health care, wealth and working conditions. In Britain, there has been a marked shift in the principal causes of death away from infectious to degenerative diseases. See: *Death Rate*; *Demography*.

Mosca, Gaetano (1858–1941). An Italian jurist and political theorist, he contributed to the sociology of elites. In *The Ruling Class* (1896), he contended that, whatever the form of government, power would be in the hands of a minority who formed the ruling class. This class, however, always had to justify its rule by appeals to the moral or legal principles which are acceptable to the governed. His ideas influenced R. Michels (q.v.) and form part of a sociological tradition concerned with elites. See: *Elite*; *Ruling Class*.

Multidimensional Scaling (MDS). MDS

refers to a group of models which portray data as a set of points in space, such that the relationships in the data are reflected spatially in the geometry of the model. Observations that are associated in different degrees in the data set will appear as points separated by distances that correspond to their coefficients of association. MDS presents complex data in a visual form that is usually easier to absorb and interpret than in tabular form. The original metric MDS had a restricted use in sociology because it assumed interval or ratio measurement levels (q.v.). Nonmetric MDS, however, represents data that are merely ordered in some way and uses this rank-order in the plotting of the co-ordinates for each point. Any sets of data which contain measures of similarity or dissimilarity can be used in such scaling. The technique is still not widely used in sociology, though there is considerable interest in its potential. It has proved useful in attitude research for the analysis of subjective perceptions of similarity and difference.

Bibl. Kruskal and Wish (1978)

Multiple Deprivation. See: *Deprivation*.

Multivariate Analysis. Multivariate techniques are used in the statistical analysis of data comprising several variables. The term describes the analysis of relationships between a number of independent and dependent variables, when techniques such as multiple correlation (q.v.), regression (q.v.), cluster analysis (q.v.), factor analysis (q.v.) and path analysis (q.v.) are employed. See: *Causal Modelling*; *Log Linear Analysis*; *Dependent/Independent Variables*; *Survey*.

Myth. A myth is a narrative account of the sacred (q.v.) which embodies collective experiences and represents the *conscience collective* (q.v.). Nineteenth-century anthropology sought to discover the origins of myths, treating them as unscientific explanations of social institutions and practices. For B. Malinowski (q.v.), myths provided legitimation (q.v.) of social arrangements. Contemporary perspectives have been profoundly influenced by C. Lévi-Strauss (q.v.), who treats myths as a system of signs from the perspective of structural linguistics. For Lévi-Strauss, myths are not legitimating charters of institutions and they do not attempt to explain social arrangements. The function of myth is essentially cognitive, namely to account for the fundamental conceptual categories of the mind. These categories are constituted by contradictory series of binary oppositions – nature and society, raw and cooked, man and woman, left and right. Myths do not carry a message which the anthropologist seeks to decipher. Any one myth is merely a variation on a theme which presents one particular combination of elements. Thus, the Oedipus myth is simply one variation on the elements of mother/son, wife/husband and father/son that are organized in relations of love, hatred, service and dominance. While this approach has proved theoretically fruitful, Lévi-Strauss's methodological presuppositions have often been criticized as arbitrary and ethnocentric. While traditional anthropology was concerned with the study of myths in primitive society, the structural analysis of myth has also been applied to modern industrial societies. For example, R. Barthes (1957) treats myths as a system of communication, consisting not only of written discourses, but also the products of cinema, sport, photography, advertising and television. The point of myth analysis is to expose what he refers to as 'the falsely obvious' world of mass communication. See: *Semiotics*; *Structuralism*.

Bibl. Leach (1967)

N

Nationalism. Nationalism is an ideology (q.v.) based on the belief that a people with common characteristics such as language, religion or ethnicity constitutes a separate and distinctive political community. Nationalists attempt to preserve this social distinctiveness to protect the social benefits which follow from national identity and membership. Nationalism locates the political legitimacy of the state in self-government by co-nationals. It is often argued that nationalism as a political doctrine did not exist before the eighteenth century and that the rise of nationalist movements coincides with the development of nation-states in Europe after the Napoleonic period. By the end of the nineteenth century, however, it was assumed by many social theorists that nationalism would tend to decline and would be replaced by internationalism and cosmopolitanism. These interpretations of industrial society suggested that: (1) the growth of trade would undermine particularistic differences between societies; (2) conflicts would be expressed through class rather than national ideologies; (3) the working class would develop a commitment to international socialism. These assumptions were shattered by the First World War when there was relatively little organized working-class opposition to a war fought on nationalist principles. Nationalism subsequently became closely associated with movements for self-determination against imperialism in the Third World.

There are three major contemporary interpretations of nationalism: (1) it was a romantic movement related to the unification of Germany and Italy, and was subsequently exported to Africa and Asia on the back of European colonialism; (2) nationalism is a form of reactive politics against colonialism in societies where traditional modes of social organization have collapsed as a result of social changes introduced by external colonialism; (3) the uneven development (q.v.) of capitalism creates profound regional imbalance, and peripheral regions embrace nationalist politics to secure a more equal distribution of wealth. An example is Scottish nationalism within the United Kingdom. In this interpretation, nationalism within advanced capitalist societies develops in response to internal colonialism (q.v.).

Nationalism is often regarded as an artificial, parasitic ideology, because it is often impossible to identify a single characteristic common to all members of a society who claim to belong to a common nation. In this view, nationalism is a myth created by intellectuals, who are the exponents of romantic notions of national language, folk heritage and national identity. Nationalism is thus also associated with political extremism and xenophobia. However, the liberal equation of nationalism and fascism tends to obscure the positive political merits of nationalist movements in the Third World, which have achieved self-government and some measure of social development.

In the classical Marxist approach to nationalism, there were three common arguments: (1) nationalism was a bourgeois ideology, because it served the class interest of the rising bourgeoisie in its opposition to the traditional aristocracy which ruled by, for example, the principle of divine right; (2) the rise of the nation-state was closely associated with the economic requirements of early capitalism, but nationalism would decline as late capitalism became more international in character; (3) national struggle was a special form of class struggle, often referred to as 'external class struggle' that is conducted on the international rather than the national level. These three arguments have not been supported by political developments in the twentieth century. Nationalism has often been associated with working-class radicalism, because nationalist politics may imply social equality for all members of the nation. Nationalism may also be part of a revolutionary socialist struggle for national autonomy against foreign domination and internal exploitation – for example, the Mexican Revolution of 1910–17. It is, furthermore, difficult to treat national struggles as a special form of class struggle and some Marxists have argued that nationalism has to be regarded as an 'autonomous force' in political struggles.

Since nationalism can take many different political directions – democracy, fascism or communism – and can be associated with different classes, it has been argued that there can be no general theory of nationalism. There is no theory which can identify a social process (such as industrialization) that will explain the emergence of all forms of nationalism, or which is able to define the essential and universal features of nationalist movements. This negative conclusion is not, however, widely shared. The consensus in social science is that, despite its empirical complexity, nationalism has the following general features: (1) it is based on the demand that governments should share the same cultural identity as the governed; (2) as a result, cultural nationalism, which seeks to preserve or recreate the national heritage through, for example, the revival of a language in Africa, prepares the basis for political nationalism, which seeks self-determination and political supremacy; (3) the development of modern systems of mass communication facilitates the dissemination of unifying nationalist ideologies; (4) nationalist ideologies have a strong appeal to subordinate classes by providing them with some economic protection against non-nationals, but the content of the ideology is typically developed by marginal intellectuals – black intellectuals, for instance, excluded from white educational establishments, were drawn to nationalism; (5) nationalism is, in the twentieth century, associated with de-colonization and the economic development of Third-World societies, and with the struggle for regional equality within existing capitalist societies. See: *Ethnic Group*; *Fascism*; *Imperialism*; *Mobilization*; *Modernization*; *Political Sociology*; *State*.

Bibl. Smith, A. D. (1971); Davis, H. B. (1978); Gellner (1983)

Natural Area. Within the theory known as urban ecology (q.v.), an area of the city inhabited by a population of a particular type (for example, the suburb or the ghetto), is known as a natural area. Such an area is relatively homogeneous socially and culturally, and the assumption is that it is created by ecological forces which drive similar populations into similar areas. See: *Chicago School*; *Concentric Zone Theory*; *Urban Way of Life*.

Natural Law. Within the natural law tradition, the justice of social laws and institutions was thought to depend on their conformity to certain universal laws of nature. All human beings, by virtue of their membership in humanity and as part of this natural order, enjoyed certain natural rights, such as a right to freedom. Natural law theory concerned itself with the moral content of laws and developed the criterion that true laws could not be unjust laws. However, the secularization of Western culture and intellectual relativism have brought into question the basic assumptions concerning the universality of human nature.

Contemporary legal theory, including the sociology of law, has inclined towards a view of law as command, supported by relevant sanctions and the coercive apparatus of the state. This is known as *positive* law. The legitimacy of law resides not in its moral content but in the procedures by which it is developed and enforced by the appropriate authorities. The positivist view of law does not provide a criterion by which the justice of governments can be assessed. See: *Legal-Rational Authority*; *Legitimacy*.

Bibl. Reasons and Rich (eds.) (1978)

Naturalism. Sociologists who argue that the methods of sociology are, for all practical purposes, the same as those of the natural sciences, propose a naturalistic account of sociology. It is commonly suggested that naturalism is equivalent to positivism (q.v.), particularly by those who oppose positivist methods in sociology. This is a mistaken view, since other doctrines opposed to positivism, for example realism (q.v.), unite the methods of natural and social sciences.

Nature/Nurture Debate. Human beings are simultaneously features of the natural world (by virtue of having bodies) and members of the cultural world (by virtue of language). The precise relationship between biology and culture in the constitution of human society has long been a controversial issue in social philosophy and social sciences. There are two extreme positions in the nature/nurture debate: (1) geneticism argues that the characteristics of individuals, groups and nations can be explained exclusively in terms of genetic inheritance; (2) cultural determinism and anti-naturalism argue that individual differences and national character are entirely explained by socialization (q.v.). Explanations in terms of genetic inheritance have been common in theories of criminal behaviour, intelligence and educational performance. Feminists have objected to the emphasis on biological sex in many accounts of the differences between men and women, on the grounds that these accounts reflect the values of patriarchy (q.v.), while differences are often socially produced by gender (q.v.). While sociologists traditionally rejected all forms of geneticism, some sociologists, like T. Parsons (q.v.), have sought a more fruitful theoretical relationship between biological and social systems. Parsons (1977) considered the parallel between symbols, information and cybernetics in social systems, and the communication of 'information' in biological systems through DNA. This approach avoids behaviourism (q.v.) which is implicit in various aspects of sociobiology (q.v.). See: *Culture*; *Intelligence*; *Mead, Margaret*; *Madness*.

Need. The concept is used in two senses. (1) As a theory of individual motivation, actions are explained by reference to needs. While it is possible to recognize certain physiologically based needs – food, sleep and shelter – which must be satisfied for human survival, needs are culturally malleable. A need for sexual satisfaction may be achieved through homosexuality, marriage, celibacy, promiscuity or prostitution. For B. Malinowski (q.v.), social institutions function to satisfy human needs. Sociologists also recognize needs which are not physiological – the need for companionship, recognition or meaning. The concept also has a critical significance; capitalist society is said to create false needs through advertising. The difficulty of 'false needs' is parallel to 'false class consciousness'. By what criteria do we judge, for example, that the need for paper underwear is false?

(2) In social systems theory, it is part of the concept of functional prerequisites (q.v.). For example, T. Parsons (q.v.) believes that any social system has four needs or 'functional imperatives' which must be met if the system is to survive. These needs correspond to four subsystems – economic, political, motivation and integration. See: *Functionalism*; *Sociobiology*; *Systems Theory*.

Bibl. Heller (1974)

Negotiated Order. Negotiated order theory regards social phenomena, particularly organizational arrangements, as emerging from the ongoing process of interaction between people. The interaction process involves constant negotiation and renegotiation of the terms of social action. Negotiated order theory emphasizes the fluidity and uncertainty of social arrangements. This perspective has been used primarily in the analysis of organizations, for example the modern hospital. Critics claim that the theory neglects the structural limitations on social action, since there are many features of society which are simply not negotiable. See: *Symbolic Interactionism*.

Bibl. Strauss (1978)

Neighbourhood. A term with a commonsense use in sociology to denote residential areas. The nature of the social ties formed in neighbourhoods was for long the subject of active investigation in urban sociology. For example, a number of studies showed that the residents of suburbs formed fairly close, family-like ties with one another, although the prevailing myth was that suburbanites had essentially private lives. See: *Affluent Worker*; *Community*; *Organization Man*; *Suburban Way of Life*.

Neo-Colonialism. See: *Imperialism*.

Neo-Evolutionism. See: *Evolutionary Theory*.

Neo-Kantianism. This term is a general label for a variety of intellectual trends in Germany between 1870 and 1920 which returned to E. Kant's philosophy. In sociology, neo-Kantianism has been important in shaping debates concerning epistemology (q.v.). In the work of G. Simmel (q.v.), for instance, the Kantian principle that mind has an active part to play in the apprehension of the natural world became a guiding feature of his sociology. Knowledge of the social world is always constructive knowledge which involves selection and interpretation and not simply a question of collecting facts. Just as Kant argued that experience of natural phenomena is determined by *a priori* categories, so Simmel attempted to show how social reality could be studied in terms of enduring social forms in which the varied content of social life was distilled. While neo-Kantianism was superseded by, for example, the debates between critical theorists and positivists, the basic assumptions of the neo-Kantian position are still influential in the philosophy of the social sciences. See: *Critical Theory*; *Hermeneutics*; *Methodenstreit*; *Positivism*; *Weber*.

Network. In family and urban sociology the notion of a network was used to describe the system of personal relationships in which each individual was involved. E. Bott (1957), for example, showed that the relationships between husband and wife depended on the interconnectedness of the networks of kin in which each was involved. Many studies attempt to map the networks of relationships within a community, often mathematically, with the aim of revealing social structure and patterns of communication. See: *Conjugal Rule*; *Sociogram*.

Bibl. Frankenburg (1966)

Neutralization. People who commit deviant acts frequently attempt to neutralize their guilt by techniques such as denying responsibility, denying that injury has occurred, blaming the victim, and criticizing those who condemn the deviant act. Neutralization is a coping response that allows deviant behaviour to continue. The phrase 'techniques of neutralization' was coined by G. Sykes and D. Matza (1957). See: *Accounts*; *Deviant Behaviour*.

New Religious Movements. It has been argued that many Western and especially European societies are undergoing a process of secularization (q.v.) whereby Christian religions lose their importance.

By contrast, several newer religious movements like the Unification Church or the Hare Krishna movement are gaining in numbers. These have often taken Eastern religions as their inspiration and have attracted considerable public attention, especially following accusations that they get converts through 'brainwashing'.

New religious movements may be conveniently divided into two main types, world-rejecting and world-affirming. The former are exclusive, seeing the outside world as threatening and asking their converts to reject their former lives. One example is the Unification Church (the Moonies). World-affirming religions (for example, Scientology), on the other hand, see the prevailing social order as having certain virtues. They tend not to be collective but are rather individualistic, promising to unlock powers latent in every individual. There is little evidence that the recruitment practices of either kind of movement do amount to brainwashing. Indeed, the turnover of membership is very high and the recruitment process is inefficient. One study of the Moonies showed that considerably fewer than 1 per cent of those initially approached were still members of the movement after two years. See: *Sociology of Religion*.

Bibl. Barker (1984); Wallis (1984)

New Working Class In the 1960s the French sociologists S. Mallet (1963), A. Gorz (1964) and A. Touraine (1969) suggested that the evolution of production technology had created a new segment within the working class. The new working class comprised people employed in advanced, high-technology industries. It was asserted that high technology required better-educated workers, organized work along communal, teamwork lines, and integrated workers into their firms. These changes promoted greater industrial and social militancy, that is, class consciousness (q.v.), because they made various 'contradictions' of capitalism more visible.

One contradiction which this new class was thought to experience acutely was between the communal production of goods and the private appropriation of profits. Their high levels of education meant the new workers understood how production processes worked and they had real control over these processes. Teamwork brought home to them the communal nature of production. They were thus able to penetrate the contradiction that was concealed from traditional workers. A second contradiction was the discrepancy between their skill, responsibility and training and their inability to influence company policy. Mallet and Gorz thought that the new class comprised both skilled manual workers and non-manual technicians and professionals operating the new technologies.

There have been several criticisms of these accounts and the concept is now discredited. (1) Other research shows that high-technology workers may have little control or understanding of the new processes. D. Gallie (1978) found that most manual workers in four oil refineries in France and Britain were little more than semi-skilled labourers. Deskilling (q.v.) may occur in high technology just as it does elsewhere. (2) There is in fact a considerable variation among the levels of skill and responsibility of the groups that make up the new working class, even within an apparently homogeneous category such as technicians. (3) In the 1970s, the French new working class was less radical and militant than the traditional workers, and was reconciled to capitalism. It is worth noting that R. Blauner (1964) argued that workers on automated systems in America were *less* alienated

than others, though his views have also been criticized. See: *Alienation*; *Automation*; *Post-Industrial Society*; *Working Class*.

Bibl. Rose, M. (1979); Hill, S. (1981)

Nisbet, Robert A. (b.1913). Currently Albert Schweitzer Professor of Humanities Emeritus at Columbia University and Scholar at the American Enterprise Institute for Public Policy Research, his approach to sociology has been remarkably consistent and influential. His work falls into two fields: the study of developmentalism in social thought; and order and disorganization in the social sphere, or community and conflict. His argument is that revolutionary social change has undermined community and communal values with the result that authority no longer has a significant social underpinning. His analysis of social change has been presented in *Tradition and Revolt* (1968), *Social Change and History* (1969) and *History of the Idea of Progress* (1980). The study of the collapse of community was a central theme of *The Quest for Community* (1953), *The Social Bond* (1970), *The Social Philosophers* (1974a) and *Prejudices* (1982). He has also been involved in a number of edited works which have been influential in the development of theoretical and applied sociology; these include *Emile Durkheim* (1965), *Contemporary Social Problems* (1961) with R. K. Merton (q.v.) and *A History of Sociological Analysis* (1980) with T. Bottomore (q.v.). He has contributed to the study of the ideas of E. Durkheim in *The Sociology of Emile Durkheim* (1974b). Nisbet's most influential book on the history of sociology is *The Sociological Tradition* (1967), in which he argues that social theory has been profoundly influenced by the French and the industrial revolutions: three systems of thought (liberalism,

167

radicalism and conservatism) emerged as responses to the disruptions following these revolutions. Sociology is primarily dependent on the conservative legacy in terms of its unit-ideas (such as status, the sacred, and community). In *Conservatism* (1986), he explores the primary themes of political conservatism and the present crisis of conservative thought.

Nominal. See: *Measurement Levels.*

Nomothetic. See: *Idiographic.*

Non-Parametric. Non-parametric statistics make no assumptions about the parameters of a distribution of values; that is, they are distribution-free, unlike many of the statistics commonly used in social science. They are useful to sociologists for three reasons: (1) they are effective with small sample sizes; (2) they are effective with the ordinal data that sociologists often work with; (3) they do not depend on assumptions that the population distribution is 'normal'. Two common techniques are the Mann-Whitney U and the Wilcoxon T.

Bibl. Siegel (1956); Senter (1969)

Non-Response. Bias in the selection of a sample can result from the refusal of some sections of the population to cooperate. Bias arises if the people who refuse to cooperate differ from those who do in some important respect, since the final sample of respondents does not represent the total population that is being investigated. The bias is greater in proportion to the numbers who fail to respond, and to the magnitude of the difference between the respondents and non-respondents. The effects of non-response can be reduced in well-designed surveys by keeping the amount of non-response down to reasonable levels and by approximately estimating the bias

that it may introduce into the results. See: *Bias.*

Bibl. Moser and Kalton (1979)

Norm. Norms are prescriptions serving as common guidelines for social action. Human behaviour exhibits certain regularities, which are the product of adherence to common expectations or norms. In this sense, human action is 'rule governed'. A social norm is not necessarily actual behaviour and normative behaviour is not simply the most frequently occurring pattern. Since the term refers to social expectations about 'correct' or 'proper' behaviour, norms imply the presence of legitimacy, consent and prescription. While deviation from norms is punished by sanctions, norms are acquired by internalization (q.v.) and socialization (q.v.). The concept is central to theories of social order (q.v.). See: *Consensus; Institution; Parsons; Role; Value.*

Normal Distribution. See: *Distribution.*

Nuclear Family. Social units comprising a man and a woman living together with their children, nuclear families are often contrasted with extended families. One theoretical position assumes a 'functional fit' between the nuclear family and industrialization, in that the nuclear family, free of wider kinship ties, is more geographically and socially mobile, gives greater emotional support via the unconstrained choice of marriage partners, and permits occupational roles to be filled by achievement criteria, all requirements of industrial society. The family structure of contemporary society is thus said to be composed of relatively isolated nuclear family households, although there will be considerable social variations.

Recent work shows that: (1) family structures before the industrial revolution were not all of the classical extended family form; (2) the *process* of industrialization was accompanied by a greater use of extended kin contacts, partly by exchange of services and financial aid; (3) there is now considerable evidence that the family structures of industrial societies are not characterized by isolated conjugal households. Contemporary families are more accurately described as modified extended families in which there are extensive contacts between kin not necessarily living together, contacts taking the form of visits, telephone calls, and the exchange of services. In this system of mutual support, non-kin will also be important, creating a modified primary group around each family.

To some extent the notion of the family as a unitary phenomenon is misleading. There are a whole variety of household structures besides the conventional nuclear one of wife, husband and children. The trend in Britain over the last two decades has been towards smaller households, more people living together before or instead of marrying, more divorces, more remarriages, and an increase in the numbers of children born outside marriage.

These changes in household structure cast some doubt on functional theories of the family current some forty or fifty years ago. Writers of this persuasion argued that the family was a universal human institution because it performed certain crucial functions for society such as socialization (q.v.), caring for the young, and reproduction. However, not only are there fewer families of this type in contemporary societies, it is also probable that the family structure also creates difficulties for society and for family members; families may be functional but they are also dysfunctional (q.v.). For example, recent writers argue that women are oppressed in the family, which also routinely causes psychological damage to the individuals concerned. See: *Conjugal Role*; *Divorce*; *Domestic Labour*; *Extended Family*; *Group*; *Kinship*; *Marriage*; *Patriarchy*; *Sexual Divisions*.

Bibl. Anderson, M. (1975); Morgan (1975); Barrett and McIntosh (1982)

Null Hypothesis. See: *Significance Test*.

O

Objectivity. The goal of scientific investigation, sociological or otherwise, is often said to be objective knowledge, free of bias or prejudice. There is a division of opinion here, some holding that objectivity in sociology is possible, others not. Five different kinds of arguments are advanced for sociology not being objective. (1) Sociological judgements are subjective, being coloured by actors' own experiences. See: *Phenomenological Sociology*. (2) All propositions are limited in their meaning to particular language contexts. See: *Ethnomethodology*; *Indexicality*. (3) All sociological theories are produced by, and limited to, particular social groups. Such a doctrine is often taken to be an outcome of the sociology of knowledge which treats all knowledge as a function of social location. See: *Mannheim*; *Relativism*. (4) All observations are necessarily theory-laden (q.v.). (5) In that all members of society have different values, sociologists will unconsciously, but necessarily, have their arguments influenced by their values. See: *Value-Freedom*; *Value-Neutrality*; *Value-Relevance*. Some sociologists argue that objectivity in some or all of the above senses is not necessarily desirable; it is argued that the sociologist, for example, should be critical and espouse particular values. See: *Sociology as Science*.

Occupational Transition. See: *Social Mobility*.

Official Statistics. Sociologists approach such data with caution, for two reasons. (1) Some official statistics are known to lack accuracy because of the way they are collected: for example, strike statistics. Inaccuracies are often systematic and do not cancel each other out, making the use of official statistics perilous: the classic example of these dangers is E. Durkheim's use of suicide statistics which under-recorded suicides in socially integrated and rural communities. (2) The categorization of data reflects the interests of government and may not be meaningful to sociologists. For example, United Kingdom unemployment statistics record as unemployed people who have registered at the local benefits office and exclude those who are out of work but do not register. Many of those excluded from the official category are women who for one reason or another fail to qualify for benefits; others include people who have taken early retirement, willingly or otherwise, rather than search for work in adverse labour market conditions. Data collected by government for its own use are in this case meaningless to sociologists concerned with, say, the incidence of unemployment among different groups.

The investigation of the social processes that lie behind the collection and categorization of official statistics, however, has proved a fertile area of research, as criminologists have demonstrated with criminal statistics (q.v.). See: *Strikes; Suicide; Unemployment.*

Bibl. Hindess (1973)

Oligarchy. In his analysis of the German Social Democratic Party in the early twentieth century, R. Michels (q.v.) (1911) argued that labour organizations with democratic aims, such as political parties and trade unions, experienced a tension between the need for efficiency and membership control of the making and execution of policy. As they grew in size, labour organizations became more complex and permanent bureaucracies developed to cope efficiently with the problems of administration. The officials, by virtue of their expertise and experience, became indispensable and difficult to change even when subject to periodic re-election. Once they occupied this strong position, the leaders began to emancipate themselves from member control and to displace member goals with their own. These goals were usually less radical than those of the members and the official party or union ideology. As they controlled the channels of communication, they manipulated the flow of information to help buttress their positions. In the final analysis, goal displacement depended on the apathy and lack of involvement of members with issues of party or union government.

The modern study of trade-union government and the internal structure of mass political parties has been deeply influenced by Michels' pessimism, though research shows that the 'iron law' of oligarchy does not always apply in such organizations. See: *Elite; Incorporation; Political Parties; Trade Unions.*

Ontology. This branch of philosophy or metaphysics is concerned with the nature of existence. Ontological assumptions are those assumptions that underpin theories about what kind of entities can exist.

Operationalization. To operationalize a concept is to provide a way of measuring and quantifying it so that it may be tested. For example, a number of scales and attitude tests have been devised to test the theory of alienation (q.v.). Some sociologists, but certainly not all, believe that if a concept cannot be operationalized, it is fruitless or meaningless.

Ordinal. See: *Measurement Levels.*

Organic Analogy. This attempts to understand the structure and function of human society by analogy with the nature of living organisms. For example, society, like an organism in nature, becomes more complex and differentiated in terms of its social structure through evolutionary change. The organic analogy is often contrasted with the mechanistic analogy of society. The former treats society as a natural phenomenon which exists independently of human planning; the latter regards society as the project of human construction just as a machine is an artefact of human design. The organic analogy is often associated with conservative thought because it suggests that society cannot be changed by political intervention. The mechanistic analogy was associated with the notion of 'social engineering' by which deliberate changes in social arrangements could be achieved. The so-called 'organistic school of sociology' was represented in

171

England by H. Spencer (q.v.). See: *Evolutionary Theory*; *Functionalism*; *Social Darwinism*; *Urban Ecology*.

Bibl. Peel (1971)

Organic Solidarity. See: *Durkheim*.

Organization Man. In *The Organization Man* (1956) W. H. Whyte identified a new breed of business executives, working for large corporations, whose lives were dominated by their firms. Firms demanded total commitment and expected executives to move from town to town, even between continents, as they were shifted from post to post. The more successful the executive, the more moves he made as he spiralled upwards within a firm. The total dedication of organization men meant they adapted their personalities to fit the bureaucratic organizational environment, they had no roots in any local community, no real friends, and little contact with their extended families. See: *Spiralist*.

Organization Theory. This describes a set of empirical and conceptual observations about (1) the factors affecting organizational structure and (2) the social behaviour of people in enterprises. It deals mainly with the administrative level of enterprises comprising clerical and managerial positions, less with other employees.

Organization theory grew out of the analysis of bureaucracy (q.v.). This led to the recognition that there are a variety of organizational forms and managerial structures. In *The Management of Innovation* (1961), T. Burns and G. M. Stalker distinguished between bureaucratic systems, which they called 'mechanistic', suitable for stable conditions such as uncompetitive markets and unchanging technology, and non-bureaucratic or 'organic' forms which maximize personal discretion, de-

centralize decision-making and minimize rule-bound behaviour where possible, which they saw as best in changing conditions. This insight fostered what is now known as the *contingency* approach, which establishes relationships among different structures and various contextual factors, notably environment, technology and size. Organizational forms differ on several dimensions: complexity; specialization of tasks; and formalization of roles and procedures. This approach is descriptive, demonstrating associations among structural and contextual variables rather than explaining causal connections. Nor are the associations particularly close and they allow for a variety of structures in any given context.

Research into business history has recently influenced the study of organizational structure. The traditional firm was an enterprise based on a single unit with all operations under one roof, or at least on one site. The rise of the giant corporation in the twentieth century has created firms that are multi-unit, operating in a variety of different industrial and commercial sectors and across vast geographical distances. Business historians note that there has been a corresponding organizational shift from a unitary organization (known as U-form), with a direct chain of command and tight control of all operations from the top of the company, to a new form of decentralization. Multi-divisionalism (M-form) groups together various subsidiary units into divisions, and each division is run as a semi-autonomous business. Corporate headquarters set financial targets, approve divisional business plans, appoint senior managerial staff, monitor performance and raise funds in the capital market, but they do not intervene in the day-to-day running of the divisions. The M-form was developed in the USA prior to the Second World War and has been adopted by large British companies over the last twenty years. Although the corporate structure is decentralized, there is no single organizational form or managerial structure within divisions.

Other approaches focus more on managerial behaviour, in particular on those aspects that are not determined by the organization's formal role prescriptions, sometimes known as 'informal' or 'emergent' behaviour. The importance of interest groups is widely recognized. The hierarchical division of managers into different strata and the horizontal division into different specialist functions create conditions for distinct subgroups to form. These often develop their own goals which may conflict with those of other groups or top management. This indicates that managerial role performance can be problematic. The officially prescribed roles which appear as the formal organizational structure do not in fact determine behaviour.

The importance of organizational power-holders for the determination of managerial structure has been emphasized by J. Child (1972). The adjustment of structure to contingencies is not automatic but mediated through top corporate managers who make strategic choices. Their choices may include the sort of structure to establish – centralized or decentralized, for example – and the contextual factors that are to surround the enterprise – which markets to enter, what technology to use and how large to let the firm grow. The main power centre is the board of directors, which controls the distribution of resources. Such control provides top management with a major source of influence over the behaviour of subordinates, since groups lower down the hierarchy need resources if they are to survive, while individuals depend on top management for access to resources and rewards in

the form of career advancement, or indeed to avoid dismissal. See: *Bounded Rationality*; *Management*; *Managerial Revolution*; *Organization Man*; *Role*; *Scientific Management*.

Bibl. Silverman (1970); Salaman (1979); Chandler and Daems (eds.) (1980)

Oriental Despotism. Contemporary debates concerning despotism originated in eighteenth-century France. For C. Montesquieu (1748), political systems were divided into republics, monarchies and despotisms according to the principles of virtue, honour and fear. The differences between monarchy and oriental despotism were: (1) monarchies were based on stable hierarchical stratification, but despotism involved general slavery; (2) in monarchy, the prince followed custom, whereas the potentate ruled by arbitrary whim; (3) in despotism, there were no intervening institutions between the subject and government. In the physiocratic tradition, the enlightened despot was expected to remove traditional constraints on progress and economic development, whereas the oriental despot was enslaved by arbitrary inclinations. For utilitarians, despotisms were the basis of tradition and ignorance, reinforced by priestly control. In Marxism, oriental despotism was associated with the Asiatic mode of production (q.v.); the arbitrary character of political life was connected with the fact that, in oriental societies, the state controlled the land. Oriental despotism was a society in which the state dominated civil society in the absence of individualism, rights of representation or personal freedoms. Oriental despotisms were arbitrary, stagnant and backward.

Recent debates have been organized around K. Wittfogel's (1957) argument that the nationalization of land under

173

Stalin involved the continuity of despotism from Tsarist to socialist Russia. Asiatic conditions were preserved in the transition from oriental to party bureaucracy. M. Weber (1950, 1951, 1958b) also argued that the political systems of the Orient were patrimonial bureaucracies; these states were arbitrary and despotic. The social conditions for patrimonial despotism were the absence of autonomous cities, rational law and private property. See: *Patrimonialism*; *Weber*.

Bibl. Venturi (1963)

Orientation to Work. Industrial sociologists often assumed that people's wants at work were universal and stable, comprising a need for community and for jobs that were intrinsically satisfying. From this it followed that contextual factors such as the type of technology or the size of a plant would have fairly consistent social consequences. J. H. Goldthorpe, D. Lockwood, F. Bechoffer and J. Platt (1968a; 1968b; 1969), however, challenged this conventional view in the Affluent Worker (q.v.) research and emphasized the importance of workers' orientations. They argued that people's social experiences outside work determined what expectations they brought to employment, and these influenced how they reacted to the work context. Orientations were a mediating variable between workplace structure and employees' perceptions and behaviour. They distinguished two major orientations: (1) *solidarism* fitted the conventional stereotype of people who expected social community and job satisfaction; (2) *instrumentalism* (q.v.) referred to workers who sought only high pay and security, who would do even such alienating work as car assembly if their instrumental wants were met; indeed, they would actively seek out such work if the pay were good.

These conclusions have been questioned by later research. (1) R. M. Blackburn and M. Mann (1979) have found little evidence that distinct orientations exist in most manual workers. (2) Among those few people who do display identifiable orientations, these are usually multistranded and combine both solidaristic and instrumental elements. (3) Solidarism is a composite of two different sets of attitudes, one concerned with intrinsic job satisfaction and the other with sociability.

Most studies deal with men in manual work. Evidence of the situation among women and non-manual employees is scarcer. R. Brown (1976) has suggested that, on theoretical grounds, women might reasonably be expected to differ from men. (1) Female socialization (q.v.) contains expectations that work will be secondary to marriage. (2) The employment opportunities open to women are more restricted than for men. (3) Women usually acquire different responsibilities during the domestic life-cycle (q.v.) which reduce the centrality of work. (4) The jobs available to women are likely to be less interesting than men's. A recent national survey of women and employment in Britain (J. Martin and C. Roberts, 1984) has found that women's orientations are also multistranded, with financial factors dominating, to be followed by intrinsic work satisfaction and then the company of other people. Life-cycle factors are significant. Married women are less likely than the unmarried to see themselves as being financially dependent on work or as working in order to provide basic essentials. Women working part time, who are usually married and often have children, have different job priorities from full-timers in that they value convenient hours of work more highly. The experience of work as providing intrinsic job satisfaction increases in higher-level,

non-manual occupations, and with age.
See: *Human Relations*.

Bibl. Hill, S. (1981)

Other-Directedness. The other-directed person depends exclusively on constant approval and support of others for confirmation of his or her self-image. This conformist personality is seen as the product of mass consumer society.

Overdetermine. This term expresses the notion within modern Marxism that even the most important element of the social structure not only determines other elements but is also affected by them. It was originally used by L. Althusser (q.v.) to indicate that what he and other Marxists saw as the basic contradiction (q.v.) in society, between capital and labour, could be modified (overdetermined) by other contradictions, for example that between urban and rural. The concept therefore forms part of his objection to economic determinism (q.v.) in Marxism.

P

Panel Study. This technique, also known as a longitudinal study, involves collecting data from the same sample at intervals over time. Panels are useful for studying trends and the effects of particular changes. Difficulties include the initial selection of the sample, when it may be hard to find people willing to join a long-term investigation; conditioning, which is a real problem as panel members may cease to be representative of the wider population simply as the result of being on the panel; and sample mortality, the consequence of panel members moving, dying or losing interest.

Paradigm. In its sociological use, this term derives from the work of T. S. Kuhn (1970) on the nature of scientific change. For Kuhn, scientists work within paradigms, which are general ways of seeing the world and which dictate what kind of scientific work should be done and what kinds of theory are acceptable. These paradigms provide what Kuhn calls 'normal science', the kind of science routinely done day after day. Over time, however, normal science produces a series of anomalies which cannot be resolved within the paradigm. Kuhn argues that at this point there is a sudden break, and the old paradigm is replaced by a new one, leading to a new period of normal science. In sociology, the term has a still vaguer usage, denoting schools of sociological work, each of which is relatively self-contained, with its own methods and theories.

Pareto, Vilfredo (1848–1923). An Italian engineer, economist and sociologist, his most significant contribution to the social sciences was as a founder of mathematical economic theory. As a sociologist, he is best known for his discussion of elites and his view that there existed a cyclical process leading to the replacement or 'circulation' of elites over time. He distinguished between elites and non-elites, and, within the ranks of the elite, between the governing fraction and the rest. In his view, 'circulation' occurred because some people (the 'lions') were more suited to the maintenance of the *status quo* under stable conditions, while others (the 'foxes') were adaptive and innovative and coped better during periods of change.

His major sociological work was *Trattato di sociologia generale*, published in Italy in 1916 and translated as *The Mind and Society* (1963), in which he put forward his elite theory and a general analytical scheme for sociology. He distinguished sociology from economics on the grounds that the latter discipline dealt only with one aspect of human action, namely logical action which was the rational choice of the most appropriate means for a given end, in this case the acquisition and allocation of scarce resources. Sociology, however, dealt with the non-logical actions that made up most of social life. These were non-logical because they did not derive from methodical observation and rational deliberation, and were determined by 'sentiments' rather than scientific method. He saw non-logical beliefs – explanations of social phenomena in terms other than those of natural science – as having a major influence in society.

Within the realm of the non-logical he distinguished *residues* and *derivations*. He saw residues as universal elements that reflected basic human sentiments and derivations as variable elements. Of six types of residue, Pareto identified two as especially important: the tendency for people to make connections even if they are unaware of any logical or observed link between the elements, which he called the 'residue of combinations'; and the propensity to preserve the things combined, which he referred to as 'residues of the persistence of aggregates'. In the circulation of elites, the 'foxes' represented the residue of combination and the 'lions' the residue of persistence. Derivations were the non-logical arguments used to justify the conclusions drawn from residues as premises, which included assertion, appeal to authority, accordance with sentiment and verbal proofs. Pareto's influence on the subsequent development of sociology has been twofold. His distinction between non-logical social action and logical economic action informed the position of the Human Relations (q.v.) school, that workers were guided by irrational sentiments whereas managerial policies were rational economic decisions. His view that societies could be analysed as systems with self-equilibrating properties, deriving from theoretical mechanics, later influenced T. Parsons (q.v.) and other structural functionalists. See: *Elite*.

Bibl. Parsons (1968b)

Park, Robert E. (1864–1944). After a varied career as journalist, student of G. Simmel and political worker, Park joined the Department of Sociology at Chicago University in 1914, where he remained for twenty years. He was a major figure in the Chicago School (q.v.) and was responsible for its focus on urban life, community and race relations, its empirical slant, and the development of participant observation (q.v.) as a research technique. With E. Burgess he wrote *Introduction to the Science of Society* in 1921. He saw social relations as being dominated by four principles: cooperation, competition, accommodation (q.v.) and assimilation (q.v.). He applied these to the study of social change in the city. His influence extended beyond his own writings, which were mainly essays, and he trained a whole generation of American sociologists. E. C. Hughes, J. Masuoka and others collected and edited Park's papers, which were published in three volumes between 1950 and 1955. See: *Urban Ecology*.

Parsons, Talcott (1902–1979). The son of a Congregational minister, T. Parsons spent the whole of his adult life in academic positions in the United States, with a short period of postgraduate training in Europe. He had a powerful influence on sociology after the Second World War, particularly in America, although, being a theorist, he was not in the dominant tradition of American empirical research. As often criticized as supported, Parsons' work was at the centre of debate in sociological theory until the mid 1970s. He wrote a great deal, his principal publications being: *The Structure of Social Action* (1937); *Toward a General Theory of Action* (1951), with E. Shils; *The Social System* (1951); *Working Papers in the Theory of Action* (1953), with R. Bales and E. Shils; *Family, Socialization, and Interaction Process* (1955), with R. Bales, J. Olds, M. Zelditch and P. Slater; *Economy and Society* (1956), with N. Smelser; *Social Structure and Personality* (1964); *Societies: Evolutionary and Comparative Perspectives* (1966); and *The System of Modern Societies* (1971).

Parsons' aim was nothing less than to provide a conceptual structure for the whole of sociology which would serve also to integrate all the social sciences. This was to be accomplished by a synthesis between the analysis of individual action and analysis of large-scale social systems. His starting point is the theory of social *action*, the essential feature of which is the relationship between actors and features of their environment, social and natural, to which they give meaning. The most important features of the environment consist of other people, which suggests further that social *interaction*, in which actors have to take notice of the actions, wishes and aims of others, should be the focus of inquiry. In these interactions, norms and values are critical as they regulate and make predictable the behaviour of others. Socialization (q.v.) ensures that individuals internalize norms and values as they grow up. Parsons treats personality and social systems as complementary, though in his analysis the latter ultimately determine the former.

Parsons notes that social interaction has a *systemic* character, hence his use of the term social system (q.v.). The concept that bridges social action and social system is that of *pattern variables*. He defines these as the fundamental dilemmas that face actors in any situation. Social systems may be characterized by the combinations of solutions offered to these dilemmas. There are four sets of dilemmas. (1) Particularism versus universalism. Actors have to decide whether to judge a person by general criteria (universalism) or criteria unique to that person (particularism). (2) Performance versus quality. Actors have to decide whether to judge persons by what they do (performance) or by their personal characteristics (quality). (3) Affective neutrality versus affectivity. Actors can either engage in a relationship for instrumental reasons without the involvement of feelings (affective neutrality) or for emotional reasons (affectivity). (4) Specificity versus diffuseness. Actors have to choose, in any situation, between engaging with others totally across a wide range of activity (diffuseness) or only for specific, restricted purposes (specificity).

These pattern variables structure any system of interaction. Such systems, however, also have certain needs of their own which have to be met, required both by relationship between the social system and its environment and by the internal workings of the system. There are four such *functional needs* (known as A G I L): adaptation, the need to relate to the environment by taking resources from it; goal attainment, the setting of goals for the system; integration, the maintenance of internal order; latency or pattern maintenance, the generation of sufficient motivation to perform tasks. In order to meet each of these functional requirements, groups of actions or sub-systems of action develop. At the most general level, for example, the cultural sub-system performs the latency function and the social sub-system the function of integration. Each of these sub-systems, in turn, is also faced by the same four functional needs and consequently each sub-system can be divided into four sub-

sub-systems. In the social system as a whole, the economy performs the function of adaptation, for example. In theory, there is no limit to the subdivision of systems and Parsons does describe in detail the structure of the economy and the relations between it and the other sub-systems of the social system.

Parsons holds that systems of social action tend to equilibrium even if they never actually reach it, and that social change is movement from one state of equilibrium to another. Change in the system is achieved by differentiation (q.v.), and in his later work Parsons used evolutionary theory (q.v.) to describe the progressive changes in society that result from this. A number of criticisms have been levelled at Parsons. (1) His is a grand theory (q.v.) of little empirical use; (2) he gives too much importance to values and norms; (3) he does not pay enough attention to social conflict; (4) he is unable to reconcile action theory and system theory, and in effect sees individual action as structurally determined; (5) his functionalism involves teleology (q.v.). See: *Action Theory*; *Agency and Structure*; *Conflict Theory*; *Freud*; *Functional Imperative*; *Functionalism*; *Internalization*; *Norm*; *Social Order*; *Stratification*; *Systems Theory*; *Value*.

Bibl. Rocher (1974); Bourricaud (1981); Hamilton (1983)

Participant Observation. In its strict usage, this refers to a research technique in which the sociologist observes a social collectivity of which he or she is also a member. Such participation allows the sociologist to observe covertly, without the collectivity being aware. This is easiest in large and 'open' communities. The classic example is the two studies of an American town known as 'Middletown', conducted by R. and H. Lynd (1929; 1937). The method has occasionally been used successfully in smaller and

more 'closed' collectivities in the study of organizations and occupations, when researchers have taken employment among the population being studied. A notable example is the study of restriction of output among industrial employees conducted by D. Roy (1952; 1953; 1955). In its looser usage, the term describes the form of observation in which the observer is known to be an outside investigator by those being studied. This is the case in ethnographic studies by anthropologists and in much sociological research.

The advantage of the covert approach is that the setting remains natural and the presence of the observer creates no artificial changes, which is a major risk of open observation. Both forms are confronted by the same problem, that the observer may gain only a restricted and partial understanding of the situation, because the observer's role may not provide access to the total population under investigation. For this reason, participant observation is sometimes supplemented by other forms of data collection.

When done well, this technique can provide data that may well have greater authenticity and validity than the more common sample survey approach. It is far more time-consuming, however, and makes greater demands on the research worker's skill and personality. See: *Ethnography*.

Bibl. Cicourel (1964)

Pastoralism. This refers to a form of subsistence economy (q.v.) in which communities derive their livelihood from tending species of domesticated animals and wander in search of adequate grazing. Historically, the relationship between nomadic and settled agriculturalists was conflictual and, in the modern period, there are strong governmental pressures to settle nomads

179

who are perceived as a threat to stable communities.

Paternalism. The use of a term describing the relationship between a father and a child to characterize that between superiors and subordinates captures much of the quality of paternalism. The father–child analogy provided M. Weber with his model of traditional political authority as patrimonialism (q.v.), in which the authority of a master over his household (patriarchalism) was extended to the administration of whole territories. In the political case, subordinates gave their loyalty and obedience to a patriarch in return for his protection. Paternalism refers to the organization of economically productive untis, agricultural and industrial, and is a way of regulating relationships between the owners of the means of production or their agents and subordinates that also draws on the patriarchal model. It has a number of features. (1) It depends on differential access to power and resources: the subordinate is unable to command sufficient resources to support himself or herself but must depend on the paternalist. (2) There is an ideological dimension that justifies subordination, emphasizing the caring role of the paternalist. (3) It is a collective form of social organization: the paternalist may be a single person, but his subordinates are treated collectively. (4) Paternalism has a tendency to become systematized and institutionalized when it occurs in modern industry, forming part of the organizational rule system. (5) Paternalism is typically a diffuse relationship which covers all aspects of subordinates' lives, which deals with the whole person rather than confining itself to specific activities.

Paternalism differs from conventional capitalist relations: (1) it assumes inequality of power, whereas the formal ideology of capitalism is that economic exchanges are contracts between equals; (2) the diffuse involvement of subordinates contrasts with the typical capitalist employment relationship based on the segmental involvement of employees and the separation of work and non-work life, where the cash nexus (q.v.) may be the only tie binding employees and employers.

The classic cases of agricultural paternalism were found in the plantations of the Old and New Worlds. Industrial paternalism in Europe and America was mainly confined to the early years of the factory system and the transition to a modern industrialized economy. In Japan, however, fully developed forms flourish among modern, large-scale corporations. In part this reflects the deliberate choice of Japanese managers to develop the system. It also reflects elements of Japanese culture which support paternalism. See: *Latifundia*; *Patron–Client Relations*.

Bibl. Abercrombie and Hill (1976)

Path Analysis. If you assume that a particular causal model explains the relationships among the variables in a data set, path analysis enables you to quantify these hypothesized causal links or connections. The geneticist S. Wright first used this technique in the 1920s, and sociologists began to use it widely in the 1960s. Path analysis is a form of multivariate analysis using regression (q.v.) techniques, which permits relations among several variables and their interaction to be studied simultaneously. The most celebrated use of path analysis in sociology was in P. M. Blau and O. D. Duncan's study (1967) of the relative importance of different factors in influencing occupational attainment in the United States. See: *Causal Modelling*; *Interaction of Variables*; *Multivariate Analysis*.

Bibl. Duncan (1966; 1975)

Patriarchy. This concept is used to describe the dominance of men over women, a dominance which appears in several quite different kinds of society. It is also used to describe a type of household organization in which an older man dominates the whole household, including younger men. While male dominance is often explained biologically, usually by reference to the necessary reproductive functions of women, most sociologists argue that patriarchy refers to social, not natural relations. There is considerable debate about the sociological explanation of patriarchy. It has been suggested, for example, that compulsory heterosexuality, male violence, the way men are organized in the workplace and socialization into gender roles are all causal factors.

There are three recent accounts of patriarchy offered by feminist sociologists. (1) Patriarchy functions as ideology. This is a view deriving from the work of the French psychoanalyst and structuralist, Jacques Lacan (1966), who argues that a society's culture is dominated by the symbol of the phallus. (2) Patriarchy is essentially based on the household in which men dominate women, economically, sexually and culturally. More narrowly, women exchange their unpaid domestic services for their upkeep. In this perspective, the marriage contract is a labour contract through which the husband controls the labour of his wife. (3) Marxist feminists have argued that the domination of women by men is intimately connected with capitalism, because patriarchy and capitalism are mutually supportive. Within the household, women's domestic labour supports men, an expense which would otherwise fall on capital. Outside the home, the segregation of women into certain occupations has, it is argued, enabled employers to keep their wages down. See: *Division of Labour*; *Domestic Labour*; *Feminism*; *Gender*; *Matriarchy*; *Mode of Production*; *Sexual Divisions*; *Stereotypes*; *Women and Work*.

Bibl. Evans (ed.) (1982)

Patrimonialism. In M. Weber's sociology, patrimonialism is a form of traditional political domination in which a royal household exercises arbitrary power through a bureaucratic apparatus. In patrimonial systems, administration and political force are under the direct, personal control of the ruler. The support for patrimonial power is provided, not by forces recruited from a landowning aristocracy, but by slaves, conscripts and mercenaries. Weber regarded patrimonialism as (1) politically unstable because it is subject to court intrigue and palace revolts, and (2) a barrier to the development of rational capitalism. Patrimonialism was thus an aspect of Weber's explanation of the absence of capitalist development in Oriental societies in which personal rulership was dominant. See: *Feudalism*; *Oriental Despotism*; *Paternalism*; *Slavery*.

Bibl. Weber (1922)

Patron–Client Relations. Unlike paternalism (q.v.), patronage involves a relationship between two individuals, namely a patron and a client. The relationship is found universally, though it is institutionally recognized and sanctioned on a limited scale since patronage offends the achievement culture of many Western societies. Patron–client relations make good the inadequacies of formal institutions, and the special relationship with someone of influence or wealth protects the subordinate client from a potentially hostile environment. Developed systems of patronage are found in Latin American and Mediterranean societies.

Bibl. Abercrombie and Hill (1976)

181

Pattern Variables. See: *Parsons.*

Peasants. Peasants are a class characterized by small-scale agricultural production, economic self-sufficiency, low division of labour and relative political isolation from urban working classes. The peasantry is often differentiated into separate social strata, according to the amount of land they cultivate and the security of their rights over land. Thus it is common for sociologists to distinguish between 'rich peasants', 'middle peasantry' and 'landless peasants', although the dividing line between these strata is often arbitrary. Peasants owning only small plots of land are typically forced to rent land in return for labour, cash or a share of the harvest (known as 'sharecropping'), or to engage in petty trade, or to become migrant, urban workers. In the twentieth century, the growth of international trade and the spread of capitalist relations of production have had a profound effect on peasants, often increasing their impoverishment through rent increases and the rising price of materials, such as fertilizers. Peasants have become increasingly dependent on the production of commercial crops for export, the prices of which are subject to major fluctuations on the world market. Peasant indebtedness to rural moneylenders typically forces the peasant into the category of landless rural proletariat. Both historically and in the contemporary situation, the nature of peasant ownership of land is complex and variable. Peasants may have customary rights to cultivation either as individuals or as a village community, they may have a legal entitlement to land, or they may be landless. In feudalism (q.v.), peasant serfdom meant that the economic surplus was raised by landlords through rent (in kind, money or labour). The development of capitalist agriculture converts the peasant into a rural labourer by undermining customary peasant ownership (typically by land enclosures) and by destroying the self-sufficiency of the peasant producer (typically by increasing rent and reducing the size of land tenures).

In the nineteenth century, a number of writers argued that the geographical isolation and economic independence of peasant communities made the peasantry a politically conservative factor in European societies. Contemporary studies, however, have concentrated on peasant participation in revolutionary changes in the Third World. Three important changes radicalize the peasantry: (1) the demographic transition (q.v.) has profoundly altered land/population ratios, leading to population pressure on agricultural resources; (2) capitalist development of agriculture, production of export commodities and land reform have disturbed traditional methods of farming and altered the range of crops produced; (3) rural society has been transformed as landowners and merchants have responded to the new market forces.

There has also been much discussion as to the nature of peasant radicalism and peasant class consciousness. In precapitalist societies, peasant rebellions against land-tenure conditions and rent increases were very widespread in Europe and 'social banditry' was a seasonal occupation for many peasants. In modern times, it has been argued that peasant consciousness is in fact traditional (in wanting to restore customary practices and village conditions) and that peasant rebelliousness cannot become genuinely revolutionary without an alliance with urban workers and external political leadership. Without political direction and political education, Marxist sociologists suggest that peasant rebelliousness will either remain traditional or ephemeral. It is thus claimed that millenarianism (q.v.) is a typical example of a traditional peasant consciousness. See: *Mobilization*; *Subsistence Economy*.

Bibl. Wolf (1971)

Pedagogical Practices. Pedagogy is the art of teaching. Different practices are informed by different educational philosophies and their assumptions about learning, the intellectual status of the child, teaching style, and curricula. Conservative or *closed* pedagogy sees learning as the absorption of specific bodies of knowledge, the child's ability as determined by hereditary and environmental factors external to the school, the appropriate teaching style as one where teachers are experts, and have authority over pupils, and direct the learning of subordinates, and the curriculum as the relevant classroom knowledge (q.v.) as defined by teachers. Liberal or *open* pedagogy conceives of learning as a process and not the acquisition of specific knowledge, the child's mind as capable of development, teaching as simply guiding this development, and curricula as tailored to suit pupils' own expressed interests.

The spread of 'progressive' and 'child-centred' teaching methods since the 1960s, the open pedagogy, has been interpreted in different ways. While P. Freire (1972) argues that it has radical political implications because it emphasizes personal autonomy rather than social control, others claim that fully developed 'progressive' methods are rarely found beyond the early years of the primary school and are unlikely to have any lasting influence on attitudes, or that open pedagogy reflects the middle-class value system and is therefore unlikely to have radical implications beyond the school. Within the school,

B. Bernstein (1977) suggests that the move towards integrated studies, an aspect of this pedagogy, may alter the power structure within the teaching staff. In principle, it also disturbs traditional authority relations between teachers and pupils, though in practice teachers resist change. The power of the hidden curriculum (q.v.) and the manner in which schools modify 'progressive' ideals in practice suggest that pedagogical practices remain fundamentally conservative.

Peer Group. Technically a peer group is any collectivity in which the members share some common characteristic, such as age or ethnicity. It most commonly refers to age groups in general, but more specifically to adolescent groups where members are closely bound together by youth culture. Adolescent peer groups tend to have: (1) a high degree of social solidarity; (2) hierarchical organization; (3) a code which rejects, or contrasts with, adult values and experience. From an adult perspective, peer groups are often deviant because delinquency is supported by the rewards of group membership. See: *Subculture*.

Penology. The scientific study of the treatment and punishment of criminals, penology is conventionally regarded as a branch of criminology (q.v.) and is associated with the movement away from retribution to correction in nineteenth-century penal reform.

Periodization. Most accounts of historical change divide the sequence of events into periods. For example, the periodization adopted by Marxist theories of history is determined by changes in the dominant mode of production (q.v.). Thus, one may speak of periods of history in which society is dominated by the feudal mode of production, or the monopoly stage of the capitalist mode of production.

Phenomenological Sociology. This is a school of sociology derived from phenomenological philosophy. It takes as its main aim the analysis and description of everyday life – the life-world (q.v.) and its associated states of consciousness. This study is carried out by 'bracketing off' judgements about social structure, that is, making no assumptions about the existence or causal powers of social structure. Phenomenologists argue that, although people generally take the everyday world for granted, a phenomenological analysis must show how it is made up.

Considered in this way, phenomenological sociology is part of that movement criticizing positivist methods in sociology. In particular, practitioners of the subject have objected to the notion that human beings are formed by social forces rather than creating the social world themselves, to the neglect of the meaning of human actions and to the use of causal analysis of human action. Phenomenologists have felt that these features tend to neglect the uniquely human character of social interaction.

Phenomenology has entered sociology largely through the work of A. Schutz (q.v.). However, the best-known sociological study informed by phenomenological principles is that by P. Berger and T. Luckmann (1967). Their starting point is a phenomenological analysis of the knowledge appropriate to everyday life. Such knowledge is almost always characterized by typification (q.v.) and is essentially orientated to solving practical problems. They then suggest that this everyday knowledge is creatively produced by individuals who are also influenced by the accumulated weight of institutionalized knowledge produced by others.

Phenomenological sociology has not greatly influenced sociology as a whole and has also been subjected to extensive criticism. It has been argued that it deals with trivial topics, is purely descriptive, has had very little empirical application, and neglects the notion of social structure. See: *Agency and Structure*; *Ethnomethodology*; *Garfinkel*; *Hermeneutics*; *Verstehen*.

Bibl. Wolff (1978)

Plural Societies. These are societies fragmented into different racial, religious, or linguistic groups. The degree of fragmentation will vary considerably from society to society, as will the relationship of social class to the different groups. In some societies race and class tend to overlap, so that certain racial groups are found mainly in particular social classes, as appears to be the case in the United States, for example. In others, Brazil for instance, races may be fairly evenly distributed in the class structure. See: *Class*; *Stratification*; *Underclass*.

Pluralism. (1) This was a political philosophy developed by English liberals and socialists in the early twentieth century. Pluralism asserted the desirability of diffusing power widely among a variety of associations – religious, economic, professional, educational and cultural – and fragmenting government into decentralized units, so that society was dominated neither by the state nor by a single class. *Laissez-faire* capitalism, which ostensibly upheld individualistic values, in practice appeared to let a minority class control employment and regulate markets, and thus coerce the majority. The centralized state apparatus found in continental Europe at the time also threatened the individual. Pluralists saw small, closely knit groups as the natural form of association and the best defence of individual rights. In pluralist political philosophy, the state was to have a greatly reduced scope, and was to act as a fairly neutral mediator between conflicting interests. In its socialist form, pluralism became guild socialism.

(2) Pluralism in modern sociology refers to social organizations, whether societies or smaller collectivities such as firms, in which power is diffused among various groups and institutions. A well-established analysis of business organizations holds that power is distributed between labour, management and capital (sometimes customers as well), that no party dominates the others, that all the parties therefore freely choose to co-operate with each other rather than being forced. This analysis has been challenged by the argument that capital and management do have far more power than labour and thus compel workers' co-operation. There has also been considerable debate among political sociologists on whether pluralism is an accurate description of the political system, since the visible and apparently pluralistic exercise of power in democracies may conceal the fact that some groups or interests actually dominate. Thus pluralism may also be an ideology that is used to describe a political system or some other imperatively coordinated social organization as pluralist when in reality it is not. See: *Conflict Theory*; *Industrial Conflict*; *Power*; *Pressure Group*; *State*.

Bibl. Lukes (1974); Hyman (1978)

Political Behaviour. A term largely specific to American political science, this refers to the political activity of individuals and its consequences for political institutions. The study of political behaviour covers issues such as participation and non-participation in politics, voting behaviour, political attitude formation and public opinion. See:

Political Culture; *Political Participation*; *Public Opinion*; *Voting*.

Political Culture. This concept describes the attitudes, beliefs and rules that guide a political system, which are determined jointly by the history of the system and the experiences of its members. It is used to characterize differences between national political systems and to analyse these in behavioural terms which draw on psychology and sociology. The study of political culture focuses on the content of this culture and the processes of socialization and internalization of political values, including the various agencies of political socialization, such as family, education, mass media, political parties, and on the compatibility of political culture with the values and attitudes current in the wider national culture, elite and mass cultures. Attempts have been made to find common elements of political culture that relate to common political structures; for example, the elements of a 'civic culture' that G. A. Almond and S. Verba (1963) have suggested is a vital ingredient of stable democracies. In the individual, this combines acceptance of and respect for political authority with a detachment and independence of such authority. The concept has proved too general in scope to be useful in comparative research. See: *Civil Religion*; *Democracy*; *Dominant Ideology Thesis*; *Ideology*.

Bibl. Pye and Verba (eds.) (1965); Almond and Powell (1978)

Political Economy. Much of the theoretical groundwork of the separate disciplines of contemporary social science was established by eighteenth- and nineteenth-century writers whose principal interest lay in the production of wealth in relation to the activities of the state. The theoretical heritage of political economy embraces the concepts of social

185

class, labour value, the division of labour (q.v.) and moral sentiments. While Marxism was a critique of 'bourgeois' political economy, K. Marx's debt to this tradition was considerable. 'Political economy' is now often used as a code word for 'Marxism'. See: *Labour Theory of Value*.

Political Participation. Taking part in the political processes which lead to the selection of political leaders and determine or influence public policy is referred to as political participation. The right to participate is a defining feature of democratic political systems, but is not fully exercised. Levels of political interest and apathy have often been taken as criteria of participation and non-participation, including party membership, expressed interest in politics and awareness of issues. Research shows that apathy is extensive and the politically concerned public is everywhere in the minority. Apart from party membership, however, these criteria do not really measure participation in the political process. The major criterion remains voting in elections, which is consistently somewhat higher than the other measures would suggest. There are wide national variations on all these indicators including voting (the United States, for example, has notably lower election turnouts than the majority of European nations). There have been attempts to correlate the different participation criteria with other variables such as occupation, age, gender, race, religion, education and social mobility. In America, where most of these studies have been conducted, there are small but consistent correlations which are not repeated for other nations. The lack of consistent relationships among the measures themselves, as well as between these measures and the other variables on an international scale, frustrates attempts to create overarching theories of political participation. See: *Democracy*; *Mobilization*; *Political Parties*; *Political Process*; *Voting*.

Bibl. Lipset (1960); Pulzer (1975)

Political Parties. These link the state to political forces in society, giving organized expression to interests and making them effective politically. The sociology of political parties covers a number of interrelated issues: the goals or political ideologies of different parties; the social bases of party support and the way support is mobilized; the distribution of power within party organizations. Parties need to mobilize the votes of non-members in elections, and this electoral necessity may constrain policies and modify goals, an aspect of the electoral process that is central to the political theory of representation though not always appreciated in studies of party organization.

Since R. Michels (q.v.) argued for the inevitability of oligarchy (q.v.) in political parties, with its consequential betrayal of parties' political philosophies and the manipulation of rank-and-file by leadership, the analysis of organizational power has received considerable attention, with goals and membership frequently being studied in relation to this. Those who believe in the importance of elites (q.v.) suggest that the leaders of political parties are composed of people with common backgrounds, interests and values, mainly drawn from the higher social classes, and that the few who enter the elite from proletarian backgrounds absorb this culture. Evidence from Britain, Canada and the United States confirms part of this argument, since all major parties are dominated by leaders recruited from restricted social backgrounds. Nevertheless, oligarchic tendencies do vary. Members of party elites do not all hold similar values and conflicts within elites may occur. These weaken leadership power and reduce the gap between members and leaders if different sections attempt to mobilize the rank-and-file in support of their views. Nor is the rank-and-file always willing to cede control of policy to leaders, and membership participation varies. Irrespective of the strength of oligarchic tendencies, parties have to retain members to maintain an effective electoral organization (except in single-party states where elections are predetermined), which limits how far leaders can ignore party goals and members' convictions.

Political systems are often studied in terms of the number of legitimate political parties which are constitutionally permitted to compete for the government of a society. F. von der Mehden (1969) considers political systems in terms of a continuum including societies without parties, one-party non-competitive states, one-party semi-competitive systems, two-party democratic systems and multi-party democratic systems. In developing societies, D. Apter (1965) has argued, the one-party system is crucial for the formation of national identity and rapid economic development, since a single political authority is more effective in the management of industrial development. Another contrast is between socialist societies (q.v.) where the party dominates the distribution of social rewards and the organization of the economy, and Western capitalist societies where there is a pluralistic competition between parties for electoral support.

Parties in Western political systems tend to polarize between left- and right-wing ideologies, though the electoral system has an effect on the number of parties and the balance of political power: proportional representation tends to produce contests between a multiplicity of parties which have to combine to create governments, while non-proportional voting is more likely to result in contests that are in effect between two major parties (even in multi-party political systems). It is sometimes suggested that left–right party divisions reflect the class divisions in capitalist society. Against this, T. Bottomore (1979) argues that: (1) parties are alliances between a variety of distinctive groups with divergent interests; (2) these alliances are unstable and this results in the periodic development of splinter groups which typically occupy a centre position between left and right; (3) political parties are relatively autonomous from their class basis. In addition, there is often a gap between local class support for a party (the 'politics of support') and the capacity of any government to fulfil these aspirations at the state level (the 'politics of government'). This gap partly explains why parties often rapidly lose electoral support when in office.

While a multi-party state is often thought to be a system which is compatible with the pluralistic features of capitalist society, in historical terms capitalism has developed under a wide variety of political systems from fascism to liberal democracy. See: *Democracy*; *Fascism*; *Miliband–Poulantzas Debate*; *Socialist Societies*; *State*; *Voting*.

Bibl. Duverger (1964); Sartori (1976); Rose, G. (1975)

Political Process. When people try to gain access to political power and to wield this for their own or group ends, they constitute the political process. The notion of a political process assumes that politics can be treated as an autonomous institutional sphere, not a view that finds much favour among contemporary sociologists. The study of this process focuses on the activities of political parties and interest groups, their internal organization, the nature of political decision-making, and the roles and backgrounds of politicians. See: *Political Parties*; *Voting*.

Bibl. Shell (1969)

Political Sociology. This is the study of politics at four levels: (1) political conflicts and struggles between states, namely the sociology of international relations; (2) the nature and role of the state within societies; (3) the nature and organization of political movements and parties; (4) the participation of individuals in politics, as shown for example in voting behaviour. See: *Authority*; *Citizenship*; *Civil Society*; *Democracy*; *Dominant Ideology Thesis*; *Elite*; *Fascism*; *Gramsci*; *Ideological State Apparatus*; *Incorporation*; *Labour Movement*; *Leninism*; *Lipset*; *Marx*; *Marxist Sociology*; *Michels*; *Miliband–Poulantzas Debate*; *Mosca*; *Nationalism*; *Oligarchy*; *Pareto*; *Pluralism*; *Political Behaviour*; *Political Culture*; *Political Participation*; *Political Parties*; *Political Process*; *Populism*; *Power*; *Psephology*; *Relative Autonomy*; *Revolution*; *Socialist Societies*; *State*; *Voluntary Associations*; *Voting*; *Weber*; *Working-Class Conservatism*.

Bibl. Dowse and Hughes (1972); Bottomore (1979)

Polity. A generic term for the set of political institutions within a society.

Popper, Karl Raimund (b. 1902). Professor of logic and scientific method at the London School of Economics until his retirement in 1969, Sir Karl Popper has contributed to a variety of philosophical debates in science and social philosophy. In the philosophy of science, he is famous for his principle of falsification, namely that a valid science aims to refute and not to defend its hypotheses. The ultimate criterion of science, as opposed to ideology, is its falsifiability. This position was developed in *The Logic of Scientific Discovery* (1959) and elaborated in *Conjectures and Refutations* (1963). In social theory, he has been critical of determinism, which he associated with historicism (q.v.) and authoritarian politics in *The Open Society and Its Enemies* (1945) and *The Poverty of Historicism* (1957). Societies should be organized like philosophical arguments: they should be open to question and conjecture. He maintains that large-scale, planned social change cannot succeed and only piecemeal social reform is possible. In his studies of physics, biology and natural sciences – *Of Clouds and Clocks* (1966), *Objective Knowledge* (1972), *Unended Quest* (1974), *The Open Universe* (1982a), *Quantum Theory and the Schism in Physics* (1982b), and *Realism and the Aim of Science* (1983) – he has defended deductivism and realism. His views on science have been challenged as artificial, because in practice scientists attempt to defend their views by verification and not by refutation; they seek to maintain not destroy existing paradigms. His perspective on the limitations on planned social change has been criticized for its conservatism. See: *Epistemology*; *Falsificationism*; *Positivism*.

Bibl. Magee (1973)

Popular Culture. Loosely referred to as the culture of the masses or of subordinate classes, there are two major theoretical divisions in the study of popular culture. (1) Critics of popular culture, for example the Frankfurt School (q.v.), define it as trivial, commercialized and passive. In this perspective, 'popular culture' is equated with 'mass culture'. Other approaches argue that popular culture is creative and authentic. (2) There is also disagreement as to whether popular culture is a specific product of modern urban society or whether it is appropriate to refer to, for example, the popular culture of the Middle Ages.

In Britain, the main sociological debate has centred on whether popular culture is an oppositional movement, challenging conventional taste and values, or whether it is conservative and commercialized. In the case of popular music, the monopolization of the market and pop groups by large corporations has generally excluded radical lyrics, ensuring a standardized musical package.

Popular culture is not necessarily a common culture; its diversity reflects the age, sex and class divisions within its audience. Sociological studies of youth culture, for example, suggest that there are a series of subcultures relating to distinctive class, regional and sexual differences. See: *Culture*; *Mass Society*; *Subculture*; *Youth Culture*.

Bibl. Hall and Jefferson (eds.) (1976); Brake (1980)

Populism. Social scientists use populism as a generic category to cover a variety of political phenomena. There has been considerable debate as to whether it is a movement or an ideology, or whether it exists at all. It is possible, however, to identify some common features. Populism is a distinctive form of political rhetoric that sees virtue and political legitimacy residing in 'the people', sees dominant elites as corrupt, and asserts that political goals are best achieved by means of a direct relationship between governments and the people, rather than being mediated by existing political institutions.

Following M. Canovan (1981), three forms of populism may be identified. (1) *Populism of the Little Man* describes the political orientation of small proprietors such as peasants, farmers and small businessmen who support private prop-

erty and cooperation between small producers, but are distrustful of big business and government. Typically, this populism decries 'progress', whether it be urbanization, industrialization, or the growth of monopoly capitalism, which it sees as leading to moral decay, and calls for a return to the virtues of past eras. It distrusts politicians and intellectuals and may lead people to support either direct popular democracy or strong leaders who share the populist ideology. Examples include the agrarian populism of the American Populist Party in the 1890s, the European peasant parties and the Canadian Social Credit Party of the early twentieth century, and the non-agrarian populism of the post-war Scottish National Party (in its early years) and the nineteenth-century Norwegian Left. (2) *Authoritarian Populism* describes charismatic leaders who bypass the political elite to appeal directly to the people, often to their reactionary sentiments. Examples include fascists such as Hitler, and right-wing leaders such as de Gaulle. (3) *Revolutionary Populism* describes the idealization of the people and their collective traditions by intellectuals who reject elitism and 'progress'. This leads to a rejection of existing political institutions in favour of the seizure of power by the people, or in favour of charismatic leaders who claim to represent the people. Examples include the Russian Populists (Narodniks), intellectuals who during the 1860s claimed that socialism could be achieved without first going through capitalism, by building on existing peasant communes, and the later support of fascism (q.v.) among certain European intellectuals.

Populism cannot be fitted easily into the conventional frameworks of political analysis. It may be either right or left, or neither. It is often reactionary, calling for a return to traditional virtues, but some populist leaders, such as Perón in Argentina, have worked for social and economic modernization and eschewed reactionary rhetoric. Nor is it possible to identify a definite pattern of social and economic conditions under which populism occurs; particular types of populism are not systematically related to particular social classes nor to specific economic circumstances.

Bibl. Ionescu and Gellner (eds.) (1969); Laclau (1977)

Positivism. A doctrine in the philosophy of science, positivism is characterized mainly by an insistence that science can only deal with observable entities known directly to experience. The positivist aims to construct general laws or theories which express relationships between phenomena. Observation and experiment will then show that the phenomena do or do not fit the theory; explanation of phenomena consists in showing that they are instances of the general laws or regularities. In sociology, positivism is identified with a conviction that sociology can be scientific in the same way as, say, physics, a marked preference for measurement and quantification, and a tendency towards social structural explanations as distinct from those which refer to human intentions and motives.

The term was introduced into sociology by A. Comte (q.v.) who held that the subject should be scientific, which meant dealing only with propositions that were directly testable. E. Durkheim (q.v.) was also a positivist in that he believed in the importation into sociology of the methods of science, in the establishment of laws of the causal relations of social phenomena, and in the rejection, in favour of social structures, of motives and intentions as causal agents. Durkheim's *Suicide* has been taken as a textbook example of a scien-

tific sociology and was particularly influential in the development of American sociology in the 1930s and in the immediate post-war period. Much research at the time favoured the minute operationalization (q.v.) of classical concepts like anomie and alienation and the importance of research techniques leading to quantifiable conclusions. In this tradition, sociological notions that were not measurable were deemed meaningless.

In much contemporary sociological debate, positivism has become a term of abuse. There are three main lines of criticism. (1) Realism (q.v.) rejects the insistence of positivism that only observable phenomena can be analysed and that explanation takes the form of showing that phenomena are instances of regularities. Realists argue that causal explanation proceeds by identifying the underlying mechanisms, perhaps unobservable, which connect phenomena. (2) If realists reject the positivist conception of science, other sociologists argue that sociology cannot be like science at all. Most radically, it is suggested that the aim of sociology is not explanation but understanding. Less extremely, it has been argued that sociological accounts must pay some attention to the intentions and motives of actors. Since these latter phenomena are unique to the social world and do not characterize the objects of the natural world, the methods of natural science cannot be utilized in sociology. (3) Members of the Frankfurt School (q.v.) were early critics of positivism, particularly in American sociology. They felt that positivism tended to stop at producing quantified facts and did not go deeper towards genuine sociological interpretation. Opinion surveys, for example, simply recorded opinions held by individuals without asking why they held them. More recently J. Habermas (q.v.) has argued that positivism in social science, as an example of technical rationality, is associated with the requirement to control societies. See: *Empiricism*; *Hermeneutics*; *Methodological Individualism*; *Naturalism*; *Phenomenological Sociology*; *Rule*; *Scientific Method*; *Sociology as Science*; *Verstehen*.

Bibl. Giddens (ed.) (1974); Keat and Urry (1975); Benton (1977)

Post-Industrial Society. This concept was first formulated in 1962 by D. Bell (q.v.), and subsequently elaborated in *The Coming of Post-Industrial Society* (1974), to describe economic and social changes in the late twentieth century. He suggests that, in modern societies, theoretical knowledge forms the 'axial principle' of society and is the source of innovation and policy formulation. In the economy this is reflected in the decline of goods-producing and manufacturing as the main form of economic activity, to be replaced by services. With regard to the class structure, the new axial principle fosters the supremacy of professional and technical occupations which constitute a new class. In all spheres – economic, political and social – decision-making is crucially influenced by new intellectual technologies and the new intellectual class.

Other writers have also commented on what they perceive as the growing power of technocrats in economic and political life: J. K. Galbraith (1967) believes that power in the United States economy, and therefore in American society as a whole, lies in the hands of a technical bureaucracy or the 'technostructure' of large corporations; A. Touraine (1969) suggests similar technocratic control of French economic and political life.

These approaches can be criticized for greatly exaggerating the power and importance of new professional and technical occupations; there is no evidence that these constitute a discrete social class, that they effectively control business corporations, or that they exercise significant political power. While it is true that theoretical knowledge has become steadily more significant as a force of production throughout this century, this implies no change in the locus of power in the economy nor within society. Somewhat similar arguments were once put forward about the new professional managers during the managerial revolution (q.v.), and were subsequently shown to have little foundation. Conversely, other writers have argued that the centrality of knowledge in modern economies has created a new working class (q.v.) of technical employees that is potentially revolutionary. See: *Convergence Thesis*; *End of Ideology Theory*; *Industrial Society*.

Poverty. Sociologists distinguish between *relative* and *absolute* poverty. Absolute poverty occurs when people fail to receive sufficient resources to support a minimum of physical health and efficiency, often expressed in terms of calories or nutritional levels. Relative poverty is defined by the general standards of living in different societies and what is culturally defined as being poor rather than some absolute level of deprivation. When poverty is defined relatively, by reference to the living standards enjoyed by the bulk of a population, poverty levels vary between societies and within societies over time; in Britain, for example, the actual living standard implied by the supplementary benefit level (the nearest thing to an officially defined 'poverty line') was higher in the late 1970s than in the early years of the welfare state after the Second World War, as was the average living standard of the bulk of the population.

It was popularly believed that poverty

had been eradicated in Britain in the quarter-century following the Second World War. Absolute poverty was abolished by high and sustained levels of economic growth which provided full employment and high wages, and a state welfare system that cared well for those who were not part of the labour market or received low incomes from their employment. Relative poverty was much lessened by more equal distribution of income and wealth. This belief has been challenged by sociologists and economists, however, who suggest that poverty (defined by reference to the prevailing supplementary benefit level) is the lot of between 12 and 15 per cent of the population. In the 1960s, retired people were the great majority of those living at or below the poverty line. In the late 1970s, retired people formed a smaller majority, partly because of the growth of occupational pension schemes with higher benefits but also because of growing numbers of non-pensioners in poverty. More single-parent families, growing unemployment and a rising proportion of unemployed people who qualified for supplementary benefits in addition to unemployment benefit, and the continuation of employment that paid wages below the poverty line, all accounted for changes in the composition of the poor population and an increase after the mid 1970s in the numbers of poor. In addition, recent research shows that the increased equality in income and wealth distribution has been exaggerated. See: *Booth*; *Deprivation*; *Distribution of Income and Wealth*; *Poverty Trap*; *Relative Deprivation*; *Unemployment*; *Welfare State*.

Bibl. Abel-Smith and Townsend (1965); Field (1982)

Poverty Trap. Many poor families in receipt of means-tested (i.e. income-related) state welfare benefits find it diffi-

cult to escape poverty if they increase their earnings from employment, because these may be offset by the loss of benefits and by the payment of income tax. See: *Poverty*.

Power. There are a number of distinctive perspectives on power. For M. Weber, it is the probability that a person in a social relationship will be able to carry out his or her own will in the pursuit of goals of action, regardless of resistance. He defined 'domination' in a similar manner as the probability that a command would be obeyed by a given group of people. This definition has the following characteristics: (1) power is exercised by individuals and therefore involves choice, agency and intention; (2) it involves the notion of agency, that is, an individual achieving or bringing about goals which are desirable; (3) power is exercised over other individuals and may involve resistance and conflict; (4) it implies that there are differences in interests between the powerful and powerless; (5) power is negative, involving restrictions and deprivations for those subjected to domination. Weber argued that, when the exercise of power was regarded by people as legitimate, it became authority (q.v.). One criticism of the Weberian approach is that, by its emphasis on agency and decision-making, it fails to recognize that non-decision-making may also be an exercise of power. For example, failure or refusal to act may be evidence of inequalities of power. Holders of power may also shape the wants or interests of subordinates. For example, advertising campaigns may involve an exercise of power through the artificial creation of needs. Weber's definition of power raises the problem of 'real' versus 'subjective' interests.

In Marxist sociology, power is regarded as a structural relationship, existing independently of the wills of individuals. The notions of agency and intentionality are not essential to the definition. The existence of power is a consequence of the class structure of societies. Thus, N. Poulantzas (1978) defined power as the capacity of one class to realize its interests in opposition to other classes. In this perspective, power has the following features; (1) power cannot be separated from economic and class relations; (2) power involves class struggle, and not simply conflicts between individuals; (3) the analysis of power cannot be undertaken without some characterization of the mode of production (q.v.)

In American sociology, power has not been seen as necessarily involving conflict and coercion. T. Parsons (q.v.) defines power as a positive social capacity for achieving communal ends; power is analogous to money in the economy as a generalized capacity to secure common goals of a social system. In these terms, it is difficult to distinguish between power and influence. Indeed, R. Dahl (1970) defines 'power', 'authority' and 'influence' as 'influence-terms', where influence is the ability of one person to change the behaviour of another. Power is thus regarded as widely diffused through society rather than being concentrated in a ruling elite. The political system is seen to be open and pluralistic, permitting the whole community to participate to some degree in the political process. It is conventional to distinguish between pluralistic, Marxist and Weberian approaches. It is held that pluralistic theories conceptualize power as diffused through the political system, whereas Marxist sociology sees power concentrated in the ruling class. Weber emphasized the importance of force and defined the state (q.v.) as an institution which had a monopoly of force. These distinctions are, however, simplistic. Dahl, for ex-

ample, noted that power was concentrated in a minority which he called the 'political class', but defended liberal democracies against the Marxist charge that an economic ruling class governed society. He also accepted implicitly the Weberian view of the state as a legitimate monopoly of force.

In American political science, the study of power involves the identification of elites and political leadership, the study of the principles by which power is allocated, and the study of government and its supporters. Since power is conceived as influence, political science is not simply the study of government and there is a long tradition of research in America into community politics. The question of power is thus translated into the study of political participation (q.v.).

These attempts to define power serve to confirm the difficulty of reconciling agency and structure (q.v.) in sociology. There is little agreement over whether power has to be intentional or whether it is structural or both. Existing definitions also fail to deal systematically with contradictory views of power as repressive and coercive, while also productive and enabling. Power is a contested concept, the use of which inevitably raises critical issues of value and perspective. See: *Authority*; *Coercion*; *Conflict Theory*; *Elite*; *Hegemony*; *Leadership*; *Marxist Sociology*; *Pluralism*; *Ruling Class*; *Sanction*; *State*; *Weber*.

Bibl. Lukes (1974); Giddens (1979)

Power Elite. See: *Elite*; *Power*.

Pragmatic Acceptance. In contrast to accounts of working-class beliefs that explain the quiescence of subordinates in the face of social and political inequality by reference to their incorporation into dominant values, or that assert on the contrary that there is a coherent oppositional ideology that for various reasons has not been effective, M. Mann (1973) argues that subordinates accept the *status quo* on a pragmatic basis that is devoid both of normative involvement and opposition. See: *Class Consciousness; Dominant Ideology Thesis; Dual Consciousness; Incorporation.*

Praxis. This concept, as part of the early work of K. Marx, has two closely related meanings. (1) It suggests action as opposed to philosophical speculation. (2) It implies that the fundamental characteristic of human society is material production to meet basic needs. Man primarily acts on the natural world – he works – and only secondarily thinks about it. See: *Marx; Materialism.*

Bibl. Lefebvre (1968)

Prejudice. This a term usually used in the literature on race relations to denote an individual attitude of antipathy or active hostility against another social group, usually racially defined. Prejudice, often the object of psychological study, is to be contrasted with *discrimination* which refers to the outcome of social processes which disadvantage social groups racially defined. Prejudiced individuals may participate in discriminatory activities but do not necessarily do so. See: *Authoritarian Personality; Racism.*

Pressure Group. These are formally constituted organizations which are designed at least partly to bring pressure to bear on government, civil service and other political institutions to achieve ends that they favour. The Confederation of British Industries is a pressure group in this sense, even if it was set up with other aims in mind as well. The idea that pressure groups play a significant part in society is related to the concept of pluralism (q.v.), since the political process is seen to result from a large number of often competing pressures. See: *State; Voluntary Association.*

Prestige. The view that the status or 'honour' of different groups is an important dimension of social stratification (q.v.) has a long tradition in American approaches to occupational inequality, going back at least to the 1920s. L. Warner's *Social Class in America* (1949) is a celebrated early contribution. Occupational prestige is determined by the system of values in a society and by the perceived functional importance of different occupations in that society. The measurement of occupational prestige is made using prestige scales, which are created by asking people to rank occupations according to their social standing or desirability. The evaluation of occupations proves remarkably stable when various measurement procedures are used, and there is also considerable consensus across different societies in the evaluation of the relative prestige of occupations.

Prestige remains somewhat ambiguous. In the European sociological tradition, M. Weber conceptualized status as social honour and saw this as a dimension of social stratification that was clearly distinct from class (q.v.). Class inequality was based on unequal access to material rewards and different life-chances (q.v.). Despite some awareness of Weber's work, the American tradition has conflated a number of dimensions of occupational inequality, and joins together income, power, educational level as well as social honour. The validity of prestige scales has also been questioned on the following grounds: (1) it is not always clear whether attitude surveys indicate what respondents believe is the actual or the desirable ranking of occupations; (2) different respondents have different knowledge of occupational structure;

(3) there are considerable variations in attitudes that are disguised when replies are consolidated into a single prestige scale. See: *Class*; *Socio-Economic Group*; *Status*; *Status Inconsistency*; *Stratification*; *Upper Class*.

Bibl. Bendix and Lipset (eds.) (1966); Parkin (1978)

Primary Group. See: *Group*.

Primary Relationship. These are interpersonal relations characterized by emotional intensity, total commitment and mutual satisfaction. In a primary relationship, the total person is involved in the interaction. In contrast, secondary relationships are partial and ephemeral. For example, interactions between strangers are secondary, while mutual love is primary. This contrast is usually associated with that between primary and secondary groups. See: *Group*.

Primitive Society. In evolutionary anthropology, primitive societies represented a particular stage from which more complex societies developed. The term often implied that modern man was more intelligent than his savage, irrational forebears. Without these prejudicial connotations, a primitive society is pre-industrial, small-scale, non-literate, technologically simple and traditional. In sociology, there is a preference for alternative terms such as 'precapitalist' or 'traditional society'. The term is commonly used in juxtaposition to modern, urban, industrial society; many of the judgemental implications of 'primitive' are still carried over into such allegedly neutral descriptions as 'traditional' society.

Privatization. A term used to describe the way in which people live their lives less in public and more in private or within the family. For example, religion is said

to be now less a matter of public acts of worship and more a question of private prayer or privately held beliefs. Similarly it is claimed that family life is more based on the home and involves parents and children only. There is less contact with neighbours, friends and wider kin and greater absorption in home-based leisure pursuits.

Some sociologists see these tendencies to privatization in spheres such as religion or the family as part of a wider process affecting all of society. They suggest that people are withdrawing more into themselves or their immediate family even to the point of being narcissistic. The public sphere, everything from participation in politics to involvement in public festivals, is thought to be decaying. The result is that people have less control over their society while at the same time having scant regard for other people beyond themselves or their immediate family. However, there is no general agreement as to whether this process of privatization is taking place, or what its causes might be. See: *Affluent Worker*; *Legitimation Crisis*; *Secularization*; *Symmetrical Family*.

Problematic. This assumes that sociological concepts do not exist separately from one another but are related together in a theoretical framework, known as a problematic.

Profane. The contrast between the profane and sacred world is a universal cultural distinction. The sacred is set apart by ritual from the profane world which is the secular, everyday reality of work, toil and domestic duties. There are two basic attitudes to the profane world: (1) world rejection, for example the mystical flight from mundane reality; (2) mastery of the profane world, for example the ascetic control of the body by prayer, diet and self-denial. The decline of the sacred in industrial society involves a secularization (q.v.) of life, which is devoid of religious significance, ritual festivity and charisma (q.v.). See: *Invisible Religion*; *Religion*; *Sacred*; *Secularization*.

Profession. G. Millerson (1964) lists these characteristics of a profession: (1) the use of skills based on theoretical knowledge; (2) education and training in these skills; (3) the competence of professionals ensured by examinations; (4) a code of conduct to ensure professional integrity; (5) performance of a service that is for the public good; (6) a professional association that organizes members. These criteria can also be used to measure the *degree* to which occupations are professionalized.

Professionals normally have high pay, high social status and autonomy in their work. Functionalists such as J. Ben-David (1963–4) explain this privileged position on the grounds that professions perform services which are socially valued. Others, for example F. Parkin (1979), suggest that exclusion strategies are used to restrict access to professions by means of educational requirements that may bear little relationship to the difficulty of professional work, and that these account for the privileges. Professions can pursue these strategies because the state gives the right to practise certain occupations to accredited members of professions. Sociologists such as T. Johnson (1972, 1977) and F. Parkin (1979) now consider the relationship of professions to state power, the location of professions within the upper class, and their ambivalent character as part of a class that carries out capital functions (q.v.) while they also perform the functions of the collective labourer (q.v.).

Another issue concerns the implications of the modern tendency for professionals to work in bureaucratic organizations, in both public and private sectors of the economy, instead of remaining independent. There may be a conflict between certain professional and organizational values: between professional ethics and organizational practices, the individual's orientation to the wider professional community and the expectation that he should become an organization man (q.v.), professional autonomy at work and bureaucratic direction. Alternatively, the professions may become proletarianized as they are subordinated to bureaucratic control and rationalization. See: *Career*; *Middle Class*; *Proletarianization*; *Social Closure*.

Progress. Most nineteenth-century sociology was based on the assumption of progress which was equated with industrialization. Technological advance was assumed to result in improvements in material welfare, reflected in enhanced standards of health and longer life expectancy. Industrialization was also associated with a growth in rights of citizenship (q.v.), literacy and education. Progress was the social manifestation of reason, knowledge and technology. With the advent of mass warfare, fascism and totalitarian governments in the twentieth century, sociology has taken a decisively pessimistic turn as confidence in the progressive nature of industrial society has evaporated.

Conventional theories of progress failed to provide adequate answers to three fundamental questions about social change. (1) Which social groups benefit from progress? (2) Who defines what is to count as progressive? (3) Who decides what personal or social costs are tolerable in relation to what degree of progress? See: *Evolutionary Theory*.

Bibl. Sklair (1970)

Proletarianization. This is a process by which parts of the middle class become effectively absorbed into the working class. The criteria by which one judges whether or not this absorption has taken place are complex and this has led to a good deal of debate, in that proletarianization may have occurred as measured by one criterion but not by another. Proletarianization of action must be distinguished from proletarianization of condition. The former is chiefly measured by voting behaviour or the propensity to join trade unions. The latter is determined by market, work and status considerations; the more closely white-collar workers' pay, holidays, chances of promotion, fringe benefits, relationships with employers, autonomy at work and status in the community approach that of manual workers, the more proletarianized they have become. Proletarianization of condition does not necessarily or immediately lead to proletarianization of action although, in the view of many, particularly Marxist, sociologists, large sections of the middle class will become proletarianized (perhaps through de-skilling (q.v.)) and this will eventually lead to their increased and more militant trade-union participation and radical political action. See: *Class*; *Middle Class*; *Trade Unions*; *Working Class*.

Bibl. Abercrombie and Urry (1983)

Proletariat. As used in sociology, proletariat is equivalent to working class (q.v.). See: *Bourgeoisie*; *Marx*.

Property. This is usually conceived in sociology as a collection of rights over both inanimate (land, houses, etc.) and animate (animals, people) objects. These rights are socially determined and thus vary from society to society and within a particular society over time. Property rights imply social relationships between people, because they define who does and does not have authorized access to

objects, because possession of property may give the possessors power over others, and because in some societies people are themselves property objects (as in slave societies and, in effect, in those feudal societies where agricultural workers were bound to the land as serfs and as such were subject to the will of the lord and could be transferred along with the land). The main concerns of sociological accounts of property are the following. (1) Acquisition, which is how individuals or collectivities gain access to property. (2) Distribution, which includes the patterns of property ownership and control, the principles that underlie these, and the institutions including law that maintain patterns of distribution. (3) The consequences of property for individuals and social structures. (4) The social values or ideologies that justify property rights.

In capitalist societies, property rarely includes rights over people. The main rights attached to property are the rights to control, benefit from and dispose of property on an exclusive basis. Historically, property was mainly private and personal and all property rights belonged to individuals (unless the disposal right was restricted by the legal device of entail), though corporate institutions such as the Church or collegiate bodies did possess collective property rights. A major change since the mid nineteenth century has been the growth of corporate property, with the rise of joint-stock companies which are owned by a number of individual shareholders but at law are considered as single entities with their own corporate personalities. In advanced capitalism productive property (property that has an economic role) is increasingly corporate and impersonal as economic activity becomes concentrated in large corporations that replace individual entrepreneurs and family firms. See: *Capitalism*; *Feudalism*; *Managerial*

197

Revolution; *Relations of Production*; *Slavery*.

Bibl. Hollowell (ed.) (1982); Abercrombie *et al.* (1986)

Protestant Ethic. Following M. Weber's two essays of 1904–5, later published as *The Protestant Ethic and the Spirit of Capitalism* (1930), it has been argued that the secular culture of capitalist society originated paradoxically in the asceticism (q.v.) of the Protestant Reformation. Protestantism emphasized the autonomy and independence of the individual rather than dependence on the Church, priesthood and ritual. The religious doctrines of Calvinism held that believers could no longer depend for their salvation on the institutionalized means of grace found in the Catholic Church (confession, eucharist, baptism), on the intermediary role of priests or on good works. Individual faith in Christ as a personal saviour of sinful humanity became the key element of Protestant doctrines. Protestants were subject to a 'salvational anxiety', since, while they believed that only the elect were predestined for salvation, they did not have complete confidence in their own personal salvation. Pastoral counselling in Protestantism maintained that the answer to such anxiety could be found in a secular vocation, self-control, hard work and communal service, because these qualities might provide a sign of election. Protestantism provided much of the cultural content of early capitalism – individualism, achievement motivation (q.v.), hostility to inherited wealth and luxury, legitimation of entrepreneurial vocations, opposition to magic and superstition, a commitment to organization and calculation in personal and public life. Protestantism provided an element in the rationalization (q.v.) of Western society. However, Weber thought that, while this ethic was supremely important in the development of the rational spirit of capitalism, the Protestant ethic was not a requirement of capitalism after its establishment.

Weber's thesis has been criticized on a number of grounds: (1) some historians object that the empirical evidence on which Weber's interpretation of Protestantism was based was too narrow and unrepresentative; (2) the precise relationship between capitalism and Protestantism was not adequately formulated; (3) there were aspects of traditional Catholic teaching which were equally compatible with capitalism; (4) Weber ignored crucial developments in Catholicism which occurred after the Reformation and which modernized Catholicism from within; (5) capitalism is contradictory in that it requires the consumption of commodities as well as saving for future investment; Protestant asceticism aids the latter, but the former may require hedonism. Despite these criticisms, Weber's thesis has shown a remarkable ability to survive damaging objections. See: *Capitalism*; *Entrepreneurship*; *Weber*.

Bibl. Marshall, G. (1982)

Psephology. This is the study of elections, particularly of voting behaviour.

Psychologism. As a term of abuse in sociology, this refers to explanations of the social structure exclusively in terms of the attributes of individual psychology. For example, adherence to religious beliefs is sometimes explained in terms of the psychological need for a way of coping with death. See: *Homans*; *Methodological Individualism*.

Public Opinion. The collection of people's opinions on topics of public interest, and the analysis of these by statistical techniques using a sample from the population in question, is what is normally meant by public opinion. Public-opinion polling techniques are widely used by market researchers and by psephologists interested in forecasting how people will vote in elections. See: *Psephology*; *Questionnaire*; *Sampling*; *Survey*.

Q

Qualitative Analysis. This refers to analysis which is not based on precise measurement and quantitative claims. Sociological analysis is frequently qualitative, because research aims may involve the understanding of phenomena in ways that do not require quantification, or because the phenomena do not lend themselves to precise measurement. For example, in participant observation (q.v.) the sociologist may simply aim to observe social behaviour without counting instances of particular behaviour; while in other cases, such as historical research, the records may be inadequate for precise measurement even if this were the researcher's aim.

Questionnaire. Used in survey research, this is a set of questions given to respondents and designed to provide information relevant to the research area. Questionnaires may be completed by the respondents themselves or be completed by an interviewer. The questions may be *closed-ended*, in which case the respondent simply selects from predetermined answers such as yes/no in the simplest form, or from a list of predetermined answers in more complicated forms. Or the questions may be *open-ended*, in which case respondents answer as they wish. When questionnaires are completed by the respondents, for example when the research is conducted by mail, or when the level of literacy among respondents is not high, it is common to use the closed-ended format as much as possible. When questionnaires are used in interviews or given to more literate respondents, the open-ended format may be used. Strictly, a questionnaire is any standardized set of questions, but some people use the term to describe only self-completed forms and refer to the interviewer-completed instrument as an *interview schedule*. See: *Attitude Scale*; *Interview*; *Public Opinion*; *Survey*.

R

Race, Sociology of. See: *Sociology of Race*.

Racism. The term may be defined as the determination of actions, attitudes or policies by beliefs about racial characteristics. Racism may be (1) overt and individual, involving individual acts of oppression against subordinate racial groups or individuals, and (2) covert and institutional, involving structural relations of subordination and oppression between social groups. While individual racism consists of intended actions, institutional racism involves the unintended consequences of a system of racial inequality. Racism may be accompanied by either implicit or explicit racist theories, which seek to explain and justify social inequality based on race. See: *Ethnic Group*; *Plural Societies*; *Prejudice*; *Stereotypes*.

Radcliffe-Brown, Alfred R. (1881–1955). He was noted, with B. Malinowski (q.v.), for his contribution to the development of functionalism (q.v.) as a theoretical perspective in British anthropology. Through a comparative approach, Radcliffe-Brown stressed the important interdependence of institutions within a social system. Society was seen as a self-regulating organism, the needs of which

were satisfied by certain basic social institutions. His major publications were *The Andaman Islanders* (1922), *Structure and Function in Primitive Society* (1952), *The Social Organization of Australian Tribes* (1931) and *Taboo* (1936). See: *Lévi-Strauss*; *Social System*; *Taboo*.

Rationalism. A philosophical tradition originating in the seventeenth and eighteenth centuries, rationalism asserts that reason is the only basis of valid knowledge of reality. Rationalist philosophers thus rejected revelation as a source of genuine knowledge. More technically, only deductive or inductive reasoning could provide precise and reliable information about the world. In sociology, rationalism was associated with positivism (q.v.) in the nineteenth century. Rationalism, however, often led to an implicit value-judgement asserting the superiority of Western civilization over other societies and over 'primitives' who were regarded as irrational. These assumptions were subsequently challenged by anthropological fieldwork which testified to the rationality of the human species at all levels of development. See: *Rationality*; *Understanding Alien Belief Systems*.

Rationality. It is important to make a

distinction between the truth of beliefs and their rationality, which refers to the grounds on which they are held. Beliefs which are coherent, not contradictory, and compatible with experience are said to be rational. It is irrational to hold beliefs which are known to be false, incoherent and contradictory. It is often suggested that science, which involves the systematic testing of propositions by observation, experiment and logical reasoning, is the example of rationality *par excellence*.

The concept of rationality, especially in anthropology and comparative sociology, does raise considerable problems. In the nineteenth century, anthropologists typically regarded magic and religion as irrational and as the product of a pre-logical mentality. It is difficult, however, to concede that a society could exist in which irrational beliefs were widespread, since the existence of language itself implies the presence of logical norms (of negation, identity and non-contradiction). There has to be some public agreement that certain terms refer consistently to specific objects and that, for example, 'up' is the opposite of 'down'. Modern anthropology argues that (1) beliefs which appear absurd, such as 'all twins are birds', are in fact reasonable once located in their appropriate cultural context; (2) understanding other beliefs is thus a matter of correct translation; (3) religious beliefs are expressive and symbolic, not informative and literal; religious beliefs are thus non-rational rather than irrational. Critics of this view have argued that by these three criteria no belief could ever be shown to be irrational. See: *Gellner*; *Rationalism*; *Understanding Alien Belief Systems*.

Bibl. Wilson, B. (ed.) (1970c)

Rationalization. This term has two very separate meanings: (1) it was employed by V. Pareto (q.v.) to refer to the use of spurious explanations to justify actions; (2) it was the master concept of M. Weber's analysis of modern capitalism, referring to a variety of related processes by which every aspect of human action became subject to calculation, measurement and control.

For Weber, rationalization involved: (1) in economic organization, the organization of the factory by bureaucratic means and the calculation of profit by systematic accounting procedures; (2) in religion, the development of theology by an intellectual stratum, the disappearance of magic and the replacement of sacraments by personal responsibility; (3) in law, the erosion of *ad hoc* law-making and arbitrary case-law by deductive legal reasoning on the basis of universal laws; (4) in politics, the decline of traditional norms of legitimacy and the replacement of charismatic leadership by the party machine; (5) in moral behaviour, a greater emphasis on discipline and training; (6) in science, the decline of the individual innovator and the development of research teams, coordinated experiment and state-directed science policies; (7) in society as a whole, the spread of bureaucracy, state control and administration. The concept of rationalization was thus part of Weber's view of capitalist society as an 'iron cage' in which the individual, stripped of religious meaning and moral value, would be increasingly subject to government surveillance and bureaucratic regulation. Like K. Marx's concept of alienation (q.v.), rationalization implies the separation of the individual from community, family and Church, and his subordination to legal, political and economic regulation in the factory, school and state. See: *Bureaucracy*; *Industrial Society*; *Metaphysical Pathos*; *Secularization*; *Weber*.

Bibl. Turner, B. S. (1981)

Realism. In opposition to positivism (q.v.), realists claim that explanation in both natural and social science consists in uncovering the (real) underlying and often unobservable mechanisms that connect phenomena causally, not merely in showing that the phenomena are instances of some observed regularity.

Sociological writers often claim that K. Marx was a realist in that he believed that the observable features of capitalist society were to be explained by the mechanisms of the capitalist mode of production (q.v.), which could not be observed directly. Marx objected to the positivist methods of his day which, he claimed, treated only the surface level of social life. Positivists would respond by arguing that Marxists, in postulating some unobservable structures or mechanisms that generate social phenomena, are not laying their theory open to test. See: *Falsificationism*; *Naturalism*.

Bibl. Keat and Urry (1975)

Reciprocity. (1) In functionalism and exchange theory the reciprocal exchange of rewards is said to be a necessary basis for social interaction between individuals. When reciprocity is not present, social actors will withdraw from interaction which has become unrewarding. The denial of reciprocity is thus an element of social control. Mutual reciprocity between social actors A and B is contrasted with univocal or directional reciprocity in which A gives to C in return for what A receives from B. The theory of reciprocal exchange suggests that social stability requires a principle of equality of rewards between social actors. Since rewards are very generally defined, the notion of reciprocity tends to be vacuous.

(2) In terms of social systems, it can be argued that the degree of reciprocity between parts of the system is variable. Where part of a social system has con-siderable functional autonomy (that is, satisfies its own requirements without being entirely dependent on the total system), there will be strong pressures to maintain that autonomy. Social systems may thus be seen in terms of a conflict between system interdependence and functional autonomy. See: *Exchange Theory*; *Functionalism*; *Social System*; *Systems Theory*.

Bibl. Ekeh (1974)

Reductionism. A sociological explanation is said to be reductionist when it attempts to account for a range of phenomena in terms of a single determining factor. It is said of some Marxist theories that they are reductionist because they explain the diversity of social behaviour by reference simply to the economy. See: *Base and Superstructure*; *Marxist Sociology*.

Reference Group. In forming their attitudes and beliefs, and in performing their actions, people will compare or identify themselves with other people, or other groups of people, whose own attitudes, beliefs, and actions are taken as appropriate measures. These groups are called reference groups. People do not actually have to be members of the groups to which they refer. For example, one explanation of working-class conservative voting is that the attitudes of these voters are formed by comparison or identification with the middle class. Furthermore, attitudes can be formed, not only by a positive identification with a reference group, but also by negative comparisons or rejections of it.

It is useful to distinguish normative from comparative functions of reference groups. The first refers simply to the manner in which people form attitudes in relation to a reference group, as in the working-class conservatism example. Reference groups may have a comparative function when they form a basis for evaluating one's own situation in life. For example, if a clerk compares herself with those of her rank who have been promoted, she is more likely to feel deprived when she is not promoted than if she compared herself with those who have not been promoted. See: *Relative Deprivation*.

Bibl. Runciman (1966)

Reflexive. Theories which are reflexive are those that refer to themselves. Theories in the sociology of knowledge (q.v.), for example, refer to themselves since they argue that all knowledge, including sociological knowledge, can be explained socially.

Registrar-General. See: *Socio-Economic Group*.

Regression. (1) A statistical term which represents the variation in one variable as being partly determined by its dependence on another, plus an error factor. Like correlation (q.v.), regression

is a measure of association. It is used, however, to estimate values of a dependent variable from the values of an independent variable. A simple linear regression is represented graphically below by means of a scatter diagram. The values of the two variables, x and y, are plotted as coordinates and the regression line of the dependent variable y on the independent variable x is a statistical construction which simply provides the line of best 'fit' to the data. Normally the regression line is expressed as an equation which provides estimates of the dependent values. Typically, regressions are used in a more complicated *multiple* form, in which a dependent variable varies with several others simultaneously. For example, a simple linear regression of road casualties and the number of vehicles on the road might show some association, but a complete analysis would require additional variables since accidents vary in relation not only to vehicle numbers but also with average vehicle mileage, average vehicle speed, the types of road

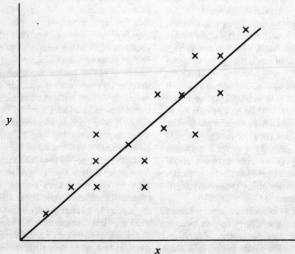

and so on. In *multivariate regression* more than one dependent variable is analysed simultaneously.

Regression assumes interval or ratio levels of measurement. Many sociological data are not measured at these levels, but a common technique is to create dichotomous 'dummy' variables which will meet the measurement requirements of regression. See: *Causal Modelling*; *Correlation*; *Dependent/Independent Variables*; *Log Linear Analysis*; *Measurement Levels*; *Path Analysis*.

(2) A psychological term which describes how individuals under stress revert to behaviour characteristic of an earlier and more impulsive stage of development; for example, when adults respond to stress by behaving in a childlike manner.

Reification. Literally meaning a process of making 'thing-like', the concept of reification was popularized by G. Lukács (q.v.). He used it to describe a situation in which social relations seem to be beyond human control because they acquire a fixed and immutable quality, almost as if they were features of the natural, rather than social, world. In Lukács's view, reification particularly arises in capitalist societies in which goods are produced for exchange, not for immediate use. These exchanges conceal the social relations involved. For example, men come to see the exchange of wages for labour as an exchange of things, rather than a social relation between people (employers and workers) which is at heart exploitative. Reification is also often related to alienation (q.v.), in that men feel alienated from the social world as they feel that its thing-like quality removes it from their control. See: *Commodity Fetishism*.

Bibl. Stedman-Jones (1971)

Relations of Production. This is a concept central to Marxist social theory. The customary view is that the economy, which for Marxists is the main determinant of social phenomena, is made up of the forces of production (q.v.) and the relations of production. The latter have always proved difficult to define. One influential view is that, in any mode of production (q.v.), the relations of production are the relations between the owners and non-owners of the means of production. The difficulty with such a definition is that ownership appears to be a legal category and, since law is something that is supposed to be determined by the economy, including the relations of production, one should not define relations of production in legal terms. Otherwise the definition of relations of production appears to include the very thing that such relations are supposed to determine.

Attempts to solve this difficulty have pursued non-legal definitions. In essence, these attempts see relations of production in terms of control and the capacity to possess the product. Thus, in capitalist societies, the relations of production are those relations that obtain between capitalist and worker such that the former both controls the means of production and can dispose of the goods and services that are produced by the worker. Of course, the capitalist can behave like this partly because he legally owns the means of production. However, this legal power does not enter into the *definition* of relations of production which could, theoretically, function without this legal sanction.

However defined, relations of production are treated as fundamental to the constitution of societies and more fundamental than the forces of production, which they organize in different ways in different societies.

The concept does not typically refer to the relations between individual capitalists and workers but is generalized to refer to social classes. Thus it is the relations of production that determine the constitution of the two classes, of capitalists and workers. Furthermore, because the relations of production are essentially antagonistic, in that the worker has his product taken away from him, so are the relations between classes. See: *Base and Superstructure*; *Class*; *Class Struggle*; *Marx*; *Marxist Sociology*.

Relative Autonomy. Marxist accounts of the state in capitalist societies traditionally regarded it as simply an outpost of the bourgeois ruling class and completely controlled by ruling-class personnel. Recent Marxist theorists, notably N. Poulantzas (1973), have suggested that the state can act with some independence or relative autonomy from this class, though it is never totally independent. Such autonomy allows the state to serve the ruling class more effectively for two reasons. (1) The ruling class tends to split into fractions according to its various economic interests, and to lack the coherence to use state power for the general interests of the class as effectively as a relatively autonomous state does. (2) The state can take a broader and longer-term view of the interests of capital than do members of the ruling class, and can pursue social and political reforms which members may oppose but which contribute to their long-term welfare; for example, raising taxation to provide a welfare state that keeps the working class content with capitalism.

Criticism of the Marxist account centres on its failure to specify how relative 'relative autonomy' is; hence its refusal to consider that the state may be far more independent of the bourgeoisie in modern industrial capitalism than Marxists are willing to concede. The Weberian analysis of the state, by contrast, has emphasized its independence

as a separate bureaucracy that follows its own rules. See: *Capital Fractions*; *Capital Logic*; *Elite*; *Miliband–Poulantzas Debate*; *State*.

Bibl. Parkin (1979)

Relative Deprivation. This concept, formulated by S. A. Stouffer *et al.* (1949) and developed by R. K. Merton (1957), suggests that people mainly experience feelings of deprivation when they compare their own situations unfavourably with those of other individuals or groups. Comparisons can be made both with individuals with whom people interact and with outsiders; what matters is which reference group (q.v.) the person or group chooses as the focus of comparison. The emphasis on people's subjective frames of reference is a useful addition to the study of deprivation (q.v.), but the concept itself does not determine at what point relative deprivation becomes objective and absolute deprivation. See: *Poverty*; *Revolution*.

Bibl. Runciman (1966)

Relativism. A theory is said to be relativistic when it cannot provide criteria of truth independent and outside of itself; beliefs, theories, or values are claimed to be relative to the age or society that produced them and not valid outside those circumstances. For example, some theories in the sociology of knowledge (q.v.) are relativist in that they suggest that all knowledge is socially produced and is therefore defective since it is distorted by social interests. Since all knowledge is thus distorted, there are no independent standards of truth. This is an important difficulty, for it implies that there is also no way of validating relativistic theories themselves. See: *Cultural Relativism*; *Understanding Alien Belief Systems*.

Reliability. The reliability of any test

employed in research is the extent to which repeated measurements using it under the same conditions produce the same results. Reliability differs from *validity*, which is the success of a test in measuring correctly what it is designed to measure. For example, an attitude scale may be reliable in that it consistently produces the same results, but have little validity since it does not in fact measure the intended attitude but some other. See: *Attitude Scale*.

Religion. In sociology, there are broadly two approaches to the definition of religion. The first, following E. Durkheim (1912), defines religion in terms of its social functions: religion is a system of beliefs and rituals with reference to the sacred which binds people together into social groups. In this sense, some sociologists have extended the notion of religion to include nationalism. This recent perspective is criticized for being too inclusive, since almost any public activity – football, for example – may have integrative effects for social groups. The second approach, following M. Weber and the theologian P. Tillich, defines religion as any set of coherent answers to human existential dilemmas – birth, sickness or death – which make the world meaningful. In this sense, religion is the human response to those things which concern us ultimately. The implication of this definition is that all human beings are religious, since we are all faced by the existential problems of disease, aging and death. See: *Civil Religion*; *Ideology*; *Invisible Religion*; *Sacred*; *Secularization*.

Bibl. Robertson (1970)

Replication. This involves the duplication or repetition of an experiment or piece of research. In sampling design it has a more technical meaning, when a number of sub-samples (rather than a single complete sample) are selected from a population with the aim of comparing the estimates of population characteristics arising from the different sub-samples. This comparison is sometimes used to estimate sampling error, but more often to highlight non-sampling errors such as the variation between interviewers who are assigned to different sub-samples in survey research.

Bibl. Moser and Kalton (1979)

Repressive State Apparatus. See: *Ideological State Apparatus*.

Reproduction of Labour Power. K. Marx argued that the reproduction of labour power (q.v.), involving the housing, feeding and health care of workers, is essential for the continuation of capitalist societies, and an understanding of the mechanisms by which this reproduction is achieved is crucial to the adequate analysis of capitalism. This idea has been used in a wide variety of Marxist analyses. The state is seen, for example, as having functions in the reproduction of labour power, particularly in respect of housing and health care. Similarly, the family and women's domestic labour perform the same general function. See: *Collective Consumption*; *Domestic Labour*; *State*.

Residue. See: *Pareto*.

Restricted Code. B. Bernstein (q.v.) introduced this concept early on in his career, contrasting it with elaborated code. Restricted code privileges context-dependent meanings, where principles are implicit, and presupposes closely shared identifications, beliefs and practices. Such a system of meanings acts selectively on syntactic and lexical choices. Elaborated codes privilege relatively context-independent systems of specialized meanings, where principles are more likely to be more explicit. Bernstein argued that the lower working class uses restricted code and the middle class uses both codes and, since the educational system transmits class-regulated elaborated codes, the working-class child is potentially at a disadvantage. Bernstein has continued to use the concepts of restricted and elaborated code in his recent theoretical and empirical work developing relationships between meanings, linguistic realizations and social context. Furthermore, they now form part of a more general theory of the transmission of forms of consciousness which relates class relations to the distribution of power, and to principles of control where language codes are positioning devices. See: *Classroom Interaction*; *Classroom Knowledge*.

Bibl. Bernstein (1977 and 1981)

Revolution. In everyday usage, a revolution is any sudden, usually violent, change in the government of a society. However, social scientists regard such events as 'palace revolutions' or *coups d'état*, reserving the term 'revolution' for a total change in the social structure, of which political changes in government are only a manifestation. The explanations of revolution may be political (for example, the failure of a government to fulfil electoral commitments or to function adequately); economic (for example, the combination of long-term poverty and short-term failures); or sociological (for example, the curtailment of social mobility). Some explanations combine a variety of factors, as in the 'J-curve theory of rising expectations' which suggests that revolutions are not the result of absolute but of relative deprivation (q.v.), occurring when long periods of rising economic prosperity are sharply reversed.

The modern debate about the nature of revolutions has been dominated by

Marxist theory in which there is a clear distinction between political changes in governments and radical changes in the economic organization of society. In his analysis of India, K. Marx suggested that periodic changes in government or dynasties did not fundamentally change the static nature of the prevailing mode of production (q.v.). For Marx, a revolution involved the replacement of one mode of production by another, as in the transition from feudalism to capitalism. Marxist approaches to revolution may, however, either emphasize the importance of the struggles between social classes – the history of societies is the history of class conflict – or the contradiction within the mode of production between the forces and the relations of production (q.v.). Marxists who treat class conflict as the essential feature of Marxist analysis are likely to see revolution as the uncertain outcome of a complex combination of forces – class consciousness (q.v.), historical circumstance, political organization and the repression of the working class. Marxists concerned with the analysis of modes of production suggest that revolutions are an inevitable outcome of contradictions in the economic base.

Revolutions have, in addition, to be considered in a global context. While Marx and Engels assumed that the revolutionary collapse of capitalism would occur in core states (such as France and Britain), the major revolutions of the twentieth century have tended to occur in the so-called peripheral regions of Latin America and Asia. L. Althusser (1966) has argued that revolution is most likely in the weak link of the chain of capitalist society, where social contradictions are most prominent. The apparent survival of European capitalism, despite political conflicts, industrial strikes and economic decline, represents a major problem for Marxist theories of revolution. The absence of working-class revolutions is typically explained in terms of the countervailing role of welfare, citizenship rights and ideology. For Marxists, revolutionary strategy in capitalism involves breaking the hegemony (q.v.) of the dominant class by a combination of political violence and education. However, there are no general propositions which hold true of all modern revolutions. See: *Citizenship*; *Conflict Theory*; *Contradiction*; *Gramsci*; *Institutionalization of Conflict*; *Marxist Sociology*; *Peasants*.

Bibl. Eckstein (1965); Stone (1965); Kramnick (1972)

Rex, John (b. 1925). Currently director of the Social Science Research Council research unit on ethnic relations at the University of Aston, Birmingham, and research professor in ethnic relations, his contribution to contemporary sociology lies in two areas. First, he has defended the classical sociological tradition in *Key Problems of Sociological Theory* (1961), *Discovering Sociology* (1973a), *Sociology and the Demystification of the Modern World* (1974) and *Social Conflict* (1981) against what he regards as the dogmatic fashions of contemporary theory. Secondly, he has contributed to the study of race relations in *Race, Community and Conflict* (1967), *Race Relations in Sociological Theory* (1970), *Race, Colonialism and the City* (1973b), *Colonial Immigrants in a British City* (1979), with S. Tomlinson, and *Race and Ethnicity* (1986).

Rites de Passage. A term first used systematically in anthropology to denote public ceremonies celebrating the transition of an individual or group to a new status, for example initiation ceremonies. Such rites, typically associated with transitions in the life-cycle (q.v.), are less prominent in industrial than in traditional societies, though they may persist in such ceremonies as marriage services.

Ritual. In anthropology, any formal actions following a set pattern which express through symbol (q.v.) a public or shared meaning are rituals. They are typically the practical aspects of a religious system and they express sacred values (q.v) rather than seek to achieve some utilitarian end. In sociology, ritual is often used to refer to any regular pattern of interaction; thus the expression 'How do you do?' as a routine method of starting conversations could be regarded as a ritual of everyday interaction.

Role. When people occupy social positions their behaviour is determined mainly by what is expected of that position rather than by their own individual characteristics – roles are the bundles of socially defined attributes and expectations associated with social positions. For example, an individual schoolteacher performs the role of 'teacher' which carries with it certain expected behaviours irrespective of his or her own personal feelings at any one time, and therefore it is possible to generalize about the professional role behaviour of teachers regardless of the individual characteristics of the people who occupy these positions. Role is sociologically important because it demonstrates how individual activity is socially influenced and thus follows regular patterns. Sociologists use roles as the units from which social institutions are constructed. For example, the school as a social institution may be analysed as a collection of teacher and pupil roles which are common across all schools.

There are broadly two approaches to the theory of social roles. The first systematic use of the concept was by G. H.

Mead (q.v.) in 1934, a forerunner of symbolic interactionism (q.v.). In this usage, roles are depicted as the outcome of a process of interaction that is tentative and creative. Meadian social psychology was primarily concerned with how children learn about society and develop their own social beings (the 'self') by *role-taking*, that is imaginatively taking the roles of *others* such as fathers, mothers, doctors, teachers. In adult social behaviour individuals were also thought to use role-taking to work out their own roles. For symbolic interactionism, every role involves interaction with other roles; for example, the role of 'teacher' cannot be conceived without the role of 'pupil' and may only be defined as expected behaviour in relation to the expected behaviour of the pupil. The interaction process means that people in roles are always testing their conceptions of other-roles, and the response of people in other-roles reinforces or questions such conceptions. This in turn leads people to maintain or change their own role behaviour. *Role-making* describes how expected behaviour is created and modified in interaction, a 'tentative process in which roles are identified and given content on shifting axes as interaction proceeds' (R. H. Turner, 1962). Symbolic interactionists attempt to avoid the extreme relativism implied by role-making, namely that roles are fluid and indeterminate and that every single interaction produces a different and unique role, and assert that role-making produces consistent patterns of behaviour which can be identified with various types of social actors. They adhere to the sociological concern with the regularities of expected behaviour.

A second approach to role theory derives from R. Linton (1936) and was subsequently incorporated into functionalism (q.v.). This moves away from role-taking as the characteristic form of interaction with role-making as its outcome, and sees roles as essentially prescribed and static expectations of behaviour, as prescriptions inherent in particular positions. These prescriptions derive from the society's culture, typically regarded in functionalist accounts as a unified cultural system, and they are expressed in the social norms (q.v.) that guide behaviour in roles. The cultural-prescriptions approach recognizes that roles are often defined in relation to other roles, but not that interaction creates or modifies roles. However, individuals may become aware of their culturally defined roles in the course of interaction with people in other roles. Carried to extremes, this approach assumes a rigid determination of behaviour that effectively makes 'role' synonymous with 'culture' and 'norms' and thus largely redundant.

Investigation of actual roles often demonstrates a considerable indeterminacy of expected behaviour associated with social positions, which is what symbolic interactionism postulates. Nevertheless, indeterminacy can also be explained from within the cultural-prescriptions approach: the cultural norms that guide behaviour may be vague and capable of various interpretations; individual roles may be subject to incompatible expectations from the other roles to which they relate (for example, the role of foreman in industry is known to be subject to conflicting pressures from the occupants of worker and managerial roles which embody different conceptions of expected foreman behaviour, even though it may be shown that both conceptions are culturally determined).

Culture and norms are rarely completely specific about concrete behaviour. Nor do they form that integrated system of mutually compatible elements which in turn are universally accepted, as functionalism postulates: the cultures of modern societies are frequently fragmented, containing diverse and inconsistent elements, and different groups (for example, workers and managers) may adhere to different elements.

Recent accounts of roles have produced several refinements. *Role distance*, a term coined by E. Goffman (1959), refers to the detachment of the performer from the role he or she is performing. This makes an important distinction between the existence of expectations concerning a social role, the performance of a role and an individual's commitment to a role. In role distance, performers of a role adopt a subjective detachment from it. *Role conflict* is used in various senses: (1) when a person finds he or she is playing two or more roles at one time that make incompatible demands, as often happens for example with those working women who have to satisfy simultaneously the role expectations of employee, wife and mother, which may conflict; (2) when a person defines his or her role in one way while those in related roles define it differently, as may happen for example when teachers adhere to their own codes of professional behaviour which are disputed by parents or local education authorities; (3) when related roles have incompatible expectations of the focal role, as is the case in the example above of foremen receiving conflicting expectations from workers and managers. Also, the freedom of individuals to role-make is now seen to vary according to the type of position they occupy: at one extreme are the bureaucratic roles found in formal organizations and the military, where rules of behaviour are explicit and formalized and the scope for improvisation is reduced – though never eliminated, as organization theory (q.v.) shows; at the other are ill-defined roles

such as parent or friend where the scope is far greater. See: *Culture*; *Institution*; *Status*.

Bibl. Gross *et al.* (1958); Biddle and Thomas (eds.) (1966); Jackson (ed.) (1972)

Rule. One school in the philosophy of social science argues that social behaviour should be understood as following a rule and not as causally generated. The best-known exponent of this position is P. Winch (1958), who argues that human behaviour is intrinsically meaningful and that one cannot *causally* understand how it is that human beings give meaning to actions. The giving of meaning is a function of following rules which are essentially social since the appeal to others' following of rules is the only way of deciding whether an attribution of meaning is correct or incorrect. For Winch, therefore, connections between actions are conceptual, not causal, and it follows that the reasons given by an actor for his or her action cannot be seen as causes of the action.

Bibl. Keat and Urry (1975)

Ruling Class. A somewhat archaic term in sociology, ruling class has come to mean a social class, usually the economically dominant class, that controls a society through whatever political institutions are available. In some societies this control may be overt, as in feudal times, while in others it may be less obvious. Many Marxists, for example, argue that parliamentary democracies are really controlled by the capitalist class, the economically powerful, although this control is by no means obvious or even deliberate, being exercised by such methods as the recruitment of members of parliament with particular class backgrounds.

Elite theorists argue that true democracy is impossible and that all societies will be dominated by a ruling class whatever their social structure. See: *Class*; *Elite*; *Mosca*; *Pareto*; *State*.

Bibl. Bottomore (1965)

Rural–Urban Continuum. In much nineteenth-century sociology it was argued that there was a definite contrast between urban and rural societies. It gradually became clear that a dichotomy of this kind was too simple; there were gradations of urban and rural. R. Redfield (1930), for example, constructed a continuum from small rural villages (or folk societies) to large cities, the more urban being more secular, more individualistic, and with a greater division of labour and consequent social and cultural disorganization. There have been many similar attempts by investigators of rural and urban communities. R. Frankenberg (1966) differentiates rural from urban by means of the concepts of role (q.v.) and network (q.v.). In urban areas there is much greater differentiation of roles and the network of social relationships is less dense. The notion of the rural–urban continuum has recently passed out of use, mainly because there no longer seem to be significant differences between urban and rural ways of life. What differences in ways of life that do exist between communities or social groups are mostly attributable to such factors as social class and not geographical location. See: *Community*; *Gemeinschaft*; *Toennies*; *Urban Way of Life*.

Bibl. Reissman (1964); Pahl (ed.) (1968)

S

Sacred. For E. Durkheim, all religious beliefs classify phenomena as either sacred or profane. The sacred includes phenomena which are regarded and experienced as extraordinary, transcendent and outside the everyday course of events. In modern societies, there has been a shrinkage of sacred reality, brought about by the rationalization (q.v.) of culture. See: *Charisma*; *Invisible Religion*; *Profane*; *Religion*; *Secularization*.

Saint-Simon, Claude H. (1760–1825). Regarded as simultaneously the founder of French socialism and sociology, Saint-Simon led a remarkable life. Born into the French aristocracy, he was a captain in the French army which fought the British in the West Indies and North America. Changing his name to Bonhomme during the Revolution, he was imprisoned under the Terror. Under the Directory and later, he was the architect of a number of educational experiments and the centre of an influential *salon*. From 1806 onwards, Saint-Simon lived in abject poverty as an independent scholar. In 1823 he attempted suicide, losing an eye as a result. While his doctrines reflect the bizarre character of his private life, Saint-Simon was particularly influential on K. Marx and, via A.

Comte and E. Durkheim, on sociology.

The principal components of his thought were: (1) the history of human society passes through three distinct stages, to which correspond distinct modes of thought – polytheism and slavery, theism and feudalism, positivism and industrialism; (2) by the application of scientific positivism (q.v.), it is possible to discover the laws of social change and organization; (3) the organization and direction of modern society should be in the hands of scientists and industrialists, since bureaucrats, lawyers and clerics are essentially unproductive and parasitic; (4) the crisis of modern society could be solved by the development of a new religion based on positivism and under the control of a new priesthood, namely sociologists.

Bibl. Taylor, K. (1975)

Sampling. For practical and cost reasons, it is often impossible to collect information about the entire population of people or things in which social researchers are interested. In these cases, a sample of the total population is selected for study. The main criteria when sampling are to ensure that a sample provides a faithful representation of the totality from which it is selected, and to know as precisely as possible the proba-

213

bility that a sample is reliable in this way. Randomization meets these criteria, because it protects against bias in the selection process and also provides a basis on which to apply statistical distribution theory which allows an estimate to be made of the probability that conclusions drawn from the sample are correct.

The basic type of random sample is known as a *simple random sample*, one in which each person or item has an equal chance of being chosen. Often a population contains various distinct groups or strata which differ on the attribute that is being researched. *Stratified random sampling* involves sampling each stratum separately. This increases precision, or reduces time, effort and cost by allowing smaller sample sizes for a given level of precision. For example, poverty is known to be most common among the elderly, the unemployed and single-parent families, so research on the effects of poverty might well sample separately each of these three strata as part of a survey of poverty in the population as a whole, which would permit the total sample size to be reduced because the investigator would know that the groups most affected by poverty were guaranteed inclusion. *Cluster sampling* is sometimes used when the population naturally congregates into clusters. For example, managers are clustered in organizations, so a sample of managers could be obtained by taking a random sample of organizations and investigating the managers in each of these. Interviewing or observing managers on this basis would be cheaper and easier then using a simple random sample of managers scattered across all organizations in the country. This is usually less precise than a simple random sample of the same size, but in practice the reduction in cost per element more than compensates for the decrease in precision.

Sampling may be done as one process or in stages, known as *multi-stage sampling*. Multi-stage designs are common when populations are widely dispersed. Thus a survey of business managers might proceed by selecting a sample of corporations as first-stage units, perhaps choosing these corporations with a probability proportionate to their size, and then selecting a sample of managers within these corporations at the second stage. Alternatively, a sample of individual factories or office buildings within each corporation could be chosen as the second-stage units, followed by a sample of managers in each of these as a third stage. Stratification can also be used in the design, if for example occupational sub-groups are known to differ from each other, by selecting strata such as personnel, production, and finance management and sampling within each of these.

For sampling to be representative, one needs a complete and accurate list of the first-stage units that make up the relevant population, a basic requirement that is not always easily met. This list forms the *sampling frame*. Selection from the frame is best done by numbering the items and using a table of random numbers to identify which items form the sample, though a quasi-random method of simply taking every *n*th item from the list is often appropriate.

The reliability of a sample taken from a population can be assessed by the spread of the sampling distribution, measured by the standard deviation (q.v.) of this distribution, called the standard error. As a general rule, the larger is the size of the sample the smaller the standard error. See: *Sampling Error*; *Significance Test*; *Survey*.

Bibl. Moser and Kalton (1979)

Sampling Error. Many sociological investigations depend on a randomly selected sample drawn from a wider population. However, a single sample may not be an accurate representation of the population, so sample estimates are subject to sampling error. Repetitive sampling would in the long run average out fluctuations between individual samples and so provide a true representation. However, it is possible to estimate the degree of sampling error from a single sample, and thus to construct confidence intervals and to use statistical significance tests. Sampling errors are more likely to be large if samples are too small or the population has a high degree of variability. See: *Bias*; *Non-Response*; *Sampling*; *Significance Test*.

Sanction. Sanctions may be either positive or negative. Positive sanctions reward behaviour that conforms to social norms, while negative sanctions restrain deviant behaviour. Sanctions are heterogeneous, ranging, for example, from financial reward or legal restraint to praise or verbal abuse. The concept has thus played an important part in the explanation of social order. Societies exist because, through the internalization (q.v.) of sanctions, human agents monitor their own behaviour in anticipation of reward or punishment from other social actors. In conflict theory (q.v.) there is a greater emphasis on the external and coercive nature of sanctions; the enforcement of sanctions is thus seen not as evidence of agreement about values but of social control and power. See: *Norm*.

Schutz, Alfred (1899–1959). Born in Austria, Schutz emigrated to the United States in 1939 where he taught and wrote part-time, only taking a full-time academic post in 1952. His main publications are: *Collected Papers* (1971); *The Phenomenology of the Social World* (1972); and, with T. Luckmann, *The Structures of the Life-World* (1974).

Schutz was a major influence in the development of phenomenological sociology in the English-speaking world. He was primarily interested in three problems: (1) he wanted to construct an adequate theory of social action, partly based on a critique of M. Weber; (2) he carried out a series of investigations into the constitution of the life-world (q.v.); (3) he tried to investigate the manner in which a sociology which took human action as important could be scientific. In a dispute with T. Parsons (q.v.), Schutz did much to advance and clarify the problems of action theory and *Verstehen* (q.v.). His posthumous works included an analysis of the role of relevance in structuring the life-world (Schutz, 1970). See: *Phenomenological Sociology*.

Bibl. Grathoff (ed.) (1978)

Scientific Management. At the end of the nineteenth century, workshop administration in manufacturing industry in America and Europe was still largely in the hands of foremen and skilled workers who, in addition to performing the physical tasks of production, decided how jobs were to be done, how the labour force was to be organized and supervised, and often who was to be hired. The scientific management movement of the early twentieth century, associated with the name of its main advocate, F. W. Taylor, attempted to transform the administration of the workplace so as to increase profitability.

Taylor put forward three principles of reorganization. (1) Greater division of labour: production processes were to be analysed systematically and broken down to their component parts, so that each worker's job was simplified and preferably reduced to a single, simple task. Greater specialization would lead to greater efficiency, while the de-skilling (q.v.) that followed simplification of

215

tasks would also allow cheaper, unskilled labour to be hired. Greater division of labour would in turn remove the planning, organizing and hiring functions from the shop floor. Greater specialization was also to be encouraged among managers. (2) Full managerial control of the workplace was to be established for the first time, and managers were to be responsible for the coordination of the production process that greater division of labour had fragmented. (3) Cost accounting based on systematic time-and-motion study was to be introduced to provide managers with the information they needed in their new roles as the controllers of the workplace.

Taylor believed that financial considerations determined employees' motivation. He assumed that if employees felt that they were sharing fairly in the increased profitability created by new workshop organization, they would willingly cooperate with management. An important aim was to design a system of payment by results that was scientific and just, to allow labour to share in the profits arising out of their efforts. In practice, companies that adopted scientific management largely ignored this aim.

Scientific management proposed two major transformations of industry simultaneously: the removal of manual skills and organizational autonomy from the work of lower-level employees; and the establishment of managing as a role distinct from ownership, with a set of technical functions to do with organization. As a movement, scientific management had some success in America prior to the First World War and later in Europe and the Soviet Union under Lenin. Its real influence, however, has been more pervasive, because it provided an important legitimation of management in the early days of the managerial revolution (q.v.) and in addition established the central philosophy of work

organization that has dominated industry to the present day. Scientific management was also linked with the revolution in manufacturing methods introduced by Henry Ford. Between 1908 and 1914, Ford pioneered mechanized mass production, notably the moving assembly line. *Fordism* is sometimes seen as separate from Taylorism, but in fact the moving line and other aspects of the mechanization of production depended on the rationalization of work outlined in the first of Taylor's principles. See: *Division of Labour*; *Human Relations*; *Labour Process Approach*; *Management*.

Bibl. Taylor, F. W. (1964); Nelson (1975); Littler (1985)

Scottish Enlightenment. In the period 1707 to 1830, Scotland experienced considerable economic growth which was associated with a flowering of Scottish culture, particularly moral and social philosophy and political economy (q.v.). The Scottish Enlightenment, which in many respects anticipated the development of sociology by A. Comte (q.v.) and H. Spencer (q.v.) in the nineteenth century, is chiefly associated with D. Hume (1711–1776), A. Ferguson (1723–1816), J. Millar (1735–1801) and A. Smith (1723–1790).

The Scottish Enlightenment's social philosophy had a number of common themes: (1) its sceptical empiricism (q.v.) emphasized the importance of observation and critical assessment of experience over religious revelation and philosophical speculation; (2) it recognized the importance of social change amd social organization in the development of morals, and the difficulties of relativism (q.v.); (3) while recognizing the material benefits brought about by industrialization, it did not suggest that social progress necessarily contributed to individual happiness; (4) the need for a new conceptual apparatus to understand the changes taking place in Scottish society was recognized.

The background to the Scottish Enlightenment was the economic and commercial development of Scotland, which reinforced the traditional division between Catholic, feudal Highlands and Protestant, capitalist Lowlands. The contrast between 'civil society' in the Lowlands (with its new system of social ranks, urban conflicts and moral change) and 'barbaric' society in the Highlands (with its traditional hierarchies, stable agrarian structure and static morality) provided the original focus of the theory of civilization. See: *Civil Society*; *Civilization*.

Bibl. Schneider (ed.) (1967)

Secondary Labour Market. See: *Dual Labour Markets*.

Sect. This is a small, voluntary, exclusive religious group, demanding total commitment from its followers and emphasizing its separateness from and rejection of society. There has been considerable debate about these characteristics and a wide variety of sub-types have been identified and studied by sociologists, but the 'church–sect typology' remains a central focus of the sociology of religion.

It is argued that, when sects are successful in recruiting members and grow in size and complexity, they tend to approximate the denomination, which is a mid-point on the church–sect continuum. Religious commitment becomes less intense, because over time members are born into rather than converted to the sect. This is often referred to as 'the second generation problem' and the whole process as 'denominationalization'. While this is true of so-called 'conversionist sects', denominationalization may not be characteristic of 'gnostic sects' which do not seek to change the world by large-scale conversion. See: *Charisma*; *Church*; *Cult*; *Secularization*.

Bibl. Wilson, B. (1982)

Secularization. B. Wilson (1966) has defined secularization as the process in which religious thinking, practice and institutions lose social significance. In Europe, secularization is held to be the consequence of the social changes brought about by urban, industrial society. Critics of this account argue: (1) it has to assume the existence of a 'golden age' of religion, when religious institutions did have widespread social significance; (2) it exaggerates the presence of rational, secular belief in modern society, ignoring the evidence of superstition and magic; (3) it cannot account for the prevalence of cults among the young, especially those deriving from Oriental religions such as Hare Krishna, Divine Light Mission and the Meher Baba movement; (4) it underestimates the importance of organized Christianity as a political force in Europe and North America; (5) in a comparative perspective, the vitality of Zionism, militant Islam, and radical Catholicism in Latin America suggests that there is no necessary connection between modernization (q.v.) and secularization; (6) by adopting a narrow definition of religion, it equates secularization with de-Christianization; (7) there are processes in modern societies which ascribe a transcendental or sacred (q.v.) significance to the self; these processes constitute an invisible religion (q.v.).

While these criticisms have not been adequately overcome, it can be argued that the diversity of religious cults and practices in modern society demonstrates that religion has become a matter of personal choice rather than a dominant feature of public life. It is further suggested that, while religion may play a part in ideological struggles against colonialism (as in modern Iran), in the long term the modernization of society does bring about secularization.

The process of secularization is, however, highly variable between different industrial societies and in some European societies (such as France, Italy and Holland), Christianity still has an important social role. Understanding secularization is thus important for any analysis of the culture of capitalist societies. See: *Church*; *Civil Religion*; *New Religious Movements*; *Profane*; *Rationalization*; *Religion*; *Sect*.

Bibl. Luckmann (1967); Martin (1978)

Segmented Labour Markets. See: *Dual Labour Markets.*

Segregated Conjugal Role. See: *Conjugal Role.*

Self. See: *Mead, G. H.*; *Role*; *Symbolic Interactionism.*

Semiology. See: *Semiotics.*

Semiotics. Used synonymously with semiology, the term semiotics is defined as the study of signs. It has had some influence in those areas of sociology which deal with communication in any form, for it seeks to provide a method for the analysis of messages, both verbal and non-verbal.

The starting point of semiotics is the distinction between signifier, signified and sign. The signifier can be a physical object, a word, or a picture of some kind. The signified is a mental concept indicated by the signifier. The sign is the association of signifier and signified. For example, a Valentine card (signifier) can signify adoration (signified). Both card and adoration can exist separately, perhaps with other signifiers or signifieds, but their association constitutes a

specific sign. The relationship between signifier and signified can be fairly direct. A photograph of a baby, for example, indicates the signified (the baby) relatively straightforwardly. In other cases, however, what signified is indicated by a signifier is largely a matter of social convention, as is the case with language, for example. Those signs relatively free of social mediation are termed iconic, while those more dependent on such mediation are arbitrary.

Signifiers may also indicate different signifieds at different levels; there may be different levels of signification or different layers of meaning of signs. A photograph of a baby, for example, may signify a baby, but it may also signify, at a second level, the innocence of childhood or the sanctity of family life. R. Barthes (q.v.) argues that there are two ways in which signs may function at a second level of signification. Firstly, they may form myths, in that a sign stands for a whole range of cultural values. Secondly, a sign not only associates an image or object with a concept, it also engenders various feelings in us; signs not only denote, they also connote.

Signs may also be organized into codes. Again cultural conventions determine how codes are constructed for they decide which signs may meaningfully go together. Particular fashions in dress may constitute a code, for example. As the word implies, some codes may be hidden and less obvious than those of fashion and it requires detailed analysis to bring them out.

Semiotics is valuable in that it identifies a problem. That is, it goes beyond the immediate impact of a sign to ask questions about the wider meanings and social functions of sign systems. There is some doubt, however, whether it does any more than provide a set of concepts for tackling these issues. Furthermore, the problem of validating a semiotic analysis has not received any distinctive solution. See: *Discourse*; *Hermeneutics*; *Ideology*; *Myth*; *Sociology of Mass Media*; *Structuralism*.

Bibl. Hawkes (1977)

Sentiment. The concept has two different meanings. (1) Sentiments are culturally patterned emotions; the emotion of rage corresponds to the sentiment of indignation. (2) In exchange theory (q.v.), interaction between individuals in social groups produces collective sentiments of loyalty, friendship, altruism and group commitment, which in turn reinforce common norms. Sentiments are not internal, subjective feelings but overt, observable signs of solidarity between individuals emerging from interaction. Both perspectives, however different, treat sentiments as an essential feature of social exchange.

Service Class. The term was coined by K. Renner and adapted by R. Dahrendorf (1959) to categorize the class position of certain higher-level, nonmanual groups such as business managers, professionals employed by institutions rather than self-employed, public officials, who exercise power and expertise on behalf of (i.e. they 'serve') corporate bodies or the capitalist class. This concept has not been widely used though it has recently been revived in the investigation of social mobility in Britain carried out by the Social Mobility Group at Nuffield College and reported in J. H. Goldthorpe (1980). See: *Middle Class*; *Social Mobility*.

Bibl. Abercrombie and Urry (1983)

Service Crimes. See: *Crimes Without Victims*.

Sexism. Sexist attitudes or actions are those that discriminate against men or women purely on grounds of their gender. While these may often be explicit, they may also be implicit, being an assumed and unrecognized part of the culture. For example, sociological studies of stratification have been accused of being sexist because they do not take account of women's place in the class structure. See: *Class*; *Gender*; *Patriarchy*; *Sexual Divisions*; *Stereotypes*.

Sexual Divisions. Sociologists increasingly investigate the manner in which the chances and opportunities available to women differ from those open to men. In the jobs taken by men and women, for example, there is a clear division between the sexes. Women are very heavily concentrated in certain occupations. Almost two-thirds of the female workforce in Britain is concentrated in ten particular occupations, while men are spread much more evenly. Furthermore, women tend to occupy the lower reaches of the occupational hierarchy. For example, some three-quarters of clerks are women, while one in twenty higher professional workers is a woman. Within occupational groupings, women will also occupy less senior positions: for example, while 90 per cent of junior primary teachers were women in the middle 1970s, only 57 per cent of headteachers were. As one would expect, these disadvantages for women are reflected in their pay. Considering gross weekly earnings, women earned 70 per cent of men's pay in 1978 in the public sector and only 58 per cent in the private sector, although women have closed the pay gap with men to some extent in the 1980s.

The sexual division of labour at work is partly engendered by differences in educational opportunity between men and women. In general, women are somewhat less well represented higher up the educational ladder. For example, at undergraduate level about two-fifths of students are female and women make up only one-quarter of postgraduates. Indeed, the evidence is that women generally receive less training of any kind. One well-known feature of gender imbalance in the education system is that women tend to take particular subjects, especially avoiding science and technology. These subject choices will in turn influence the kinds of career open to women.

Women's occupational disadvantages must also be related to their role, or potential role, in the family. While the main burden of domestic labour falls on women, they will be constrained in their occupational choice. Furthermore, both employers and other workers will be influenced by the prevailing belief that a woman's place is in the home and will act accordingly. Lastly, women are themselves socialized to believe that they are better suited to being housewives than seeking equality with men in employment. See: *Class*; *Division of Labour*; *Domestic Labour*; *Dual Labour Markets*; *Educational Attainment*; *Human Capital*; *Patriarchy*; *Social Reproduction*; *Stereotypes*; *Underclass*; *Women and Work*.

Bibl. Barrett (1980); Bilton *et al.* (1981)

Shame. In anthropology, there is a distinction between guilt-cultures in which social control operates through internal sanctions and shame-cultures in which individuals are controlled by public threats to personal reputation and honour. Public shame reflects not only on the individual, but on his family and kin, and there are, therefore, strong familial sanctions on deviation from communal norms. Shame as a mechanism of social control can only operate in small groups where visibility and intimacy are prominent, and is thus characteristic of village rather than urban existence.

Sharecropping. See: *Peasants*.

Sick Role. The concept was first outlined by L. J. Henderson (1935) and then elaborated by T. Parsons (q.v.) (1951). From a sociological perspective, illness can be regarded as a form of social deviance, in which an individual adopts a specific role. This sick role has four major characteristics; (1) the incumbent is exempted from normal social responsibilities; (2) the sick person is not blamed for being sick; (3) the person is expected to seek out competent professional help, since the illness is socially undesirable; (4) the incumbent of a sick role is expected to comply with the regimen prescribed by a competent physician. Since doctors in Western society have a professional monopoly, they are the principal legitimators of the sick role. The concept of the sick role has been criticized on a number of grounds: (1) it fails to distinguish between the patient and the sick role, since being sick does not automatically lead to the adoption of a patient status; (2) it does not recognize the possibility of conflicting interests between physician and patient; (3) the concept does not have universal application, since some 'conditions' (alcoholism, physical disability or pregnancy) do not necessarily result in a suspension of normal social responsibilities; (4) the concept is useful in the analysis of acute but not chronic illness; (5) there are problems related to so-called 'abnormal illness behaviour' (like hypochondriasis and Munchausen's syndrome) where there is a conflict of definitions of illness between doctor and patient; (6) the concept does not provide a phenomenology of the experience of being ill. For some critics, Parsons' model of the sick role is itself a legitimation of the power of doctors over patients. It did, however, lay the foundations for a sociological critique of the medical model (q.v.).

See: *Sociology of Health and Illness.*
Bibl. Levine and Kozloff (1978)

Sign. See: *Semiotics.*

Significance Test. When researchers study a sample drawn from a population rather than investigating the whole population, they need to know how far they can trust the quantities calculated on the basis of the elements of the sample. Values derived from samples may be subject to sampling error (q.v.) and so be inaccurate as estimates of population values. For example, if a public opinion poll were to show that a sample was divided into one-third opposing and two-thirds supporting the reintroduction of capital punishment, the investigator would need to know the likelihood that this result was due simply to sampling error; the problem is to know whether the same statistic would have emerged if a different sample of people had been chosen.

Significance testing starts with a *null hypothesis*, which in this example states that there is no significant difference between the observed sample estimates, because they are chance results due to random variations in the population. A test statistic is calculated, and if its value falls within a specified range which has a small probability of occurring under the null hypothesis, the hypothesis will be rejected. In this example, rejection means that it is highly probable that there *is* a real difference in the proportions who support or reject capital punishment. Significance tests can be used at various *levels* of significance or confidence, most commonly in sociology at the ·01 or ·05 levels which indicate, respectively, a 1 in 100 or 5 in 100 probability that the null hypothesis has been rejected when it is true. Various statistics exist for the testing of means, proportions, variances, correlations and goodness of fit.

Sociologists distinguish between *sta-tistical* and *substantive* significance. Findings may have substantive significance in terms of a theory or because they reinforce other results, even though they fail to reach statistical significance at a given level. This often occurs when the total sample size or the size of individual subgroups within the sample are small. Conversely, certain findings may have statistical but not substantive significance, when the observations are unimportant in terms of the substance of an investigation.

Signifier/Signified. See: *Semiotics.*

Simmel, Georg (1858–1918). A German professor of philosophy who wrote extensively on aesthetics, epistemology (q.v.), the philosophy of history as well as sociology, Simmel's views were formed by opposition both to the structural sociology of writers like A. Comte (q.v.) and to the German tradition of *Geisteswissenschaften* (q.v.), in which social and historical events were to be seen as unique and not generalizable. Simmel's solution was to picture society as a web of interactions between people. He stressed the interaction. For example, in his analysis of power, he argued that the powerful could not exercise their power without the complicity of their subordinates; power is an interaction. If there are social structures like the family, they are to be considered as mere crystallizations of interactions between individuals.

Simmel's proposed method of analysing human interactions was by formal sociology (q.v.). He suggested that one could isolate the form of interactions from their content, so that apparently very different interactions (with different contents) could be shown to have the same form. For example, the relationship between a writer and an aristocrat in eighteenth-century England

and the relationship between a peasant and his landlord in twentieth-century Latin America are apparently different interactions. However, they do have the same form, in that they are both examples of patronage relationships. Simmel was particularly fascinated by numbers. For example, he argued that social situations involving two or three parties have the same formal similarities whether the parties are people or nation states. This similarity of form means that certain properties of the relationships are manifested in very different situations. For example, the options open to three nation states, and their consequent behaviour, are much the same as those applying to three people. Another way in which Simmel applied his formal sociology was in the analysis of social types. Thus he argued that certain social types, the stranger for example, appear in different societies at different times and the behaviour of the stranger, and the behaviour of others towards him or her, is very similar in these different social situations.

Although subsequent commentators have concentrated on his formal sociology, his analyses of social interaction and his views about the functions of social conflict, Simmel was also concerned with the study of social development, as characterized by social differentiation and the emergence of a money economy. The translation into English of *The Philosophy of Money* (1900), which, among other topics, presents an alternative to the Marxist labour theory of value (q.v.), has inspired a new interest in the whole corpus of Simmel's work. The evolution of economic exchange from barter to paper money to credit represents a rationalization (q.v.) of daily life. This economic quantification of social interaction was a further illustration of the separation of the form from the content of social life. Simmel's analysis of money provided a phenomenological alternative to Marxist economic categories.

Simmel's main works available in English include *The Philosophy of History* (1892) and two collections of essays: *The Sociology of Georg Simmel*, ed. K. Wolff (1950) and *Conflict and the Web of Group Affiliation* (1955). See: *Conflict Theory*; *Neo-Kantianism*.

Bibl. Frisby (1981; 1984)

Skewness. The degree of asymmetry in a distribution. See: *Distribution*.

Skill. See: *De-Skilling*.

Slavery. As an institution, slavery is defined as a form of property which gives to one person the right of ownership over another. Like any other means of production, the slave is 'a thing'. Slave labour has existed under a variety of social conditions – in the ancient world, in the colonies of the West Indies and in the plantations of the southern states of America. From the point of view of efficient production, slave labour presents a number of problems. (1) A barrack slave system does not reproduce itself and slaves have to be obtained either through purchase on a slave market or by conquest; slave systems tend, therefore, to experience acute labour shortages. (2) Slaves require considerable political surveillance, because of the threat of slave revolts. (3) It is difficult to force slaves to perform skilled labour tasks without additional incentives. These problems suggest that slavery does not provide an appropriate basis for long-term economic growth. There is some debate as to whether slavery is compatible with a capitalist economy: M. Weber (1922) has argued that capitalism requires free labour markets if it is to fulfil its potential; while B. Moore (1966) believes that slavery is incompatible only with a particular form of capitalism – competitive, democratic capitalism – and not with capitalism as such.

Slavery presupposes the existence of private property and, in Marxism, is an economic rather than a political category. Support for the view that the essential feature of slavery is not political domination can be found in classical Greece and Mameluke Egypt where slaves often performed crucial administrative and military roles. While in Marxism the slave mode of production (q.v.) is often regarded as a distinctive form, there are few systematic treatments of this mode of production and the nature of the transition between slavery and feudalism remains obscure. For example, the dividing line between serfdom in feudalism and servitude in slavery is empirically fluid and uncertain.

It is generally acknowledged, however, that classical Greece and Rome were based on slave labour. In antiquity, the dominant class was an urban citizenry which drew its wealth from the countryside, in which slave labour was preponderant. Because slaves were acquired largely through conquest, every citizen was threatened by the prospect of servitude. While slaves provided certain obvious economic benefits – as highly movable commodities – it has been argued by P. Anderson (1974) that slavery inhibited the development of the forces of production because there was little incentive to develop labour-saving technology.

While slavery was the basis of the classical societies of Greece and Rome, it also flourished in the plantation system of the Americas. Cotton produced by slave labour in the southern states of North America played a crucial role in the development of American industrial capitalism. Marxists regard these south-ern states as a form of agrarian capitalism employing slave labour and not as a slave mode of production as such. As a capitalist system, the plantation economy of the southern states had distinctive characteristics: it was a rural, not urban, form and gave rise to an aristocratic rather than a bourgeois culture.

In a comparative perspective, it has also been argued that slavery in North America was far more repressive than in Latin America. There are a number of reasons for this. (1) The Protestants of North America regarded the slave as sinful and in need of sexual restraint, while Catholicism in South America was more tolerant. (2) The ethnic diversity of Latin America was extensive and therefore the division between black and white was less sharply drawn. (3) It was possible for slaves to purchase their freedom in South America, but this was uncommon in North America. Although the American Civil War put an end to slavery, the legacy of racial hatred has been a decisive influence on contemporary politics in North America. See: *Capitalism*; *Feudalism*; *Property*; *Racism*.

Bibl. Davis, B. D. (1970)

Social Change. The problem of explaining social change was central to nineteenth-century sociology. This preoccupation arose from (1) an awareness of the radical social effects of industrialization on European societies, and (2) an appreciation of the fundamental gap between European industrial societies and so-called 'primitive societies'. Theories of social change thus centred on the nature of capitalist or industrial development and the apparent absence of social development in those societies which had become part of the colonial empire of Europe. These theories of social change were concerned with long-term and large-scale or macro-development.

Sociological theories of change, especially nineteenth-century ones, may be divided into theories of social evolution and theories of revolution. In the first, social change was thought to involve basic stages of development such as 'military society' and 'industrial society', by which society progressed from simple, rural, agrarian forms to more complex, differentiated, industrial-urban ones. This type of evolutionary theory (q.v.) was developed by A. Comte (q.v.), H. Spencer (q.v.) and E. Durkheim. The analysis of social change in functionalism (q.v.) continues to depend, to some extent, on evolutionary theory by regarding change as the adaptation of a social system to its environment by the process of mental differentiation and increasing structural complexity. Theories of revolutionary social change, particularly deriving from K. Marx, emphasized the importance of class conflict, political struggle and imperialism as the principal mechanisms of fundamental structural changes.

This distinction between evolutionary and revolutionary theories is a fundamental analytical division, but theories of social change can be further classified in terms of: (1) the level of analysis (whether macro or micro); (2) whether change derives from factors internal or external to the society, institution or social group; (3) the cause of social change (variously demographic pressure, class conflict, changes in the mode of production (q.v.), technological innovation or the development of new systems of belief); (4) the agents of change (innovative elites of intellectuals, social deviants, the working class); (5) the nature of change (whether a gradual diffusion of new values and institutions, or a radical disruption of the social system).

Although the issue of long-term structural change is still alive in con-temporary social science, it is widely agreed that a general theory of change is necessarily too vague to be of much use in the explanation of historical change. The trend in twentieth-century sociology has been towards middle-range theory (q.v.) which accounts for the development of particular institutions, social groups, items of culture, or particular beliefs rather than for the transformation of societies as a whole. See: *Differentiation*; *Historical Materialism*; *Marx*; *Revolution*; *Underdevelopment*.

Bibl. Etzioni and Etzioni (1964); Smith, A. D. (1973)

Social Closure. Used by M. Weber to describe the action of social groups who maximize their own advantage by restricting access to rewards (usually economic opportunities) to their members thus closing access to outsiders, this term was re-introduced into the modern analysis of social class by F. Parkin (1974; 1979) who treats closure as an aspect of the distribution of power between classes. Parkin identifies strategies of *exclusion*, by which collectivities with privileged access to rewards attempt to exclude outsiders and pass on privileges to their own kind, and *usurpation*, by which outsiders, often organized collectively, try to win a greater share of resources. See: *Caste*; *Class*.

Social Contract. Contract theory seeks to explain the origins and binding force of mutual obligations and rights in society. T. Hobbes, in *Leviathan* (1651), argued that in the pre-social 'state of nature' people enjoy absolute personal freedom, but this very freedom means that they are exposed to the threat of physical violence and exploitation. In order to remove this threat, people enter into a social contract with each other whereby they surrender their absolute individual freedom to a third party (the state) which then acts to guarantee social order and stability. Social contract theory simultaneously legitimates state power and provides a right of revolution if the state fails to guarantee the minimum conditions of civilized life.

It should be recognized that social contract theory does not literally assume that at a given period in history people decided to band together to form society. To form a contract presupposes that people possess a language in which the terms of a contract could be formulated. The existence of human language in turn presupposes the existence of social relations. Contract theory suggests that we examine the relationship between state and society 'as if' people were bound by mutual obligations and privileges. In other words, it is an early theoretical attempt to analyse the basis of consensus (q.v.) and coercion (q.v.). In social theory, the idea of a contract has played an important analytical role in justifying power relations and for limiting the boundaries of the state in relation to individual rights. The theory of social contract was a crucial ingredient of J. Locke's analysis of property rights, and of J.-J. Rousseau's account of the 'general will' as the basis of government. In contemporary sociology, T. Parsons (1937) has attempted to show that the fundamental basis of society is not social contract and the coercive apparatus of the state, but the existence of a consensus over values and norms. The classical theory of the social contract has thus been replaced in sociology by theories of consensus, reciprocity and exchange. See: *Social Order*.

Bibl. Wolin (1961)

Social Control. The majority of sociologists argue that social control is achieved through a combination of compliance, coercion and commitment to social values. For example, T. Parsons (1951) defined it as the process by which, through the imposition of sanctions, deviant behaviour is counteracted and social stability maintained. In contemporary sociology the concept is primarily encountered in the analysis of deviant behaviour, where it is an aspect of labelling theory (q.v.). It is argued that, paradoxically, the attempt to increase forms of coercive social control by, for example, increasing police surveillance of particular crimes or social groups tends to amplify deviance rather than diminish it. The implication is that social control depends more on the stability of social groups, community relations and shared values than it does on mere coercion. The concept is somewhat vague and embraces a number of other, more precise, sociological categories. See: *Coercion*; *Deviancy Amplification*; *Deviant Behaviour*; *Parsons*; *Sanction*; *Social Order*.

Social Darwinism. Late nineteenth-century sociology was dominated by various theories of social evolution, one of which was Social Darwinism – nothing to do with C. Darwin himself. This doctrine, most prominent in the United States, took various forms but most versions had two central assumptions. (1) There are underlying, and largely irresistible, forces acting in societies which are like the natural forces which operate in animal and plant communities. One can therefore formulate social laws similar to natural ones. (2) These social forces are of such a kind as to produce evolutionary progress through the natural conflicts between social groups. The best adapted and most successful social groups survive these conflicts, raising the evolutionary level of society generally ('the survival of the fittest').

Such a theory, like that of H. Spencer

(q.v.), has been interpreted as well suited to *laissez-faire* conceptions of society. It also, in some authors, especially L. Glumpowicz and, to a lesser extent, W. Sumner, had racial overtones, with the belief that some races, being innately superior, were bound to triumph over inferior ones. In other authors the doctrine took a weaker form. A. Small, for example, based his sociology on the notion that social groups necessarily had interests which conflicted. See: *Competition*; *Evolutionary Theory*; *Organic Analogy*; *Urban Ecology*.

Bibl. Timasheff (1967)

Social Distance. This term refers to the perceived feelings of separation or social distance between social groups. A social distance scale (the Bogardus scale) attempts to measure degrees of tolerance or prejudice between social groups. This scale is assumed to be cumulative. For example, a respondent who is prepared to contemplate marriage between blacks and whites is likely also to be prepared to live in the same street as blacks.

Social Division of Labour. See: *Division of Labour*.

Social Fact. E. Durkheim (1895) used this term to describe social phenomena that were external to the individual yet constrained his or her actions. Social facts were (1) external to individuals; (2) coercive; (3) objective, that is, not merely a product of subjective definitions. Law provided a good illustration of these characteristics. He defined the task of sociology as the study of these social facts, which devalued explanations of social action in terms of individual free will. See: *Durkheim*.

Social Mobility. A concept used in the sociological investigation of inequality, social mobility refers to the movement of individuals between different levels of the social hierarchy, usually defined occupationally. The study of mobility looks at mobility rates, mobility patterns (whether short-range between adjacent hierarchical levels or long-range between widely separated levels), who is recruited to various positions and the determinants of this selection. *Intergenerational* mobility compares the present position of individuals with those of their parents. *Intragenerational* mobility compares the positions attained by the same individual at different moments in the course of his or her worklife.

Sociological interest in mobility has been informed by several issues. S. M. Lipset and R. Bendix (1959) believed that mobility was essential for the stability of modern industrial society, since open access to elite positions would allow able and ambitious people to rise from lower social levels, acting as a safety valve that reduced the likelihood of revolutionary collective action by lower classes. Others have been more concerned with issues of efficiency and social justice, P. M. Blau and O. D. Duncan (1967) arguing that the efficiency of modern societies requires mobility if the most able people are to perform the most important jobs, and D. V. Glass (1954) that justice in a democratic society depends on an egalitarian opportunity structure.

Three of the findings of the Social Mobility Group at Nuffield College, Oxford, reported in J. H. Goldthorpe (1980), have challenged traditional beliefs about social mobility in Britain: (1) absolute mobility rates since the war are higher than previously believed; (2) there is considerable long-range mobility from the working class into the upper class (which is called the 'service' class) as well as short-range mobility; (3) membership of the upper ('service') and intermediate classes is more fluid than expected. What others have called the *occupational transition*, that is the growth of professional, technical, managerial and lower-level white-collar occupations and the contraction of manual jobs which all advanced industrial societies have experienced, is the main explanation of why mobility is high and the class hierarchy appears fluid and open at the top. Goldthorpe (1980) adjusts the Nuffield data to 'allow' for structural changes in the occupational system, and suggests that class structure would have been stable without much openness but for these changes. One limitation of this research is that it deals only with the mobility of men.

The comparison of mobility rates and patterns between societies is difficult, given differences between occupational structures. However, taking two bench marks which provide fairly crude indicators of mobility at two important levels of stratification, mobility into the elite, and across the manual/non-manual line, permits some comparison. Czechoslovakian evidence suggests that socialist societies may be open, with low ascription (q.v.) and scope for individual merit or achievement. Among Western societies, Australia and Sweden appear the most open, Britain, Canada and the United States have intermediate mobility rates, while West Germany and Japan are among the least open. See: *Career*; *Class*; *Educational Attainment*; *Middle Class*; *Service Class*; *Sponsored Mobility*; *Stratification*; *Working Class*.

Bibl. Heath (1981)

Social Movements. The term covers various forms of collective action aimed at social reorganization. In general, social movements are not highly institutionalized, but arise from spontaneous social protest directed at specific or widespread grievances. Examples include millenarianism (q.v.), syndicalism, and movements for moral reform. Despite attempts to make the term precise and rigorous, 'social movements' embraces a bewildering variety of very different groups. See: *Collective Behaviour*; *Revolution*; *Urban Social Movement*.

Bibl. Smelser (1962)

Social Order. The explanation of order and cohesion in society is a central concern of social theory. Three types of explanation may be identified. (1) The utilitarian approach suggests that it is in the self-interest of all individuals to maintain social order, particularly in complex societies where division of labour (q.v.) is high and people are interdependent. Utilitarianism (q.v.) has had less influence on sociological than economic theory, except in exchange theory (q.v.), and enlightened self-interest does not figure prominently in sociological accounts of order. (2) The cultural approach emphasizes the role of shared norms and values, E. Durkheim and T. Parsons being influential sociological exponents of value consensus. (3) The compulsion approach emphasizes power and domination – variously military, judicial, spiritual, economic – and the capacity of those who dominate to enforce order. Among sociological theorists, K. Marx and M. Weber are notable exponents of compulsion, though neither denies the contributory role of values. See: *Authority*; *Coercion*; *Conflict*; *Consensus*; *Dominant Ideology Thesis*; *Durkheim*; *Gramsci*; *Hegemony*; *Ideological State Apparatus*; *Marx*; *Parsons*; *Power*; *Social Contract*; *Social Control*; *Value*; *Weber*.

Bibl. Abercrombie *et al.* (1980)

Social Pathology. This nineteenth-century notion is based on an analogy between organic disease or pathology and social deviance. In E. Durkheim's discussion of crime and suicide, social pathology was based on a distinction between normal and abnormal social conditions rather than individual deviance. Furthermore, he argued that the distinction was objective rather than a moral judgement and that social pathology could be scientifically measured. Unfortunately, Durkheim's use of the concept is confused and treated social pathology as merely the obverse of social normality. See: *Durkheim*; *Organic Analogy*; *Suicide*.

Social Problems. The definition of a social problem is fraught with difficulty for a variety of reasons. (1) Cultural relativism means that what is a social problem for one group may be nothing of the sort for another. (2) Historically, the nature of social problems has changed over time with changes in law and mores (q.v.). (3) There is a political dimension, that the identification of a 'problem' may involve one group in the exercise of social control over another. Sociologists reject taken-for-granted views that social problems have an objective status like some organic pathology, and search for the socially created definitions of what constitutes a 'problem'.

Symbolic interactionists, for example, suggest that social problems are not social facts (q.v.), and that some problems result simply from processes of social change that create conflicts between groups, when one group succeeds in winning public acceptance of its claim that the other's behaviour should be labelled as problematic. Mass media, official agencies and 'experts' typically exaggerate the extent of social problems and over-react to social pressures. The concept of a moral panic (q.v.) illustrates how the media of communication help define social problems and create public anxiety.

Other sociologists criticize the assumption implicit in many official definitions of social problems, particularly in the area of social welfare policy, that such problems derive from the personal characteristics of individuals rather than from structural features of the social system over which individuals have little influence. For example, emphasis on the 'problem' that many people are unemployed because they are 'work-shy' diverts attention from the actual causes of mass unemployment, some of which may be the actions of government. See: *Addiction*; *Alcoholism*; *Criminology*; *Deviancy Amplification*; *Deviant Behaviour*; *Divorce*; *Labelling Theory*; *Poverty*; *Symbolic Interactionism*; *Unemployment*.

Bibl. Merton and Nisbet (eds.) (1961); Doublas, J. D. (ed.) (1973)

Social Reproduction. Just as people reproduce physically over the generations, so they also tend to reproduce their social organization, and social reproduction is the name given to this phenomenon. In Marxist sociology it has a more restricted sense, meaning reproduction of labour power and the relations of production (q.v.). See: *Collective Consumption*; *Cultural Reproduction*; *Reproduction of Labour Power*; *Socialization*.

Social Structure. This is a concept often used in sociology but rarely discussed at any length. It has been defined simply as any recurring pattern of social behaviour. However, for most sociologists such a definition might tend to include trivial behaviours as well as the significant ones. A more generally preferred approach is to say that social structure refers to the enduring, orderly and patterned relationships between elements of a society, a definition that prompted some nineteenth-century sociologists to compare societies with machines or organisms. There is some disagreement as to what would count as an 'element'. A. R. Radcliffe-Brown (q.v.), for example, thought of social structures as relationships of a general and regular kind between people. S. F. Nadel, on the other hand, suggested roles (q.v.) as the elements. Even more generally, social institutions (q.v.), as organized patterns of social behaviour, are proposed as the elements of social structure by a wide range of sociologists, particularly functionalists, who then define societies in terms of functional relations between social institutions. Furthermore, for them, certain elements of social structure – social institutions – are necessary because they are functional prerequisites (q.v.).

Sociologists typically wish to use concepts of social structure to explain something, and this usually means that the explanation is a causal one. Such a view can present difficulties in that social structures are not directly observable entities but are rather abstract formulations. This and other difficulties have led to criticism of the use of social structure. Thus it has been seen as a reified concept, as unobservable and therefore unverifiable, and as denying human creativity and freedom by suggesting that human action is determined by structures. One solution to these criticisms is to demonstrate, as P. Berger and T. Luckmann (1967) do, the way in which social structures are themselves the creation of active human beings. See: *Agency and Structure*; *Functionalism*; *Hermeneutics*; *Methodological Individualism*; *Organic Analogy*; *Phenomenological Sociology*; *Realism*; *Social System*; *Spencer*; *Structuralism*; *Structuration*.

Bibl. Bottomore (1962); Keat and Urry (1975)

Social System. The notion of 'system' is not peculiar to sociology, but is a conceptual tool with widespread currency in the natural and social sciences. A system is any collection of interrelated parts, objects, things or organisms. It is often seen to be purposeful or functional, that is, it exists to satisfy some purpose or goal. In the work of T. Parsons (1951), a *social* system is defined in terms of two or more social actors engaged in more or less stable interaction within a bounded environment. The concept is not, however, limited to interpersonal interaction, and refers also to the analysis of groups, institutions, societies and inter-social entities. It may, for example, be employed in the analysis of the university or the state as social systems which have structures of interrelated parts. There are two further features typically associated with the concept: (1) social systems tend over time towards equilibrium or 'homoeostasis', because they are 'boundary-maintaining systems'; (2) social systems can be regarded, from a cybernetic point of view, as information systems or input-output systems. In functionalism (q.v.) in the 1950s, it was common to draw an analogy between living organisms and social systems as homoeostatic systems. For example, exercise in human beings increases the blood sugar level, heart rate and temperature. We perspire, which has the effect of controlling our body temperature. The body depends on a variety of such feedback mechanisms in order to maintain an equilibrium. Similarly, the parts of a social system are linked together by media of exchange which include a variety of information-carrying symbols such as language, money, influence, or commitments. Equilibrium may thus be defined as a balance between inputs and outputs.

The concept of social system has been used most explicitly and self-consciously in modern functionalism, but it was

229

implicit in much nineteenth-century social thought. Any social theory which treats social relations, groups or societies as a set of interrelated parts which function to maintain some boundary or unity of the parts is based implicitly or explicitly on the concept of 'social system'. For some theorists, therefore, the concept is inescapable as the basis of a scientific approach to social data. See: *Boundary Maintenance*; *Functional Imperative*; *Holism*; *Pareto*; *Parsons*; *Reciprocity*; *Social Structure*; *Society*; *Systems Theory*.

Bibl. Buckley (1967)

Socialist Societies. While there are various strands of socialist thought (such as utopian and scientific), most socialists identify the following as the important characteristics of socialist societies: (1) there is common ownership of the means of production and distribution; (2) economic activities are planned by the state and the market plays little or no role in the allocation of resources; (3) with the disappearance of private property, economic classes also disappear and hence the state has an administrative rather than repressive function; (4) there are important changes in criminal and property law, since the legal system is now primarily concerned with administration; (5) these structural changes also bring about the disappearance of ideology, especially religion; (6) human alienation (q.v.) will be abolished with the disappearance of private property.

Three claims are typically made about the superiority of socialist over capitalist societies: (1) socialist societies are more efficient economically, because in a command economy they do not experience the waste (unemployment, overproduction, idle machinery, inflation and stagnation) associated with capitalist market economies; (2) socialist societies do not have colonial markets, because they do not require an outlet for capital or commodities; (3) socialist societies are more democratic than capitalist societies, because decisions about the satisfaction of human needs are taken collectively and publicly. Socialist economic development is thus regarded as the only successful alternative to capitalism in the Third World, because it offers the possibility of growth without dependency.

Critics of socialist societies argue that, in practice, the societies that have emerged in Russia, eastern Europe, Asia and Africa that claim to be socialist do not exhibit these characteristics. The following arguments are typically raised: (1) socialist societies have not proved more economically efficient and dynamic than capitalist societies, since they are dependent on the West for imports of food, technology and skill, without which they could not satisfy the needs of their populations; (2) socialist societies are not democratic, because major decisions are taken by the Party, which controls all appointments to important political and social positions in society; (3) they have proved to be imperialist because, to satisfy the requirements of rapid industrialization and economic accumulation, they are forced to exploit their indigenous workers or the peasants of underdeveloped nations; (4) while economic classes may have become less important with the abolition of private ownership, social stratification persists in the form of income inequality, differences in prestige, and inequalities of power; (5) inequality is determined not by the market but by the Party and its bureaucratic apparatus, which enjoys a monopoly of power; (6) in practice, it is difficult to remove entirely the operation of economic markets within a planned economy and the black market serves to reinforce social inequalities associated with political monopoly; (7) ideology is important in legitimating Party power, although it has not proved particularly effective (for example, the persistence of Catholicism in Poland or Protestant opposition in Russia).

In defence of socialist societies, it is often claimed that: (1) these empirical departures from socialism are defects of the transition to advanced socialist society rather than inevitable and inherent failures; (2) socialist societies cannot fully develop in a global situation which is still dominated by capitalist societies, since capitalism is able to impose certain restraints on independent socialist development; (3) more radically, societies like the Soviet Union are not socialist but 'state capitalist', since the state has merely replaced private owners in the exercise of capitalist functions. See: *Convergence Thesis*; *Industrial Society*.

Bibl. Parkin (1971); Lane (1985)

Socialization. Sociologists use this term to describe the process whereby people learn to conform to social norms, a process that makes possible an enduring society and the transmission of its culture between generations. The process has been conceptualized in two ways. (1) Socialization may be conceived as the internalization of social norms: social rules become internal to the individual, in the sense that they are self-imposed rather than imposed by means of external regulation and are thus part of the individual's own personality. The individual therefore feels a need to conform. (2) It may be conceived as an essential element of social interaction, on the assumption that people wish to enhance their own self-image by gaining acceptance and status in the eyes of others; in this case, individuals become socialized as they guide their own actions to accord with the expectations of others. The two conceptualizations may be combined, as in the work of T. Parsons (q.v.).

Socialization may be divided into three stages: the primary stage involves the socialization of the young child in the family; the secondary stage involves the school; and the third stage is adult socialization, when actors enter roles for which primary and secondary socialization may not have prepared them fully (for example, becoming an employee, a husband or wife, a parent).

In the mid twentieth century, particularly in Parsonian functionalism (q.v.), sociologists displayed what D. H. Wrong (1961) called the 'oversocialized conception of man'; that is, they saw socialization as all-powerful and effective rather than as a more tentative process that influences but may not determine actors' behaviours and beliefs. Symbolic interactionists have also criticized the conventional usage, emphasizing socialization as a process of transaction between individual and society, in which both are mutually influential. It is now accepted that individuals are rarely totally moulded by the culture of their society. See: *Agency and Structure*; *Internalization*; *Mead, G. H.*; *Role*.

Bibl. Danziger (1971)

Societal. This term refers to the characteristics of a society as a whole.

Society. The concept is a commonsense category in which 'society' is equivalent to the boundaries of nation-states. While sociologists in practice often operate with this everyday terminology, it is not adequate because societies do not always correspond to political boundaries (as in 'Palestinian society'). Some Marxists, in order to avoid this difficulty, have substituted 'social formation' for 'society', but in practice these two terms are equivalent. It is more useful to argue that sociology is the analysis of the social, which can be treated at any level (for example, dyadic interaction, social groups, large organizations or whole societies). See: *Sociology*.

Socio-Economic Groups. The Registrar General in Britain has classified occupations into S E Gs since the 1951 census. These contain people whose life-styles (q.v.) are similar with respect to social, cultural and leisure behaviour, and people are allocated to the various S E Gs on the basis of their occupation and employment status. There were originally thirteen S E Gs which increased to seventeen in 1961. There is a condensed version of six *socio-economic classes* which are described as (1) professional; (2) employers and managers; (3) intermediate and junior non-manual; (4) skilled manual and self-employed non-professionals; (5) semi-skilled manual and personal service; (6) unskilled manual. Sociologists rarely use these classifications in class analysis, however, and modern class theories distinguish different class boundaries. See: *Class*.

Sociobiology. Associated particularly with E. O. Wilson (1975), sociobiology attempts to explain the social organization of animals, including man, by reference to biological characteristics such as genetic constitutions and population constraints. While making a useful contribution to the understanding of animal nature, sociobiology so far has not adequately accounted for the additional properties of social behaviour that are created in human interaction and as the result of social structure. See: *Ethology*; *Nature/Nurture Debate*; *Organic Analogy*.

Sociodrama. A term used to describe events, usually games or rituals, that have come to have a particular symbolic significance for certain social groups or society at large; it is as if these events were dramas, watched, perhaps via the mass media, by a society. For example, it has been suggested that the coronation of Queen Elizabeth II unified British society. Similarly, cricket or football matches may dramatize social conflicts that might otherwise be really acted out.

Sociogram. Relationships among members of a group may be presented diagrammatically in a sociogram which plots, for example, who interacts with whom and who are the effective leaders. See: *Sociometry*.

Sociology. The term has two stems – the Latin *socius* (companion) and the Greek *logos* (study of) – and literally means the study of the processes of companionship. In these terms, sociology may be defined as the study of the bases of social membership. More technically, sociology is the analysis of the structure of social relationships as constituted by social interaction, but no definition is entirely satisfactory because of the diversity of perspectives which is characteristic of the modern discipline.

The study of society can, of course, be traced back to Plato and Aristotle in Greek philosophy, Ibn Khaldun in Islamic jurisprudence and to the European and Scottish Enlightenment (q.v.), but the term 'sociology' dates from the correspondence of A. Comte (q.v.) in 1824 and became more publicly used through his *Cours de philosophie positive* (1838). The sociological approach of C. H. Saint-Simon (q.v.), Comte, and H. Spencer (q.v.) was based on the optimistic belief that positivism (q.v.) would provide a scientific basis for the study of society. Sociology would discover general laws of social change similar to those found in Newtonian physics or Darwinian biology, but these aims proved overly ambitious. By the end of the nineteenth century, sociologists adopted far more limited goals for the new discipline.

For M. Weber, sociology would have to concern itself with the meaning of social action and the uniqueness of historical events rather than with the fruitless search for general laws. By contrast, E. Durkheim exhibited a far more confident view of the achievements of sociology, claiming that it had shown how certain moral and legal institutions and religious beliefs were the same in a wide variety of societies, and that this uniformity was the best proof that the social realm was subject to universal laws.

While Durkheim's research attempted to show that sociology was an autonomous and distinctive science of social phenomena, there is considerable disagreement with respect to sociology's place in the social sciences. Against Durkheim, it can be argued that: (1) sociology is not a separate discipline, but one that integrates the findings of economics, politics and psychology, since the social is not an autonomous datum but is constituted by the intersection of economics, politics, geography, history and psychology; (2) sociology is a perspective or a form of imagination which seeks to ground individuals and events in a broad social context, and this imagination is not peculiar to the discipline of sociology but is shared by historians, geographers, economists, journalists, etc.; (3) for some Marxists, sociology does not have a scientific status, because it has no definite object of analysis, no distinctive methodology and no scientific frame of analysis, and should be seen as an ideology (q.v.) appropriate to a particular stage of capitalist development.

Sociology is sometimes seen as the intellectual and often conservative response to the specific social problems which were produced by the French Revolution and the transition from a traditional to an industrial society. It attempted to measure and analyse urban poverty, political instability, mortality rates, disease, crime, divorce, suicide, etc.

However, the subject was also deeply influenced by Saint-Simon (q.v.), K. Marx and F. Engels (q.v.) in its analysis of social structure (q.v.), class (q.v.) and social change (q.v.). The philosophical and political inheritance of sociology is complex and no single tradition can be regarded as entirely dominant.

While there is disagreement about the nature of sociology, there is some agreement about its importance. A defence of the discipline could rightly claim: (1) it has contributed in detail, through numerous empirical studies, to knowledge and understanding of modern societies; (2) it raises important questions about the nature of individual responsibility in law and morality by studying the social context of action; (3) it has contributed significantly to developments in other disciplines, especially history, philosophy and economics; (4) it can be regarded as a new form of consciousness, particularly sensitive to the dilemmas of a secular, industrial civilization. See: *Sociology as Science*.

Bibl. Nisbet (1967); Coser (1971); Bottomore and Nisbet (eds.) (1978); Bilton *et al.* (1981)

Sociology as Science. A long-standing controversy in sociology is to what extent or in what ways sociology is a science. Sciences are commonly understood as having certain objectives and using particular methods to reach those objectives. Most fundamentally, they aim at causal explanation (by means of theories) of regularities in the natural world. They attempt to provide theories which in turn generate testable hypotheses. Theories, generalizations or even laws may survive this process of testing and become more and more firmly accepted, only being rejected if they are shown to be logically incoherent or if evidence piles up against them. One of the most important ways in which evidence is brought to bear on theory is by experiments, which can be repeated and which will often involve an attempt to quantify variables, provide techniques of measurement and apply mathematical and statistical methods to the results.

Many sociologists (often called positivists) believe that their subject has many of these features of sciences. They are interested in causal explanations of phenomena in the social world by confronting theories with empirical evidence which is often quantified. It is even said that certain types of causal modelling (q.v.) may be equivalent to the experimental method. It should be noted here that much practice in the natural sciences does not in fact conform precisely to this scheme. For example, it is often difficult to repeat experiments in the same form, while some branches of science, such as the theory of evolution in biology, do not use experiments in the strict sense. Even positivist sociologists, however, will concede that sociology cannot conform to the scientific method precisely. It is certainly very difficult to experiment with social behaviour in such a way that variables can be controlled precisely and experiments can be repeated.

There are, however, more fundamental objections to the view that sociology is, with some relatively minor exceptions, like the natural sciences. These objections are of two kinds. First, it has been argued that human beings cannot be treated in the same way as objects in the natural world because, among other things, they have the capacity to reason and to make active sense of their world. Sociologists, on this view, cannot aim to produce theories which give causal explanations of social behaviour but only ones which provide understanding, perhaps by the operation of *Verstehen* (q.v.). One extreme version of this position is provided by P. Winch (1958), who argues that social behaviour cannot be seen as causally regular behaviour but must be seen as rule-following behaviour. Sociologists do not causally explain, they detect rules. The second objection to the positivist view of sociology is that, unlike natural science, sociology cannot be separated from value judgements about social behaviour. Because sociologists are themselves members of the society that they study, they simply cannot make objective studies of society; they can only see social reality as it is filtered through a set of value judgements. See: *Causal Explanation*; *Empathy*; *Empiricism*; *Ethnomethodology*; *Experimental Method*; *Falsificationism*; *Grounded Theory*; *Hermeneutics*; *Hypothesis*; *Hypothetico-Deductive Method*; *Induction*; *Methodenstreit*; *Naturalism*; *Neo-Kantianism*; *Objectivity*; *Operationalization*; *Phenomenological Sociology*; *Positivism*; *Qualitative Analysis*; *Realism*; *Replication*; *Understanding Alien Belief Systems*; *Value Freedom*; *Value Neutrality*; *Value Relevance*.

Sociology of Development. This involves the analysis of the social and political effects of industrialization on Third-World societies. In the 1960s, the sociology of development was dominated by perspectives and assumptions drawn from functionalism (q.v.) and regarded industrial change as largely beneficial. In the 1970s, Marxist sociology (q.v.) emphasized the negative effects of capitalist industrialization by arguing that development programmes, which were financed by Western societies, did not necessarily result in economic growth or social improvement. See: *Capitalism*; *Centre/Periphery*; *Conver-*

gence Thesis; Dependency; Differentiation; Dual Economy; Imperialism; Industrialization; Internal Colonialism; Migration; Mobilization; Modernization; Nationalism; Peasants; Secularization; Social Change; Underdevelopment; Uneven Development; Urbanization.

Bibl. Bernstein, H. (1973); Hoogvelt (1976)

Sociology of Education. The main focus of British educational sociology in the 1950s and 1960s was on the contribution of education to social mobility and life-chances, social class differences in educational attainment and the explanation of these. Since the early 1970s the subject has developed in several ways. (1) School ethnographies provided descriptions of the social systems of schools, and drew attention to the significance of pupil–teacher interactions for educational attainment. (2) Reflecting the interest within mainstream sociology in accounts of ideologies, educational sociologists have looked at schools as agencies of cultural reproduction and purveyors of a hidden curriculum. (3) Feminist sociologists have recently begun to investigate the role of the school in reinforcing gender stereotypes among children. (4) Empirical research into teaching methods attempts to identify the effectiveness of different teaching styles. See: Bernstein; Class; Classroom Interaction; Classroom Knowledge; Cultural Capital; Cultural Deprivation; Cultural Reproduction; Educational Attainment; Hidden Curriculum; Intelligence; Life-Chances; Nature/Nurture Debate; Pedagogical Practices; Restricted Code; Sponsored Mobility; Stereotypes.

Sociology of the Family. This is the study of how human sexual reproduction is institutionalized and of how children, which are the product of sexual unions, are assigned places within a kinship system. Two issues have dominated contemporary sociological approaches to the family. (1) The relationship between types of family structure and industrialization has been debated. (2) Critics of modern family life suggest that a woman's place in the home compounds female inequality in society at large and that the modern family based on intimacy and emotional attachment in fact masks a system of exploitation of wives by husbands and children by parents. See: Conjugal Role; Demography; Descent Groups; Divorce; Domestic Labour; Extended Family; Marriage; Maternal Deprivation; Matriarchy; Nuclear Family; Patriarchy; Sexual Divisions; Symmetrical Family.

Bibl. Morgan (1975)

Sociology of Gender. The sociology of gender considers the ways in which the physical differences between men and women are mediated by culture and social structure. These differences are culturally and socially elaborated so that (1) women are ascribed specific feminine personalities and a 'gender identity' through socialization; (2) women are often secluded from public activities in industrial societies by their relegation to the private domain of the home; (3) women are allocated to inferior and typically degrading productive activities; (4) women are subjected to stereotypical ideologies which define women as weak and emotionally dependent on men.

There have been two major debates within the sociology of gender. The first has addressed the issue of whether gender is a separate and independent dimension of social stratification (q.v.) and of the social division of labour (q.v.). The second debate concerns the appropriateness of general theoretical perspectives for the analysis of gender differences and divisions in society. For example, one aspect of the debate is whether feminism is compatible with Marxism. See: *Class*; *Division of Labour*; *Domestic Mode of Production*; *Dual Labour Markets*; *Educational Attainment*; *Feminism*; *Gender*; *Maternal Deprivation*; *Mead, Margaret*; *Orientation to Work*; *Patriarchy*; *Sexual Divisions*; *Sociology of the Family*; *Stereotypes*; *Women and Work*.

Bibl. Oakley (1972; 1981); Barrett (1980)

Sociology of Health and Illness. This term is often preferred to the sociology of medicine (q.v.), because it reflects the theoretical interests of sociology rather than the professional interests of medicine. The sociological study of health and illness has the following features: (1) it is critical of the medical model (q.v.) and treats the concepts of health and illness as highly problematic and political; (2) it is concerned with the phenomenology of health and illness and gives special attention to how patients experience and express their distress; (3) it has been significantly influenced by the concept of the sick role (q.v.) but is also critical of this legacy; (4) it argues that modern societies have a residual conception of health, because the medical profession (q.v.) has been primarily concerned with illness; (5) it has been critical of the medicalization (q.v.) of social problems. In practice, there is considerable overlap between the sociology of medicine and the sociology of health and illness. See: *Clinical Sociology*.

Bibl. Twaddle (1982)

Sociology of Industry and Work. Industrial sociologists are mainly concerned with two issues: (1) to investigate the nature of the social relations involved in the production of goods and services, broadly to determine whether these are cooperative and harmonious, or conflictual; (2) to determine whether the tasks that people perform at work provide for the satisfaction of human needs.

Early work was heavily influenced by a Durkheimian perspective, that conflict was pathological rather than inherent, and a belief that the low morale of employees, interpreted as the result of uninteresting jobs and work that provided little opportunity to participate in a social community in the firm, was a major cause of conflict. Although associated with the old Human Relations movement, these views retain some influence with the recent concern in some quarters to 'humanize' jobs and to increase employees' sense of belonging to their companies. Sociologists broke with Human Relations in the 1960s to argue that employees did not have fixed or universal expectations of work, and that boring jobs and lack of community did not necessarily lead to low morale. The older approach was also accused of technological determinism, believing that technology was responsible for the nature of social relations at work and individual job satisfaction. A further shift of perspective occurred towards the end of the 1970s, with the revival of the Marxist view that capitalism contains an inherent conflict of interest between capital and labour and the parallel interest in M. Weber's belief that all modern organizations, whether in capitalist or socialist economies, dominate the individual. Interest now centres on the history of the social relationships involved in production, the labour process, managerial control systems and employee resistance, and the effects of technological change. Alternative forms of organizing the enterprise, such as industrial democracy, self-management and cooperatives, are also studied. The idea of human needs reappears with the notion of alienation. The position of women and ethnic groups in employment is a growing area of research.

In the course of this evolution, the scope of the sociology of industry and work has widened, from the focus on a restricted selection of factors internal to the enterprise that largely ignored labour markets, trade unions and management, to a more complete analysis of the structure of enterprises which also includes their social, economic and political environments. At its margins, the subject increasingly merges with mainstream sociology. See: *Affluent Worker*; *Alienation*; *Automation*; *Bureaucracy*; *Capitalism*; *Class Imagery*; *Collective Bargaining*; *Cooperative*; *Corporatism*; *Dual Labour Markets*; *Human Capital*; *Human Relations*; *Industrial Conflict*; *Industrial Democracy*; *Institutionalization of Conflict*; *Labour Movement*; *Labour Process Approach*; *Management*; *Managerial Revolution*; *Organization Theory*; *Orientation to Work*; *Paternalism*; *Pluralism*; *Privatization*; *Scientific Management*; *Socio-Technical Systems*; *Strikes*; *Technology*; *Trade Unions*; *Unemployment*; *Unionateness*; *Women and Work*.

Bibl. Hill, S. (1981)

Sociology of Knowledge. This is a branch of sociology often mentioned but only slightly developed. In its earlier stages it was dominated by the debate with the ideas of K. Marx, and K. Mannheim (q.v.), an early practitioner, spent much effort showing that forms of belief or knowledge could not all be explained by the economy or the class structure. Since Mannheim the subject has become defined very generally as the relation between knowledge and a social base. In much sociology of knowledge this relation is understood causally; social base produces particular kinds of knowledge. This point has been attacked by hermeneutics (q.v.).

Not a great deal of empirical work has been done in the sociology of knowledge itself, but there has been considerable activity in some of its branches, particularly in the sociologies of literature and science. The former typically asks how social institutions influence particular literary forms or novelists. In the latter, these macrosociological questions are left aside in favour, for example, of investigations of how scientists decide what is to count as knowledge. See: *Base and Superstructure*; *Critical Sociology*; *Discourse*; *Frankfurt School*; *Ideology*; *Marx*; *Marxist Sociology*; *Semiotics*; *World-View*.

Bibl. Merton (1957); Abercrombie (1980)

Sociology of Law. This field of sociology involves the study of how social conditions influence the making and enforcement of law. One controversy within the subject is between Marxist and Weberian sociologists concerning the relationship of law to the economy. For Marxists, the law ultimately serves the interests of the dominant class by, for example, protecting property rights, whereas M. Weber argued that a stable system of abstract, general law was a requirement of capitalism. Symbolic interactionists have also argued that sociologists should not study why people break laws but why the laws are made in the first place. See: *Criminal Statistics*; *Criminology*; *Deviant Behaviour*; *Durkheim*; *Ideological State Apparatus*; *Labelling*; *Legitimacy*; *Natural Law*; *Property*; *State*; *Symbolic Interactionism*.

Bibl. Reasons and Rich (eds.) (1978)

Sociology of the Mass Media. Three main issues currently preoccupy practitioners in this subject. (1) The study of media messages is a major concern and various approaches have been suggested. However, there are still no widely agreed procedures as to the proper methods of analysing the content of, say, television programmes. (2) One way of understanding how particular messages are produced is to study media institutions and personnel. There have been many investigations of the ownership and control of newspapers and television companies and of the background, education, and basic assumptions of journalists in these media. (3) Studies of audiences have not been so common in recent years, although most investigations of the mass media do speculate as to the effects of the media on the audience. In work done after the Second World War, audiences were thought to be passive while the media were all-powerful. This view was replaced by an account of audiences as active, selecting and often rejecting media opinions. More recent work suggests some compromise between these two. See: *Content Analysis*; *Discourse*; *Dominant Ideology Thesis*; *Ideological State Apparatus*; *Ideology*; *Mass Society*; *Semiotics*.

Bibl. Gurevitch *et al.* (eds.) (1982)

Sociology of Medicine. Although medical sociology emerged rather late in the 1950s as a specialized area of sociology, it has subsequently developed rapidly, partly because the medical profession has recognized the importance of sociology in the education of medical students. There are now a number of important journals dealing with the subject – *Journal of Health and Social Behavior*; *Millbank Memorial Fund Quarterly*; *Social Science and Medicine*; *Sociology of Health and Illness*.

Medical sociology covers a variety of topics: (1) the sociology of the healing professions; (2) the sociology of illness, illness behaviour and 'help-seeking' behaviour; (3) medical institutions and health service organizations; (4) social factors in the aetiology of illness and disease; (5) social factors in fertility and mortality; (6) social factors influencing the demand for and use of medical facilities; (7) the sociology of doctor–patient interaction; (8) the social effects of different medical systems, such as between private and public provision of health care; (9) international patterns of illness and health services.

It is important to recognize a distinction between sociology *in* medicine and sociology *of* medicine as perspectives in research. The former involves the use of sociology to clarify medically defined problems and objectives, such as the nature of patient compliance to medical regimens. J. Roth (1962) claims that sociology in medicine exhibits a 'management bias', because research is guided by the dominant values of professional medicine. Controversial issues, such as medical malpractice, tend to be ignored. By contrast, the sociology of medicine has been more concerned with issues of power between doctors and patients, and between medicine and the state. For example, writers like I. Illich (1977) have drawn attention to the issue of iatrogenesis, that is, the risks to human health brought about by medical intervention itself. Medicalization (q.v.) has produced dependency on antibiotics, amphetamines and barbiturates which can be harmful to health. In the USA in 1979, for example, there were 65 million prescriptions for tranquillizers written by physicians. There has been a corresponding shift in paradigms from symbolic interactionism (q.v.) and functionalism (q.v.), which neglected the politics of medicine, to various Marxist paradigms which adopt a far more critical perspective on health service organizations and healing professions. Another radical perspective on medicine has come from feminism (q.v.) which regards inequalities in health provision and differences in illness behaviour as the products of patriarchy (q.v.) and gender (q.v.). Feminist critics have argued: (1) that modern medicine converts women into 'natural' patients by regarding women as emotional and complaining; (2) modern surgery often inflicts unnecessary procedures on women as patients (such as mastectomy and hysterectomy) where the benefit of these operations is uncertain; (3) modern obstetrics prevents women from exercising some control over the birth of their children; (4) medicine in general prevents women from having control over their bodies (especially with respect to reproduction). These critical perspectives in contemporary medical sociology argue that the health of human populations is not a consequence of medical intervention but of the sociopolitical environment. See: *Clinical Sociology*; *Demography*; *Epidemiology*; *Gerontology*; *Sick Role*; *Sociology of Health and Illness*.

Bibl. Mechanic (1968); Navarro (1977); Mumford (1983)

Sociology of Race. Since sociologists do not believe that the biological notion of 'race' has any relevance to the study of human society, the first task of this branch of sociology has been to deny the scientific validity of the 'race' concept, and many sociologists prefer 'race relations' or 'ethnic relations' as the description of their field of inquiry. The sociology of race relations comprises the following issues: (1) the study of racialist ideologies which suggest that social inequality between ethnic groups is caused by genetic endowment; (2) the analysis of the structures which support racism and racialist ideologies; (3) the study of the interaction between social class and ethnicity in social stratification, giving rise to both vertical and horizontal segments in the social structure of societies; (4) the historical inquiry into

the origins of race and racism, with special reference to colonialism and anti-colonialism; (5) the study of the location of ethnic groups within the labour market; (6) the contribution of these social, historical and cultural factors to the contemporary inequality between ethnic communities within industrial society. A major recent debate has been whether ethnicity is a separate and independent dimension of social stratification, or whether it can be subsumed under status, prestige or social class. Race relations research in Britain has sometimes been criticized for viewing ethnic cultures primarily from the perspective of the dominant culture and unwittingly sanctioning popular white stereotypes of coloured minorities, and for neglecting white racism institutionalized in economic and political structures. See: *Accommodation*; *Assimilation*; *Caste*; *Dual Labour Markets*; *Ethnic Group*; *Ghetto*; *Heredity*; *Imperialism*; *Intelligence*; *Internal Colonialism*; *Plural Societies*; *Prejudice*; *Racism*; *Slavery*; *Social Closure*; *Social Stratification*; *Stereotypes*; *Stigma*; *Underclass*.

Sociology of Religion. In classical sociology, the study of religion was primarily concerned with two broad issues: (1) how did religion contribute to the maintenance of social order? (2) what was the relationship between religion and capitalist society? These two issues were typically combined in the argument that industrial capitalism would undermine traditional religious commitment and thereby threaten the cohesion of society. More recently, the subject has been narrowly defined as the study of religious institutions. See: *Church*; *Civil Religion*; *Cult*; *Durkheim*; *Freud*; *Halévy Thesis*; *Invisible Religion*; *Millenarianism*; *Myth*; *New Religious Movements*; *Profane*; *Protestant Ethnic*; *Rationalization*; *Religion*; *Ritual*; *Sacred*; *Sect*; *Seculariza-*

tion; *Taboo*; *Theodicy*; *Weber*; *Witch-craft*.

Bibl. Turner, B. S. (1983)

Sociometry. This attempts to study small-group social relations using sociograms (q.v.) and is associated with the social psychologist J. L. Moreno. It has not proved influential in sociology. See: *Network*.

Socio-Technical Systems. This term was coined by members of the Tavistock Institute of Human Relations to describe their view that industry would operate efficiently only if both the social needs of employees, for satisfying tasks and group working, and the technical requirements of production were met simultaneously. Their research suggested that production technology could often be redesigned so as to meet social needs without any loss of technical efficiency. See: *Alienation*; *Human Relations*; *Labour Process Approach*; *Technology*.

Bibl. Hill, S. (1981)

Sorokin, Pitirim A. (1880–1968). Born and educated in Russia, Sorokin was exiled in 1922 and eventually came to the United States. He became the first professor of sociology at Harvard University in 1930. His main interests included: social mobility in *Social Mobility* (1927); assessments of sociological theory in *Contemporary Sociological Theories* (1928), *The Social Philosophies of an Age of Crisis* (1950), *Fads and Foibles in Modern Sociology* (1956) and *Sociological Theories of Today* (1966); and analysis of social change in *Social and Cultural Dynamics* (1937–41) and *Sociocultural Causality, Space, Time* (1943).

Spencer, Herbert (1820–1895). The principal feature of Spencer's sociology was its attempt to combine utilitarian individualism with an organic model of the evolution of social systems. Influenced by the biological theories of natural selection, Spencer used two separate versions of social evolution. First, he argued that social systems, like organisms, adapt to their environments by a process of internal differentiation and integration. Second, the evolutionary progress of societies was from simple homogeneity in 'militant' society to complex heterogeneity in industrial society. The political doctrine which Spencer derived from his sociology was that social planning, social welfare and state intervention interfered with the natural process of social evolution and progress, which guaranteed personal freedom in industrial society. Spencerian sociology is often associated with the principle of 'the survival of the fittest' and Social Darwinism (q.v.), but Spencer thought that competitive struggle was only dominant in early militant societies. An advanced industrial society would rely on cooperation, persuasion and altruism rather than aggression and conflict. Spencer contributed to the emergence of functionalism (q.v.), but little of his work has survived in contemporary sociology. See: *Differentiation*; *Evolutionary Theory*; *Organic Analogy*; *Social System*.

Bibl. J. Turner (1985)

Spiralist. This term describes the typical organization man (q.v.), whose upward career movement is a spiralling progression of new posts that involve frequent relocation around the country and abroad. C. Bell (1968) contrasts *burghers*, locally based middle-class people who stay in one place and run family businesses or professional practices.

Sponsored Mobility. R. H. Turner (1960) contrasted the British and American educational systems with respect to upward social mobility in terms of 'sponsored' and 'contest' mobility. Until the introduction of comprehensive schools, sponsorship in Britain involved the early identification of able children, by means of the 11 + examination, who were chosen to progress through selective secondary education and to attain high-level occupations. The American system delayed selection as long as possible, at least to the tertiary stage of education, and was seen as more egalitarian, because social mobility depended on a contest open to all. The notion has become dated with the abolition of selection in British state schools and the realization that mobility patterns in America and Britain do not greatly differ. See: *Social Mobility*.

SPSS. These initials refer to the *Statistical Package for the Social Sciences*, the most widely used standard computer programme for the analysis of sociological research data.

Standard Deviation. To measure the variability of any set of data, the standard deviation and its square, the variance (q.v.), are the most commonly used statistics. The standard deviation measures the spread of the distribution (q.v.) about the mean value of the data. It is calculated by measuring the deviation (x) of each datum from the mean, taking the squared value of each deviation(x^2), summing these squared deviations (Σx^2), dividing the sum of the squared deviations by the total number (N) of elements in the set to establish the average squared deviation, and extracting the square root to convert squared back into linear units. Thus the basic formula for the standard deviation (σ) is:

$$\sigma = \sqrt{\frac{\Sigma x^2}{N}}$$

In the analysis of survey data, it is important that the likely accuracy of a single sample estimate can be assessed, for which a measure of the variability or the fluctuations of the various sample estimates is needed. This measure is provided by the *standard error of the mean* (or the *proportion*, if the relevant estimates are proportions rather than means), which is partly determined by the standard deviation of the population. In practice, of course, population values are usually unknown and the actual standard deviation cannot be used. However, from any one randomly selected sample it is possible to estimate the likely average magnitude of sampling fluctuations (i.e. the variability) using the variability in the sample which is measured by the standard deviation of the sample. For large numbers, the sampling distribution (q.v.) of the sample mean is approximately Normal, and statistical theory provides procedures for assessing the sample results. See: *Sampling; Sampling Error; Significance Test*.

Bibl. Moser and Kalton (1979)

State. The modern state is a set of institutions comprising the legislature, executive, central and local administration, judiciary, police and armed forces. Its crucial characteristic is that it acts as the institutional system of political domination and has a monopoly of the legitimate use of violence. In various historical societies, the state was amorphous because the legitimate use of force was diffused; for example, to feudal lords, kinship groups or corporate bodies. The variety of institutions that comprise the modern state indicate that it may not always act as a unitary and homogeneous entity.

Sociological accounts of the state broadly fall into three categories. (1) There are those like M. Weber who see the state in capitalist and socialist

241

societies as an independent force that has its own rules of action – the legal-rational rules of bureaucracy – and dominates all social groups. (2) There are Marxist accounts of the state in capitalist societies which regard it as tied to the interests of capital and the dominant class. 'Instrumentalist' Marxism sees the state as simply an outpost of the dominant class because its personnel are drawn from this class. 'Structuralist' Marxism maintains that the state furthers the interests of capital or the capitalist class even though the state has relative autonomy (q.v.) of the class. (3) Pluralist accounts steer a middle course, regarding the state as a partly independent force which, via the workings of the democratic process, may still be influenced by the different interests that are represented politically. See: *Authority*; *Capitalism*; *Citizenship*; *Civil Society*; *Feudalism*; *Ideological State Apparatus*; *Legitimation*; *Miliband–Poulantzas Debate*; *Pluralism*; *Power*; *Pressure Group*; *Socialist Societies*; *Weber*.

Bibl. Poggi (1978); Parkin (1979)

State Capitalism. See: *Capitalism*; *Socialist Societies*.

Status. This has two sociological uses. (1) R. Linton (1936) defined status simply as a position in a social system, such as 'child' or 'parent'. Status refers to what a person is, whereas the closely linked notion of role (q.v.) refers to the behaviour expected of people in a status. (2) Status is also used as a synonym for honour or prestige, when social status denotes the relative position of a person on a publicly recognized scale or hierarchy of social worth. M. Weber employed *status group* as an element of social stratification distinct from class to describe certain collectivities distinguished from other social groups in a society by socially defined criteria of

status, such as caste (q.v.) or ethnicity. See: *Class*; *Prestige*; *Status Inconsistency*; *Stratification*; *Weber*.

Status Crystallization. See: *Status Inconsistency*.

Status Group. See: *Status*.

Status Inconsistency. In multi-dimensional systems of stratification, individuals may occupy inconsistent statuses. For example, individuals with a high level of educational attainment, which provides a high social status along one stratification dimension, may be employed in occupations that are poorly paid and carry low prestige, indicating low status along other dimensions. G. Lenski (1954) coined this term along with *status crystallization*, which denotes consistency between an individual's various statuses. He cites four important statuses: income, occupational prestige, education and ethnicity. Inconsistency is believed to promote resentment among individuals, who may therefore either favour radical social change designed to alter the system of stratification or attempt to crystallize their own statuses by changing their own personal situations (in the above example, by raising their occupational level). See: *Class*; *Prestige*; *Status*; *Stratification*.

Stereotypes. A stereotype is a one-sided, exaggerated and normally prejudicial view of a group, tribe or class of people, and is usually associated with racism (q.v.) and sexism (q.v.). Stereotypes are often resistant to change or correction from countervailing evidence, because they create a sense of social solidarity.

Sociologists have long used the notion in the analysis of deviant behaviour (q.v.), notably to explain deviancy amplification (q.v.), and of race relations. Recently it has been used in accounts of gender stereotyping in education and at work. Schools, it is claimed, reinforce gender stereotyping by socializing children into traditional male and female roles: school books depict girls helping mothers with domestic chores and boys helping fathers repair cars, for example, while teachers believe that boys are more suited to technical and scientific subjects and girls to domestic subjects, the humanities or biology, and instil these ideas in their pupils. At work, employers stereotype all women as being more likely than men to be absent from work or to interrupt their careers because of their family commitments, regardless of whether an individual woman employee in fact fits the stereotype, and have fixed ideas about what is appropriate 'women's work', thus denying women equal opportunities with men on the basis of the ascriptive criterion of gender. See: *Ascription*; *Dual Labour Markets*; *Prejudice*; *Socialization*; *Stigma*; *Women and Work*.

Stigma. A stigma is a social attribute which is discrediting for an individual or group. There are stigmas of the body (blemishes and deformities), of character (homosexuality) and of social collectivities (race or tribe). Stigma theories explain or justify the exclusion of stigmatized persons from normal social interaction. See: *Goffman*; *Symbolic Interactionism*.

Bibl. Goffman (1964)

Strata. See: *Sampling*; *Stratification*.

Stratification. Social differences become social stratification when people are ranked hierarchically along some dimension of inequality, whether this be income, wealth, power, prestige, age, ethnicity, or some other characteristic. Members of the various *strata* which constitute each level of the stratification hierarchy tend to have common life-chances (q.v.) and life-styles (q.v.) and may display an awareness of communal identity, and these characteristics further distinguish them from other strata. Sociologists normally identify three major types of stratification: caste, estate and class. There is some debate as to whether stratification is universal.

American sociologists have often argued that America does not fit the class type of stratification found in other industrial societies. There are a number of views. (1) Ranking is based on different criteria which include income, occupation, power, ethnicity, religion and education; individuals may have high status or prestige on some criteria but be low on others, producing parallel lines of stratification and making any structured stratification system unlikely. (2) The hierarchy is a single line, usually based on occupation, in which the income and prestige associated with occupations combine to produce a finely graded system containing a large number of strata with no sharp breaks between them. (3) L. Warner (1963) defined stratification in status terms and identified five or six discrete groups. Multiple strata, the importance of status differences, and exaggerated beliefs about the possibilities of individual social mobility in America, lead sociologists to assume that the life-chances, life-styles and collective awareness common in European societies are not characteristic of this system.

The *functional theory of stratification* was important in American discussions of inequality in the 1950s and 1960s. K. Davis and W. E. Moore (1945) asserted that in all societies there are positions that objectively have more functional importance than others, and need special skills if they are to be performed adequately. These skills, however, are in short supply, because talent is scarce and training is costly of people's time and resources. So there must be adequate rewards to induce the right people to develop their skills. Such rewards are typically a mix of monetary inducements and high social status or prestige. Stratification is universal and results from the need to fill positions of functional importance. It should be noted that Davis and Moore recognized that the existence of inherited wealth and property might prevent a tight relationship between material rewards and functional importance, and also that they made fewer assumptions than other functionalists about a social consensus of occupational importance. T. Parsons (1953, and in two papers originally published in 1949 and reprinted in Parsons (1954)), developed a theory of stratification that contained a number of assumptions. (1) Achievement values had replaced ascriptive criteria in industrial societies, and a merit system placed people in occupations. (2) Occupations were arranged in a hierarchy of material rewards and social prestige according to their functional importance to society, that is, their capacity for producing some service or good required by society. (3) High rewards were necessary to motivate people to do functionally important jobs. (4) There was a social consensus about the importance of occupations.

Functionalist accounts were criticized in a long-running debate popularly referred to as the *Davis–Moore debate*, despite the fact that some of the positions under attack cannot be attributed to these authors. The main contributions have been collected into one volume edited by R. Bendix and S. M. Lipset (1966). Various criticisms include the following: that functional importance cannot be specified and the theory is circular, because high-paying jobs are defined as functional simply because they are high paying; that conflict and power as aspects of stratification are under-

emphasized; that the significance of wealth and property is ignored; that the extent to which inequality reflects achievement is exaggerated; that the consensual element is overemphasized; that the theory favours social stability rather than change; that it ignores the inheritance of class position. The theory has been exposed as an ideological justification of existing patterns of inequality in America that was concerned to deny the reality of social class. Within the last decade class analysis has emerged in America, influenced by Marxist sociology. See: *Caste*: *Class*; *Estate*; *Functionalism*; *Prestige*; *Status*; *Status Inconsistency*; *Teleology*.

Bibl. Parkin (1978)

Strikes. Industrial sociologists regard strike action, the refusal of employees collectively to continue working, as an instance of industrial conflict and are mainly concerned with this broader phenomenon rather than strikes as such. Researchers concerned with strikes as such have approached these in three ways. (1) Case studies, for example A. Gouldner (1955b), T. Lane and K. Roberts (1971), and E. Batstone *et al.* (1978), provide detailed ethnographic accounts of individual strikes. (2) Official statistics on strike activity are analysed to find trends over time and between different industries, often on a comparative basis among different countries. (3) Strike activity is taken as an indicator of something else, worker militancy and sometimes even class consciousness.

The second and third approaches face methodological and substantive problems. The methodological problem is that official strike statistics are known to be inaccurate. They depend on employers, often voluntarily, reporting stoppages and their causes, which leads to underrecording and misclassification. Unofficial strikes (those not sanctioned by a union) are notably prone to under-recording, particularly when the stoppages are of short duration or in countries where such activity is illegal. Different societies have different criteria of what counts as a strike: some exclude all small stoppages; others disregard 'political' strikes. Employers' perceptions of the causes of strikes are often highly contentious. Comparative analysis compounds inaccuracies because different national statistics are biased in different ways. The substantive problem is that strikes are not necessarily good indicators of workers' attitudes: strike activity also depends on contextual factors such as the efficacy of collective bargaining, managerial attitudes and behaviour, the organizational strength of unions, labour market conditions and the legal framework of industrial relations. Workplace militancy may not even show up in strike data if labour is powerful and managements give way without strikes. See: *Collective Bargaining*; *Industrial Conflict*; *Official Statistics*; *Trade Unions*.

Structuralism. This term is frequently used to refer to a particular style of sociological work, although it is not at all distinctive. At its most general level it simply refers to a sociological perspective based on the concept of social structure (q.v.) and the view that society is prior to individuals. However, the label is also used in a more specific sense for those theorists who hold that there are a set of social structures that are unobservable but which generate observable social phenomena. The best-known exponent of this position is the anthropologist, C. Lévi-Strauss (q.v.), who is a member of an intellectual movement, particularly in France, that embraces anthropology, sociology, linguistics and literary criticism. He holds that cultural forms, especially myths, typically take the form of the combination of opposite qualities, called

binary oppositions, such as sweet and sour or red and green. Analysis of myths, and by extension of literary texts, takes the form of showing what binary oppositions are manifested. For Lévi-Strauss, explanation of the form of myths is to be found in unvarying qualities (structures) of the human mind. Certain Marxists, particularly L. Althusser (q.v.), have adopted a structuralist framework in seeking to explain social phenomena by reference to the underlying structures of the mode of production (q.v.). These contemporary structuralist positions have been heavily criticized as ahistorical, unverifiable, and neglectful of human creative activity. See: *Agency and Structure*; *Althusser*; *Barthes*; *Foucault*; *Myth*; *Realism*.

Bibl. Keat and Urry (1975); Bottomore and Nisbet (1978a)

Structuration. This is a concept, employed by A. Giddens (q.v.), which expresses the mutual dependency, rather than opposition, of human agency and social structure. Social structures should not be seen as barriers to action and as repressive of the agent's ability to act, but are intimately involved in the production of action. The structural properties of social systems provide the means by which people act and they are also the outcomes of those actions. Giddens has been criticized in a number of respects, chiefly for a failure to provide empirical illustration. See: *Agency and Structure*; *Social Structure*.

Bibl. Giddens (1979)

Subculture. This is a system of values, attitudes, modes of behaviour and life-styles of a social group which is distinct from, but related to the dominant culture of a society. In modern society there are a great diversity of such subcultures, but the concept has been of most use in sociology in the study of youth and deviancy. For example, it has been argued that delinquent or criminal subcultures provide a solution to the problems faced by their members, who find in membership of a subculture some compensation for their 'failure' in conventional society. Youth cultures (q.v.), which are often treated as deviant, develop around the adoption of styles of dress or music that differentiate them from others. Some analysts see this as expressing an opposition to the dominant culture. There are two central analytical problems with the concept. (1) It is not clear what are the main determinants of subcultures. It has been argued, for example, that most contemporary subcultures are in fact manifestations of working-class deviation from the culture of the dominant class. (2) The concept implies the existence of an identifiable dominant culture, but the fragmentation of contemporary culture makes the identification of such a common or dominant culture problematic. See: *Culture*; *Deviant Behaviour*; *Gang*; *Popular Culture*.

Bibl. Brake (1980)

Subject/Subjectivity. The concept of 'the subject' in contemporary structuralism (q.v.) has a paradoxical and contradictory significance. The subject implies agency, action and authorship, but also subjection. While the term is often used synonymously with 'the person' or 'the actor', it has the merit of bringing out the complexity of the debate over determinism (q.v.), since 'the subject' suggests both agency and subjection. In structuralist theories of literature, the text is analysed as a product which is independent of the author (subject). In contemporary Marxism, the function of ideology (q.v.) is to constitute subjects as the occupants of roles and bearers of social structures. Both perspectives thus deny

the creative agency of human subjects.

'Subjectivity' is the self-conscious awareness of subjects, but it is also suggested in structuralism that subjectivity is a mode of awareness which is historically specific to modern Western culture. Recent developments in psychoanalysis, Marxism and structuralism have brought into question most traditional assumptions about subjective agency and the primacy of subjectivity. Subjectivity and self-consciouness are, in these approaches, no longer seen as innate, a part of human nature, but as socially constructed in different forms in different societies. See: *Action Theory*; *Agency and Structure*; *Freud*; *Lacan*; *Methodological Individualism*; *Objectivity*; *Semiotics*.

Bibl. Benoist (1975)

Subsistence Economy. Also referred to as a 'self-sufficient economy' or 'natural economy', economic subsistence is characterized by the following: (1) the unit of production, such as the peasant family, produces for its own immediate consumption; (2) the unit does not depend on the market for consumption; (3) there is little specialization or division of labour. The subsistence economy is regarded as typical of pre-capitalism or peripheral regions where capitalism has not penetrated. It is thus defined by the absence of economic exchange within a market. The concept has been criticized, since so-called 'self-sufficient' economies do in fact buy and sell on the market. Subsistence economies are thus in reality dependent on external market forces, which in the modern world force them into dependency (q.v.).

See: *Peasants*; *Underdevelopment*.

Sub-system. See: *Parsons*; *Social System*.

Suburban Way of Life. It has been argued that those who live in suburbs have a distinctive way of life, described as quasi-primary, involving close, almost family-like, relationships with neighbours and friends. Early work suggested that this way of life was in some way caused by suburban location. However, it is clear that it rather depends on social class and stage in the life-cycle. See: *Metropolitan Fringe*; *Primary Relationship*; *Urban Way of Life*.

Bibl. Gans (1968)

Suicide. A major sociological tradition derives from E. Durkheim's theory that suicide rates and different types of social context are related, in particular that suicide is related to the level of social integration so that increased disintegration leads to increased numbers of suicides. Three other characteristics of Durkheim's works have also been adopted: (1) a concern with aggregate rates of suicide rather than individual acts and motives; (2) a positivistic approach that relates suicide rates to 'objective', external variables; (3) the use of government statistics as the data source. M. Halbwachs (1930) concluded that Durkheim's analysis could be simplified to an inverse relationship between social complexity and suicide rates, demonstrated by the fact that suicides were lower in rural areas where life-styles were simpler than in towns. Modern theories usually assume that rapid changes of socio-economic status are the cause of suicide, though unlike Durkheim they include various psychological factors to explain why only certain individuals commit suicide in these circumstances. Outside the Durkheimian tradition, 'ecological' accounts such as R. Cavan's (1928) also focus on social disorganization, which is conceptualized in terms of population variables such as high rates of social mobility and social complexity that weaken the influence of social values on individuals.

The devastating criticisms of sociological theories made by J. B. Douglas (1967) indicate that existing accounts lack foundation and are misguided. He shows that official statistics are highly inaccurate and systematically biased in ways that support disintegration theories: suicides are more accurately reported in towns than rural areas, highly integrated groups are more likely than poorly integrated ones to conceal suicides by ensuring that other causes of death are recorded; the medical competence of those who categorize deaths for official purposes varies and may be assumed to be greater as societies modernize (and grow more complex). Thus Durkheimian and ecological theories simply and uncritically reproduce the distortions inherent in official statistics. Existing theories are also misguided, because they impute social meanings to suicide such as 'egoistic' and 'anomic' acts that are based merely on untested commonsense judgements and ignore the actual meanings for those involved. In Douglas's view, particular social acts like suicides cannot be explained by abstract social meanings such as values favouring suicide. See: *Durkheim*; *Official Statistics*; *Social Pathology*.

Bibl. Atkinson, J. M. (1980)

Superstructure. See: *Base and Superstructure*.

Surplus Value. In Marxist analysis, this is the value remaining when the worker's daily costs of subsistence have been subtracted from the value that he produces. Let say the worker has a working day of ten hours. In a portion of this, say eight hours, the worker will produce goods of a value equal to his costs of subsistence. In the two hours remaining the worker will be creating surplus value, which is appropriated by the capitalist. For K. Marx, this theory provided an account of exploitation in capitalist societies, but it has been criticized: (1) there is no absolute definition of necessary labour time, because the costs of subsistence vary from society to society; (2) the labour theory of value (q.v.) is deficient. See: *Labour Power*; *Marx*; *Marxist Sociology*.

Survey. Survey research is the systematic gathering of information about individuals and collectivities, using interview or mail questionnaire methods to elicit information directly and interpreting the resulting data by means of statistical analysis. It provides an alternative to the experimental method (q.v.) or participant observation (q.v.) and is widely used in sociology. Surveys may use sampling (q.v.) in order that inferences may be made from the sample to a wider population with a known degree of accuracy, as in government surveys and the investigation of public opinion. When the populations are small, sociological surveys may cover whole groups rather than samples. Even when taking a sample from a wider population sociologists may treat the sample as a self-contained whole and may not attempt to generalize to the wider population from the sample. Surveys may be used in case-study (q.v.) research.

The purpose of surveying may be description or causal analysis. Large-scale descriptive surveys have a long history in social research, including two notable surveys of poverty in Britain in the 1890s, C. Booth's *Life and Labour of the People in London* (1889–91) and B. S. Rowntree's *Poverty: a Study of Town Life* (1902) based on York, and the national sample surveys carried out by government such as the *New Earnings Survey* and *Family Expenditure Survey* in Britain.

Sociologists are often less interested in description as such than in charting relationships among variables and the analysis of causation. This interest influences the design of surveys, but its main effect is on the data analysis; whereas descriptive surveys mainly analyse their findings as percentage frequency counts which are presented in a tabular form, sociologists are more likely to use various statistical techniques of multivariate analysis (q.v.) or engage in causal modelling (q.v.) in order to test theoretical hypotheses. A recent trend has been the re-analysis of existing surveys – rather than designing and administering their own surveys, a number of sociologists have used modern statistical techniques for the causal analysis of survey material collected by others. This poses problems when, as is often the case, the aims of the original survey differ from those of the re-analyst. See: *Booth*; *Interview*; *Mass Observation*; *Public Opinion*; *Questionnaire*.

Bibl. Moser and Kalton (1979)

Survival of the Fittest. See: *Evolutionary Theory*; *Organic Analogy*; *Social Darwinism*; *Spencer*; *Urban Ecology*.

Symbol. Any gesture, artefact, sign or concept which stands for, signifies or expresses something else is a symbol. The study of symbols is important because they are public and convey shared emotions, information or feeling, and may therefore function for social cohesion and commitment. However, they may also have social dysfunctions representing social conflicts and, like ritual (q.v.), 'symbol' is often defined so broadly that it includes all human culture.

Symbolic Interactionism. In the 1970s, this was seen to be a major alternative to functionalism (q.v.) and social systems theory, especially as developed by T. Parsons, which then formed the dominant paradigm (q.v.) in American sociology. In addition, this approach was important in sociology as a critique of positivism (q.v.). It has its intellectual roots in the concept of the self as developed by G. H. Mead (q.v.), who argued that reflexivity was crucial to the self as a social phenomenon. Social life depends on our ability to imagine ourselves in other social roles, and this taking the role of the other depends on our capacity for an internal conversation with ourselves. Society was conceived by Mead as an exchange of gestures which involves the use of symbols. Symbolic interactionism is thus the study of the self–society relationship as a process of symbolic communications between social actors. The perspective has made important contributions to the analysis of role (q.v.), socialization (q.v.), communication and action. It has been particularly influential in the sociology of deviance for the concept of career (q.v.) in the study of criminal behaviour (q.v.). The interactionist perspective provided the theoretical basis for labelling theory (q.v.), stereotypes (q.v.) and stigma (q.v.). It has been valuable in medical sociology for the study of doctor–patient interaction and the sick role (q.v.). While Mead emphasized his social objectivism (society has an objective existence and is not merely the subjective awareness of actors), modern symbolic interactionism tends to see society as emerging from the infinite transactions of social actors, and it has been criticized for failing to give sufficient weight to the objective restraints on social action. See: *Action Theory*; *Chicago School*; *Ethnomethodology*; *Dramaturgical*; *Goffman*; *Symbol*.

Bibl. Rock (1979)

Symmetrical Family. A term employed by Young and Willmott (1973) to describe the family form which they believe is emerging in modern Britain. There are

three characteristics of the symmetrical family. (1) Husband and wife, especially when children are young, are centred on the home. (2) The extended family (q.v.) counts for less and the nuclear family (q.v.) for more. (3) There is less division of labour between husband and wife in domestic work. Men are taking more responsibility for housekeeping and childcare, and married women are working outside the home rather more.

The symmetrical family represents a third stage in the development of the family. In the first stage, the family was the unit of production, with all family members working together in home and field. Stage two, corresponding to industrialization, saw a disruption of the family unit with men working outside the home, women confined to the home as domestic workers, and children in compulsory schooling. The symmetrical family represents a reuniting of the family, but around consumption not production. See: *Domestic Labour*; *Sociology of the Family*.

Systems Theory. This was the dominant paradigm (q.v.) in sociology in the 1950s and 1960s, being associated in particular with a group of social theorists centred around T. Parsons (q.v.) at Harvard University. Much of the early inspiration for systems theory came from an attempt to establish parallels between physiological systems in medical science and social systems in the social sciences. In Parsons (1951), a voluntaristic theory of action is combined with a systemic approach to two-person interactions. In later work, Parsons provided a general theory of social systems as problem-solving entities, which sought to integrate sociological theory with developments in biology, psychology, economics and political theory. Every social system has four sub-systems corresponding to four functional imperatives (q.v.), namely adaptation (A), goal-attainment

(G), integration (I) and pattern-maintenance or latency (L). These four subsystems can be conceptualized at various levels so that, for example, the basic AGIL pattern also corresponds to the economy, polity, societal community and institutions of socialization. In adapting to their internal and external environments, social systems have to solve these four problems in order to continue in existence, and they evolve by greater differentiation of their structures and by achieving higher levels of integration of their parts. Parsons attempted to show the validity of the systems approach through a diversity of studies – of the university, politics, religion and professions.

Although widely influential in the study of political processes, industrialization, development, religion, modernization, complex organizations, international systems, and sociological theory, the theory has been extensively criticized. The arguments against social systems theory are: (1) it cannot deal adequately with the presence of conflict and change in social life; (2) its assumptions about equilibrium and social order are based on a conservative ideology; (3) it is couched at such a level of abstraction that its empirical referents are often difficult to detect and hence the approach is of little value in actual sociological research; (4) its assumptions about value consensus in society are not empirically well grounded; (5) it is difficult to reconcile notions about structural processes and functional requirements with the theory of action which emphasizes the centrality of purposeful choice by individual actors; (6) the teleological assumptions of systems theory cannot explain why certain societies experience underdevelopment or deindustrialization; (7) many of the propositions of the theory are tautological and vacuous. For example, in the last analysis the existence of a social system is the only real evidence of its adaptation to its environment. In short, modern systems theory appears to reproduce all the essential weaknesses of nineteenth-century evolutionary theory (q.v.).

In the late 1950s and early 1960s, critics of functionalism (q.v.) and systems theory argued in favour of conflict theory (q.v.) as an alternative perspective. In the 1970s, Marxist theory, with its focus on change, conflict and contradiction, came to be seen as the major alternative to systems theory. However, there has been a growing recognition that: (1) Marxist theory itself is based on a concept of the social system; (2) systems theory is not inevitably tied to assumptions about static equilibria or to a conservative ideology; (3) there are models of systems other than those developed in the biological sciences, which do not depend on an organic analogy (q.v.). For example, cybernetic models of social systems provide an alternative to crude analogies between social and biological systems by examining the importance of information in exchanges between sub-systems. Further possibilities for the development of systems theory have been opened up by J. Habermas (q.v.) in the analysis of the *legitimation crisis* (1973) of contemporary capitalism. Systems theory does not in principle preclude notions of contradiction, conflict and change in the analysis of social systems. The consequence of these developments is that the concept of social system is not uniquely tied to any particular branch of sociology, but is a concept which is basic to all sociological paradigms. With the death of Parsons in 1979, there has been a revival of interest in Parsonian sociology, especially in Germany. In turn, this development has produced a re-evaluation of systems theory. See: *Social System*.

Bibl. Wallace (1969); Alexander (1982; 1984)

T

Taboo (tabu). The term, which came into the English language from Captain Cook's travels in Polynesia, refers to anything (food, place, activity) which is prohibited and forbidden. For E. Durkheim, observation of a taboo has the social consequence of binding a social group together behind common rituals and sentiments. The taboo is the symbol of group membership. Contemporary analysis of totemism (q.v.) has been revolutionized by C. Lévi-Strauss (q.v.) for whom the taboo is a message, a symbolic system, which gives expression to the interchange between nature and culture, animality and society. See: *Symbol*.

Taxonomy. This is a classification of phenomena as opposed to their explanations. For example, T. Parsons' (q.v.) notion of pattern variables is intended to offer a taxonomy of human action.

Taylorism. See: *Scientific Management*.

Technical Division of Labour. See: *Division of Labour*.

Technical Rationality. See: *Habermas*; *Rationality*.

Techniques of Neutralization. See: *Accounts*; *Delinquent Drift*; *Neutralization*.

Technological Determinism. This is the notion that social change is produced by changes in productive technique, such as the invention of the steam engine. The industrial revolution, in this light, is then simply a bundle of such techniques. Most sociologists regard such an account as misleading since it neglects the social changes that are necessary for technical inventions to be made and applied. See: *Industrial Society*; *Marx*.

Technology. In sociological usage, technology embraces all forms of productive technique, including handworking, and is not synonymous with machinery as in some popular accounts. In the sociology of industry, the term also includes the physical organization of production, i.e. the way in which production hardware is arranged in the place of work, and thus embraces the division of labour and organization of work that is built into or required for efficient operation by the production technique. Productive techniques and the organization of production are social products, the consequences of human decision-making, and so technology can

251

be analysed as the outcome of social processes.

Industrial sociologists in the Human Relations (q.v.) tradition focused on the relationships between technology and employee morale and alienation, specifically on the direct worker–machine interaction and on the influence of technology on work groups, both of which were shown to have some limited effects on morale. Recently, attention has turned to technology as an aspect of social class and class relations. Several Weberian theories of class see 'work situation' as a criterion of class position and technology as a major determinant of work situation. The Marxist labour process approach (q.v.) treats technology as a manifestation of the relations between social classes, arguing that new productive techniques which dominate and control employees are developed in order to alleviate the consequences of an inherent conflict of interests between employees (labour) and management (capital) in capitalist economies. In addition, research has been conducted on the social values of engineers and how these influence the development of technology. See: *Alienation*; *Automation*; *Class*; *De-skilling*; *Division of Labour*; *Labour Process*; *Scientific Management*; *Socio-Technical Systems*.

Bibl. Hill, S. (1981)

Teleology. Sociological explanations are teleological when they try to explain social processes, particularly processes of social change, by reference to an end-state to which they are alleged to be working, or to an ultimate function which they are said to serve. For example, A. Comte (q.v.) argued that human societies necessarily evolved to higher and higher states of civilization. T. Parsons (q.v.) and other functionalists are often said to be offering teleological accounts when they explain, say, systems

of stratification by reference to the 'need' which societies have for the efficient discharge of tasks. Thus the cause of a social phenomenon is said to be its effects on some other phenomenon, a circular or tautological explanation. See: *Functionalism*; *Stratification*; *Systems Theory*.

Bibl. Ryan (1970)

Theodicy. A theodicy in religion justifies divine justice, despite the existence of evil. The concept was used by M. Weber to explore how religious beliefs may legitimate social privilege or compensate the suffering of the disprivileged. The most frequently quoted illustration of a theodicy is

> The rich man in his castle,
> The poor man at his gate –
> God made them high and lowly,
> And ordered their estate.

Like charisma (q.v.), the term illustrates how sociology often takes its vocabulary from other disciplines. See: *Religion*.

Theories of the Middle Range. See: *Middle-Range Theory*.

Theory-Laden. A proposition or empirical finding is theory-laden if it is necessarily produced by, or only makes sense in the context of, a particular theory; it is not theory-neutral. Such propositions are already influenced by the theory that they are intended to support. Some sociologists argue that all sociological findings are necessarily theory-laden. See: *Objectivity*.

Bibl. Keat and Urry (1975)

Time Series. Data that are ordered in time, typically at regular intervals, constitute a time series. In sociological research, the most commonly used time-series data are derived from censuses or panel studies. See: *Census*; *Panel Study*.

Tocqueville, Alexis de (1805–1859). A French aristocrat who wrote on comparative political systems. He visited the United States in 1831–2 to examine the prison system. His views on the negative psychological effects of solitary confinement and the problems of comparative criminology (q.v.) were reported (with Gustave de Beaumont) in *On the Penitentiary System in the United States* (1833). His major contribution to political sociology was *Democracy in America*, which was published in two sections in 1835 and 1840. Tocqueville made a comparison between the highly centralized and powerful apparatus of the state (q.v.) in France and the decentralized democratic system of government in the United States. His primary focus in the first part was the principle of equality (q.v.), which eroded traditional distinctions of status (q.v.) and was the fundamental principle of modern societies. Although he admired the American system, he argued that the universal franchise would produce a tyranny of the majority, which would obliterate hierarchy, local differences and regionalism. He thought that in a democracy voluntary associations would be crucial as a counter-weight to the tyranny of the majority. In the second part, he considered the consequences of political democracy on religion, philosophy, art and science. While the egalitarian principle was dominant at the political level, he argued that American culture was thoroughly penetrated by individualism (q.v.).

In *The Old Regime* (1856), he reflected on the causes of the French Revolution, arguing that revolution (q.v.) occurs when there is a sudden improvement in social conditions or when there is a deterioration after a period of social improvement. He argued that the French Revolution was caused by the contradiction between the new principles of individualism emerging with the growth of trade, markets and a money economy, and the traditional principles of hierarchy and status characteristic of French feudalism (q.v.) and aristocracy. *The Old Regime* can also be regarded as an exercise in the comparative method (q.v.). The absence of a violent revolution in England was a consequence of the fact that the English class system was relatively open and fluid, without a rigid system of privilege. Reflecting on the Revolution of 1848 in France, Tocqueville came, in the posthumously published *Recollections* (1893), to a set of conclusions rather similar to K. Marx (q.v.), namely that the Revolution of 1848 was a continuation of the social processes underlying the Revolution of 1789, primarily the struggle by the working class (q.v.) for a new set of principles associated with democracy and equality. The development of a comparative political sociology can be regarded as an elaboration of the sociological studies of Montesquieu (q.v.). See: *Political Sociology*.

Bibl. Aron (1965c); Poggi (1972)

Toennies, Ferdinand (1855–1936). A German sociologist and a founder of the German Sociological Association, he is best known for his distinction between 'community' and 'association' which he elaborated in *Gemeinschaft und Gesellschaft* (1887). Toennies identified three separate branches of sociology: pure or theoretical, applied, and empirical. The distinction between 'community' (*Gemeinschaft*) and 'association' (*Gesellschaft*) constituted the core of his theoretical sociology. These 'fundamental concepts' were to guide empirical and applied sociology in the study of the transformation of society from communal to associational relationships. Although they are ideal types, Toennies wanted to use his pair of concepts to describe the historical transformation of Germany from a rural to an industrial society. He was influenced by the philosophy of A. Schopenhauer (1788–1860) and F. Nietzsche (1844–1900), from whom he adopted the notion of 'the will to life'. Toennies argued that social relations are the products of human will; he identified two types of will. Natural will (*Wesenwille*) is the expression of instinctual needs, habit, conviction or inclination. Rational will (*Kurwille*) involves instrumental rationality in the selection of means for ends. Whereas natural will is organic and real, rational will is conceptual and artificial. These forms of will correspond to the distinction between community and association, since communal life is the expression of natural will and associational life is a consequence of rational will. See: *Gemeinschaft*; *Ideal Type*; *Teleology*; *Rural–Urban Continuum*; *Urban Way of Life*.

Bibl. Atoji (1984)

Total Institution. E. Goffman (1961b) defined this as 'a place of residence and work where a large number of like-situated individuals, cut off from the wider society for an appreciable period of time, together lead an enclosed, formally administered round of life' (p. 11). Examples include prisons, mental hospitals, monastic settlements, boarding schools and work camps. Goffman's primary interest is in the inmate culture of such institutions, by which inmates adapt to and modify the formal system of surveillance. See: *Goffman*.

Totemism. A totem is a plant, animal or object which is the symbol (q.v.) of a social group, particularly a clan or tribe. The totem is taboo (q.v.). A totem animal or plant may be eaten on ritual occasions (the totemic feast), but otherwise it is carefully avoided as sacred (q.v.). In the 1950s, A. R. Radcliffe-Brown (q.v.) argued that totemism is essentially a system of classification with respect to the relationship between man and nature. This view provided the basis of structuralist interpretations in which totemism as a mode of classification provides an analysis of the structure of human thought. See: *Lévi-Strauss*.

Trade Unions. These are organizations of employees who have joined together to improve pay and conditions at work. Sociological interest in trade unions has a variety of foci. (1) The contribution that unions make to the institutionalization of conflict (q.v.) in society and industry. In this context, attention is paid to collective bargaining (q.v.), the extent to which union officials represent their members when they negotiate, and the likelihood that members will honour bargains. It is generally agreed that unions have been fairly effective in institutionalization, and Marxist sociologists criticize them for promoting among workers a commitment to reformism and piecemeal improvement that inhibits the development of a revolutionary class consciousness. (2) Trade-union democracy has been of concern since R. Michels (q.v.) claimed that union administrations inevitably developed into oligarchies that no longer represented members' interests. Oligarchic tendencies clearly exist, but modern research suggests that representativeness is maintained under certain conditions, notably when there are strong workplace rank-and-file organizations based on shop stewards. (3) The amount of power unions have to pursue members' interests is sometimes raised, with research suggesting that unions are normally weaker than employers, particularly large corporations, the precise power imbalance varying with economic conditions. (4) The relationship between unions and politics was debated in the 1970s, when the notion of corporatism (q.v.) was used to describe a certain political strategy regarding trade unions. (5) Marxists have been exercised by the effects of unions on the unity of labour, since occupationally based unionism, which once dominated Britain and America and still has some force, divides labour into segments that inhibit united action or consciousness. (6) A tendency has been to use union membership as an indicator of proletarianization (q.v.). Union membership as such bears no relation to class consciousness or proletarian social imagery, since the reasons people join unions range from ideological commitment to the labour movement, through a calculative assessment of the benefits unions bring, to coercion when closed-shop arrangements force people into unions against their will. However, sociologists sometimes argue that the rapid unionization of white-collar employees in Britain since the early 1960s reflects their proletarianization (q.v.). It remains unclear how much white-collar unionization has been influenced by this change in class position, since non-proletarianized occupations such as doctors, university teachers and top civil servants have also become union members on a large scale. See: *Citizenship*; *Class Consciousness*; *Class Imagery*; *Collective Bargaining*; *Industrial Conflict*; *Labour Movement*; *Leninism*; *Middle Class*; *Oligarchy*; *Strikes*; *Unionateness*; *Working Class*.

Bibl. Hill, S. (1981); Crouch (1982)

Tradition. In its literal sense, tradition refers to any human practice, belief, institution or artefact which is handed down from one generation to the next. While the content of traditions is highly variable, it typically refers to some element of culture regarded as part of the common inheritance of a social group. Tradition is often regarded as a source of social stability and legitimacy (q.v.), but appeals to tradition may also provide the basis for changing the present. The concept is important in sociology in making a contrast with modern society and in debates on the nature of authority (q.v.).

Bibl. Shils (1981)

Traditional Society. See: *Primitive Society*.

Transmitted Deprivation. See: *Deprivation*.

Typification. The great bulk of knowledge of the life-world (q.v.) is typified. That is, it refers, not to the individual or unique qualities of things or persons, but to their typical features. Typification refers to the process by which people typify the world around them. See: *Phenomenological Sociology*.

U

Underclass. It has been suggested that, in many Western societies, women and ethnic minorities are placed in the lowest-paid, least secure and most unpleasant occupations, and constitute under-classes. *Status* group characteristics – gender and ethnicity – are thus trans-formed into *class* attributes that relegate these groups to the bottom of the class hierarchy, separated from the working class as a whole by these characteristics. The concept has proved useful in illu-minating dual labour markets (q.v.) and the position of migrant workers in cer-tain industrialized societies. See: *Class*; *Sexual Divisions*; *Status*; *Women and Work*; *Working Class*.

Bibl. Giddens (1973)

Underdevelopment. Against the classical view that trade produces mutual advan-tages to societies involved in exchange, underdevelopment theory demonstrates that capitalist development retards in-dependent economic change in peri-pheral regions, because the conditions of exchange are unequal. The penetration of capitalism does not necessarily trans-form traditional society, but creates backward socio-economic conditions. Underdevelopment involves dependence on the export of raw materials and on manufactured imports. Because com-modities are subject to external price fluctuations, underdeveloped economies are exposed to inflationary pressures. Underdeveloped societies have small industrial sectors, combined with large backward sectors. Local markets are blocked by imports, low wages and low productivity. Underdevelopment theory is critical of modernization theory and Marxist development theory, both of which assumed the inevitability of capital-ist development. See: *Centre/Periphery*; *Dependency*; *Development*; *Dual Econ-omy*; *Imperialism*; *Internal Colonialism*; *International Division of Labour*; *Modernization*; *Uneven Development*; *World-System Theory*.

Bibl. Amin (1976)

Understanding. See: *Empathy*; *Her-meneutics*; *Rule*; *Understanding Alien Belief Systems*; *Verstehen*.

Understanding Alien Belief Systems. Insofar as sociology attempts to arrive at propositions which have general validity, comparative study of cultures is a necessary feature of sociological re-search. While some sociologists have adopted a thorough relativism (q.v.), most sociologists argue that valid know-ledge of other cultures is in principle possible, despite the difficult methodological problems which such knowledge involves. The problems of comparative understanding can be illustrated by two issues. (1) How can we know that what counts as X (honour, religion, madness, etc.) in our culture also counts as X in some other culture? (2) How can we know that a sociological explanation of X in our culture will be valid for another culture? Cross-cultural comparisons involve difficulties of identification and explanation.

Followers of philosophers like L. Wittgenstein and P. Winch have argued that understanding X in terms of the actor's own definition of the situation (q.v.) is the best way of avoiding misidentification, since we no longer impose our categories on their behaviour. However, this procedure can be criticized on two grounds: (1) it involves 'contextual charity' to such an extent that no behaviour or belief in another culture could ever be regarded as irrational once it is located in its appropriate cultural context; (2) sociologists and anthropologists often, regardless of their intentions, inherit frameworks (or discourses) which organize culture in such a way as to rule out any genuine understanding of the subjective experience of actors in other cultures. Good intentions not to impose alien categories are never in themselves sufficient to rule out bias. See: *Comparative Method*; *Cultural Relativism*; *Rationality*; *Rule*.

Bibl. Peel (1969b)

Unemployment. After three decades of relatively full employment, unemployment in advanced capitalist economies grew substantially from the mid 1970s. In 1986, the average rate in these developed countries was 8·1 per cent of the workforce according to OECD figures. The causes of modern unemployment are low economic growth-rates, structural economic changes such as higher productivity for each person employed and the decline of older, labour-intensive industries, and an increase in the size of the potential labour force as the result of population growth and more women seeking employment.

Unemployment statistics reflect the assumptions of those who collect the information as well as the actual number of people who may be regarded as out of work, and rates will vary according to how unemployment is defined and how the size of the workforce is calculated. In Britain, government made sixteen separate changes in the way the unemployment rate was calculated between 1981 and early 1986. The cumulative effect was to reduce both the numbers of people defined as being unemployed and unemployment as a proportion of the workforce. Official figures put unemployment at 3·3 million in the middle of 1986, that is 11·7 per cent of the workforce defined as including the self-employed. Using a different basis of calculating the size of the workforce, the OECD estimated British unemployment as 13·3 per cent. Whatever their basis, most figures on unemployment in Britain are likely to underestimate the numbers seeking work, or underemployed, for several reasons: (1) a number of workers, especially women, do not register when made redundant; (2) there is the so-called 'silent reserve', those who only start to look for work when the job market improves; (3) temporary employment schemes take increasingly large numbers out of the 'normal' labour market for a while; (4) many workers are underemployed by being on short-time working. It was once possible to conceive of unemployment as a 'flow': people flow out of work into unemployment, and then back into work after a short interval. This model still holds good for part of the unemployed population, but betweeen one-third and a half of those without work in the mid 1980s failed to find a job within one year: for them, the 'flow' petered out. Some groups are more affected by unemployment than others. The young, the old, the disabled, the low-paid, ethnic minorities, the unskilled and inhabitants of depressed regions are all disproportionately unemployed. In Britain, the growth of jobs for women, particularly in part-time work, has kept female unemployment reasonably low.

The social consequences of un-employment for those out of work include higher incidences of poverty, ill-health and death, demoralization, and strained family relationships. For society as a whole, they include the failure to realize the social investment in 'human capital' (q.v.) made through the educational system, and a loss of tax revenue combined with increased outgoings in unemployment benefits that threaten the financing of other parts of the welfare state. Some authors have argued that changes in the nature of industrial production, particularly the growth in automation and the increase in size of the service sector, will produce higher permanent rates of unemployment and that full employment is not possible. See: *Automation*; *De-industrialization*; *Official Statistics*; *Poverty*; *Women and Work*.

Bibl. Hawkins (1979); Daniel (1981)

Unequal Exchange. See: *World-System Theory*.

Uneven Development. The notion of 'combined and unequal development' was first employed by L. Trotsky and V. Lenin to analyse the uneven features of Russian capitalist development prior to the Revolution. They argued that capitalist development is not a smooth, upward trajectory from traditional to modern society by noting that pre-capitalist social structures are often conserved and reinforced by capitalist economic growth, and development is a contradictory and complex process. See: *Underdevelopment*.

Unintended Consequences. See: *Latent Function*.

Unionateness. This concept has been proposed as a measure of the commitment of employees' collective organizations to the principles and ideology of trade unionism. It defines the relevant characteristics of 'unionate' organizations in Britain as collective bargaining, willingness to take industrial action against employers (especially to strike), and affiliation to the Trades Union Congress and to the Labour Party. The concept has been used to compare manual trade unions with those of non-manual workers, the latter typically fulfilling all the conditions of union-ateness except party affiliation, though several do even this. It has also been the basis of comparison among non-manual organizations. such as unions, staff and professional associations. Some of these latter associations do display certain unionate characteristics, such as collective bargaining and a willingness to take forms of industrial action against employers. See: *Trade Unionism*.

Bibl. Blackburn and Prandy (1965)

Unobtrusive Measures. These research techniques are 'non-reactive' since they involve no interaction between the investigator and the population being studied, unlike research that involves interviewing, observation or even self-completed questionnaires. For example, the effect of changing the social conditions within a workplace might be assessed by company records of absenteeism, sickness and output rather than by direct investigation of the employees concerned. Unobtrusive measures can be used imaginatively in sociological research and are a useful addition to more conventional methods, but they do not entirely remove reactive error or subjective judgement.

Bibl. Webb *et al.* (1966)

Upper Class. The upper class can be distinguished from the middle class (q.v.) and the working class (q.v.) by its wealth, its coherence, and its power.

Wealth is unevenly distributed in the UK. The top 1 per cent of wealth-holders own one-third of the nation's wealth. This proportion has fallen considerably from an estimated two-thirds before the First World War, but in the 1980s the proportion has, if anything, actually increased. The upper class should be seen very much in terms of families. Wealth is apparently distributed among close family members, both by means of inheritance and by gifts designed to avoid taxes on death. Similarly, family background continues to be important in gaining certain upper-class occupations. For example, almost half of the bank directors listed in *Who's Who* in 1973 also had fathers listed there. Family and kinship give a certain coherence to the class, which is reinforced by similar educational experiences and continuing friendship and business contacts. For instance, three-quarters of clearing-bank directors studied in 1970 were from public schools and one in three was from Eton. These same people are likely also to have contacts in business, at least partly by means of interlocking directorships – the practice of companies having directors on each other's boards.

The way in which elite positions are interconnected by a variety of factors may also give the upper class real power. Those who hold senior jobs in business, politics, the civil service, the Church and the army, tend to have a similar educa-

tion, giving a similarity of outlook as well as frequency of contact. Those without these common experiences are likely to be socialized into the outlook of the class. It should be pointed out, however, that common origins and education do not, of themselves, *necessarily* mean common interests or common action, and little in fact is known about how holders of upper-class positions *actually* interact. See: *Class*; *Distribution of Income and Wealth*; *Elite*; *Management*; *Power*; *Prestige*; *Stratification*.

Bibl. Scott (1982)

Urban Ecology. The Chicago School (q.v.) introduced ecological theory into urban studies. It derives from the organic analogy (q.v.), specifically from the attempted application of C. Darwin's theory of natural selection to social life. The city is defined as an environment like those found in nature. All parts of the environment are interdependent and are moved by natural forces. The most important of these forces is competition. Competition between social groups for scarce urban resources, especially land, means that the best-adapted, the fittest, groups become dominant. Competition also forces societies to a greater division of labour which, by promoting more efficient social organization, provides greater adaptive capacity. The competitive struggle also tends to create numbers of sub-environments or natural areas (q.v.) within the city. Each of these areas is occupied by a distinctive social group which has adapted to it in much the same way as a plant or animal species adapts to a specialized natural environment. The city tends to equilibrium (q.v.) and any disturbance is met by forces which restore equilibrium. One illustration of this is the process of succession. If a social group (defined largely by racial or national characteristics) leaves a natural area, its place will

259

be taken by another group, which will be subject to the same ecological forces, eventually even having, for example, the same rate of delinquency. Urban ecologists used their theory in a large number of empirical studies. The concepts of competition, natural area and succession are best illustrated in the concentric zone theory (q.v.).

The crucial assumption of urban ecology is that the social structure of the city is formed by underlying natural and impersonal forces. It suggests, therefore, that social structure is not greatly influenced by individual interventions such as planning. Culture also takes on a secondary role; ecologists argued that culture only had significance when ecological forces had already established an equilibrium. The neglect of culture, and the conviction that cities operated like environments in nature, formed the basis of a critique of urban ecology and ultimately its collapse. Although there have been attempts to revive ecological thinking, it has degenerated into the minute statistical examination of urban areas.

Bibl. Reissmann (1964); Saunders (1981)

Urban Managerialism. As codified by R. Pahl (1975), this approach in urban sociology concentrates on the role of various managers, for example council housing officials or building society managers, in the distribution of urban resources. Studies have been done on such managers, often concentrating on the values and ideologies which guide their decisions. The approach has been criticized because it tends to assume that urban managers are relatively independent and have freedom of action. More recent studies have stressed the way that managers are constrained by economic factors or by bureaucratic rules, and have limited independence. See:

Housing Class; *Rural–Urban Continuum*. Bibl. Norman (1975); Saunders (1981)

Urban Social Movement. A term derived from contemporary Marxist urban sociology and popularized by M. Castells (1977; 1978), urban social movements arise out of the politicization of access to various publicly provided and generally urban goods and services, for example, housing, education or transport. The argument is that the provision of these services necessarily becomes increasingly restricted – there is a crisis in collective consumption (q.v.) – which, after a period of active political organization, generates urban social movements in protest. Since a restricted access to collective consumption tends to affect all classes, urban social movements will be an alliance of classes. Class struggles promoted by urban social movements will not, however, engender fundamental change, if they have any effect at all, since that can only come from change in the ownership and control of the forces of production (q.v.). The concept has been heavily criticized as not being empirically productive. It is not clear how specific urban social movements are related to crises in collective consumption, most movements are not class alliances, and the term has been overgeneralized to include any urban protest movement, whatever its origins or effects. See: *Social Movements*; *State*.

Bibl. Pickvance (1976)

Urban Way of Life. In an article said to be the most widely cited in sociology, L. Wirth (1938) attempted to describe and explain a way of life peculiar to cities. For Wirth, cities have a whole range of features including the loss of primary relationships (q.v.), weaker social control, a great division of labour, greater importance of the mass media and the tendency for urbanites to treat each other instrumentally. These features are caused by three basic factors – the numbers, density and heterogeneity of the population. In this theory Wirth was faithful to the principles of urban ecology (q.v.) in holding that fundamental features of the urban environment produce the entire range of urban social behaviour. He has been criticized, firstly because empirical research showed that there was not one urban way of life but several, and, secondly, because it does not seem possible to derive all aspects of urban life from the three basic factors.

Other sociologists, G. Simmel (q.v.), for example, regard anonymity as the principal characteristic of urban life. See: *Chicago School*; *Division of Labour*; *Rural–Urban Continuum*; *Suburban Way of Life*; *Zone of Transition*.

Bibl. Morris (1968)

Urbanization. Urbanization refers properly to a growth in the *proportion* of a country's population living in urban centres of a particular size. Although cities have always been socially, politically and economically important, the urbanization of industrialized Western societies in the nineteenth century was very rapid: for example, in the United Kingdom in 1800 some 24 per cent of the population was urban, while by 1900 it was 77 per cent. For almost all these societies urbanization has followed an S-shaped curve, building up very slowly, expanding very quickly, and then slowing down, or even reversing slightly, with greater suburban development. The proportional increase in urban populations in the nineteenth century was largely by migration from the countryside. However, in contemporary underdeveloped societies, which are urbanizing even more rapidly, the increase comes rather more from simple growth in the urban population, as

public health and medical facilities have improved, and tends to be concentrated in a single city.

In general, periods of urbanization appear to be associated with industrialization (q.v.). There is, however, some controversy about the nature of the association and about the role that capitalism plays in the process. Urbanization has contradictory consequences for economic growth, since it cheapens the cost of providing services such as health and education while increasing the cost of labour that can no longer supplement its wages by small-scale agricultural production. See: *Demographic Transition*; *Industrial Society*; *Modernization*; *Rural–Urban Continuum*.

Bibl. Davis, K. (1967); Friedmann and Wulff (1975)

Use Value. See: *Labour Theory of Value*.

Utilitarianism. This social philosophy, associated with J. Bentham and J. S. Mill (though precursors such as T. Hobbes, J. Locke, and D. Hume are sometimes called utilitarians as well) placed the satisfaction of the individual's wants (utility) at its core. Consequently, the greatest good was defined simply as the greatest happiness of the greatest number of people. Its main impact on the social sciences has been via its model of social action in which individuals rationally pursue their own self-interests, and its conception of society as the aggregation of atomized individuals united by self-interest. Behavioural psychology and economics have been influenced by these conceptions, as has exchange theory (q.v.) in sociology. Sociology, however, has been more influenced by the French collectivist tradition that gave society greater weight than the individual and saw social order as the outcome of cultural traditions that were not reducible to individuals' interests, mainly via the work of E. Durkheim. See: *Social Contract*; *Social Order*.

Bibl. Parsons (1968c)

Utopia. K. Mannheim (q.v.) used this term to describe the beliefs of subordinate classes, expecially beliefs which emphasized those aspects of a society which pointed to the future collapse of the established order. By contrast, the ideology of the dominant class emphasized the enduring stability of existing social arrangements. While Mannheim suggested that utopian thought would not be characteristic of the twentieth century, some sociologists claim that modern pessimism over, for example, nuclear warfare represents dystopian thought – a collapse of civilization without a subsequent social reconstruction. See: *Millenarianism*.

V

Validity. See: *Reliability*.

Value. In Parsonian sociology, social order depends on the existence of general, shared values which are regarded as legitimate and binding, and act as a standard by means of which the ends of action are selected. The linkage between social and personality systems is achieved by the internalization (q.v.) of values through the process of socialization (q.v.). Values cannot be reduced to or explained by interests, biological need or class. Three criticisms of this interpretation of values are pertinent: (1) societies exist despite considerable disgreement over values; (2) values may be accepted pragmatically rather than normatively; (3) it disregards the constraining force of social structures.

In Marxism, value has an entirely different meaning in the labour theory of value (q.v.), where the exchange value of a commodity is determined by the labour time it contains. See: *Coercion*; *Consensus*; *Norm*; *Parsons*; *Pragmatic Acceptance*; *Social Order*.

Value Freedom. In sociology, this has a variety of meanings: (1) sociology can successfully exclude ideological or non-scientific assumptions from research; (2) sociologists should not make evaluative judgements about empirical evidence; (3) value judgements should be restricted to the sociologist's area of technical competence; (4) sociologists are indifferent to the moral implications of their research; (5) sociologists should make their own values open and clear; (6) sociologists should refrain from advocating particular values. See: *Objectivity*; *Value Neutrality*; *Weber*.

Bibl. Gouldner (1975)

Value Neutrality. While research topics, approaches and perspectives are selected according to the criterion of value relevance (q.v.), social science is not in a privileged position to pronounce on social values, because there is a logical gap between empirical evidence and moral actions. Empirical discoveries about the nature of poverty, inequality or suicide do not tell us what we *ought* to do. It is consequently argued that sociologists have to strive for value neutrality with respect to research and policy formation. Value neutrality operates at two levels: (1) at a personal level, sociologists should make clear their own values; (2) at an institutional level, sociologists should not use their professional status as teachers to dictate values to students.

There are three objections to this conventional account. (1) Despite personal declarations of neutrality, values may unwittingly obtrude in research. (2) It is not clear that neutrality, even in principle, is possible. (3) It is not always evident that value neutrality is desirable; on some questions nobody should be neutral. See: *Value Freedom*; *Weber*.

Bibl. Gouldner (1975)

Value Relevance. In M. Weber's discussion of the philosophy of social science, there is a definite but complex distinction between value judgement and value interpretation. As social scientists, sociologists have to avoid making *ad hoc*, personal value judgements on social phenomena and, in particular, they are not in a position to recommend courses of action by suggesting that their recommendations are necessary and inevitable deductions from objective facts. However, given that Weber thought sociology involved the interpretative understanding of social action, interpretation depends on value interpretation. The values of a social scientist determine which questions will be asked in any inquiry, which topics will be selected for investigation and which methods will be employed for gathering data. For Weber, value relevance operates at three levels. (1) There is philological interpretation which establishes the meaning of texts and documents. (2) There is ethical interpretation in assigning a value to an object of inquiry. (3) There is rational interpretation in which the sociologist seeks the meaningful relationship between phenomena in terms of causal analysis. The point of value interpretation is to establish the values towards which an activity is directed; it is not to judge such activities as either good or bad. See: *Objectivity*; *Value Freedom*; *Value Neutrality*; *Weber*.

Bibl. Freund (1966)

Variance. This is a statistical measure of

variability or dispersion closely related to the standard deviation (q.v.). The *analysis of variance* is a commonly used technique for the evaluation of differences among several groups.

Veblen, Thorstein (1857–1929). An American social critic who held university posts at Chicago, Stanford and Missouri but remained an outsider in the academic community. He developed an economic sociology of capitalism that criticized the acquisitiveness and predatory competition of American society and the power of the corporation. His best-known publication was *The Theory of the Leisure Class* (1899). In this he argued that the dominant class in American capitalism, which he labelled as the 'leisure class', pursued a life-style of conspicuous consumption, ostentatious waste and idleness. In *The Higher Learning in America* (1918a), he claimed that the universities were dominated by considerations of profitability, economic patronage, and self-interest, and had no commitment to true academic values.

In *The Instinct of Workmanship* (1914), *The Place of Science in Modern Civilization* (1918b) and *The Engineers and the Price System* (1921), Veblen optimistically suggested that engineers, who embodied the spirit of science and technology, would replace the parasitic leisure class. In *The Theory of the Business Enterprise* (1904) and *Absentee Ownership and Business Enterprise* (1923) he considered the distinctive features of US capitalism, namely the separation of ownership and control and the oligopolistic power of the giant corporation.

During the First World War, he published *Imperial Germany and the Industrial Revolution* (1915). He regarded warfare as a threat to economic productivity, which he defined as the production of useful commodities and services. Contrasting the authoritarian politics of Germany with the British democratic tradition, he noted that in Germany industrialization had not produced a progressive political culture. He contributed to the analysis of American diplomatic strategy in *An Inquiry into the Nature of Peace and its Perpetuation* (1917).

Bibl. Diggins (1978)

Verification. See: *Falsificationism*; *Significance Test*.

Verstehen. Usually translated as 'understanding', this concept has formed part of a critique of positivist or naturalist sociology. It is argued that sociology should not analyse human action from 'the outside' by copying the methods of natural science. Instead, sociology should recognize the meanings that people give to their actions. *Verstehen* is the procedure by which sociologists can have access to these meanings. The concept has come into sociology largely via the work of M. Weber, who defined sociology as being concerned with meaningful action. *Verstehen* consists of placing oneself in the position of other people to see what meaning they give to their actions, what their purposes are, or what ends they believe are served by their actions. For example, if sociologists wish to analyse the social circumstances of waving, they must have some basis for deciding which cases of flapping one's arm up and down are waving and which mean something else. Not to be able to investigate the meaning of the actions may be seriously misleading, in that actions might all be put together in one category when they actually belong in different ones. To some extent, the inspection of meaning involved here is simply an extension of everyday attempts to understand action.

However, Weber wishes to go further, by reconciling interpretation of action by *Verstehen* with causal explanation. It is not entirely clear what is meant here and interpreters of Weber have variously suggested that *Verstehen* merely generates causal hypotheses or that meanings can function as causes.

The use of *Verstehen* has been criticized from two points of view. On the one hand sociologists have argued that there is no way of validating *Verstehen* interpretations, while, on the other, it has been suggested that the attempt to reconcile causal and *Verstehen* analysis actually ends up by denying the actors' point of view. See: *Agency and Structure*; *Empathy*; *Ethnomethodology*; *Geisteswissenschaften*; *Hermeneutics*; *Meaningful Action*; *Naturalism*; *Phenomenological Sociology*; *Positivism*; *Rule*; *Social Structure*; *Understanding Alien Belief Systems*; *Weber*.

Bibl. Outhwaite (1975)

Vocabulary of Motives. See: *Accounts*.

Voluntarism. This term is applied to those sociological theories based on the intentions or motives of actors who are thus assumed to act 'voluntarily' and not as 'determined' by the social structure. Sociologists often dislike voluntaristic explanations, because in neglecting the role of social structure they appear to be anti-sociological. See: *Action Theory*; *Agency and Structure*; *Methodological Individualism*; *Parsons*; *Psychologism*.

Voluntary Associations. Participation in voluntary associations such as political parties, churches, trade-union and professional bodies has been regarded as integrating marginal groups such as immigrants and ethnic minorities into society. In America, voluntary associations are regarded as important elements in participatory democracy. As secondary groups, they bridge the gulf between the individual or family and the wider society. See: *Group*; *Pressure Group*.

Bibl. Ross (1972)

Voting. The social scientific analysis of voting behaviour in Britain and America has, since the 1950s, rested heavily on what is known as the *party identification* model. This suggests that voting patterns in elections are associated primarily with the socio-economic factors that form the basis of party loyalty via long-term political socialization, rather than being moulded by the political campaigns of parties at election time. The model has also focused on the social correlates of voting and the lack of understanding among most voters of all except the most important political issues. However, the outcome of any election will largely be decided by the minority of voters who do change their party allegiance or abstain.

For the first thirty years of the post-war era in Britain, as in many Western nations, the main influence on voting appears to have been the family: political socialization in the home means that people tend to vote like their parents. Class was also closely associated with voting: typically in the post-war period about two-thirds of the manual working class voted Labour and four-fifths of the non-manual, middle class voted Conservative. Parental and class influences are difficult to disentangle, since parental occupation is also a major determinant of the class position of offspring. The other important influence has been community: middle-class voters living in predominantly working-class communities are more likely to vote Labour than if they lived in a middle-class area; conversely, working-class voters in middle-class areas show some tendency to vote Conservative.

Other factors may be influential: fewer women than men vote Labour; voters under the age of forty-five are more likely to support Labour than other voters; religion is significant in Wales where Nonconformists tend to vote Labour or Liberal, and in Ulster, Glasgow and Liverpool where Catholics tend to vote Labour; regional imbalances are noticeable, with Conservative support far greater in the South than the North, and the reverse for Labour.

Since the mid 1970s, voting behaviour has changed. More people vote against their 'natural' class alignment, a process known as *class dealignment*. There has been growing support for the Liberal–SDP Alliance in the 1980s, which seems likely to transform British politics into a three-party contest. Even among the core supporters of the Labour and Conservative parties, there has been some *partisan dealignment*, a weakening of support for party policies. The party identification model has been challenged by two other theories that claim to account for these shifts. One group of authors suggests that voting should be viewed as a form of rational decision-making that involves choice based on an understanding of the issues; for example, I. Crewe (1981; 1982) and H. T. Himmelweit *et al.* (1981). P. Dunleavy and C. T. Husbands (1985) put forward a different account, the radical-structural model, which identifies the political correlates of recent structural changes in British society. They suggest that there are new constellations of interests which cut across traditional political ties. These include: whether people depend on public services such as transport, housing, health and social security, or make private provision; whether or not they are trade unionists; and whether they are employed in the private or public sectors of the economy. Manual workers who are not members of a trade union, work in the private sector, and own their homes have a low probability of voting Labour despite their class position. See: *Political Parties*; *Working-Class Conservatism*.

W

Wealth. See: *Distribution of Income and Wealth.*

Weber, Max (1864–1920). Weber is often regarded as the founder of modern sociology, because: (1) he provided a systematic statement of the conceptual framework of the sociological perspective; (2) he developed a coherent philosophy of social science, which recognized the essential problems of explanation of social action; (3) in a variety of substantive fields, he grasped the basic characteristics of a modern, industrial civilization; (4) through these empirical studies of modern society, he identified a number of key issues which have become the foci of the principal debates within the discipline; (5) his own life in many respects provides a forceful example of sociology as a vocation.

The details of Weber's life have been fully and sympathetically examined in an extensive biography by his wife, Marianne Weber (1975). Born in Erfurt, Weber grew up in a family context characterized by merchant wealth, liberal politics and Protestant pietism. Attending the universities of Heidelberg, Göttingen and Berlin, Weber completed his academic training by research on the history of commercial societies in the Middle Ages and on Roman agrarian history.

While Weber held professorial posts at Freiburg, Heidelberg and Munich, his teaching and research were interrupted by illness, following a mental breakdown in 1897. Despite this, his academic productivity was formidable. Weber has suffered in English translation from a highly selective and discontinuous publication of his work, much of which originally took the form of essays, papers, lectures and even speeches. However, the major German text, *Wirtschaft und Gesellschaft* (1922), published posthumously, has been translated in its entirety as *Economy and Society* in 1968.

The complex and controversial nature of Weber's sociology has been repeatedly illustrated by the contradictory interpretations of his work. Both the nature of his work and the diversity of exegesis can be examined by summarizing Weber's contribution to modern social science under the following topics: (1) philosophy of social science (1949; 1975); (2) rationalization (1922; 1930); (3) the Protestant Ethic thesis (1930); (4) Weber's relationship to Marx and Marxism (1922); (5) his analysis of power politics in relation to German society (1946; 1978).

(1) Weber's analysis of the methodological and philosophical problems of sociology is conventionally regarded as a form of Neo-Kantianism (q.v.). In

267

his early commentaries on the methodology appropriate to sociology, Weber denied: (i) that sociology could discover universal laws of human behaviour comparable with those of natural science; (ii) that sociology could confirm any evolutionary progress in human societies; (iii) that sociology could provide any evaluation of, or any moral justification for, any existing or future state of affairs; (iv) that sociology could develop any collective concepts (like 'the state' or 'the family') unless they could be stated in terms of individual action. Sociology had to aim at the understanding of the meaning of actions, on the basis of which sociology could work towards formal models or ideal types of action on a comparative basis. Concepts in sociology like 'bureaucracy' would have the same analytical status as those in economics such as 'perfect competition'. Sociology was not simply a subjective interpretation of action, because sociologists were guided by certain public norms (such as 'value neutrality') and their findings were open to academic scrutiny and criticism. Weber regarded statistics and social surveys as an essential aid to sociological research, but statistical data still had to be interpreted and evaluated. While Weber rejected as unwarranted the claims of positivism (q.v.) and Marxism, it is not clear from his actual studies of society that he fully adhered to his own methodological principles.

(2) Having denied the possibility of developmental laws in sociology, Weber implicitly presented rationalization as the master trend of Western capitalist society. Rationalization is the process whereby every area of human relationships is subject to calculation and administration. While Marxists have noted the prominence of rational calculation in factory discipline and the labour process, Weber detected ration-

alization in all social spheres – politics, religion, economic organization, university administration, the laboratory and even in musical notation. Weber's sociology as a whole is characterized by a metaphysical pathos (q.v.) whereby the process of rationalization eventually converted capitalist society into a meaningless 'iron cage'.

(3) One source of rationalization in Western societies lay in the cultural changes brought about by the Protestant Ethic. Protestantism was not a direct cause of capitalism, but it did provide a culture which emphasized individualism, hard work, rational conduct and self-reliance. This ethic had an 'affinity' with early capitalism, but Weber thought that advanced capitalist societies would no longer require any religious legitimation.

(4) It is conventional to regard Weber as one of the major critics of Marx and Marxism. The reasons for this position are: (i) Weber's emphasis on the role of culture, especially religion, in shaping human action appears to be a refutation of economic determinism (q.v.); (ii) the importance of subjective orientation of individuals in Weber's analysis of social relations is said to be in contrast to the analysis of objective structural effects in Marxism; (iii) Weber's account of status groups and markets appears to run counter to Marx's emphasis on economic class and relations of production; (iv) Weber was explicitly critical of Marxist analyses of the imminent collapse of capitalism, since Weber argued that the planned economy in socialist society would enhance rationalization, not terminate it. An alternative view is that: (i) Weber regarded Marx, along with Nietzsche, as one of the most important thinkers of the nineteenth century; (ii) Weber's criticisms were directed at institutionalized Marxism (in the form of the German Democratic Party) rather than at Marx; (iii) the Protestant Ethic

thesis was not intended to be a refutation of Marx; (iv) Weber often wrote in a manner that suggests a strong element of determinism; (v) Weber's description of the nature of capitalism as an 'iron cage' was often very close to Marx's analysis and, in particular, there is a close relationship between the concepts of alienation (q.v.) and rationalization; (vi) Weber came to regard capitalist society as having a logic which operated independently of the subjective attitudes of social actors.

(5) Weber's sociology and his attitude towards Marxism have to be seen in the context of German society between 1870 and 1918. For Weber, Germany lacked an independent, politically educated middle class, while the working class was underdeveloped, partly because of the late development of industrialization. The political and economic development of Germany had been brought about by a strong state under Bismarck and political power rested in the hands of the feudal land-owning class of Junkers. With the death of Bismarck, the German bureaucracy and state lacked leadership, which neither the middle nor working class could provide. This political vacuum partly explains the importance of power and power-conflicts in Weber's writing on authority and charisma (q.v.). There are basically two responses to Weber's political sociology. (i) Marxists tend to regard Weber's analysis of German politics as a precursor of fascism. (ii) Liberals suggest that Weber's sociology is in fact grounded in an anxiety that rationalization will destroy individual freedom and creativity. There is evidence for both views since Weber thought Germany would require strong state leadership to beat off the economic threat posed by the United States and Great Britain, but he also sought to encourage a situation in which the importance of the individual could be maximized. The debate about the political implications of Weber's sociology has continued to be important in modern Germany, while controversy about his contribution to contemporary sociology continues unabated.

Weber also contributed to the sociology of comparative religions (1951; 1952; 1958a), urban sociology (1958b), the sociology of music (1958c), economic history (1950), the sociology of law (1922; 1977); and to the analysis of ancient civilizations (1976). See: *Action Theory*; *Authority*; *Bureaucracy*; *Capitalism*; *Class*; *Ideal Type*; *Legal-Rational Authority*; *Marx*; *Marxist Sociology*; *Meaningful Action*; *Methodological Individualism*; *Protestant Ethic*; *Rationality*; *Rationalization*; *Social Closure*; *Status*; *Value Freedom*; *Value Neutrality*; *Value Relevance*; *Verstehen*.

Bibl. Bendix (1960); Seyfarth and Schmidt (1977); Turner, B. S. (1981)

Welfare State. The basic premise of a welfare state is that government has the responsibility for the well-being of its citizens and that this cannot be entrusted to the individual, private corporation or local community. Welfare states typically protect people against poverty by means of unemployment benefits, family allowances, income supplements for the poorly paid, and old-age pensions; they provide comprehensive medical care, free education, public housing. These services are financed by state insurance schemes and taxation.

The earliest state welfare programme was the national social insurance system that Bismarck introduced to Germany in the 1880s, and which Lloyd George imitated in Britain in 1911 with national insurance for health and unemployment. W. H. Beveridge (q.v.), whose vision was of state care 'from the cradle to the grave', had a key influence over the British measures and the subsequent introduction of the first comprehensive welfare state by the Labour government of 1945–50, which included the National Health Service. Labour intended both to promote welfare and at the same time to use welfare spending, financed out of taxation that bore more heavily on the rich, as a means to reduce social inequality by redistributing resources. The British welfare state has had real success in caring for its citizens, though the nation's relative economic stagnation since the 1960s means that most programmes are now increasingly underfunded, and the family and voluntary organizations still perform welfare roles. However, it has not achieved as much as was once expected in redistributing resources. Most Western European and Scandinavian societies have comprehensive welfare states, as do Australia and New Zealand, leaving America and Japan with the most poorly developed welfare provision among advanced industrial societies. See: *Citizenship*; *Deprivation*; *Distribution of Income and Wealth*; *Poverty*; *State*; *Unemployment*.

Bibl. Pinker (1979)

Weltanschauung. See: *World View*.

White-Collar Crime. As originally used by E. Sutherland (1945), this referred to crimes committed by members of the business community and large corporations, including false advertising, infringement of copyright, unfair competition, tax evasion, fraud and unfair labour practices. The concept has since been broadened to include the large volume of hidden crime committed by white-collar employees at work (for example, pilfering and fiddling expenses). While such activities are technically illegal, white-collar crime is often not regarded by public opinion as crime, because this activity does not necessarily carry a criminal stigma (q.v.),

and because they are often crimes against institutions rather than people. White-collar crimes are not obvious or violent, unlike rape or assault; their consequences are usually diffuse rather than directly affecting single individuals. The legal response to such crimes tends, therefore, to be lenient. See: *Criminal Statistics*.

White-Collar Worker. A term sometimes used to describe all non-manual employees, but increasingly confined to the lower levels of this occupational hierarchy.

Willmott, Peter (b. 1923). A British sociological researcher and currently a senior fellow at the Policy Studies Institute, Willmott has been chiefly active in studies of family, community and youth, especially in association with Michael Young and the Institute of Community Studies. His best-known works are: *Family and Kinship in East London* (1957) and *Family and Class in a London Suburb* (1960) (both with M. Young), which are studies of the relationship of family with community and the relevance of the extended family to modern life in different parts of the city; *The Evolution of a Community* (1963) and *Adolescent Boys of East London* (1966), both investigations of East London; and *The Symmetrical Family* (1973), also with M. Young, which is a study of changing family forms. See: *Symmetrical Family*.

Wilson, Bryan R. (b. 1926). Currently reader in sociology at Oxford and fellow of All Souls, he has made a major contribution to the contemporary sociological study of religion, with special reference to the religious sect (q.v.). In *Patterns of Sectarianism* (1967) and *Religious Sects* (1970a) he has formulated an ideal type of sectarian groups which has resolved many of the traditional problems in the classical legacy of M. Weber. Wilson has also defended a strong version of the theory of secularization (q.v.), and argues that religious institutions have been robbed of their social significance, in *Religion in Secular Society* (1966) and *Religion in Sociological Perspective* (1982). He has evaluated his analyses of sects and secularization on a world scale in *Magic and the Millennium* (1973) and *Contemporary Transformations of Religion* (1976). Wilson has also taken a critical stand in relation to contemporary educational issues, youth culture and modern values, in *Youth Culture and the Universities* (1970b). The general theme of his sociology is that the powerful and transformative values which characterized both primitive Christianity and Protestantism have declined, leaving the modern world exposed to social processes which have trivialized contemporary culture and intellectual activity.

Witchcraft. In anthropology, this is defined as the belief that members of a community employ supernatural means to harm others in ways which are socially disapproved. Witchcraft is occasionally distinguished from sorcery, which is the use of ritual (q.v.) to control supernatural forces in ways that do not evoke strong social disapproval. Various explanations have been offered for the presence of witchcraft beliefs: (1) they provide an account for the misfortunes of everyday life; (2) they are a vehicle for interpersonal conflict in small communities; (3) witchcraft accusations serve to re-affirm more general social values, such as cooperation or neighbourliness; (4) since most suspects were women, witchcraft accusations were an expression of male control; (5) accusations and trials of witches were a form of social control over deviants. The decline of witchcraft is seen as a consequence of changes in communal life with urbanization and in changes in intellectual life with secularization (q.v.).

Bibl. Douglas, M. (ed.) (1970)

Women and Work. There has been a major shift in the employment patterns of Western industrialized economies over the last quarter of a century, as women have increasingly sought paid employment in the labour market. For example, in the USA in 1963 approximately 38 per cent of women aged over 16 were employed, and by 1983 this proportion had risen to 53 per cent. In the UK, 37 per cent were employed in 1961, rising to 48 per cent by 1984. In America in 1981, about one-fifth of all women employees worked part-time, while in Britain the proportion was two-fifths. Most of the growth in employment since the 1950s can be accounted for by the increasing proportions of married women returning to work after bearing children and choosing to spend less time out of the labour market for domestic reasons. Women now account for about 44 per cent of the total labour force in the USA and 43 per cent in the UK. The typical female career pattern in postwar Britain has been bimodal, women working full-time until they decide to start a family, when they leave the labour market, and returning to work (usually part-time) in their middle to late 30s. Evidence collected in 1980 by J. Martin and C. Roberts (1984) suggests that in Britain the period women spend out of paid employment has declined sharply and they now work for a longer period over their lifetime, although only 4 per cent of the women with children in the survey worked continuously throughout their adult lives. US evidence shows the same pattern of more extended labour-force participation among women (F. D. Blau and M. A. Ferber, 1985).

The reasons for the shifting pattern of employment may be divided into demand and supply. Among the factors leading to a greater demand for women employees are: the growth of routine non-manual work and services where women have traditionally been employed; interest among employers in hiring part-time employees to match fluctuations in work flow; the fact that part-timers are often less well protected by employment legislation and collective agreements negotiated by trade unions, and are therefore cheaper to hire and easier to dismiss; labour shortages in the 1960s and early 1970s when the supply of male labour was inadequate. Among the factors increasing the supply of female labour are: limitations on family size, giving women more opportunity to work and for longer periods; changing social conceptions of women's roles; the increasing qualification of women via the educational system; the desire to increase household income.

In comparison with men, women in Britain and elsewhere work in a narrow range of occupations (occupational segregation), few of them have top jobs (vertical segregation), and on average they earn less. The occupational classification used in official British statistics contains eighteen occupational orders (aggregated from 253 occupational units), and in 1980 the three orders with the highest percentages of women employees accounted for 69 per cent of all women's jobs, while four occupations had less than 1 per cent. Clerical employment accounted for 33 per cent of working women, catering, cleaning and hairdressing for 23 per cent, and the professions in health, education and welfare employed 13 per cent. Among men, the three highest orders contained only 43 per cent of men's jobs and none had less than 1 per cent. Moreover, women are proportionately under-represented in higher-status occupations and in senior jobs within the three feminized occupational orders. On average, men earn more than women in all Western economies, although the gap has somewhat closed in most countries over the last fifteen years.

There is no agreed explanation of occupational and vertical segregation, or of differential remuneration. Human capital (q.v.) explanations point to the significance of the greater education and training, and the continuous work experience of men. Others point to discrimination as the reason women enter only a few jobs, fail to reach senior positions and tend to be poorly paid. Discrimination within the family leads to different patterns of childhood socialization, so that boys and girls have different aspirations, and later assigns women domestic roles that prevent them participating fully in work. Discrimination may also occur in the labour market when employers fail to treat men and women on equal terms, and in the workplace when male employees insist on women being treated unequally. Trade unions and professional associations dominated by men are likely to reinforce women's disadvantage. J. O'Neill (1984) discusses the earnings differential between men and women and estimates that, after allowing for women's lack of continuous work experience which is the major cause of lower earnings, there remains a residual of 10 to 25 per cent that has to be explained by factors which may include discrimination.

Legislation may redress discrimination. In Britain, the Equal Pay Act and the Sexual Discrimination Act (both of which became fully operational in 1975) have together accounted for some closing of the earnings differential between men and women, although as yet they do not seem to have led to much change in the patterns of segregation. The maternity provisions of the 1975 Employment Protection Act provided for maternity pay and the right to return to a job for women who met the qualifying conditions. Elsewhere in Europe, improvements in women's relative pay seem to have owed less to legislation.

The lifetime employment patterns of women workers clearly reflect a sexual division of labour that gives men and women different roles in relation to the family and domestic organization. These patterns in turn are part of any explanation of the inequalities of condition that occur. Equally, women's attitudes to work are influenced by their family roles, since women appear to have distinctive orientations to work (q.v.) that relate to their life-cycles.

It is often said that women are part of the secondary market in a system of dual labour markets (q.v.). Occupational segregation means that women in the main sell their labour in a separate market from men, and this is an indicator of dualism. However, the evidence that the market for female labour is 'secondary', in the sense that it provides low pay, unstable jobs, little chance to acquire skills, and little career progression, is not completely clear cut. Different groups of women are in different sorts of market: professional occupations have many 'primary' labour-market characteristics; the nature of clerical employment varies from employer to employer; while catering, cleaning and hairdressing do have 'secondary' characteristics. See: *Class*; *Division of Labour*; *Domestic Labour*; *Feminism*; *Gender*; *Middle Class*; *Patriarchy*; *Sexual Divisions*; *Sociology of Gender*; *Stereotypes*.

Bibl. Hakim (1979); Amsden (ed.) (1980); West (ed.) (1982)

Women's Studies. See: *Sociology of Gender*.

Work Situation. See: *Class*; *Technology*.

Working Class. The working class in Britain, following the traditional but now disputed definition of this as manual workers, is declining, from 75 per cent of the employed population in 1911 to 49 per cent in 1981. Changes in the occupational structure have led to a steady increase in the number of non-manual jobs along with the contraction of manual work. The distinctiveness of the working class has not, however, been eroded: on average it has lower incomes, less job security and more unemployment, a greater likelihood of poverty, more boring jobs and worse conditions of employment, fewer chances of a structured career, higher rates of morbidity and an earlier age of mortality, and less chance of success within the educational system than the intermediate and upper classes. There is some blurring of class differences because low-level white-collar occupations are increasingly proletarianized (this has prompted some sociologists to re-classify these as working class), which does not necessarily indicate a convergence of classes. Recent sociological interest has focused on two issues: (1) why the working class appears to tolerate such inequalities of condition and does not organize more effectively to reduce the depth of class divisions; (2) how far the working class is unified and internally homogeneous.

(1) Investigations of working-class consciousness typically reveal dualism: people simultaneously reject and accept the social, economic and political structures that create such inequalities, and their views are incoherent. Evidence indicates that proletarian class imagery (q.v.) is widespread but does not develop into a radical class consciousness (q.v.). Sociologists have advanced various reasons for this, though none is universally accepted: (i) the embourgeoisement

(q.v.) of manual workers; (ii) the ideological hegemony (q.v.) of those who benefit from and dominate the existing structures; (iii) the pragmatic acceptance (q.v.) by the working class of its lot. The failure to organize effectively is seen to derive partly from the lack of a coherent and single-minded commitment to change, and also from the failure of working-class organizations such as trade unions and the Labour Party to press for change. This in turn may be seen as a consequence of oligarchical tendencies in these organizations and processes of incorporation (q.v.), and as a result of the growth of rights of citizenship (q.v.), the institutionalization of conflict (q.v.), and social welfare which, by allowing for some amelioration of living and working conditions, give the appearance of change without effecting major transformations.

(2) Homogeneity relates partly to the above issue, in that the less homogeneous the working class the less likely its members are to share a common consciousness or act in concert. Historically, in Britain, the labour aristocracy (q.v.) marked a major division within the class. Skill divisions have become less significant as the result of de-skilling (q.v.) and declining differentials in the areas of pay and working conditions. Since the war other divisions have been postulated, including the typology in the Affluent Worker (q.v.) research of affluent, traditional-proletarian, and traditional-deferential workers, and the notion of a new working class (q.v.). Neither has withstood scrutiny. More significant divisions appear to be those of gender and ethnicity, women and ethnic minorities constituting something of an underclass (q.v.). Given that social mobility takes people out of the working class but does not replace them with outsiders from other classes because the class is shrinking, and that the shift from agricul-

ture to industry has long been complete and with it the influx of peasants and agricultural workers into the industrial working class, the working class is fairly homogeneous except for the underclasses. Whether working-class ethnic minorities will in time become better integrated is unclear, but immigration restrictions in the 1970s and 1980s have in any case greatly reduced the inflow of new working-class immigrants from the Commonwealth. Elsewhere, in Western Europe and America, the movement of population from agriculture to industry and recent waves of immigration make homogeneity less. In America, a highly developed dual labour market creates a privileged stratum that also divides the working class. See: *Career*; *Class*; *Deferential Worker*; *Distribution of Income and Wealth*; *Dominant Ideology Thesis*; *Dual Consciousness*; *Dual Labour Markets*; *Labour Process Approach*; *Leninism*; *Michels*; *Middle Class*; *Migration*; *Proletarianization*; *Social Mobility*; *Unemployment*; *Upper Class*; *Welfare State*; *Working-Class Conservatism*.

Bibl. Roberts (1978); Hill, S. (1981)

Working-Class Conservatism. A substantial minority of the British manual working class, varying between about one-third and two-fifths, has voted Conservative in post-war elections. Since this behaviour deviates from the class norm and, for some commentators, appears to be against workers' class interests, it has aroused sociological interest. Explanations have included embourgeoisement (q.v.), the deferential worker (q.v.), and the prevalence of a false class consciousness as the result of the ideological hegemony (q.v.) of the ruling class. Voting behaviour in the 1970s showed a relative weakening of class-based decisions for all classes, as more middle-class individuals voted Labour as well as workers voting Conservative. Among the factors associated with working-class Conservatism were cross-pressures, such as individuals in manual occupations whose spouses had middle-class jobs or whose parents or parents-in-law were middle class, an increased Conservative vote among skilled manual workers, regional variations (the South being more Conservative than the North), and gender (women being more Conservative than men). See: *Affluent Worker*; *Class Consciousness*; *Class Imagery*; *Class Interest*; *Dominant Ideology Thesis*; *Voting*.

Bibl. Butler and Stokes (1974)

World-System Theory. A perspective on the origins and development of capitalism as a global economic system, this theory was originally outlined by I. Wallerstein (1974). The theory argues: (1) the economic organization of modern capitalism is on a global, not national, basis; (2) this system is composed of core regions, which are economically and politically dominant, and peripheries which are economically dependent on the core; (3) core regions are developed as industrial systems of production, whereas the peripheries provide raw materials, being thereby dependent on prices set in the core regions; (4) there are also semi-peripheries which have a mixture of social and economic characteristics from both core and periphery; (5) this world economic order began to develop in Europe in the fifteenth century with the slow evolution of capitalist agriculture. Wallerstein makes the important point that pre-modern empires had a common political-bureaucratic structure but diverse economic systems, whereas the modern world has diverse political systems but a common interlocking economic organization. The principal im-plication of this approach is that we cannot understand the nation-state in isolation, because the 'internal' economic processes of any society will be completely shaped by its location in the world-system.

World-system theory has been criticized on the following issues: (1) it is not entirely evident that peripheral societies are underdeveloped by core regions, because most trade and investment takes place between societies which are already developed and industrialized; (2) it is not clear how socialist societies fit into the world-system; (3) it is not clear that external forces of the world economy are more significant for social change than internal processes (such as class struggle); (4) by emphasizing economic processes, world-system theory has neglected cultural change, and some theorists, such as Robertson and Lechner (1985), have argued that there is a world-system of global culture which is entirely autonomous from the economic processes of capitalism. See: *Capitalism*; *Centre/Periphery*; *Dependency*; *Feudalism*; *Imperialism*; *Industrialization*; *International Division of Labour*; *Marxist Sociology*; *Peasants*.

World View. A term used synonymously with world-vision and the German *Weltanschauung*, world view refers to the set of beliefs constituting an outlook on the world characteristic of a particular social group, be it a social class, generation or religious sect. For example, the world view of the nineteenth-century entrepreneur is said to comprise individualism, thrift, a sense of family propriety, moral order and moderate religious devotion. Sociologists of knowledge will want to explain why a particular group holds a particular world view. However, the analytical problem consists in what justification the sociologist has for putting particular elements into a world view, for it will never be the case that all members of a group believe all elements of the world view that is ascribed to them. See: *Hermeneutics*.

Wrong, Dennis Hume (b. 1923). Formerly editor of *Social Research* (1962–4) and *Contemporary Sociology* (1972–4), and currently Professor of Sociology at New York University, his early work was concerned with demography (1966), but he is best known for his criticisms of functionalism (q.v.), theories of socialization (q.v.) and functionalist theories of social stratification. His criticisms emphasized the continuing importance of conflict, opposition and resistance to cultural integration, against the sociology of T. Parsons (q.v.). In his evaluation of socialization theory, Wrong drew upon the work of S. Freud (q.v.), to reassert the significance of the conflict between sexual needs and social order within the Freudian tradition. Many of these influential articles have been reprinted in *Skeptical Sociology* (1977). In his recent research (1979), he has turned to the perennial problems of power. He has identified various forms of power, such as force, manipulation, persuasion and authority, and located the bases of power in various individual and collective resources. While Wrong has made a significant contribution to modern sociological theory, his influence spreads far beyond the formal academy, especially through his contributions to *Commentary* and *Dissent*.

Y

Youth Culture. Since the Second World War, there has been an increasing emphasis in many countries on youth as a social category. Young people, between the ages of 12 and about 20, have acquired a distinctive social identity, with their own tastes in clothes and music, for example. There are a number of reasons for this trend, the most important of which are the rise in disposable incomes available to young people and a lengthening of the period between childhood and adulthood caused partly by the raising of the school-leaving age.

Three features distinguish youth culture: (1) it is a culture of leisure rather than work; (2) social relationships are organized around the peer group, not families or individual friends; (3) youth groups are particularly interested in *style*.

While youth culture can be discussed as a general phenomenon, there is obviously a range of different specific youth cultures, differentiated by gender, class or ethnicity, that adopt different styles. The most important sociological issue concerning youth cultures is their relationship to parent or dominant cultures. While many young people are relatively conforming, some youth cultures are notable for their non-conformity, for example skinheads or punks. Most of these cultures are working class and often involve a transformation of elements of the parental or dominant culture into an oppositional culture. See: *Adolescence*; *Aging*; *Generation*; *Subculture*.

Bibl. Frith (1984)

Z

Zone of Transition. E. Burgess (1923) invented the term 'zone in transition' in his Concentric Zone Theory (q.v.), although the common usage is now 'zone of transition', to describe the area of the city immediately adjacent to the city centre. As economic activity in the centre expands, land in the zone of transition is developed for offices, big shops or large hotels, for example. As a result the zone of transition is typically a run-down area, landlords being reluctant to improve property since they are waiting for land-values to rise so that they can sell profitably. In Burgess's view, the outcome is that the zone of transition (or *inner city* in contemporary idiom) is an area of marginal light manufacturing or service industry, houses in multi-occupation, a shifting population without any sense of community and a high crime rate. Many recent studies confirm this view of the inner city but others suggest that there may be more community life in slums than there appears. See: *Chicago School*; *Urban Ecology*; *Urban Way of Life*.

Bibl. Rex and Moore (1967)

Bibliography

Where a book was originally published in a foreign language, or some time ago, we have given the original date of publication in the text and in the bibliography, followed by bibliographical details of an accessible English edition. In many cases, as with the work of M. Weber or J. Habermas, for example, the work available in English is extracted or selected from the original foreign-language source. For these references we have given the date of the first English edition, not of the often rather different original.

Abel-Smith, B., and Townsend, P. (1965), *The Poor and the Poorest*, London, Bell

Abercrombie, N. (1980), *Class, Structure and Knowledge*, Oxford, Blackwell

Abercrombie, N., and Hill, S. (1976), 'Paternalism and patronage', *British Journal of Sociology*, vol. 27, pp. 413–29

Abercrombie, N., Hill, S., and Turner, B. S. (1980), *The Dominant Ideology Thesis*, London, Allen & Unwin

Abercrombie, N., Hill, S., and Turner, B. S. (1986), *Sovereign Individuals of Capitalism*, London, Allen & Unwin

Abercrombie, N., and Urry, J. (1983), *Capital, Labour and the Middle Classes*, London, Allen & Unwin

Abrams, P. (1982), *Historical Sociology*, Shepton Mallet, Open Books

Adorno, T. W. (1967), *Prisms: Cultural criticism and society*, London, Spearman

Adorno, T. W. (1974), *Minima Moralia: Reflections from a damaged life*, London, New Left Books

Adorno, T. W., Frankel-Brunswik, E., Levinson, D. J., and Sanford, R. N. (1950), *The Authoritarian Personality*, New York, Harper

Adorno, T. W., and Horkheimer, M. (1973), *Dialectic of Enlightenment*, London, Allen Lane The Penguin Press

Albrow, M. C. (1970), *Bureaucracy*, London, Macmillan

Ald, R. (1970), *The Youth Communes*, New York, Tower

Alexander, J. C. (1982), *Theoretical Logic in Sociology*, vol. 1, London, Routledge & Kegan Paul

Alexander, J. C. (1984), 'The Parsons revival in German sociology', in R. Collins (ed.), *Sociological Theory 1984*, San Francisco, Jossey-Bass, pp. 394–412

Almond, G. A., and Powell, G. B. (1978), *Comparative Politics*, 2nd ed., Boston, Little Brown

Almond, G. A., and Verba, S. (1963), *The Civic Culture: Political attitudes and democracy in five nations*, Princeton, Princeton University Press

Althusser, L. (1966), *For Marx*, London, Allen Lane The Penguin Press, 1969

Althusser, L. (1971), *Lenin and Philosophy and Other Essays*, London, New Left Books

Althusser, L., and Balibar, E. (1968), *Reading Capital*, London, New Left Books, 1970

Amin, S. (1976), *Unequal Development: An essay on the social formations of peripheral capitalism*, Hassocks, Harvester Press

Amsden, A. H. (ed.) (1980), *The Economics of Women and Work*, Harmondsworth, Penguin Books

Anderson, M. (1975), *Sociology of the Family*, Harmondsworth, Penguin Books

Anderson, P. (1976a), 'The Antimonies of Antonio Gramsci', *New Left Review*, No. 100, pp. 5–80

Anderson, P. (1976b), *Considerations on Western Marxism*, London, New Left Books

Andorka, R. (1978), *Determinants of Fertility in Advanced Societies*, New York, Free Press

Anthony, P. O. (1977), *The Ideology of Work*, London, Tavistock

Apter, D. W. (1965), *The Politics of Modernization*, Chicago, Chicago University Press

Aries, P. (1960), *Centuries of Childhood*, Harmondsworth, Penguin Books

Aron, R. (1935), *German Sociology*, London, Heinemann, 1957

Aron, R. (1938), *Introduction to the Philosophy of History: An essay on the limits of historical objectivity*, Boston, Beacon Press, 1961

Aron, R. (1951), *The Century of Total War*, New York, Doubleday, 1954

Aron, R. (1955), *The Opium of the Intellectuals*, London, Secker & Warburg, 1957

Aron, R. (1961), *Peace and War: A theory of international relations*, New York, Doubleday, 1966

Aron, R. (1963a), *The Great Debate: Theories of nuclear strategy*, New York, Doubleday, 1965

Aron, R. (1963b), *Eighteen Lectures on industrial Society*, London, Weidenfeld & Nicolson, 1967

Aron, R. (1965a), *Democracy and Totalitarianism*, New York, Praeger, 1969

Aron, R. (1965b), *An Essay on Freedom*, New York, World, 1970

Aron, R. (1965c), *Main Currents in Sociological Thought*, New York, Basic Books, 1965, 1967, 2 vols.

Aron, R. (1966), *The Industrial Society: Three essays on ideology and development*, New York, Simon & Schuster

Aron, R. (1968a), *De Gaulle, Israel and the Jews*, New York, Praeger, 1969

Aron, R. (1968b), *The Elusive Revolution: Anatomy of a student revolt*, New York, Praeger, 1969

Aron, R. (1969), *Progress and Disillusion: The dialectics of modern society*, New York, Praeger

Aron, R. (1973a), *History and the Dialectic of Violence: An analysis of Sartre's Critique de la raison dialectique*, Oxford, Blackwell, 1975

Aron, R. (1973b), *The Imperial Republic: The United States and the World 1945–1973*, Englewood Cliffs, New Jersey, Prentice-Hall, 1974

Aron, R. (1976), *Clausewitz*, London, Routledge & Kegan Paul, 1983

Aron, R. (1978), 'Introduction' to M. B. Conant (ed.), *Politics and History: Selected essays by Raymond Aron*, New York, Free Press, pp. xvii–xxx

Atkinson, A. B. (ed.) (1980), *Wealth, Income and Inequality*, 2nd ed., Oxford, Oxford University Press

Atkinson, J. M. (1978), *Discovering Suicide*, London, Macmillan

Atkinson, P. (1985), *Language, Structure and Reproduction: An Introduction to the sociology of Basil Bernstein*, London, Methuen

Atoji, Y. (1984), *Sociology at the Turn of the Century: On G. Simmel in comparison with F. Toennies, M. Weber and E. Durkheim*, Tokyo, Dobunkan

Austin, J. L. (1962), *How to Do Things with Words*, Oxford, Clarendon Press

Averitt, R. T. (1968), *The Dual Economy: The dynamics of American industry structure*, New York, Norton

Babbage, C. (1832), *On the Economy of Machinery and Manufactures*, London, Knight

Bailey, A., and Llobera, J. R. (eds.) (1981), *The Asiatic Mode of Production: Science and politics*, London, Routledge & Kegan Paul

Banks, O. (1976), *The Sociology of Education*, 3rd ed., London, Batsford

Baran, P. (1957), *The Political Economy of Growth*, New York, Monthly Review Press

Barker, E. (1984), *The Making of a Moonie: Choice or brainwashing?*, Oxford, Blackwell

Barratt Brown, M. (1974), *The Economics of Imperialism*, Harmondsworth, Penguin Books

Barrett, M. (1980), *Women's Oppression Today*, London, New Left Books

Barrett, M., and McIntosh, M. (1982), *The Anti-Social Family*, London, Verso

Barthes, R. (1953), *Writing Degree Zero*, London, Cape, 1967

Barthes, R. (1957), *Mythologies*, London, Cape, 1972

Barthes, R. (1970), *S/Z*, London, Cape, 1975

Barthes, R. (1971), *Sade, Fourier, Loyola*, London, Cape, 1977

Barthes, R. (1975), *The Pleasure of the Text*, London, Cape, 1976

Batstone, E., Boraston, I., and Frenkel, S. (1978), *The Social Organization of Strikes*, Oxford, Blackwell

Bauman, Z. (1978), *Hermeneutics and Social Science*, London, Hutchinson

Becker, H. (1932), *Systematic Sociology*, New York, Wiley

Becker, H. S., *et al.* (1961), *Boys in White: Student culture in the medical world*, Chicago, Chicago University Press

Becker, H. S. (1963), *Outsiders: Studies in the sociology of deviance*, Glencoe, Free Press

Becker, H. S., *et al.* (1968), *Making the Grade: The academic side of college life*, New York, Wiley

Becker, H. S. (1970a), *Campus Power Struggle*, Chicago, Aldine

Becker, H. S. (1970b), *Sociological Work, Method and Substance*, Chicago, Chicago University Press

Bell, C. (1968), *Middle-Class Families*, London, Routledge & Kegan Paul

Bell, C., and Newby, H. (1971), *Community Studies*, London, Allen & Unwin

Bell, D. (1960), *The End of Ideology*, New York, Collier

Bell, D. (1974), *The Coming of Post-Industrial Society*, New York, Basic Books

Bell, D. (1976), *The Cultural Contradictions of Capitalism*, New York, Basic Books

Bellah, R. N. (1967), 'Civil religion in America', *Daedalus*, vol. 96, pp. 1–21

Bellah, R. N. (1970), *Beyond Belief*, New York, Harper & Row

Bellah, R. N. (1974), 'American civil religion in the 1970s', in R. Richey and D. Jones (eds.), *American Civil Religion*, New York, Harper & Row, pp. 255–72

Bellah, R. N. (1975), *The Broken Covenant*, New York, Seabury

Bellah, R. N., and Hammond, P. E. (1980), *Varieties of Civil Religion*, New York, Harper & Row

Belsey, C. (1980), *Critical Practice*, London, Methuen

Ben-David, J. (1963–4), 'Professions in the class system of present day societies: a trend report and bibliography', *Current Sociology*, vol. 12

Bendix, R. (1936), *Work and Authority in Industry: Ideologies of management in the course of industrialization*, New York, Wiley; 2nd ed., New York, Harper, 1963

Bendix, R. (1960), *Max Weber: An intellectual portrait*, New York, Doubleday

Bendix, R. (1964), *Nation-Building and Citizenship: Studies of our changing social order*, New York, Wiley

Bendix, R., and Lipset, S. M. (eds.) (1966), *Class, Status and Power: Social stratification in comparative perspective*, 2nd ed., New York, Free Press

Benoist, J.-M. (1975), *The Structural Revolution*, London, Weidenfeld & Nicolson, 1978

Benton, T. (1977), *Philosophical Foundations of the Three Sociologies*, London, Routledge & Kegan Paul

Berg, I. (ed.) (1981), *Sociological Perspectives on Labor Markets*, New York, Academic Press

Berger, P. L. (1969), *The Social Reality of Religion*, London, Faber & Faber

Berger, P. L., and Berger, B. (1976), *Sociology: A biographical approach*, Harmondsworth, Penguin Books

Berger, P. L., and Luckmann, T. (1963), 'Sociology of religion and sociology of knowledge', *Sociology and Social Research*, vol. 74, pp. 417–27

Berger, P. L., and Luckmann, T. (1967), *The Social Construction of Reality*, London, Allen Lane The Penguin Press

Berle, A. A., and Means, G. C. (1932), *The Modern Corporation and Private Property*, New York, Macmillan

Bernstein, B. B. (1961), 'Social class and linguistic development: a theory of social learning', in A. Halsey, J. Floud, and C. A. Anderson (eds.), *Education, Economy and Society*, New York, Free Press, pp. 288–314

Bernstein, B. B. (1971, 1973, 1975), *Class, Codes and Control*, vols. 1–3, London, Routledge & Kegan Paul

Bernstein, B. B. (1977), *Class, Codes and Control*, vol. 3, 2nd ed., London, Routledge & Kegan Paul

Bernstein, H. (1973), *Underdevelopment and Development*, Harmondsworth, Penguin Books

Bernstein, R. J. (1976), *The Restructuring of Social and Political Theory*, Oxford, Blackwell

Biddle, B. J., and Thomas, E. J. (eds.) (1966), *Role Theory: Concepts and research*, New York, Wiley

Bilton, T., Bonnett, K., Jones, P., Stanworth, M., Sheard, K., and Webster, A. (1981), *Introductory Sociology*, London, Macmillan

Blackburn, R. M., and Mann, M. (1979), *The Working Class in the Labour Market*, London, Macmillan

Blackburn, R. M., and Prandy, K. (1965), 'White-collar unionization: a conceptual framework', *British Journal of Sociology*, vol. 16, pp. 111–22

Blalock, H. M., and Blalock, A. B. (eds.) (1968), *Methodology in Social Research*, New York, McGraw-Hill

Blau, F. D., and Ferber, M. A. (1985), 'Women in the labor market: The last twenty years', in L. Larwood, A. H. Stromberg and B. A. Guteck (eds.), *Women and Work: An annual review*, pp. 19–49, Beverly Hills, Sage

283

Blau, P. M. (1955), *The Dynamics of Bureaucracy: A study of interpersonal relations in two government agencies*, Chicago, Chicago University Press

Blau, P. M. (1964), *Exchange and Power in Social Life*, New York, Wiley

Blau, P. M., and Duncan, O. D. (1967), *The American Occupational Structure*, New York, Wiley

Blau, P. M., and Schoenherr, R. A. (1971), *The Structure of Organizations*, New York, Basic Books

Blau, P. M., and Scott, W. R. (1962), *Formal Organizations: A comparative approach*, San Francisco, Chandler

Blauner, R. (1964), *Alienation and Freedom*, Chicago, Chicago University Press

Bloch, M. (1961), *Feudal Society*, London, Routledge & Kegan Paul

Bocock, R. (1983), *Sigmund Freud*, London, Tavistock

Bonar, J. (1942), *Malthus and his Work*, London, Cass

Bonte, P. (1981), 'Marxist theory and anthropological analysis: the study of nomadic pastoralist societies', in J. S. Kahn and J. R. Llobera (eds.), *The Anthropology of Pre-capitalist Societies*, London, Macmillan, pp. 22–56

Booth, C. (1889–91), *Life and Labour of the People in London*, London, Macmillan

Bott, E. (1957), *Family and Social Network*, London, Tavistock

Bottomley, K., and Pease, K. (1986), *Crime and Punishment: Interpreting the data*, Milton Keynes, Open University Press

Bottomore, T. B. (1962), *Sociology*, London, Allen & Unwin

Bottomore, T. B. (1965), *Classes in Modern Society*, London, Allen & Unwin

Bottomore, T. B. (1966), *Elites and Society*, Harmondsworth, Penguin Books

Bottomore, T. B. (1975), *Marxist Sociology*, London, Macmillan

Bottomore, T. B. (1978), 'Marxism and sociology', in T. B. Bottomore and R. Nisbet (eds.), *A History of Sociological Analysis*, New York, Basic Books, 1978, pp. 118–48

Bottomore, T. B. (1979), *Political Sociology*, London, Hutchinson

Bottomore, T. B. (ed.) (1983), *A Dictionary of Marxist Thought*, Oxford, Blackwell

Bottomore, T. B. (1984), *Sociology and Socialism*, Brighton, Wheatsheaf

Bottomore, T. B. (1985), *Theories of Modern Capitalism*, London, Allen & Unwin

Bottomore, T. B., and Goode, P. (eds.) (1978), *Austro-Marxism*, Oxford, Oxford University Press

Bottomore, T. B., and Nisbet, R. (1978a), 'Structuralism', in T. B. Bottomore and R. Nisbet (eds.), *A History of Sociological Analysis*, New York, Basic Books, 1978, pp. 557–98

Bottomore, T. B., and Nisbet, R. A. (eds.) (1978b), *A History of Sociological Analysis*, New York, Basic Books

Bottomore, T. B., and Rubel, M. (eds.) (1961), *Karl Marx: Selected writings in sociology and social philosophy*, Harmondsworth, Penguin Books

Bourdieu, P. (1973), 'Cultural reproduction and social reproduction', in Brown, R. (ed.), *Knowledge, Education and Cultural Change*, London, Tavistock, pp. 71–112

Bourdieu, P. (1977a), *Outline of a Theory of Practice*, Cambridge, Cambridge University Press

Bourdieu, P. (1977b), *Reproduction in Education, Society and Culture*, London, Sage

Bourdieu, P. (1984), *Distinction*, London, Routledge & Kegan Paul

Bourricaud, F. (1981), *The Sociology of Talcott Parsons*, Chicago, University of Chicago Press

Bowlby, J. (1953), *Child Care and the Growth of Love*, Harmondsworth, Penguin Books

Bowles, S., and Gintis, H. (1976), *Schooling in Capitalist America*, London, Routledge & Kegan Paul

Boyers, R., and Orrill, R. (1972), *Laing and Anti-Psychiatry*, Harmondsworth, Penguin Books

Box, S. (1971), *Deviance, Reality and Society*, London, Holt, Rinehart & Winston

Box, S. (1983), *Power, Crime, and Mystification*, London and New York, Tavistock

Bradley, K., and Gelb, A. (1983), *Cooperation at Work*, London, Heinemann Educational Books

Brake, M. (1980), *The Sociology of Youth Culture and Youth Subcultures*, London, Boston & Henley, Routledge & Kegan Paul

Braudel, F. (1966), *The Mediterranean and the Mediterranean World of Philip II*, Glasgow, Collins, 1972–3

Braudel, F. (1969), *On History*, Chicago, Chicago University Press, 1980

Braudel, F. (1979), *Civilization and Capitalism*, Glasgow, Collins, 1981–2

Braverman, H. (1974), *Labor and Monopoly Capitalism: The degradation of work in the twentieth century*, New York, Monthly Review Press

Brown, R. (1976), 'Women as employees: some comments on research in industrial sociology', in D. L. Barker and S. Allen (eds.), *Dependence and Exploitation in Work and Marriage*, London, Longman, pp. 1–46

Brown, M., and Madge, N. (1982), *Despite the Welfare State*, London, Heinemann Educational Books

Buckley, W. (1967), *Sociology and Modern Systems Theory*, Englewood Cliffs, New Jersey, Prentice-Hall

Burawoy, M. (1979), *Manufacturing Consent: Changes in the labor process under monopoly capitalism*, Chicago, Chicago University Press

Burke, P. (1980), *Sociology and History*, London, Allen & Unwin

Burnham, J. (1941), *The Managerial Revolution: What is happening in the world*, New York, Day

Burns, T., and Stalker, G. M. (1961), *The Management of Innovation*, London, Tavistock

Burridge, K. O. L. (1960), *Mambu – a Melanesian Millennium*, London, Methuen

Burrow, J. W. (1966), *Evolution and Society: A study of Victorian social theory*, Cambridge, Cambridge University Press

Butler, D. E., and Stokes, D. (1974), *Political Change in Britain*, 2nd ed., London, Macmillan

Callinicos, A. (1976), *Althusser's Marxism*, London, Pluto Press

Canovan, M. (1981), *Populism*, New York, Harcourt Brace

Castles, S., and Kosack, G. (1973), *Immigrant Workers and Class Structure in Western Europe*, London, Oxford University Press

Cavan, R. (1928), *Suicide*, Chicago, Chicago University Press

Chandler, A. D., and Daems, H. (1980), *Managerial Hierarchies: Comparative perspectives on the rise of the modern industrial enterprise*, Cambridge, Mass., Harvard University Press

Child, J. (1969), *The Business Enterprise in Modern Industrial Society*, London, Collier-Macmillan

Child, J. (1972), 'Organisational structure, environment and performance: the role of strategic choice', *Sociology,* vol. 6, pp. 1–22

Cicourel, A. (1964), *Method and Measurement in Sociology*, New York, Free Press

Clinard, M. B. (1965), 'Criminological research', in Robert K. Merton *et al.*, *Sociology Today*, New York, Harper, vol. 2, pp. 509–36

Cloward, R. A., and Ohlin, L. E. (1960), *Delinquency and Opportunity*, New York, Free Press

Cloward, R. A., and Piven, F. F. (1979), 'Female protest, the channeling of female innovative resistance', *Signs*, vol. 4, pp. 661–9

Cohen, A. K. (1955), *Delinquent Boys: The culture of the gang*, New York, Free Press

Cohen, P. S. (1968), *Modern Social Theory*, London, Heinemann Educational Books

Cohen, S. (ed.) (1971), *Images of Deviance*, Harmondsworth, Penguin Books

Cohen, S. (1972), *Folk Devils and Moral Panics*, London, Paladin

Comte, A. (1838), *The Positive Philosophy of Auguste Comte*, London, Bell, 1896

Connerton, P. (ed.) (1976), *Critical Sociology*, Harmondsworth, Penguin Books

Connor, W. D. (1979), *Socialism, Politics and Equality: Hierarchy and change in Eastern Europe and the U.S.S.R.*, New York, Columbia University Press

Cooley, C. H. (1902), *Human Nature and the Social Order*, New York, Scribner's

Cooley, C. H. (1909), *Social Organization*, New York, Scribner's

Coombs, R. (1985), 'Automation, management strategies and labour-process change', in D. Knights, H. Willmott and D. Collinson (eds.), *Job Redesign: Critical perspectives on the labour process*, Aldershot, Gower, pp. 142–70

Coser, L. A. (1956), *The Functions of Social Conflict*, New York, Free Press

Coser, L. A. (1968), 'Conflict: social aspects', in D. L. Sills (ed.), *International Encyclopedia of the Social Sciences*, vol. 3, pp. 232–6, New York, Macmillan and Free Press

Coser, L. A. (1971), *Masters of Sociological Thought: Ideas in historical and social context*, New York, Harcourt Brace

Cosin, B. R., Dale, I. R., Esland, G. M., Mackinnon, D., and Swift, D. F. (eds.) (1977), *School and Society: A sociological reader*, London, Routledge & Kegan Paul

Coulbourn, R. (ed.) (1956), *Feudalism in History*, Princeton, Princeton University Press

Cousins, M., and Hussain, A. (1984), *Michel Foucault*, New York, St Martin's Press

Cox, O. C. (1959), *Caste, Class and Race*, New York, Monthly Review Press

Cox, P. R. (1970), *Demography*, Cambridge, Cambridge University Press

Cressey, D. R. (1955), 'Changing criminals: The application of the theory of differential association', *The American Journal of Sociology*, vol. 61, pp. 112–18

Crewe, I. (1981), 'Why the Conservatives won', in H. R. Penniman (ed.), *Britain at the Polls, 1979*, Washington, D.C., American Enterprise Institute for Public Policy Research, pp. 263–305

Crewe, I. (1982), 'The Labour Party and the electorate', in D. Kavanagh (ed.), *The Politics of the Labour Party*, London, Allen & Unwin, pp. 9–49

Crompton, R. (1976), 'Approaches to the study of white-collar unionism', *Sociology*, vol. 10, no. 3, pp. 407–26

Crompton, R., and Gubbay, J. (1978), *Economy and Class Structure*, London, Macmillan

Crompton, R., and Jones, G. (1984), *White-Collar Proletariat*, London, Macmillan

Crompton, R., and Mann, M. (eds.) (1986), *Gender and Stratification*, Oxford, Polity Press

Crouch, C. (1982), *Trade Unions: The logic of collective action*, Glasgow, Fontana

Crozier, M. (1964), *The Bureaucratic Phenomenon*, London, Tavistock

Cuff, E. C., and Payne, G. C. F. (eds.) (1979), *Perspectives in Sociology*, London, Allen & Unwin

Culler, J. (1983), *Barthes*, Glasgow, Fontana

Cutler, A., Hindess, B., Hirst, P., and Hussain, A. (1977), *Marx's 'Capital' and Capitalism Today*, London, Routledge & Kegan Paul

Dahl, R. A. (1970), *Modern Political Analysis*, 2nd ed., Englewood Cliffs, New Jersey, Prentice-Hall

Dahrendorf, R. (1959), *Class and Class Conflict in an Industrial Society*, London, Routledge & Kegan Paul

Dahrendorf, R. (1967a), 'Conflict after Class', Noel Buxton Memorial Lecture, Longmans for the University of Essex

Dahrendorf, R. (1967b), *Society and Democracy in Germany*, New York, Doubleday

Dahrendorf, R. (1975), *The New Liberty*, London, Routledge & Kegan Paul

Dahrendorf, R. (1979), *Life Chances*, London, Weidenfeld & Nicolson

Daniel, W. W. (1981), *The Unemployed Flow*, London, Policy Studies Institute

Danziger, K. (1971), *Socialization*, Harmondsworth, Penguin Books

Davies, J. C. (1962), 'Toward a theory of revolution', *American Sociological Review*, vol. 27, pp. 5–19

Davis, B. D. (1970), *The Problem of Slavery in Western Culture*, Harmondsworth, Penguin Books

Davis, H. B. (1978), *Toward a Marxist Theory of Nationalism*, New York and London, Monthly Review Press

Davis, K. (1967), 'The urbanization of the human population', in *Cities*, Harmondsworth, Penguin Books, pp. 11–32

Davis, K., and Moore, W. E. (1945), 'Some principles of stratification', *American Sociological Review*, vol. 10, pp. 242–9; reprinted in R. Bendix and S. M. Lipset (eds.) (1966), *Class, Status and Power*, 2nd ed., New York, Free Press

Dawe, A. (1978), 'Theories of social action', in T. B. Bottomore and R. Nisbet (eds.), *A History of Sociological Analysis*, New York, Basic Books, pp. 362–417

Diggins, J. P. (1978), *The Bard of Savagery: Veblen and modern social theory*, Hassocks, Harvester Press

Ditton, J. (1979), *Contrology: Beyond the new criminology*, London, Macmillan

Ditton, J. (ed.) (1980), *The View from Goffman*, London, Macmillan

Doeringer, P. B., and Piore, M. J. (1971), *Internal Labor Markets and Manpower Analysis*, Lexington, Heath

Donzelot, J. (1977), *The Policing of Families*, New York, Pantheon, 1979

Dore, R. P. (1958), *City Life in Japan*, London, Routledge & Kegan Paul

Dore, R. P. (1959). *Land Reform in Japan*, London, Oxford University Press

Dore, R. P. (1965), *Education in Tokugawa Japan*, London, Routledge & Kegan Paul

Dore, R. P. (1973), *British Factory, Japanese Factory: The origins of national diversity in industrial relations*, London, Allen & Unwin

Dore, R. P. (1976), *The Diploma Disease*, London, Allen & Unwin

Dore, R. P. (1978), *Shinohata: A portrait of a Japanese village*, London, Allen Lane The Penguin Press

Dore, R. P. (1986), *Flexible Rigidities: Industrial policy and structural adjustment in the Japanese economy*, London, Athlone

Douglas, J. B. (1967), *The Social Meanings of Suicide*, Princeton, Princeton University Press

Douglas, J. D. (ed.) (1973), *Introduction to Sociology*, New York, Free Press

Douglas, M. (ed.) (1970), *Witchcraft Confessions and Accusations*, London, Tavistock

Downes, D., and Rock, P. (1982), *Understanding Deviance*, Oxford, Oxford University Press

Dowse, R. E., and Hughes, J. (1972), *Political Sociology*, New York, Wiley

Doyal, L. (1979), *The Political Economy of Health*, London, Pluto Press

Dumont, L. (1970), *Homo Hierarchicus*, Chicago, Chicago University Press

Duncan, O. D. (1966), 'Path analysis: sociological examples', *American Journal of Sociology*, vol. 72, pp. 1–16

Duncan, O. D. (1975), *Introduction to Structural Equation Models*, New York, Academic Press

Dunleavy, P., and Husbands, C. T. (1985), *British Democracy at the Crossroads: Voting and party competition in the 1980s*, London, Allen & Unwin

Durkheim, E. (1893), *The Division of Labor in Society*, Glencoe, Free Press, 1960

Durkheim, E. (1895), *The Rules of Sociological Method*, Glencoe, Free Press, 1958

Durkheim, E. (1897), *Suicide: A study in sociology*, Glencoe, Free Press, 1951

Durkheim, E. (1912), *The Elementary Forms of the Religious Life*, London, Allen & Unwin, 1954

Durkheim, E. (1978), *On Institutional Analysis*, Chicago, Chicago University Press

Durkheim, E., and Mauss, M. (1903), *Primitive Classification*, Chicago, Chicago University Press, 1963

Duster, T. S. (1970), *The Legislation of Morality: Law, drugs and moral legislation*, New York, Free Press

Duverger, M. (1964), *Political Parties*, London, Methuen

Eckstein, H. (1965), 'On the etiology of internal wars', *History and Theory*, vol. 4, pp. 133–63

Edwards, R. (1979), *Contested Terrain*, London, Heinemann Educational Books

Ehrenreich, B., and Ehrenreich, J. (1970), *The American Health Empire: Power, profits and politics*, New York, Random House

Eisenstadt, S. N. (1956), *From Generation to Generation*, Glencoe, Free Press

Eisenstadt, S. N. (1968a), 'Evolution: social evolution', in D. L. Sills (ed.), *International Encyclopedia of the Social Sciences*, vol. 5, pp. 228–34, New York, Macmillan and Free Press

Eisenstadt, S. N. (1968b), 'Social institutions: the concept', in D. L. Sills (ed.), *International Encyclopedia of the Social Sciences*, vol. 14, pp. 409–21, New York, Macmillan and Free Press

Eisenstadt, S. N. (1968c), 'Social institutions: comparative study', in D. L. Sills (ed.), *International Encyclopedia of the Social Sciences*, vol. 14, pp. 421–9, New York, Macmillan and Free Press

Ekeh, P. (1974), *Social Exchange Theory: The two traditions*, London, Heinemann Educational Books

Elias, N. (1939a), *The Civilizing Process: The history of manners*, vol. 1, Oxford, Blackwell, 1978

Elias, N. (1939b), *The Civilizing Process: State formation and civilization*, vol. 2, Oxford, Blackwell, 1982

Elias, N. (1969), *The Court Society*, Oxford, Blackwell, 1983

Elias, N. (1970), *What is Sociology?*, London, Hutchinson University Library, 1978

Elias, N. (1982), *The Loneliness of the Dying*, Oxford, Blackwell, 1985

Elias, N. (1986), *Involvement and Detachment*, Oxford, Blackwell

Elias, N., and Scotson, J. L. (1965), *The Established and the Outsiders*, London, Cass

Emmanuel, A. (1972), *Unequal Exchange*, London, New Left Books

Emmanuel, A. (1974), 'Current myths of development', *New Left Review*, no. 85, pp. 61–82

Engels, F. (1845), *The Condition of the Working Class in England*, Oxford, Blackwell, 1958

Engels, F. (1877–8), *Anti-Dühring: Herr Eugen Dühring's revolution in science*, Moscow, Foreign Languages Publishing House, 1959

Engels, F. (1884), *The Origin of the Family, Private Property and the State*, New York, International Publishers, 1942

Engels, F. (1952), *Dialectics of Nature*, New York, International Publishers, 1960

Etzioni, A. (1968), 'Mobilization as a macrosociological conception', *British Journal of Sociology*, vol. 19, pp. 243–53

Etzioni, A., and Etzioni, E. (1964), *Social Change: Sources, patterns and consequences*, New York, Basic Books

Evans, M. (ed.), *The Woman Question*, London, Fontana Books

Everitt, B. S. (1980), *Cluster Analysis*, 2nd ed., London, Heinemann Educational Books

Faris, R. E. L. (1970), *Chicago Sociology*, Chicago, Chicago University Press

Ferguson, A. (1767), *An Essay on the History of Civil Society*, Edinburgh, Edinburgh University Press, 1966

Festinger, L. (1957), *A Theory of Cognitive Dissonance*, Evanston, Row

Feuerbach, L. (1841), *The Essence of Christianity*, New York, Harper, 1957

Field, F. (1982), *Poverty and Politics*, London, Heinemann Educational Books

Fine, B. (1975), *Marx's 'Capital'*, London, Macmillan

Fletcher, R. (1971), *The Making of Sociology: Beginnings and foundations*, vol. 1, London, Nelson

Foucault, M. (1961), *Madness and Civilization*, London, Tavistock, 1971

Foucault, M. (1963), *The Birth of the Clinic*, London, Tavistock, 1973

Foucault, M. (1966), *The Order of Things: An archaeology of the human sciences*, London, Tavistock, 1974

Foucault, M. (1969), *The Archaeology of Knowledge*, London, Tavistock, 1974

Foucault, M. (1973), *I Pierre Rivière, Having Slaughtered My Mother, My Sister and My Brother . . .*, London, Tavistock, 1978

Foucault, M. (1975), *Discipline and Punish: The birth of the prison*, London, Tavistock, 1977

Foucault, M. (1976), *History of Sexuality*, London, Tavistock, 1979

Fox, A. (1974), *Beyond Contract: Work, power and trust relations*, London, Faber & Faber

Frank, A. G. (1969), *Capitalism and Underdevelopment in Latin America*, New York, Monthly Review Press

Frankenburg, R. (1966), *Communities in Britain*, Harmondsworth, Penguin Books

Freeman, D. (1983), *Margaret Mead and Samoa: The making and unmaking of an anthropological myth*, Canberra, Australian National University Press

Freire, P. (1972), *Pedagogy of the Oppressed*, Harmondsworth, Penguin Books

Freud, S. (1900), *The Interpretation of Dreams*, London, Hogarth, 1958

Freud, S. (1901), *The Psychopathology of Everyday Life*, London, Hogarth, 1960

Freud, S. (1905a), *Jokes and their Relation to the Unconscious*, Harmondsworth, Penguin Books, 1976

Freud, S. (1905b), *Three Essays on the Theory of Sexuality*, London, Hogarth, 1953

Freud, S. (1910), *Leonardo da Vinci: A memory of his childhood*, London ARK edition, 1984

Freud, S. (1910 and 1926), *Two Short Accounts of Psycho-Analysis*, Harmondsworth, Penguin Books, 1962

Freud, S. (1914), *On the History of the Psycho-Analytical Movement*, New York, Norton, 1966

Freud, S. (1923), *The Ego and the Id*, London, Hogarth, 1961

Freud, S. (1925), *An Autobiographical Study*, London, Hogarth, 1959

Freud, S. (1927), *The Future of an Illusion*, London, Hogarth Press

Freud, S. (1930), *Civilization and Its Discontents*, London, Hogarth Press

Freud, S. (1934–8), *Moses and Monotheism: Three essays*, London, Hogarth Press

Freud, S., and Breuer, J. (1895), *Studies on Hysteria*, Harmondsworth, Penguin Books, 1974

Freund, J. (1966), *The Sociology of Max Weber*, London, Allen Lane The Penguin Press, 1968

Friedman, A. L. (1977), *Industry and Labour*, London, Macmillan

Friedman, J., and Wulff, R. (1975), *The Urban Transition*, London, Arnold

Frisby, D. (1981), *Sociological Impressionism: A reassessment of Georg Simmel's social theory*, London, Heinemann Educational Books

Frisby, D. (1984), *Georg Simmel*, London, Tavistock

Frith, S. (1984), *The Sociology of Youth*, Ormskirk, Causeway Press

Froomkin, J. N. (1968), 'Automation', in D. L. Sills (ed.), *International Encyclopedia of the Social Sciences*, vol. 1, pp. 480–88, New York, Macmillan and Free Press

Galbraith, J. K. (1967), *The New Industrial State*, London, Hamish Hamilton

Gallie, D. (1978), *In Search of the New Working Class: Automation and social integration within the capitalist enterprise*, Cambridge, Cambridge University Press

Gans, H. J. (1968), 'Urbanism and suburbanism as ways of life', in R. E. Pahl, *Readings in Urban Sociology*, Oxford, Pergamon Press, pp. 95–118

Garfinkel, H. (1967), *Studies in Ethnomethodology*, Englewood Cliffs, New Jersey, Prentice-Hall

Gellner, E. (1959), *Words and Things*, London, Routledge & Kegan Paul

Gellner, E. (1964), *Thought and Change*, London, Weidenfeld & Nicolson

Gellner, E. (1969), *Saints of the Atlas*, London, Weidenfeld & Nicolson

Gellner, E. (1974), *Legitimation of Belief*, Cambridge, Cambridge University Press

Gellner, E. (1982), *Muslim Society*, Cambridge, Cambridge University Press

Gellner, E. (1983), *Nations and Nationalism*, Oxford, Blackwell

Gellner, E. (1985), *The Psychoanalytic Movement or The Coming of Unreason*, London, Paladin Books

Geoghegan, V. (1981), *Reason and Eros: The social theory of Herbert Marcuse*, London, Pluto Press

Geras, N. (1971), 'Fetishism in Marx's *Capital*', New Left Review, no. 65, pp. 69–85

Gerth, H. H., and Mills, C. W. (eds.) (1946), *From Max Weber: Essays in sociology*, New York, Oxford University Press

Giddens, A. (1971), *Capitalism and Modern Social Theory*, Cambridge, Cambridge University Press

Giddens, A. (1972), *Politics and Sociology in the Thought of Max Weber*, London, Macmillan

Giddens, A. (1973), *The Class Structure of the Advanced Societies*, London, Hutchinson

Giddens, A. (ed.) (1974), *Positivism and Sociology*, London, Heinemann Educational Books

Giddens, A. (1976), *New Rules of Sociological Method*, London, Hutchinson

Giddens, A. (1977), *Studies in Social and Political Theory*, London, Hutchinson

Giddens, A. (1978), *Durkheim*, London, Fontana

Giddens, A. (1979), *Central Problems in Social Theory*, London, Macmillan

Giddens, A. (1981), *A Contemporary Critique of Historical Materialism*, London, Macmillan

Giddens, A. (1982), *Sociology: A brief but critical introduction*, London, Macmillan

Giddens, A. (1983), *Profiles and Critiques in Social Theory*, London, Macmillan

Giddens, A. (1984), *The Constitution of Society: Outline of the theory of structuration*, Cambridge, Polity Press

Giddens, A. (1985), *The Nation-State and Violence: Volume two of a contemporary critique of historical materialism*, Cambridge, Polity Press

Gilbert, G. N. (1981), *Modelling Society*, London, Allen & Unwin

Gill, C. (1985), *Work, Unemployment and the New Technology*, Cambridge, Polity Press

Giner, S. (1976), *Mass Society*, London, Martin Robertson

Glaser, B. G., and Strauss, A. L. (1968), *The Discovery of Grounded Theory: Strategies for qualitative research*, Chicago, Aldine and Atherton

Glaser, D. (1956), 'Criminality theories and behavioral images', *The American Journal of Sociology*, vol. 61, pp. 433–45

Glasgow University Media Group (1980), *More Bad News*, London, Routledge & Kegan Paul

Glass, D. V. (ed.) (1954), *Social Mobility in Britain*, London, Routledge & Kegan Paul

Glass, D. V., and Eversley, D. E. C. (eds.) (1965), *Population in History*, London, Arnold

Glass, D. V., and Revelle, R. (1972), *Population and Social Change*, London, Arnold

Glassner, B., and Freedman, J. A. (1979), *Clinical Sociology*, New York and London, Longman

Goffman, E. (1959), *The Presentation of Self in Everyday Life*, Garden City, New York, Doubleday Anchor

Goffman, E. (1961a), *Encounters: Two studies in the sociology of interaction*, Indianapolis, Bobbs-Merrill

Goffman, E. (1961b), *Asylums*, Harmondsworth, Penguin Books

Goffman, E. (1963), *Behavior in Public Places: Notes on the social organization of gatherings*, New York, Free Press

Goffman, E. (1964), *Stigma: Notes on the management of spoiled identity*, Englewood Cliffs, New Jersey, Prentice-Hall

Goffman, E. (1967), *Interaction Ritual: Essays in face-to-face behavior*, Chicago, Aldine

Goffman, E. (1969), *Strategic Interaction*, Philadelphia, University of Philadelphia Press

Goffman, E. (1971), *Relations in Public: Microstudies of the public order*, New York, Basic Books

Goffman, E. (1974), *Frame Analysis: An essay on the organization of experience*, Cambridge, Mass., Harvard University Press

Goffman, E. (1979), *Gender Advertisements*, London, Macmillan

Goldthorpe, J. H. (1980), *Social Mobility and Class Structure in Britain*, Oxford, Clarendon Press

Goldthorpe, J. H. (ed.) (1985), *Order and Conflict in Contemporary Capitalism*, Oxford, Oxford University Press

Goldthorpe, J. H., and Hope, K. (1974), *The Social Grading of Occupations: A new approach and scale*, Oxford, Clarendon Press

Goldthorpe, J. H., Lockwood, D., Bechhofer, F., and Platt, J. (1968a), *The Affluent Worker: Industrial attitudes and behaviour*, Cambridge, Cambridge University Press

Goldthorpe, J. H., Lockwood, D., Bechhofer, F., and Platt, J. (1968b), *The*

Affluent Worker: Political attitudes and behaviour, Cambridge, Cambridge University Press

Goldthorpe, J. H., Lockwood, D., Bechhofer, F., and Platt, J. (1969), *The Affluent Worker in the Class Structure*, Cambridge, Cambridge University Press

Goode, W. J. (1964), *The Family*, Englewood Cliffs, New Jersey, Prentice-Hall

Gordon, D. M., Edwards, R., and Reich, M. (1982), *Segmented Work, Divided Workers*, Cambridge, Cambridge University Press

Gorz, A. (1964), *Strategy for Labour*, Boston, Beacon Press, 1967

Gouldner, A. W. (1954), *Patterns of Industrial Bureaucracy*, New York, Free Press

Gouldner, A. W. (1955a), 'Metaphysical pathos and the theory of bureaucracy', *American Political Science Review*, vol. 49, pp. 496–507

Gouldner, A. W. (1955b), *Wildcat Strike*, London, Routledge & Kegan Paul

Gouldner, A. W. (1965), *Enter Plato: Classical Greece and the origins of social theory*, New York, Basic Books

Gouldner, A. W. (1970), *The Coming Crisis of Sociology*, New York, Basic Books

Gouldner, A. W. (1975), *For Sociology: Renewal and critique in sociology today*, Harmondsworth, Penguin Books

Gouldner, A. W. (1976), *The Dialectic of Ideology and Technology*, New York, Seabury Press

Gouldner, A. W. (1979), *The Future of Intellectuals and the Rise of the New Class*, New York, Seabury Press

Gouldner, A. W. (1980), *The Two Marxisms: Contradictions and anomalies in the development of theory*, New York, Seabury Press

Gouldner, A. W. (1985), *Against Fragmentation: The origins of Marxism and the sociology of intellectuals*, Oxford, Oxford University Press

Gouldner, A. W., and Peterson, R. A. (1962), *Notes on Technology and the Moral Order*, New York, Bobbs-Merrill

Gove, W. R. (1975), *The Labeling of Deviance: Evaluating a perspective*, Beverley Hills, Sage

Gramsci, A. (1971), *Selections from the Prison Notebooks*, London, New Left Books

Granovetter, M. (1981), 'Toward a sociological theory of income differences', in I. Berg (ed.), *Sociological Perspectives on Labor Markets*, New York, Academic Press

Grathoff, R. (ed.) (1978), *The Theory of Social Action: The correspondence of Alfred Schutz and Talcott Parsons*, Bloomington and London, Indiana University Press

Gray, R. (1981), *The Aristocracy of Labour in Nineteenth-Century Britain c. 1850–1914*, London, Macmillan

Gross, N., Mason, W. S., and McEachern, A. W. (1958), *Explorations in Role Analysis: Studies of the school superintendency role*, New York, Wiley

Gurevitch, M., Bennett, T., Curran, J., and Woollacott, J. (eds.) (1982), *Culture, Society and the Media*, London, Methuen

Habakkuk, H. J. (1963), 'Population problems and European economic development in the late eighteenth and nineteenth century', *American Economic Review*, vol. 53, pp. 607–18

Habermas, J. (1963), *Theory and Practice*, London, Heinemann Educational Books, 1973

Habermas, J. (1968), *Knowledge and Human Interests*, London, Heinemann Educational Books, 1971

Habermas, J. (1970a), 'On systematically distorted communication', *Inquiry*, vol. 13, pp. 205–18

Habermas, J. (1970b), 'Towards a theory of communicative competence', *Inquiry*, vol. 13, pp. 360–75

Habermas, J. (1970c), *Towards a Rational Society*, London, Heinemann Educational Books, 1971

Habermas, J. (1973), *Legitimation Crisis*, London, Heinemann Educational Books, 1976

Habermas, J. (1979), *Communication and the Evolution of Society*, London, Heinemann Educational Books

Habermas, J., and Luhmann, N. (1971), *Theorie der Gesellschaft oder Sozialtechnologie?*, Frankfurt, Suhrkamp Verlag

Hakim, C. (1979), *Occupational Segregation*, Department of Employment Research Paper No. 9, London, Her Majesty's Stationery Office

Halbwachs, M. (1930), *Les Causes du suicide*, Paris, Alcan

Halévy, E. (1962), *A History of the English People in the Nineteenth Century*, 2nd ed., vols. 1 and 2, London, Benn

Hall, J. A. (1981), *Diagnoses of Our Time: Six views of our social condition*, London, Heinemann Educational Books

Hall, J. A. (1985), *Powers and Liberties: The causes and consequences of the rise of the West*, Oxford, Blackwell

Hall, R. (1969), *Occupations and the Social Structure*, Englewood Cliffs, New Jersey, Prentice-Hall

Hall, S., and Jefferson, T. (eds.) (1976), *Resistance through Rituals*, London, Hutchinson

Halsey, A. H. (1957), *Social Class and Educational Opportunity*, London, Heinemann

Halsey, A. H. (1961), *Education, Economy and Society*, New York, Free Press

Halsey, A. H. (1965), *Power in Co-operatives*, Oxford, Blackwell

Halsey, A. H. (1968), *Social Survey of the Civil Service*, London, Her Majesty's Stationery Office

Halsey, A. H. (1971), *The British Academics*, London, Faber & Faber

Halsey, A. H. (1972), *Trends in British Society since 1900*, London, Macmillan

Halsey, A. H. (1977), *Heredity and Environment*, London, Methuen

Halsey, A. H. (1978), *Change in British Society*, Oxford, Oxford University Press

Halsey, A. H., Heath, A. F., and Ridge, J. M. (1980), *Origins and Destinations: Family, class, and education in modern Britain*, Oxford, Clarendon Press

Halsey, A. H., and Karabel, J. (1977), *Power and Ideology in Education*, Oxford, Oxford University Press

Hamilton, P. (1983), *Talcott Parsons*, London, Tavistock

Hammersley, M., and Woods, P. (eds.) (1976), *The Process of School: A sociological reader*, London, Routledge & Kegan Paul

Haralambos, M. (1980), *Sociology: Themes and perspectives*, Slough, University Tutorial Press

Harman, H. H. (1967), *Modern Factor Analysis*, 2nd ed., Chicago, Chicago University Press

Harris, C. C. (1969), *The Family*, London, Allen & Unwin

Hart, N. (1976), *When Marriage Ends: A study in status passage*, London, Tavistock

Hawkes, T. (1977), *Structuralism and Semiotics*, London, Methuen

Hawkins, K. (1979), *Unemployment*, Harmondsworth, Penguin Books

Hawthorne, G., and Busfield, J. (1968), 'A sociological approach to British fertility', in J. Gould (ed.), *Penguin Social Science Survey*, Harmondsworth, Penguin Books, pp. 168–210

Heath, A. (1981), *Social Mobility*, Glasgow, Fontana

Hechter, M. (1975), *Internal Colonialism: The Celtic fringe in British national development, 1536–1966*, London, Routledge & Kegan Paul

Hegel, G. W. F. (1937), *The Philosophy of History*, New York, Dover, 1956

Held, D. (1980), *Introduction to Critical Theory*, London, Hutchinson

Heller, A. (1974), *The Theory of Need in Marx*, London, Allison & Busby

Henderson, L. J. (1935), 'Physician and patient as a social system', *New England Journal of Medicine*, vol. 212, pp. 819–23

Herberg, W. (1955), *Protestant, Catholic, Jew*, New York, Doubleday

Hill, M. (1973), *A Sociology of Religion*, London, Heinemann Educational Books

Hill, S. (1976), *The Dockers: Class and tradition in London*, London, Heinemann Educational Books

Hill, S. (1981), *Competition and Control at Work*, London, Heinemann Educational Books

Himmelweit, H. T., *et al.* (1981), *How Voters Decide*, London, Academic Press

Hinde, R. A. (1982), *Ethology,* Glasgow, Fontana

Hindess, B. (1973), *The Use of Official Statistics in Sociology*, London, Macmillan

Hindess, B. (1977), 'The concept of class in Marxist theory and Marxist politics', in J. Bloomfield (ed.), *Class, Hegemony and Party*, London, Lawrence & Wishart, pp. 95–108

Hindess, B., and Hirst, P. Q. (1975), *Pre-Capitalist Modes of Production*, London, Routledge & Kegan Paul

Hirsch, F., and Goldthorpe, J. H. (eds.) (1978), *The Political Economy of Inflation*, London, Martin Robertson

Hobbes, T. (1651), *Leviathan*, Glasgow, Fontana, 1962

Hofstadter, R. (1955), *Social Darwinism in American Thought*, Boston, Beacon Press

Holloway, J., and Picciotto, S. (eds.) (1978), *State and Capital*, London, Arnold

Hollowell, P. (ed.) (1982), *Property and Social Relations*, London, Heinemann Educational Books

Holsti, O. R. (1969), *Content Analysis for the Social Sciences and Humanities*, Reading, Mass., Addison-Wesley

Holton, R. J. (1985), *The Transition from Feudalism to Capitalism*, London, Macmillan

Homans, G. C. (1950), *The Human Group*, New York, Harcourt Brace

Homans, G. C. (1961), *Social Behavior: Its elementary forms*, New York, Harcourt Brace

Homans, G. C. (1962), *Sentiments and Activities*, New York, Free Press

Homans, G. C. (1964), 'Bringing men back in', *American Sociological Review*, vol. 29, pp. 809–18

Homans, G. C. (1967), *The Nature of Social Science*, New York, Harcourt Brace

Hoogvelt, A. M. (1976), *The Sociology of Developing Societies*, London, Macmillan

Hough, M., and Mayhew, P. (1985), *Taking Account of Crime: Key findings from the second British Crime Survey*, Home Office Research Paper No. 85, London, Her Majesty's Stationery Office

Hughes, E. C., and Masuoka, J. (1950–55), *Collected Papers of Robert Ezra Park*, 3 vols., New York, Free Press

Hunt, A. (1978), *The Sociological Movement in Law*, London, Macmillan

Hyman, R. (1977), *Strikes*, 2nd ed., Glasgow, Fontana

Hyman, R. (1978), 'Pluralism, procedural consensus and collective bargaining', *British Journal of Industrial Relations*, vol. 16, pp. 16–40

Illich, I. (1977), *Limits to Medicine*, Harmondsworth, Penguin Books

Ionescu, G., and Gellner, E. (eds.) (1969), *Populism*, London, Weidenfeld & Nicolson

Jackson, J. A. (ed.) (1970), *Professions and Professionalisation*, Cambridge, Cambridge University Press

Jackson, J. A. (ed.) (1972), *Role*, Cambridge, Cambridge University Press

Jackson, J., and Jobling, R. (1968), 'Towards an analysis of contemporary cults', in *A Sociological Yearbook of Religion in Britain*, vol. 1, pp. 94–105

Jay, M. (1973), *The Dialectical Imagination: A history of the Frankfurt School and the Institute of Social Research 1923–50*, Boston, Little Brown

Jay, M. (1984), *Adorno*, London, Fontana

Jerrome, D. (ed.) (1983), *Ageing in Modern Society: Contemporary approaches*, London, Croom Helm

Johnson, E. S., and Williamson, J. B. (1980), *Growing Old: The social problems of aging*, New York, Holt, Rinehart & Winston

Johnson, T. J. (1972), *Professions and Power*, London, Macmillan

Johnson, T. J. (1977), 'The professions in the class structure', in R. Scase (ed.), *Industrial Society: Class, cleavage and control*, London, Allen & Unwin

Keat, R., and Urry, J. (1975), *Social Theory as Science*, Routledge & Kegan Paul

Keddie, N. (1971), 'Classroom knowledge', in M. F. D. Young (ed.), *Knowledge and Control*, London, Collier-Macmillan, pp. 133–61

Keesing, R. M. (1975), *Kin Groups and Social Structure*, New York, Holt, Rinehart & Winston

Kerr, C., *et al.* (1962), *Industrialism and Industrial Man*, London, Heinemann Educational Books

Keynes, J. M. (1936), *The General Theory of Employment, Interest and Money*, London, Macmillan

Kitchen, M. (1976), *Fascism*, London, Macmillan

Kolakowski, L. (1978a), *Main Currents of Marxism*, vol. 1, Oxford, Oxford University Press

Kolakowski, L. (1978b), *Main Currents of Marxism*, vol. 2, Oxford, Oxford University Press

Kramnick, I. (1972), 'Reflections on revolution; definition and explanation in recent scholarship', *History and Theory*, vol. 2, pp. 26–63

Kruskal, J. B., and Wish, M. (1978), *Multidimensional Scaling*, London, Sage

Kuhn, A., and Wolpe, A. (eds.) (1978), *Feminism and Materialism: Women and modes of production*, London, Routledge & Kegan Paul

Kuhn, T. S. (1970), *The Structure of Scientific Revolutions*, 2nd ed., Chicago, Chicago University Press

Kumar, K. (1978), *Prophecy and Progress: The sociology of industrial and post-industrial society*, Harmondsworth, Penguin Books

Lacan, J. (1966), *Ecrits: A selection*, London, Tavistock, 1977

Laclau, E. (1977), *Politics and Ideology in Marxist Theory: Capitalism, fascism, populism*, London, New Left Books

Ladurie, E. Le Roy (1975), *Montaillou*, Harmondsworth, Penguin Books, 1978

Laing, R. D. (1959), *The Divided Self*, London, Tavistock

Lane, D. (1971), *The End of Inequality?*, Harmondsworth, Penguin Books

Lane, D. (1985), *Soviet Economy and Society*, Oxford, Blackwell

Lane, T., and Roberts, K. (1971), *Strike at Pilkingtons*, London, Fontana

Lanternari, V. (1963), *The Religions of the Oppressed: A study of modern messianic cults*, London, MacGibbon & Kee

Larrain, J. (1979), *The Concept of Ideology*, London, Hutchinson

Laslett, P. (ed.) (1972), *Household and Family in Past Time*, Cambridge, Cambridge University Press

Lazarsfeld, P. F. (1954), *Mathematical Thinking in the Social Sciences*, New York, Russell & Russell

Lazarsfeld, P. F. (1971), *Qualitative Analysis: Historical and critical essays*, Boston, Allyn & Bacon

Lazarsfeld, P. F., and Katz, E. (1955), *Personal Influence: The part played by people in the flow of mass communications*, New York, Free Press

Lazarsfeld, P. F., and Henny, N. W. (1968), *Latent Structure Analysis*, New York, Houghton Mifflin

Lazarsfeld, P. F., *et al.* (1969), *The People's Choice: How the voter makes up his mind in a presidential campaign*, 3rd ed., New York, Columbia University Press

Leach, E. R. (1967), *The Structural Study of Myth and Totemism*, London, Tavistock

Leach, E. R. (1970), *Lévi-Strauss*, London, Fontana

Le Bon, G. (1895), *The Crowd*, New York, Macmillan, 1947

Lefebvre, H. (1968), *The Sociology of Marx*, London, Allen Lane The Penguin Press

Lemaire, A. (1977), *Lacan*, London, Routledge & Kegan Paul

Lemert, E. M. (1951), *Social Pathology: A systematic approach to the study of sociopathic behavior*, New York, McGraw-Hill

Lemert, E. M. (1967), *Human Deviance, Social Problems and Social Control*, New Jersey, Prentice-Hall

Lemon, N. (1973), *Attitudes and Their Measurement*, London, Batsford

Lenin, V. I. (1902), 'What is to be done?', *Collected Works*, vol. 5, Moscow, Foreign Languages Publishing House, 1961

Lenin, V. I. (1951), *Imperialism, as the Highest Stage of Capitalism*, Moscow, Progress Publishers

Lenski, G. E. (1954), 'Status crystallization: a non-vertical dimension of social status', *American Sociological Review*, vol. 19, 405–14

Lerner, D. (1958), *The Passing of Traditional Society*, Glencoe, Free Press

Lessnoff, M. (1974), *The Structure of Social Science*, London, Allen & Unwin

Lévi-Strauss, C. (1949), *The Elementary Structures of Kinship*, London, Eyre & Spottiswoode, 1969

Lévi-Strauss, C. (1955), *Tristes Tropiques*, New York, Atheneum, 1968

Lévi-Strauss, C. (1958), *Structural Anthropology*, London, Allen Lane The Penguin Press, 1968

Lévi-Strauss, C. (1962a), *Totemism*, Harmondsworth, Penguin Books, 1969

Lévi-Strauss, C. (1962b), *The Savage Mind*, Chicago, Chicago University Press, 1966

Lévi-Strauss, C. (1964), *Introduction to a Science of Mythology*, 4 vols., London, Cape, 1970–81

Levine, S., and Kozloff, M. A. (1978), 'The sick role: assessment and overview', *Annual Review of Sociology*, vol. 4, pp. 317–43

Lindesmith, A. R. (1968), *Addiction and Opiates*, Chicago, Aldine

Linton, R. (1936), *The Study of Man: An introduction*, New York, Appleton

Lipset, S. M. (1950), *Agrarian Socialism, The Co-operative Commonwealth Federation in Saskatchewan: A study of political sociology*, Berkeley, University of California Press

Lipset, S. M. (1960), *Political Man: The social bases of politics*, Garden City, N. Y., Doubleday

Lipset, S. M. (1963), *The First New Nation: The United States in historical and comparative perspective*, New York, Basic Books

Lipset, S. M. (1969), *Revolution and Counter-Revolution*, London, Heinemann Educational Books

Lipset, S. M., and Bendix, R. (1959), *Social Mobility in Industrial Society*, Berkeley, University of California Press

Lipset, S. M., and Raab, E. (1971), *The Politics of Unreason*, London, Heinemann Educational Books

Lipset, S. M., Trow, M. A., and Coleman, J. S. (1956), *Union Democracy: The internal politics of the International Typographical Union*, Glencoe, Free Press

Littler, C. R. (1982), *The Development of the Labour Process in Capitalist Societies*, London, Heinemann Educational Books

Littler, C. R. (1985), 'Taylorism, Fordism and job design', in D. Knights, H. Willmott and D. Collinson (eds.), *Job Redesign: Critical perspectives on the labour process*, Aldershot, Gower, pp. 30–51

Lockwood, D. (1956), 'Some remarks on "The Social System"', *British Journal of Sociology*, vol. 7, pp. 134–46

Lockwood, D. (1958), *The Blackcoated Worker*, London, Allen & Unwin

Lockwood, D. (1964), 'Social integration and system integration', in G. K. Zollschan and W. Hirsch (eds.), *Explorations in Social Change*, London, Routledge & Kegan Paul, pp. 244–57

Lockwood, D. (1966), 'Sources of variation in working-class images of society', *Sociological Review*, vol. 14, pp. 249–67

Luckmann, T. (1967), *The Invisible Religion: The problem of religion in modern society*, New York, Macmillan

Lukács, G. (1923), *History and Class Consciousness*, London, Merlin Press, 1971

Lukács, G. (1955), *The Historical Novel*, London, Merlin Press, 1962

Lukács, G. (1954), *The Destruction of Reason*, London, Merlin Press

Lukács, G. (1964), *Essays on Thomas Mann*, London, Merlin Press

Lukács, G. (1968), *Goethe and his Age*, London, Merlin Press

Lukács, G. (1972), *Studies in European Realism*, London, Merlin Press

Lukács, G. (1978), *The Ontology of Social Being*, London, Merlin Press

Lukes, S. (1967), 'Alienation and anomie', in P. Laslett and W. G. Runciman (eds.), *Philosophy, Politics and Society*, Third Series, Oxford, Blackwell, pp. 134–56

Lukes, S. (1972), *Émile Durkheim, his Life and Work: A historical and critical study*, London, Allen & Unwin

Lukes, S. (1974), *Power: A radical view*, London, Macmillan

Lynd, R. S., and Lynd, H. M. (1929), *Middletown: A study in contemporary American culture*, New York, Harcourt Brace

Lynd, R. S., and Lynd, H. M. (1937), *Middletown in Transition: A study in cultural conflicts*, New York, Harcourt Brace

Magee, B. (1973), *Popper*, London, Fontana

Malinowski, B. (1922), *Argonauts of the Western Pacific*, London, Routledge & Kegan Paul

Malinowski, B. (1927), *Sex and Repression in Savage Society*, London, Routledge & Kegan Paul

Malinowski, B. (1935), *Coral Gardens and their Magic*, London, Allen & Unwin

Malinowski, B. (1944), *A Scientific Theory of Culture*, Oxford, Oxford University Press

Malinowski, B. (1948), *Magic, Science and Religion and Other Essays*, Glencoe, Free Press

Mallett, S. (1963), *The New Working Class*, Nottingham, Spokesman, 1975

Mandel, E. (1975), *Late Capitalism*, London, New Left Books

Mangen, S. P. (1982), *Sociology and Mental Health*, Edinburgh, Churchill Livingstone

Mann, M. (1973), *Consciousness and Action in the Western Working Class*, London, Macmillan

Mannheim, H. (1965), *Comparative Criminology*, London and Boston, Routledge & Kegan Paul

Mannheim, K. (1936), *Ideology and Utopia*, London, Routledge & Kegan Paul

Mannheim, K. (1940), *Man and Society in an Age of Reconstruction*, London, Routledge & Kegan Paul

Mannheim, K. (1943), *Diagnosis of Our Time*, London, Kegan Paul/Trench, Trubner

Mannheim, K. (1951), *Freedom, Power and Democratic Planning*, London, Routledge & Kegan Paul

Mannheim, K. (1952), *Essays on the Sociology of Knowledge*, London, Routledge & Kegan Paul

Mannheim, K. (1953), *Essays on Sociology and Social Psychology*, London, Routledge & Kegan Paul

Mannheim, K. (1956), *Essays on the Sociology of Culture*, London, Routledge & Kegan Paul

March, J. G., and Simon, H. A. (1958), *Organizations*, New York, Wiley

Marcuse, H. (1954), *Reason and Revolution: Hegel and the rise of social theory*, New York, Humanities Press

Marcuse, H. (1955), *Eros and Civilization: A philosophical inquiry into Freud*, Boston, Beacon Press

Marcuse, H. (1961), *Soviet Marxism: A critical analysis*, New York, Columbia University Press

Marcus, H. (1964), *One-Dimensional Man: Studies in the ideology of advanced industrial society*, London, Routledge & Kegan Paul

Marcuse, H. (1968), *Negations: Essays in critical theory*, London, Allen & Unwin

Marcuse, H. (1969), *An Essay in Liberation*, London, Allen Lane The Penguin Press

Marshall, G. (1982), *In Search of the Spirit of Capitalism*, London, Hutchinson

Marshall, T. H. (1963), *Sociology at the Crossroads*, London, Heinemann Educational Books

Marshall, T. H. (1965), *Social Policy in the Twentieth Century*, London, Hutchinson, 1985 (5th edition by A. M. Rees)

Marshall, T. H. (1981), *The Right to Welfare and Other Essays*, London, Heinemann Educational Books

Martin, D. (1965), *Pacifism: A sociological and historical study*, London, Routledge & Kegan Paul

Martin, D. (1967), *A Sociology of English Religion*, London, SCM Press

Martin, D. (1969a), *The Religious and the Secular*, London, Routledge & Kegan Paul

Martin, D. (1969b), *Anarchy and Culture*, London, Routledge & Kegan Paul

Martin, D. (1973), *Tracts against the Times*, London, Lutterworth Press

Martin, D. (1978a), *A General Theory of Secularization*, Oxford, Blackwell

Martin, D. (1978b), *The Dilemmas of Contemporary Religion*, Oxford, Blackwell

Martin, D. (1980), *The Breaking of the Image*, Oxford, Blackwell

Martin, J., and Roberts, C. (1984), *Women and Employment: A lifetime perspective*, London, Her Majesty's Stationery Office

Marx, K. (1845), *Theses on Feuerbach*, reprinted in K. Marx and F. Engels, *Selected Works*, London, Lawrence & Wishart, 1970

Marx, K. (1847), *The Poverty of Philosophy*, Moscow, Progress Publishers, 1956

Marx, K. (1852), *The Eighteenth Brumaire of Louis Bonaparte*, Moscow, Progress Publishers, 1934

Marx, K. (1867, 1885, 1894), *Capital*, London, Lawrence & Wishart, 1970

Marx, K. (1964), *The Economic and Philosophical Manuscripts of 1844*, New York, International Publishers

Marx, K. (1973), *Grundrisse*, Harmondsworth, Penguin Books

Marx, K., and Engels, F. (1845a), *The Holy Family*, Moscow, Progress Publishers, 1956

Marx, K., and Engels, F. (1845b), *The German Ideology*, London, Lawrence & Wishart, 1965

Marx, K., and Engels, F. (1848), *Manifesto of the Communist Party*, in K. Marx and F. Engels, *Selected Works*, London, Lawrence & Wishart, 1968

Matza, D. (1964), *Delinquency and Drift*, New York, Wiley

Matza, D. (1969), *Becoming Deviant*, New Jersey, Prentice-Hall

Mauss, M. (1925), *The Gift*, New York, Free Press, 1954

McCarthy, T. (1978), *The Critical Theory of Jürgen Habermas*, London, Hutchinson

McClelland, D. C. (1961), *The Achieving Society*, Princeton, Princeton University Press

McHugh, P. (1968), *Defining the Situation: The organization of meaning in social interaction*, Indianapolis, Bobbs-Merrill

McLellan, D. (1973), *Karl Marx*, London, Macmillan

McLellan, D. (1977), *Engels*, Glasgow, Fontana

Mead, G. H. (1934), *Mind, Self and Society*, Chicago, Chicago University Press

Mead, G. H. (1938), *The Philosophy of the Act*, Chicago, Chicago University Press

Mead, G. H. (1959), *The Philosophy of the Present*, Seattle, Open Court Publishing

Mead, M. (1928), *Coming of Age in Samoa*, Harmondsworth, Penguin Books, 1961

Mead, M. (1930), *Growing Up in New Guinea*, Harmondsworth, Penguin Books, 1967

Mead, M. (1935), *Sex and Temperament in Three Primitive Societies*, New York, Morrow, 1963

Mead, M. (1949), *Male and Female: A study of the sexes in a changing society*, New York, Morrow, 1963

Mead, M. (1956), *New Lives for Old*, New York, Morrow

Mead, M. (1970a), *Culture and Commitment: A study of the generation gap*, London, Bodley Head

Mead, M. (ed.) (1970b), *Science and the Concept of Race*, New York, Columbia University Press

Mead, M. (1972), *Twentieth Century Faith: Hope and survival*, New York, Harper

Mechanic, D. (1968), *Medical Sociology*, New York, Macmillan

Mennell, S. (1985), *All Manners of Food: Eating and taste in England and France from the middle ages to the present*, Oxford, Blackwell

Merquior, J. G. (1980), *Rousseau and Weber: Two studies in the theory of legitimacy*, London, Routledge & Kegan Paul

Merton, R. K. (1957), *Social Theory and Social Structure*, New York, Free Press

Merton, R. K., and Nisbet, R. (eds.) (1961), *Contemporary Social Problems*, New York, Harcourt Brace

Michels, R. (1911), *Political Parties: A sociological study of the oligarchical tendencies of modern democracy*, New York, Free Press, 1962

Miliband, R. (1969), *The State in Capitalist Society*, London, Weidenfeld & Nicolson

Miliband, R. (1970), 'The capitalist state: reply to Nicol Poulantzas', *New Left Review*, no. 59, pp. 53–60

Millerson, G. L. (1964), *The Qualifying Association*, London, Routledge & Kegan Paul

Mills, C. W. (1940), 'Situated actions and vocabularies of motive', *American Sociological Review*, vol. 5, pp. 904–93

Mills, C. W. (1951), *White Collar: The American middle classes*, New York, Oxford University Press

Mills, C. W. (1956), *The Power Elite*, New York, Simon & Schuster

Mills, C. W. (1959), *The Sociological Imagination*, New York, Oxford University Press

Mommsen, W. J. (1980), *Theories of Imperialism*, London, Weidenfeld & Nicolson

Montesquieu, C.-L. (1721), *Persian Letters*, Harmondsworth, Penguin Books, 1973

Montesquieu, C.-L. (1734), *Considérations sur les causes de la grandeur des*

Romains et de leur décadence, in *Oeuvres complètes de Montesquieu*, N.R.F., Bibliothèque de la Pléiade, vol. 2, 1951

Montesquieu, C.-L. (1748), *The Spirit of the Law*, New York, Hafner, 1962

Moore, B. (1950), *Soviet Politics – The Dilemma of Power: The role of ideas in social change*, Cambridge, Mass., Harvard University Press

Moore, B. (1954), *Terror and Progress USSR: Some sources of change and stability in the Soviet dictatorship*, Cambridge, Mass., Harvard University Press

Moore, B. (1958), *Political Power and Social Theory*, Cambridge, Mass., Harvard University Press

Moore, B. (1967), *Social Origins of Dictatorship and Democracy: Lord and peasant in the making of the modern world*, London, Allen Lane The Penguin Press

Moore, B. (1972), *Reflections on the Causes of Human Misery and upon Certain Proposals to Eliminate Them*, Boston, Beacon Press

Moore, B. (1978), *Injustice: The social bases of obedience and revolt*, White Plains, New York, M. E. Sharpe

Moore, B. (1984), *Privacy: Studies in social and cultural history*, New York, Pantheon Books

Moore, B., and Wolff, K. H. (eds.) (1967), *The Critical Spirit: Essays in honour of Herbert Marcuse*, Boston, Beacon Press

Moorhouse, H. F. (1976), 'Attitudes to class and class relationships in Britain', *Sociology*, vol. 10, pp. 469–96

Moorhouse, H. F. (1978), 'The Marxist theory of the labour aristocracy', *Social History*, vol. 3, pp. 61–82

Morgan, D. (1975), *Social Theory and the Family*, London, Routledge & Kegan Paul

Morris, R. (1968), *Urban Sociology*, London, Allen & Unwin

Mosca, G. (1896), *The Ruling Class*, New York, McGraw-Hill, 1939

Moser, C. A., and Kalton, G. (1979), *Survey Methods in Social Investigation*, 2nd ed., London, Heinemann Educational Books

Mosteller, F. (1968), 'Errors: nonsampling errors', in D. L. Sills (ed.), *International Encyclopedia of the Social Sciences*, vol. 5, pp. 113–32, New York, Macmillan and Free Press

Mouffe, C. (ed.) (1979), *Gramsci and Marxist Theory*, London, Routledge & Kegan Paul

Mouzelis, N. P. (1967), *Organisations and Bureaucracy*, London, Routledge & Kegan Paul

Mumford, E. (1983), *Medical Sociology: Patients, providers and policies*, New York, Random House

Nandan, Y. (1977), *The Durkheimian School*, Westport, Conn., Greenwood

Navarro, V. (1977), *Medicine under Capitalism*, London, Croom Helm

Nelson, D. (1975), *Managers and Workers*, Madison, University of Wisconsin Press

Neuwirth, G. (1969), 'A Weberian outline of a theory of community: its application to the "Dark Ghetto"', *British Journal of Sociology*, vol. 20, pp. 148–63

Newby, H. (1977), *The Deferential Worker*, London, Allen Lane

Nisbet, R. A. (1953), *The Quest for Community: A study in the ethics of order and freedom*, New York, Oxford University Press

Nisbet, R. A. (ed.) (1965), *Emile Durkheim*, Englewood Cliffs, New Jersey, Prentice-Hall

Nisbet, R. A. (1967), *The Sociological Tradition*, London, Heinemann Educational Books

Nisbet, R. A. (1968), *Tradition and Revolt: Historical and sociological essays*, New York, Random House

Nisbet, R. A. (1969), *Social Change and History*, New York, Oxford University Press

Nisbet, R. A. (1970), *The Social Bond: An introduction to the study of society*, New York, Knopf

Nisbet, R. A. (1974a), *The Social Philosophers: Community and conflict in Western thought*, London, Heinemann Educational Books

Nisbet, R. A. (1974b), *The Sociology of Emile Durkheim*, London Heinemann Educational Books

Nisbet, R. A. (1976), *Sociology as an Art Form*, London, Heinemann Educational Books

Nisbet, R. A. (1980), *History of the Idea of Progress*, New York, Basic Books

Nisbet, R. A. (1982), *Prejudices: A philosophical dictionary*, Cambridge, Mass., Harvard University Press

Nisbet, R. A. (1986), *Conservatism*, Milton Keynes, Open University Press

Norman, P. (1975), 'Managerialism: Review of recent work', in M. Harloe (ed.), *Proceedings of the Conference on Urban Change and Conflict (1975)*, London, Centre for Environmental Studies, pp. 62–86

Nozick, R. (1974), *Anarchy, State and Utopia*, New York, Basic Books

Oakeshott, R. (1978), *The Case for Workers' Co-ops*, London, Routledge & Kegan Paul

Oakley, A. (1972), *Sex, Gender and Society*, Melbourne, Sun Books

Oakley, A. (1974), *The Sociology of Housework*, London, Martin Robertson

Oakley, A. (1981), *Subject Women*, Oxford, Martin Robertson

O'Connor, J. (1973), *The Fiscal Crisis of the State*, New York, St Martin's Press

Ogburn, W. F. (1950), *On Culture and Social Change*, Chicago, Chicago University Press

Ollman, B. (1971), *Alienation: Marx's critique of man in capitalist society*, Cambridge, Cambridge University Press

O'Neill, J. (1984), 'Earnings differentials: empirical evidence and causes', in G. Schmid and R. Weitzel (eds.), *Sex Discrimination and Equal Opportunity: The labour market and employment policy*, Aldershot, Gower

Ossowski, S. (1963), *Class and Class Structure in the Social Consciousness*, London, Routledge & Kegan Paul

Outhwaite, W. (1975), *Understanding Social Life*, London, Allen & Unwin

Pahl, R. E. (ed.) (1968), *Readings in Urban Sociology*, Oxford, Pergamon Press

Pahl, R. E. (1975), *Whose City?*, Harmondsworth, Penguin Books

Panitch, L. (1980), 'Recent theorizations of corporatism', *British Journal of Sociology*, vol. 31, pp. 159–87

Pareto, V. (1973), *The Mind and Society: A treatise on general sociology*, New York, Dover

Park, R. E. (1950), *Collected Papers of Robert Ezra Park*, New York, Free Press

Park, R. E., and Burgess, E. (1921), *Introduction to the Science of Sociology*, Chicago, Chicago University Press, 2nd ed., 1929

Parkin, F. (1971), *Class, Inequality and Political Order*, London, MacGibbon & Kee

Parkin, F. (1974), 'Strategies of social closure in class formation', in F. Parkin (ed.), *The Social Analysis of the Class Structure*, London, Tavistock, pp. 1–18

Parkin, F. (1978), 'Social stratification', in T. Bottomore and R. Nisbet (eds.), *A History of Sociological Analysis*, New York, Basic Books, pp. 599–632

Parkin, F. (1979), *Marxism and Class Theory: A bourgeois critique*, London, Tavistock

Parkin, F. (1982), *Max Weber*, London, Tavistock

Parsons, T. (1937), *The Structure of Social Action*, New York, McGraw-Hill

Parsons, T. (1951), *The Social System*, New York, Free Press

Parsons, T. (1953), 'A revised analytical approach to the theory of social stratification', in R. Bendix and S. M. Lipset (eds.), *Class, Status and Power: A reader in social stratification*, Glencoe, Free Press

Parsons, T. (1954), *Essays in Sociological Theory*, rev. ed., New York, Free Press

Parsons, T. (1963), 'On the concept of political power', *Proceedings of the American Philosophical Society*, vol. 107, pp. 232–62

Parsons, T. (1964), *Social Structure and Personality*, New York, Free Press

Parsons, T. (1966), *Societies: Evolutionary and comparative perspectives*, Englewood Cliffs, New Jersey, Prentice-Hall

Parsons, T. (1967), *Sociological Theory and Modern Society*, New York, Free Press

Parsons, T. (1968a), 'Durkheim, Emile', in D. L. Sills (ed.), *International Encyclopedia of the Social Sciences*, vol. 4, pp. 311–20, New York, Macmillan and Free Press

Parsons, T. (1986b), 'Pareto, Vilfredo: contributions to sociology', in D. L. Sills (ed.), *International Encyclopedia of the Social Sciences*, vol. 11, pp. 411–15, New York, Macmillan and Free Press

Parsons, T. (1968c), 'Utilitarianism: sociological thought', in D. L. Sills (ed.), *International Encyclopedia of the Social Sciences*, vol. 16, pp. 229–36, New York, Macmillan and Free Press

Parsons, T. (1971), *The System of Modern Societies*, Englewood Cliffs, New Jersey, Prentice-Hall

Parsons, T. (1977), *Social Systems and the Evolution of Action Theory*, New York, Free Press

Parsons, T., Bales, R. F., Olds, J., Zelditch, M., and Slater, P.E. (1955), *Family, Socialization and Interaction Process,* New York, Free Press

Parsons, T., Bales, R. F., and Shils, E. A. (1953), *Working Papers in the Theory of Action*, New York, Free Press

Parsons, T., and Shils, E. A. (eds.) (1951), *Toward a General Theory of Action*, Cambridge, Mass., Harvard University Press

Parsons, T., and Smelser, N. (1956), *Economy and Society*, New York, Free Press

Peel, J. D. Y. (1969a), 'Spencer and the Neo-Evolutionists', *Sociology*, vol. 3, pp. 173–92

Peel, J. D. Y. (1969b), 'Understanding alien belief systems'. *British Journal of Sociology*, vol. 20, pp. 69–84

Peel, J. D. Y. (1971), *Herbert Spencer: The evolution of a sociologist*, London, Heinemann Educational Books

Petersen, W. (1979), *Malthus*, London, Heinemann Educational Books

Phillipson, C. (1982), *Capitalism and the Construction of Old Age*, London, Allen & Unwin

Pickvance, C. G. (1976), *Urban Sociology*, London, Tavistock

Pinker, R. (1979), *The Idea of Welfare*, London, Heinemann Educational Books

Poggi, G. (1972), *Images of Society: Essays on the sociological theories of Tocqueville, Marx and Durkheim*, Stanford, Stanford University Press

Poggi, G. (1978), *The Development of the Modern State: A sociological introduction*, Stanford, Stanford University Press

Poole, M. (1975), *Workers' Participation in Industry*, London, Routledge & Kegan Paul

Popham, R. E. (ed.) (1970), *Alcohol and Alcoholism*, Toronto, University of Toronto Press

Popper, K. R. (1945), *The Open Society and Its Enemies*, 2 vols., London, Routledge & Kegan Paul

Popper, K. R. (1957), *The Poverty of Historicism*, London, Routledge & Kegan Paul

Popper, K. R. (1959), *The Logic of Scientific Discovery*, London, Hutchinson

Popper, K. R. (1963), *Conjectures and Refutations: The growth of scientific knowledge*, London, Routledge & Kegan Paul

Popper, K. R. (1966), *Of Clouds and Clocks*, St. Louis, Washington University Press

Popper, K. R. (1972), *Objective Knowledge: An evolutionary approach*, Oxford, Clarendon Press

Popper, K. R. (1974), *Unended Quest*, Glasgow, Fontana

Popper, K. R. (1982a), *The Open Universe*, London, Hutchinson

Popper, K. R. (1982b), *Quantum Theory and the Schism in Physics*, London, Hutchinson

Popper, K. R. (1983), *Realism and the Aim of Science*, Totowa, New Jersey, Rowman & Littlefield

Poulantzas, N. (1969), 'The problems of the capitalist state', *New Left Review*, no. 58, pp. 67–78

Poulantzas, N. (1973), *Political Power and Social Classes*, London, New Left Books, 1971

Poulantzas, N. (1974), *Fascism and Dictatorship*, London, New Left Books

Poulantzas, N. (1978), *State, Power, Socialism*, London, New Left Books

Prawer, J., and Eisenstadt, S. N. (1968), 'Feudalism', in D. L. Sills (ed.), *International Encyclopedia of the Social Sciences*, vol. 5, pp. 393–403, New York, Macmillan and Free Press

Pulzer, P. G. J. (1975), *Political Representation and Elections in Britain*, 3rd ed., London, Allen & Unwin

Punnett, R. M. (1980), *British Government and Politics*, 4th ed., London, Heinemann Educational Books

Pye, L. W., and Verba, S. (eds.) (1965), *Political Culture and Political Development*, Princeton, Princeton University Press

Radcliffe-Brown, A. R. (1922), *The Andaman Islanders*, New York, Free Press

Radcliffe-Brown, A. R. (1931), *The Social Organization of Australian Tribes*, Glencoe, Free Press

Radcliffe-Brown, A. R. (1936), *Taboo*, Cambridge, Cambridge University Press

Radcliffe-Brown, A. R. (1952), *Structure and Function in Primitive Society*, London, Cohen & West

Rawls, J. (1971), *A Theory of Justice*, Oxford, Oxford University Press, 1973

Reasons, C. E., and Rich, R. M. (eds.), (1978), *The Sociology of Law*, London, Butterworth.

Redfield, R. (1930) *Tepoztlan, a Mexican Village: A study of folk life*, Chicago, Chicago University Press

Reich, M., Gordon, D. M., and Edwards, R. C. (1973), 'A theory of labour market segmentation', *American Economic Review*, vol. 63, pp. 359–65

Reich, W. (1933), *The Mass Psychology of Fascism*, Harmondsworth, Penguin Books, 1975

Reissmann, L. (1964), *The Urban Process*, New York, Free Press

Rex, J. (1961), *Key Problems of Sociological Theory*, London, Routledge & Kegan Paul

Rex, J. (1970), *Race Relations in Sociological Theory*, London, Weidenfeld & Nicolson

Rex, J. (1973a), *Discovering Sociology: Studies in sociological theory and method*, London, Routledge & Kegan Paul

Rex, J. (1973b), *Race Colonialism and the City*, London, Routledge & Kegan Paul

Rex, J. (1974), *Sociology and the Demystification of the Modern World*, London, Routledge & Kegan Paul

Rex, J. (1981), *Social Conflict: A conceptual and theoretical analysis*, London, Longman

Rex, J. (1986), *Race and Ethnicity*, Milton Keynes, Open University Press

Rex, J., and Moore, R. (1967), *Race, Community and Conflict: A study of Sparkbrook*, London, Oxford University Press

Rex, J., and Tomlinson, S. (1979), *Colonial Immigrants in a British City*, London, Routledge & Kegan Paul

Rigby, A. (1974), *Alternative Realities*, London, Routledge & Kegan Paul

Roberts, K. (1978), *The Working Class*, London, Longman

Roberts, K., Cook, F. G., Clark, S. C., and Semeonoff, E. (1977), *The Fragmentary Class Structure*, London, Heinemann Educational Books

Robertson, R. (1970), *The Sociological Interpretation of Religion*, Oxford, Blackwell

Robertson, R. (1974), 'Towards the identification of the major axes of sociological analysis', in J. Rex (ed.), *Approaches to Sociology: An introduction to major trends in British sociology*, London, Routledge & Kegan Paul, pp. 107–124

Robertson, R., and Lechner, F. (1985), 'Modernization, globalization and world-systems theory', *Theory, Culture and Society*, vol. 2(3), pp. 103–17

Rocher, G. (1974), *Talcott Parsons and American Sociology*, London, Nelson

Rock, P. (1979), *The Making of Symbolic Interactionism*, London, Macmillan

Rodwin, V. G. (1984), *The Health Planning Predicament: France, Quebec, England and the United States*, Berkeley, University of California Press

Rogers, R. E. (1969), *Max Weber's Ideal Type Theory*, New York, Philosophical Library

Rose, G. (1975), *The Problem of Party Government*, London, Macmillan

Rose, M. (1975), *Industrial Behaviour*, London, Allen Lane

Rose, M. (1979), *Servants of Post-Industrial Power?*, London, Macmillan

Ross, J. C. (1972), 'Towards a reconstruction of voluntary association theory', *British Journal of Sociology*, vol. 23, pp. 20–32

Roth, J. (1962), 'Management bias in social science research', *Human Organization*, vol. 21, pp. 47–50

Rowntree, B. S. (1902), *Poverty: A study of town life*, London, Longman

Roy, D. (1952), 'Quota restriction and goldbricking in a machine shop', *American Journal of Sociology*, vol. 57, pp. 427–42

Roy, D. (1953), 'Work satisfaction and social reward in quota achievement: an analysis of piecework incentive', *American Sociological Review*, vol. 18, pp. 507–14

Roy, D. (1955), 'Efficiency and "the fix": informal intergroup relations in a piecework machine shop', *American Journal of Sociology*, vol. 60, pp. 255–66

Royal Commission on the Distribution of Income and Wealth (1980), *An A to Z of Income and Wealth*, London, Her Majesty's Stationery Office

Runciman, W. G. (1966), *Relative Deprivation and Social Justice*, London, Routledge & Kegan Paul

Runciman, W. G. (1972), *A Critique of Max Weber's Philosophy of Social Science*, Cambridge, Cambridge University Press

Rutter, M. (1972), *Maternal Deprivation Reassessed*, Harmondsworth, Penguin Books

Rutter, M., Maughan, B., Mortimore, P., and Ouston, J. (1979), *Fifteen Thousand Hours: Secondary schools and their effects on children*, London, Open Books

Ryan, A. (1970), *The Philosophy of the Social Sciences*, London, Macmillan

Sahlins, M. (1977), *The Use and Abuse of Biology: An anthropological critique of sociobiology*, London, Tavistock

Salaman, G. (1979), *Work Organizations*, London, Longman

Salmon, J. W. (ed.) (1984), *Alternative Medicines: Popular and policy perspectives*, London, Tavistock

Santos, T. Dos (1970), 'The structure of dependence', *American Economic Review*, vol. 60, pp. 231–6

Sartori, G. (1976), *Parties and Party Systems: A framework for analysis*, Cambridge, Cambridge University Press

Saunders, P. (1980), *Urban Politics*, Harmondsworth, Penguin Books

Saunders, P. (1981), *Social Theory and the Urban Question*, London, Hutchinson

Scheff, T. J. (1966), *Being Mentally Ill: A sociological theory*, London, Weidenfeld & Nicolson

Schneider, L. (ed.) (1967), *The Scottish Moralists, on Human Nature and Society*, Chicago, Chicago University Press

Schumpeter, J. A. (1934), *The Theory of Economic Development*, Cambridge, Mass., Harvard University Press

Schumpeter, J. A. (1950), *Capitalism, Socialism, and Democracy*, 3rd ed., London, Allen & Unwin

Schumpeter, J. A. (1951), *Imperialism and Social Classes*, New York, Kelley

Schur, E. M. (1965), *Crimes without Victims*, Englewood Cliffs, New Jersey, Prentice-Hall

Schutz, A. (1970), *Reflections on the Problem of Relevance*, ed. R. M. Zaner, New Haven, Conn., Yale University Press

Schutz, A. (1971), *Collected Papers*, vols. 1 and 2, The Hague, Nijhoff

Schutz, A. (1972), *The Phenomenology of the Social World*, London, Heinemann Educational Books

Schutz, A., and Luckmann, T. (1974), *The Structures of the Life-World*, London, Heinemann Educational Books

Scott, J. (1979), *Corporations, Classes and Capitalism*, London, Hutchinson

Scott, J. (1982), *The Upper Class: Property and privilege in Britain*, London, Macmillan

Scott, M. B., and Lyman, S. M. (1968), 'Accounts', *American Sociological Review*, vol. 33, pp. 46–62

Seeman, M. (1959), 'On the Meaning of Alienation', *American Sociological Review*, vol. 24, pp. 783–91

Senter, R. J. (1969), *Analysis of Data: Introductory statistics for the behavioral sciences*, Glenview, Illinois, Scott, Foresman

Seyfarth, C., and Schmidt, G. (1977), *Max Weber Bibliographie – eine Dokumentation der sekundar Literatur*, Stuttgart

Sharpe, S. (1979), *Just Like a Girl: How girls learn to be women*, Harmondsworth, Penguin Books

Shell, K. L. (1969), *The Democratic Political Process*, Waltham, Mass., Blaisdell

Sheridan, A. (1980), *Michel Foucault: The will to truth*, London, Tavistock

Shils, E. (1962), 'The theory of mass society', *Diogenes*, vol. 39, pp. 45–66

Shils, E. (1975), *Center and Periphery: Essays in macrosociology*, Chicago, Chicago University Press

Shils, E. (1981), *Tradition*, London, Routledge & Kegan Paul

Shonfield, A. (1965), *Modern Capitalism*, London, Oxford University Press

Shorter, E. (1977), *The Making of the Modern Family*, Glasgow, Fontana

Siegel, S. (1956), *Nonparametric Statistics for the Behavioral Sciences*, New York, McGraw-Hill

Silverman, D. (1970), *The Theory of Organisations*, London, Heinemann Educational Books

Simey, T. S., and Simey, M. B. (1960), *Charles Booth, Social Scientist*, Oxford, Oxford University Press

Simmel, G. (1892), *The Problems of the Philosophy of History*, New York, Free Press, 1977

Simmel, G. (1900), *The Philosophy of Money*, London, Routledge & Kegan Paul, 1978

Simmel, G. (1955), *Conflict and the Web of Group Affiliations*, New York, Free Press

Sklair, L. (1970), *The Sociology of Progress*, London, Routledge & Kegan Paul

Smart, B. (1985), *Michel Foucault*, Chichester, Ellis Horwood, and London, Tavistock

Smelser, N. J. (1959), *Social Change in the Industrial Revolution*, London, Routledge & Kegan Paul

Smelser, N. J. (1962), *Theory of Collective Behavior*, New York, Free Press

Smith, A. (1776), *An Inquiry into the Nature and Causes of the Wealth of Nations*, ed. E. Cannan, London, Methuen, 1950

Smith, A. D. (1971), *Theories of Nationalism*, London, Duckworth

Smith, A. D. (1973), *The Concept of Social Change*, London, Routledge & Kegan Paul

Smith, D. (1983), *Barrington Moore Jr: A critical appraisal*, Armonk, New York, M. E. Sharpe

Social Trends 16 (1986), London, Her Majesty's Stationery Office

Sociology (1978), special issue on *Language and practical reasoning*, vol. 12, no. 1

Sohn-Rethel, A. (1978), *Intellectual and Manual Labour: A critique of epistemology*, London, Macmillan

Sombart, W. (1930), 'Capitalism', in A. Johnson and E. R. A. Seligman (eds.), *Encyclopaedia of the Social Sciences*, vol. 3, pp. 195–208, New York, Macmillan

Sorokin, P. A. (1927), *Social Mobility*, New York, Harper

Sorokin, P. A. (1928), *Contemporary Sociological Theories*, New York, Harper

Sorokin, P. A. (1937–41), *Social and Cultural Dynamics*, New York, American Book Company

Sorokin, P. A. (1943), *Sociocultural Causality, Space, Time*, Durham, Duke University Press

Sorokin, P. A. (1950), *The Social Philosophies of an Age of Crisis*, republished as *Modern Historical and Social Philosophies*, New York, Dover, 1963

Sorokin, P. A. (1956), *Fads and Foibles in Modern Sociology*, Chicago, Regnery

Sorokin, P. A. (1966), *Sociological Theories of Today*, New York, Harper

Spencer, H. (1876–96), *Principles of Sociology*, New York, Appleton

Spencer, H. (1884), *The Data of Ethics*, London, Williams & Norgate

Stanworth, M. (1983), *Gender and Schooling: A study of sexual divisions in the classroom*, London, Hutchinson

Stedman-Jones, G. (1971), 'The Marxism of the Early Lukács', *New Left Review*, no. 70. pp. 27–64

Stokman, F., Ziegler, R., and Scott, J. (1985), *Networks of Corporate Power: A comparative analysis of ten countries*, Cambridge, Polity Press

Stone, L. (1965), 'Theories of revolution', *World Politics*, vol. 18, pp. 159–76

Stouffer, S. A., *et al.* (1949), *The American Soldier*, vol. 1, Princeton, Princeton University Press

Strauss, A. (1964), *George Herbert Mead on Social Psychology*, Chicago, Chicago University Press

Strauss, A. (1978), *Negotiations, Varieties, Contexts, Processes and Social Order*, San Francisco, Jossey-Bass

Sturmthal, A., and Scoville, J. G. (1973), *The International Labor Movement in Transition*, Urbana, University of Illinois Press

Sumner, W. G. (1906), *Folkways*, New York, Dover

Sutherland, E. H. (1934), *Principles of Criminology*, Chicago, Lippincott

Sutherland, E. H. (1939), *Principles of Criminology*, Philadelphia, Lippincott, rev. ed., 1955

Sutherland, E. H. (1945), 'Is "white-collar crime" crime?', *American Sociological Review*, vol. 10, pp. 132–9

Sutherland, E. H., and Creasey, D. R. (1955), *Principles of Criminology*, Chicago, Lippincott

Swingewood, A. (1977), *The Myth of Mass Culture*, London, Macmillan

Sykes, G., and Matza, D. (1957), 'Techniques of neutralization, a theory of delinquency', *American Sociological Review*, vol. 22, pp. 664–70

Szasz, T. (1971), *The Manufacture of Madness*, London, Paladin

Tawney, R. H. (1931), *Equality*, New York, Barnes & Noble

Taylor, F. W. (1964), *Scientific Management*, New York, Harper

Taylor, I., Walton, P., and Young, J. (1973), *The New Criminology: For a social theory of deviance*, London, Routledge & Kegan Paul

Taylor, K. (1975), *Henri Saint-Simon 1760–1825: Selected writings on science, industry and social organisation*, London, Croom Helm

Therborn, G. (1980), *The Ideology of Power and the Power of Ideology*, London, New Left Books

Thomas, W. I. (1927), 'The behavior pattern and the situation', *Publications of the American Sociological Society*, papers and proceedings, 22nd Annual Meeting, vol. 22, pp. 1–13

Thomas, W. I. (1928), *The Child in America, Behavior Problems and Programs*, New York, Knopf

Thomas, W. I. (1966), *On Social Organization and Social Personality*, Chicago, Chicago University Press

Thompson, E. P. (1979), *The Poverty of Theory*, London, Merlin Press

Thompson, P. (1983), *The Nature of Work: An introduction to debates on the labour process*, London, Macmillan

Thornley, J. (1981), *Workers' Co-operatives: Jobs and dreams*, London, Heinemann Educational Books

Thrasher, F. M. (1927), *The Gang: A study of 1,313 gangs in Chicago*, Chicago, Chicago University Press

Timasheff, N. S. (1967), *Sociological Theory*, New York, Random House

Tocqueville, A. de (1835 and 1840), *Democracy in America*, Glasgow, Collins, 1968

Tocqueville, A. de (1856), *The Old Regime and the French Revolution*, New York, Doubleday, 1955

Tocqueville, A. de (1893), *Recollections*, New York, Doubleday, 1970

Tocqueville, A. de, and Beaumont, G. de (1833), *On the Penitentiary System in the United States and Its Application to France*, Carbondale and Edwardsville, Southern Illinois University Press, 1964

Toennies, F. (1887), *Community and Association*, Michigan, Michigan State University Press, 1957

Touraine, A. (1969), *The Post-Industrial Society*, New York, Random House, 1971

Troeltsch, E. (1912), *The Social Teaching of the Christian Churches*, New York, Macmillan, 1931

Turner, B. S. (1981), *For Weber: Essays on the sociology of fate*, London, Routledge & Kegan Paul

Turner, B. S. (1983), *Religion and Social Theory: A materialist perspective*, London, Heinemann Educational Books

Turner, B. S. (1986a), *Citizenship and Capitalism: The debate over reformism*, London, Allen & Unwin

Turner, B. S. (1986b), *Equality*, London, Tavistock

Turner, J. H. (1985), *Herbert Spencer: A renewed appreciation*, London, Sage

Turner, R. (ed.) (1974), *Ethnomethodology*, Harmondsworth, Penguin Books

Turner, R. H. (1960), 'Sponsored and contest mobility and the school system', *American Sociological Review*, vol. 25, pp. 855–67

Turner, R. H. (1962), 'Role taking: process versus conformity', in A. M. Rose (ed.), *Human Behavior and Social Processes*, Boston, Houghton Mifflin, pp. 20–40

Twaddle, A. (1982), 'From medical sociology to the sociology of health:

some changing concerns in the sociological study of sickness and treatment', in T. Bottomore, S. Nowak and M. Sokolowska (eds.), *Sociology: The state of the art*, London and Beverly Hills, Sage, pp. 323–58

Urry, J. (1980), *The Anatomy of Capitalist Society – the Economy, Civil Society and the State*, London, Macmillan

Urry, J., and Wakeford, J. (eds.) (1973), *Power in Britain: Sociological readings*, London, Heinemann Educational Books

Vallier, I. (ed.) (1971), *Comparative Methods in Sociology*, Berkeley, University of California Press

van der Mehden, F. R. (1969), *Politics of the Developing Nations*, Englewood Cliffs, New Jersey, Prentice-Hall

Veatch, R. M. (1981), 'The medical model, its nature and problems', in A. L. Caplan, H. T. Englehardt and J. J. McCartney (eds.), *Concepts of Health and Disease: Interdisciplinary perspectives*, London, Addison, pp. 523–54

Veblen, T. (1899), *The Theory of the Leisure Class*, New York, Mentor, 1953

Veblen, T. (1904), *The Theory of the Business Enterprise*, New York, Kelley, 1965

Veblen, T. (1914), *The Instinct of Workmanship and the State of the Industrial Arts*, New York, Norton, 1964

Veblen, T. (1915), *Imperial Germany and the Industrial Revolution*, New York, Kelley, 1964

Veblen, T. (1917), *An Inquiry into the Nature of Peace and the Terms of its Perpetuation*, New York, Kelley, 1964

Veblen, T. (1918a), *The Higher Learning in America*, Gloucester, Mass., Peter Smith

Veblen, T. (1918b), *The Place of Science in Modern Civilization and Other Essays*, New York, Russell & Russell, 1961

Veblen, T. (1921), *The Engineers and the Price System*, New York, Harcourt, 1963

Veblen, T. (1923), *Absentee Ownership and Business Enterprise in Recent Times*, Boston, Beacon Press, 1967

Venturi, F. (1963), 'Oriental despotism', *Journal for the History of Ideas*, vol. 24, pp. 133–42

Wallace, W. L. (1969), *Sociological Theory: An introduction*, London, Heinemann Educational Books

Wallerstein, I. (1974), *The Modern World-System: Capitalist agriculture and the origins of the European world-economy in the sixteenth century*, New York, Academic Press

Wallis, R. (1984), *The Elementary Forms of the New Religious Life*, London, Routledge & Kegan Paul

Warner, L. (1949), *Social Class in America: A manual of procedure for the measurement of social status*, New York, Harper, 1960

Waxman, C. I. (ed.) (1986), *The End of Ideology Debate*, New York, Funk & Wagnalls

Webb, E. J., *et al.* (1966), *Unobtrusive Measures: Nonreactive research in the social sciences*, Chicago, Rand McNally

Weber, M. (1922), *Economy and Society: An outline of interpretive sociology*, New York, Bedminster Press, 1968

Weber, M. (1930), *The Protestant Ethic and the Spirit of Capitalism*, London, Allen & Unwin

Weber, M. (1946), *From Max Weber: Essays in sociology*, London, Routledge & Kegan Paul, edited by H. H. Gerth and C. W. Mills

Weber, M. (1949), *The Methodology of the Social Sciences*, Glencoe, Free Press, edited by E. Shils and H. Finch

Weber, M. (1950), *General Economic History*, New York, Collier

Weber, M. (1951), *The Religion of China*, New York, Macmillan

Weber, M. (1952), *Ancient Judaism*, Glencoe, Free Press

Weber, M. (1958a), *The Religion of India*, Glencoe, Free Press

Weber, M. (1958b), *The City*, Glencoe, Free Press

Weber, M. (1958c), *The Rational Foundations of Music*, Carbondale, Southern Illinois University Press

Weber, M. (1968), *Economy and Society*, New York, Bedminster

Weber, M. (1975), *Roscher and Knies: The logical problems of historical economics*, New York, Free Press

Weber, M. (1976), *The Agrarian Sociology of Ancient Civilizations*, London, New Left Books

Weber, M. (1977), *Critique of Stammler*, New York, Free Press

Weber, M. (1978), *Selections in Translation*, Cambridge, Cambridge University Press, edited by W. G. Runciman

Weitz, S. (1977), *Sex Roles: Biological, psychological and social foundations*, New York, Oxford University Press

West, J. (ed.) (1982), *Work, Women and the Labour Market*, London, Routledge & Kegan Paul

Whyte, W. F. (1956), *The Organisation Man*, New York, Simon & Schuster

Whyte, W. F. (1961), *Street Corner Society: The social structure of an Italian slum*, 2nd ed., Chicago, Chicago University Press

Wilkins, L. (1965), 'Some sociological factors in drug addiction control', in D. Wilner and G. Kassebaum (eds.), *Narcotics*, New York, McGraw-Hill

Wilkins, L. T. (1964), *Social Deviance: Social policy, action and research*, London, Tavistock

Williams, R. (1973), 'Base and Superstructure', *New Left Review*, no. 82, pp. 3–16

Willmott, P. (1963), *The Evolution of a Community*, London, Routledge & Kegan Paul

Willmott, P. (1966), *Adolescent Boys of East London*, London, Routledge & Kegan Paul

Willmott, P., and Young, M. (1960), *Family and Class in a London Suburb*, London, Routledge & Kegan Paul

Wilson, B. (1966), *Religion in a Secular Society*, London, Watts

Wilson, B. (1967), *Patterns of Sectarianism: Organization and ideology in social and religious movements*, London, Heinemann Educational Books

Wilson, B. (1970a), *Religious Sects: A sociological study*, London, Weidenfeld & Nicolson

Wilson, B. (1970b), *Youth Culture and the Universities*, London, Faber & Faber

Wilson, B. (ed.) (1970c), *Rationality*, Oxford, Blackwell

Wilson, B. (1973), *Magic and the Millennium: A sociological study of religious movements of protest among tribal and third-world peoples*, London, Heinemann Educational Books

Wilson, B. (1976), *Contemporary Transformations of Religion*, London, Oxford University Press

Wilson, B. (1982), *Religion in Sociological Perspective*, London, Oxford University Press

Wilson, E. O. (1975), *Sociobiology*, Cambridge, Mass., Harvard University Press

Winch, P. (1958), *The Idea of a Social Science*, London, Routledge & Kegan Paul

Wirth, L. (1931), 'Clinical sociology', *American Journal of Sociology*, vol. 37, pp. 49–66

Wirth, L. (1938), 'Urbanism as a way of life', *American Journal of Sociology*, vol. 44, pp. 1–24

Wittfogel, K. A. (1957), *Oriental Despotism: A comparative study of total power*, New Haven, Yale University Press

Wolf, E. (1971), *Peasant Wars of the Twentieth Century*, London, Faber & Faber

Wolff, K. H. (ed.) (1950), *The Sociology of Georg Simmel*, New York, Free Press

Wolff, K. H. (1978), 'Phenomenology and Sociology', in T. B. Bottomore and R. Nisbet (eds.), *A History of Sociological Analysis*, New York, Basic Books, 1978, pp. 499–556

Wolfgang, M. (1957), 'Victim-precipitated criminal homicide', *Journal of Criminal Law, Criminology and Police Science*, vol. 48, pp. 1–11

Wolfgang, M., Savitz, L., and Johnston, N. (eds.) (1970), *The Sociology of Crime and Delinquency*, New York, Wiley

Wolin, S. S. (1961), *Politics and Vision: Continuity and innovation in Western political thought*, London, Allen & Unwin

Wolpe, H. (ed.) (1980), *The Articulation of Production*, London, Routledge and Kegan Paul

Wood, S. (ed.) (1982), *The Degradation of Work?*, London, Hutchinson

Woolf, S. J. (ed.) (1968), *The Nature of Fascism*, New York, Random House

Wright, E. O. (1976), 'Class boundaries in advanced capitalist societies', *New Left Review*, no. 98, pp. 3–41

Wrigley, E. A. (ed.) (1966), *An Introduction to English Historical Demography from the Sixteenth to the Nineteenth Century*, London, Weidenfeld & Nicolson

Wrigley, E. A. (1969), *Population and History*, London, Weidenfeld & Nicolson

Wrigley, E. A., and Schofield, R. (1982), *The Population History of England 1541–1871: A reconstruction*, London, Arnold

Wrong, D. H. (1961), 'The oversocialized conception of man in modern sociology', *American Sociological Review*, vol. 26, pp. 183–93

Wrong, D. H. (1966), *Population and Society*, New York, Random House

Wrong, D. H. (1977), *Sceptical Sociology*, London, Heinemann Educational Books

Wrong, D. H. (1979), *Power: Its forms, bases and uses*, Oxford, Blackwell

Yablonsky, L. (1967), *The Violent Gang*, Harmondsworth, Penguin Books

Young, J. (1971), *The Drugtakers: the social meaning of drug use*, London, Paladin

Young, M. (1958), *The Rise of the Meritocracy*, London, Thames & Hudson

Young, M., and Willmott, P. (1957), *Family and Kinship in East London*, London, Routledge & Kegan Paul

Young, M., and Willmott, P. (1973), *The Symmetrical Family*, Harmondsworth, Penguin Books

Zimbalist, A. (ed.) (1979), *Case Studies on the Labor Process*, New York, Monthly Review Press

Zola, I. K. (1972), 'Medicine as an institution of social control: the medicalizing of society', *Sociological Review*, vol. 20, pp. 487–504

Zollschan, G. K., and Hirsch, W. (eds.), *Explorations in Social Change*, London, Routledge & Kegan Paul

READ MORE IN PENGUIN

In every corner of the world, on every subject under the sun, Penguin represents quality and variety – the very best in publishing today.

For complete information about books available from Penguin – including Puffins, Penguin Classics and Arkana – and how to order them, write to us at the appropriate address below. Please note that for copyright reasons the selection of books varies from country to country.

In the United Kingdom: Please write to *Dept. JC, Penguin Books Ltd, FREEPOST, West Drayton, Middlesex UB7 0BR*

If you have any difficulty in obtaining a title, please send your order with the correct money, plus ten per cent for postage and packaging, to *PO Box No. 11, West Drayton, Middlesex UB7 0BR*

In the United States: Please write to *Penguin USA Inc., 375 Hudson Street, New York, NY 10014*

In Canada: Please write to *Penguin Books Canada Ltd, 10 Alcorn Avenue, Suite 300, Toronto, Ontario M4V 3B2*

In Australia: Please write to *Penguin Books Australia Ltd, 487 Maroondah Highway, Ringwood, Victoria 3134*

In New Zealand: Please write to *Penguin Books (NZ) Ltd,182–190 Wairau Road, Private Bag, Takapuna, Auckland 9*

In India: Please write to *Penguin Books India Pvt Ltd, 706 Eros Apartments, 56 Nehru Place, New Delhi 110 019*

In the Netherlands: Please write to *Penguin Books Netherlands B.V., Keizersgracht 231 NL–1016 DV Amsterdam*

In Germany: Please write to *Penguin Books Deutschland GmbH, Friedrichstrasse 10–12, W–6000 Frankfurt/Main 1*

In Spain: Please write to *Penguin Books S. A., C. San Bernardo 117–6° E–28015 Madrid*

In Italy: Please write to *Penguin Italia s.r.l., Via Felice Casati 20, I–20124 Milano*

In France: Please write to *Penguin France S. A., 17 rue Lejeune, F–31000 Toulouse*

In Japan: Please write to *Penguin Books Japan, Ishikiribashi Building, 2–5–4, Suido, Tokyo 112*

In Greece: Please write to *Penguin Hellas Ltd, Dimocritou 3, GR–106 71 Athens*

In South Africa: Please write to *Longman Penguin Southern Africa (Pty) Ltd, Private Bag X08, Bertsham 2013*

READ MORE IN PENGUIN

DICTIONARIES